D0930579

LIBRARY
MURRAY STATE UNIVERSITY

Frontier Musicians on the
Connoquenessing, Wabash, and Ohio

Frontier Musicians

on the Connoquenessing, Wabash, and Ohio

A History of the Music and Musicians
of George Rapp's Harmony Society
(1805-1906)

Richard D. Wetzel

OHIO UNIVERSITY PRESS: ATHENS

ML
200.4
W 48

© 1976 by Richard D. Wetzel

Library of Congress Catalog Number: 74-80809
ISBN: 8214-0208-0
All Rights Reserved.

Manufactured in the United States of America by
Oberlin Printing Company.

To my parents, Violet Witmer Wetzel and Myles Henry Wetzel, and to the many German-Americans who through faith in God and honesty in labor gave much good to our country, but especially to the memory of our beloved Harmonists.

Richard D. Wetzel
Chesterhill, Ohio

284127

LIBRARY
MURRAY STATE UNIVERSITY

Contents

PLATES

Preface

The contributions made by communally governed societies and conclaves to the settlement and colonization of America were myriad. Most members of these communal groups were religiously or humanistically oriented; they were firm believers in the dignity of labor, and they knew, often from bitter experience, the need for social unity and cooperation. Frequently unheralded and even more frequently misunderstood, they helped shape that spirit which was and still is the very heartbeat of America.

The purpose for writing this book has been to provide a comprehensive account of the musical life of a distinctive nineteenth-century German-American communal society, George Rapp's Harmony Society. Descriptions of the Society's vocal and instrumental ensembles, their repertoires and performance practices (still overlooked by most histories of American music), provide the basic material for the text. The four appendixes, the last of which is a catalog of the more than 800 items remaining of the Harmonists' music library, document it with examples. But in this book, as in others which describe the economic, religious and social aspects of life in the Harmony Society, it is the people themselves who emerge as the predominant subject. Indeed, the personalities of those who were most dedicated to the religious and social principles of the Society and who most willingly suppressed personal desires and ambitions to advance the common good, often emerge as sharply and distinctly as public figures contemporary to them in the world outside the Society. It is also interesting to note that the most conspicuous of these were often the Society's leading musicians.

Reduced to simple terms, the success of the Harmony Society was achieved by maintaining a delicate balance between religion, economics, education, and the arts. When any one was ignored or overemphasized the community became uneasy. Considering the religious and social peculiarities which the Society espoused, this may appear contradictory. But the generosity with which they dealt with those outside the Society and the respect in which they held the government of the United States revealed a pragmatic as well as religious approach to life. Far from being fatalistic or fanatical, they maintained an almost perfect balance between the preaching of their religion and its practical application in their daily lives on the American frontier.

Music was both encouraged and controlled. Their skills did not equal those of their Moravian brethren whom they greatly admired; but, when most American cities were struggling to establish cultural organizations and educational institutions, the Harmonists had well-established schools, an impressive library, a museum, and between 1825 and 1831, an orchestra equal to those orchestras (and there were very few) in the cities on the eastern seaboard. In addition, through their communal and religious beliefs, the Harmonists created distinctive kinds of art and made unique contributions to the cultural life of our country during its formative years.

Although concerned primarily with the music of the Harmonists, the following pages occasionally give glimpses of nineteenth-century American life outside the Society. The Harmonists built towns in Pennsylvania and Indiana, and influenced the building of others in Ohio, Louisiana, and Texas and because they were caught up in the Industrial Revolution, their business associations extended over much of what was then the United States. Consequently, the information found in this book was acquired by following a route which was filled with surprising and unexpected turns. During the research the author became indebted to a host of librarians, museum curators, teachers, business persons, and descendants of Harmonists who willingly contributed information and encouragement to the project. In particular, the author's thanks are extended to Theodore M. Finney, former chairman of the Music Department, University of Pittsburgh; Noel Barstad, Assistant Professor of German, Ohio University; Fletcher Hodges, Jr., curator of the Stephen Foster Memorial Museum of Pittsburgh; George McMaster Jones, librarian of the Darlington Library of Pittsburgh; Irene Millen, librarian of the Music Division of the Carnegie Library of Pittsburgh; Norris L. Stephens, music librarian of the University of Pittsburgh; and the staffs of the Historical Society of Western Pennsylvania; the Historical Society of Lehigh County, Pennsylvania; the Music Division of the New York Public Library; the Workingman's Institute, New Harmony, Indiana; the Fairfield Public Library of Lancaster, Ohio; the Cincinnati Public Library; and Zoar Village, Zoar, Ohio.

Special thanks are extended to Robert Sutherland Lord, organist of the University of Pittsburgh, who first introduced me to the music of the Harmonists; to Olive Cavanaugh Wilson, Doris Dorr and Reginald H. Fink for their assistance in preparing the typed and musical texts; and to Daniel B. Reibel, curator of Economy Village, who has enthusiastically encouraged every effort to preserve and catalog the music and made possible its performance in public concerts at Economy Village.

The influence on this study of Dr. Karl J. R. Arndt is readily apparent. His writings laid the foundation for all subsequent Harmonist research and chapter one of this volume draws heavily from his *George Rapp's Harmony Society 1785-1847*. Beyond this, I am indebted to him for his careful reading of the text. Throughout, I have retained Harmonist grammatical and spelling practices which are frequently inconsistent and contradictory, especially in the area of hymnody, and Dr. Arndt has labored valiantly to separate my errors from those of the Harmonists.

Finally, the financial support of the Harmonie Associates, a civic organization dedicated to the preservation of the Harmonist legacy, made possible the restoration of the music catalog, a prerequisite to the writing of this work. A special acknowledgment is extended to the Sinfonia Foundation of Phi Mu Alpha Sinfonia Fraternity, Evansville, Indiana, which awarded the author a research grant in American Music in 1972, and helped make this publication possible.

Frontier Musicians on the
Connoquenessing, Wabash, and Ohio

An Historical Sketch of George Rapp's
Harmony Society: 1805-1906

Between the years 1663 and 1806 there were no less than one hundred and thirty communal settlements founded by immigrant religious groups in the United States.[1] Many exhibited features which characterized the monastic movement of the Catholic Church in Europe during the Middle Ages, such as celibacy and community of property. These early American communal villages were comprised of Protestant Separatists who were products of the splintering process which took place in the Lutheran Church during the seventeenth and eighteenth centuries.

The first attempt at establishing a communal society in America was made by a group of Dutch Mennonites, followers of Pieter Plockhoy, who in 1663 settled in what is now Sussex County, Delaware. "Plockhoy's Commonwealth," as it was called, endured peacefully for one year, but in 1664 the English conquered New Netherlands and in the process plundered ". . . what belonged to the Quaking Society of Plockhoy to a very naile."[2]

Twenty years later, a second attempt at communal settlement was made when the followers of the Protestant mystic, Jean de Labadie, founded Bohemian Manor in what is now Cecil County, Maryland. This group suffered from a common ailment of communal living—internal dissension. Established in 1683 the Labadist colony endured until 1698, when disagreement among the members resulted in its dissolution.[3] The Labadists were the last community to come to America from the Dutch and North German areas. The following wave of immigration originated primarily in southern Germany and by the end of the eighteenth century, immigrants from this area had contributed to the founding of eighteen communal villages in America. Between the years 1800 and 1860, no fewer than one hundred and ten more communal societies were established in the United States, many by immigrants from southern Germany.

The numerous political and religious extremists who left Germany during the 18th and 19th centuries were expressing the frustration caused by generations of social and religious turmoil and war.[4] From 1440 to 1493 wars had raged between the German princes, the free states, and the Catholic Church. During the sixteenth century Germany was a country in which ecclesiastical sovereigns, armed with the dreaded weapon of excommunication, ruled with absolute power. The only property secure from the ravages of war was that owned by the Church. The unsettled state of government led to the aggrandizing of ecclesiastics who were protected against prosecution even for the most atrocious crimes, and they and the wealthy privileged classes were freed from the obligation to support or defend the state. The oppression of the lower classes consequently led to peasant insurrections. The four which occurred between 1476 and 1513 were further intensified as a result of the invention of printing which increased dissemination of the writings of humanists such as Erasmus of Rotterdam, whose translations of the early church fathers expanded the theological dimensions of the crises and made conditions appear even more intolerable to the poor.[5] Further, the crowning of Charles V as Holy Roman emperor, a man whose ambitions ran counter to the Reformation, imperial reform, and the German national economy, coincided with Luther's excommunication in 1520. This led to the Knights' War of 1522 and another Peasants' Revolt in 1525. Finally, in 1547, Charles attacked the Protestants at Mühlberg and defeated them, but the Germanic empire was now hopelessly divided.

The beginning of the seventeenth century brought little to relieve the existing religious enmities. The Thirty Years' War between Catholics and Protestants ultimately engulfed much of Europe and so devasted the Rhineland that it did not fully recover for generations. Disease and pestilence were inevitable consequences of the war. Epidemics, such as the one in Eilenberg in 1637 in which eight thousand persons died, were common. The population of Germany shrank from sixteen to six million and, though the war ended in 1648, the effects lasted for more than a century.[6]

Religious tolerance was slowly becoming established, at least in principle, by the middle of the seventeenth century and the Lutheran Church became an important institution in German life. But it experienced dissension within and harassment from without from religious dissidents, Pietists and Separatists, who preached a return to a more primitive Christianity. Many of these attracted large numbers of followers and some eventually formed religious sects of their own.

This religious fragmentation within German Protestantism came about largely through the preaching of Philip Spener (1635-1705), who inaugurated a second Reformation with his "Collegia Pietatis," or "cottage prayer-meetings," which he began to hold in 1670 while he was pastor in Frankfurt-on-the-Main. Spener felt that the Lutheran Church had grown smug in its earlier victories and that the service, with its formal creeds and sacraments, was dominated by the organ which embroidered the chorales and separated the stanzas with unnecessary interludes.[7] The doctrines of Spener, along with the writings of earlier mystics such as Jacob Böhme (1575-1624), influenced the thinking of a host of Separatist preachers who emerged in Germany during the eighteenth century. One of these was Johann Georg Rapp, a Separatist preacher from Iptingen, a village of Württemberg. (See Plate 1)

Johann Georg Rapp, the son of Hans Adam Rapp, a moderately successful farmer, was born 1 November 1757. The second-born in a family of five children, Georg was a good student and early in life showed a strong inclination toward religion. After completing traditional Lutheran church schooling and being confirmed in 1771, he worked at the trade of weaving. He spent several years abroad as a journeyman (where he traveled is not known) and, upon his return to Iptingen in 1783, he married Christine Benzinger of Fiolzheim who bore him two children.[8]

Rapp's religious inclinations increased during the next decade, and he came under the scrutiny of both civil and religious authorities, no small distinction in Württemberg at this time when anything less than a veritable prophet caused little stir in the religious mainstream. He did, in fact, declare himself just that during an official investigation of his preaching activities held at Maulbronn in June, 1791. According to Karl J. R. Arndt, his most comprehensive biographer, Rapp's words to his inquisitors were, "I am a prophet and am called to be one."[9] Moreover, the intensity of his belief was shared by his followers, who were convinced that they constituted a society formed under the special guidance of God, whose Kingdom was near at hand.[10]

Rapp's preaching was based largely upon his interpretation of the Book of Revelation. He was certain that a new heaven and a new earth would come in his lifetime and that he and his followers would have a major role in that event. This intense millenialism fostered a distrust of secular authority in every form and a flaunting of Lutheran doctrine, particularly that regarding the sacraments of baptism and the Lord's Supper. The clergy, outraged when Rapp's followers baptized their own children and boycotted observances of the Lord's Supper, urged the civil authorities to administer disciplinary action. The civil authorities sensed the potential danger of the situation, because Rapp's following, which reportedly numbered in the thousands, came from no less than ten districts, with some walking as much as twelve to fifteen hours to attend meetings at Iptingen. Consequently, the authorities feared an uprising and handled the issue circumspectly despite the fact that Rapp's followers were keeping their children out of the schools which they felt to be, along with the churches, "idols of Baal."[11]

Continued pressure from the Lutheran Church resulted in Rapp's imprisonment in 1791. Considering his extreme position, the sentence was a brief one and he was treated leniently. Over the next six years his religious activities intensified and he was greatly encouraged by his increasing prominence and his growing congregation. In the spring of 1798 he was called before the Württemberg authorities to clarify his religious and political views. On behalf of his congregation, he drafted a document which explained their position on seven major issues.

> . . . we believe in a Christian church . . . on the basis and plan of the holy Apostles and fathers of the first church. . . . This is to be seen from I Cor. 14:27-32. . . . We consider it better to conduct our meetings according to the manner of the first Christians in our homes. . . .
>
> . . . We recognize [baptism] as the seal of Christianity, but as useful only to him who has first been moved by God and, through passionate repentance . . . has been made passive and contrite . . . therefore it will be better not to baptize children . . . they ought to be blessed, however, by tried men according to Mark 10:13-16.
>
> . . . We hold communion several times a year, but only according to the ancient constitution of the noble fathers of the church. . . . There is confession, secret and public. . . . When all disagreements have been settled and unity has been renewed. . . . a meal is prepared and eaten in common.
>
> The institutions [schools] of our land are quite proper and well equipped . . . but it is considered better by us to teach our children ourselves or that we be allowed to keep a teacher, for Deut. 6:6,7 gives us considerable evidence that men living righteousness and seeking it also care best for their children. . . .
>
> . . . Since we notice and know from experience that children about to be confirmed are not interested in the vow which they are about to take but rather in the new clothes, which according to evil custom, they receive at this time . . . we cannot admit our children to take part in the ceremonies.
>
> . . . Our feeling toward the government is still warm. . . . The fact that we do not bind ourselves with physical oaths is not meant to convey any evil intent. . . . Yea, yea, and nay, nay, shall be truth, and shall thus be interpreted and accepted by us.
>
> . . . Those who possess the inner peace of God do not like to hurt creatures and accordingly they may bear no weapons of war. . . .[12]

The Articles of Faith of 1798, as they were to be called, were prepared to meet a civil demand but they embodied most of the religious tenets of Rapp's preaching. The subject of Revelation had been skirted, as had other theological peculiarities which would become important later. But, even lacking these, the document was generally a definitive statement of the beliefs of George Rapp and his Associates, as they came to be known, and was a significant step toward eventual communal organization.

At the close of the eighteenth century, political and military events took on a character not unlike that which had existed in Württemberg during the Reformation. The ascendancy of Napoleon and the devastation accompanying his conquests were watched with great interest by the prophet Rapp because they figured into his calculation regarding the Second Coming of Christ.[13]

Rapp was later influenced by Johann Gottfried Herder's *Ideen zur Philosophie der Geschichte der Menschheit* (Outlines of a Philosophy of the History of Man), a four-volume work published in 1784-1791.[14] To Herder, history was the scene of God's activity, the fulfillment of His plan, and the sole purpose of man's existence was the advancement of humanity toward the Creator's goal. After Rapp read Herder's works, he placed special significance in Revelation 12:6 which he conveyed to his followers when he preached the coming of a new heaven and a new earth, leading them to feel the promise of imminent escape from what was to him a morally bankrupt society. By this time Rapp had lost all hope of realizing his dreams in his homeland and had begun to contemplate emigration. Convinced of his calling, his concern now was to found the New Jerusalem, that place in the wilderness for his society ". . . where she hath a place prepared of God."

THE FIRST MIGRATION

Emigration from the Rhineland reached such great proportions during the eighteenth century that for a time it appeared as if the entire area would be depopulated. Large numbers left the Palatinate, Alsace, and Württemberg, some at the invitation of the British government which hoped to establish them in colonies in America.[15] Others migrated to Russia, Hungary, and other European countries. Rapp's thoughts, like those of the majority of his countrymen, were toward America, and he first considered purchasing land in Louisiana.

> As Napoleon was First Consul at that time, I wrote him in 1802 that he permit us to settle in Louisiana, which then belonged to France. Through his Embassy, I soon received Napoleon's answer that permission for us to settle in Louisiana had been granted and that we could travel there shortly on two French government ships. Fifteen hundred of us planned to leave, but during our preparations our government put so many obstacles in our way that, in the meantime, Napoleon sold Louisiana to the United States and informed us that we should be allowed to settle in France, in the Pyrenees region. For a variety of reasons we could not accept this offer, and we decided to emigrate to the United States. But, as no one of us had acquaintances there, I was elected with two others by our Society to come here first and find a place.[16]

Rapp and his companions left Iptingen in midsummer of 1803, and the congregation was left under the direction of his most trusted follower, Frederick Reichert, a stonemason by profession but a man of many talents, who was completely devoted to his leader and his cause. By Christmas of 1803, the members of the congregation had made a decision to sell their property and prepare to leave. There were 100 families, or about 500 persons, in the group, and Frederick was made the guardian of a common treasury. On 1 May 1804, the first emigration of Rapp's followers set out from Iptingen for Amsterdam from which they set sail for America.[17]

On 4 July 1804, the ship *Aurora* landed at Baltimore bearing three hundred of Rapp's followers. This first group had traveled under the direction of Dr. David Gloss, a physician. A second group numbered two hundred and fifty-seven, under the direction of Frederick Reichert, who was later to become Rapp's adopted son, sailed into Philadelphia on Friday, 14 September, aboard the ship *Atlantic*. A third group arrived aboard the *Margaret*, 19 September 1804, and another group arrived aboard the same ship the following year, on 26 August 1805.[18]

A tract of land of approximately five thousand acres was purchased in Butler County, Pennsylvania, near present-day Zelienople, 22 December 1804. After considerable effort, Rapp gathered his people to this place and the building of a community was begun. They called the village "Harmony," a name which eventually took on the connotation of supreme economic and spiritual unity and which was applied to the Society as well as to the town. During the first year they erected buildings to house most of their families. These houses, eighteen by twenty-four feet, were made of logs. They also built a large barn and a gristmill, to which a race was dug of nearly three-quarters of a mile in length. A stone inn was built in 1806, along with another large barn, a dyer's shop, and a tannery. More buildings, including a store in which to sell their products, were built in 1807. Six hundred bushels of grain and 3,000 gallons of whiskey were sold during that year. In 1808 more stables and barns were built along with a brick church and a bridge across the Connoquenessing Creek. In the same year 2,000 bushels of grain were sold and 1,400 bushels were made into whiskey.[19] By 1810 the Harmony Society consisted of 140 families—more than 700 persons—who cultivated about 3,000 acres and owned large herds of sheep and cattle.

This prosperity was made possible primarily through communal government of the Society, the terms of which were outlined in a document drawn up by Rapp and signed by the members 15 February 1805. It contained six "Articles of Agreement," the first three stating the obligations of the members, and the last three stating those of George Rapp and his Associates. The basic content of the document was as follows:

1. The members renounced all claim to personal property.
2. The members pledged submission to all rules and laws of the congregation.
3. In case any chose to leave the group, no demand would be made for payment or reward for the subscriber or his children.
4. The members were entitled to attend all religious services, all meetings, and were eligible for instruction in the school and church.

5. All the necessities of life—food, shelter, clothing— would be supplied.

6. In case of withdrawal, property brought in would be restored, without interest, in two or three annual installments.

The group was blessed by the business genius of Frederick Rapp (formerly Reichert) who had a unique capacity for gaining cooperation both from members and business associates. He was a good example of the spirit of the Industrial Revolution, and became in the business realm of the Society what Father Rapp was in the spiritual. By the year 1810, three-fifths of the land was under cultivation and large surpluses were sold. Frederick, however, envisioned the Society as more than an agricultural community and desired more diversification of industries, a prospect which was proving difficult in Butler County because of poor transportation and inaccessibility of markets.[20] Limited soil fertility and the rapid settlement of adjacent areas by people unsympathetic to their way of life and envious of their material success led them to search for a location which would permit them to better fulfill their newly awakened industrial ambitions.

THE SECOND MIGRATION

In 1814 George Rapp and two companions set out to find a new site for settlement. After some investigating, it was decided that 25,000 acres near the banks of the Wabash River in the state of Indiana would be purchased. Harmony in Butler County was sold and the Society moved to Harmony on the Wabash during the year 1814-15. Here both agriculture and manufacturing were expanded and the Harmony Society became a major economic power both in the state of Indiana and in the country.

While unity through community of property had been achieved, there were constant internal difficulties in the Society. Father Rapp had as early as 1801 favored the adoption of celibacy. While not in the Articles of Agreement by which the Society was governed, an unwritten rule evolved forbidding, or at least strongly discouraging, marriage and sexual intercourse.[21] Rapp believed that "Adam, as described in Genesis 1:26, 27, was a bi-sexual being, and the female part of him was separated from him as a result of the Fall, which consisted of his discontent with his original state. Sexual intercourse, therefore, was not intended by God and is polluting to man. It can be tolerated in marriage, but only for propagation of the species."[22] And, since the millenium was imminent, there was no sense in having more children who would then be forced to stand in the judgment which was coming.[23] Rapp frequently preached on the subject and, since failure to comply could result in banishment from the Society, it was a source of grave emotional concern to all, with tragic consequences in some instances.[24]

On the Wabash they were confronted with other problems which they had not experienced in Butler County. Fever and illness, largely due to the change in climate, took a heavy toll of Harmonist lives. The death rate, averaging five per year from 1805 to 1810, rose to forty-nine in 1814 and in 1815 seventy members died. Bills and letters at this time frequently have postscripts for Dr. Müller, the Society physician, which reflect an urgency and common knowledge that the Harmonists were having health problems. Isaac Bean, a Pittsburgh merchant, added a note to his bill: "the medicines for Doctor Müller I thought best to send as perhaps he needs them."[25] The quantity in which medicines were bought indicates the scope of the problem, as in the following: "1 keg of medicine for Dr. Müller wt. 123; 3 boxes medicine for Dr. Müller wt. 213."[26] The summer season seemed to bring the most sickness, and a bill received in November, 1814, bears the note, "I am extremely happy to hear of our people at the Wabash recovering their health. . . ."[27]

Visitors to New Harmony also spoke of oppressive heat, heavy rains, prairie fires, and hostile Indians.[28] Still, the productivity of the Society appears not to have suffered. In December, 1815, a steam engine was purchased. Factories were built and markets extended into Louisville, New Orleans, and to other large cities by entrusting representatives with power of attorney to buy and sell and collect debts for them. Many people grew to depend upon the Harmonists for raw materials and manufactured products. Some of their neighbors were suspicious of them, but many depended upon them for domestic essentials as well as for the more luxurious items of frontier living, as the following letters show:

> "please to let bearer have a half bushel salt, 3 lbs. sugar, 3 lbs. coffee, and 1 gallon of your good vinegar. I am just gitting able to stur about. I will be able to see you on Friday if possible. My pork will be lost without salt. I have no money by me owing to sickness. . . ."[29]
> "Sir with respect I wish to inform you that I would be glad to have 2 more of your barls of whiskey on the same credit your let me have the others and you may either put it in the same note or take Burnsides note and i will let my name to it as before. I am a bout building and clearing this summer whitch takes a good deal of licker in this country. . . ."[30]

Buying and selling reached a high point in 1817. This year also saw the largest increase in membership with 130 persons arriving from Württemberg.[31] Dozens of men, women, and children were bought out of indenture by the Society. Contacts, such as the merchant Abishai Way of Pittsburgh, were instructed to greet and care for German immigrants, frequently at considerable expense to the Society.[32]

The spring and summer of 1819 saw a change in the national economy. Frederick Rapp in a letter to James Olds, a business acquaintance in New Orleans, states that "almost half the banks in New York and Philadelphia have failed." A return letter from Olds in September, 1819, says "our city for the past six weeks has been so sickly that almost all kinds of business is at a standstill. . . ." Even Abishai Way declared that because of severe business conditions he could not take "goods on account," a barter-like arrangement he had maintained with the Society.[33]

Domestic difficulties continued as well. Grumbling within the Society as to which families had brought in the most money at its founding had led Rapp to burn the record book in 1818. By 1821 Rapp was so thoroughly disgusted with the moral laxity in the Society, particularly with the new members, that he insisted that new and more specific agreements be drawn up for those who were now coming in.[34]

In addition, transportation continued to be a problem because the Harmonists were frequently at the mercy of the rivers. "The changes in the river and unavoidable accidents excepted" was a clause in most shipping contracts. Abishai Way writes to Frederick Rapp in October, 1818: "one hundred boats lay at dock in the river [Pittsburgh] unable to move for weeks because of a drought which made travel impossible."[35] Frequently the Society ordered merchandise, anticipated its use, only to receive a letter stating that the boat carrying it "got a ground by the shore and sunk wetting most of the goods on board. . . ."[36]

Mounting discontent led the Society to consider still another move and, in 1824, a piece of land was purchased northwest of Pittsburgh. The winter of 1824 was the mildest and the spring of 1825 the most pleasant the area round Harmony, Indiana, had experienced for many years. It was an auspicious year to show a prospective buyer the lands and buildings owned by the Harmony Society. The property had been turned over to an agent, Richard Flower, an Englishman whose antislavery views had gotten him into difficulty with the people in Illinois.[37] Back in England he advertised Harmony as follows:

2,000 acres of highly cultivated land, 15 of it in vineyard, 35 in apple orchard . . . 1 store, a large tavern, 6 large frame buildings used as mechanics shops, 1 tanyard of 50 vats, 3 frame barns 50 x 100, with 1 threshing machine, 3 large sheep stables, 6 two-story brick buildings 60 x 60, 40 two-story brick and frame buildings, 86 log dwellings, all houses have stables and gardens; 2 distilleries, 1 brewery, and factories.[38]

Robert Owen, another Englishman who had had vast experience with the New Lanark Mills in Scotland, was looking for a place to put into practice his ideas which he felt would effect a communitarian transformation of society.[39] He toured Harmony, Indiana, and made the decision to buy it on New Year's Day, 1825.[40] Flower negotiated the deal in which Owen paid $150,000 for the property and $40,000 additional for part of the stock and equipment. Flower received $5,000 commission for his work, but the sale was not particularly profitable for the Harmonists.[41] George Rapp, however, does not appear to have been greatly concerned, for long before the sale he had gone to the 3,000 acre tract near Pittsburgh and, with some of the members, had begun to erect houses to accommodate the Society which would make its third and final migration in the spring.

ECONOMY—LAND OF SILK AND MONEY

The smaller acreage of the new site indicated a decrease in emphasis on agriculture, and the name given to it, Economy, had specific industrial connotations which the village soon reflected. By January, 1826, factories were in operation. The manufacturing of silk, which reached its peak in the 1840s, was begun at this time under the direction of George Rapp's granddaughter, Gertrude Rapp (the daughter of his son, John, who died at the Butler County settlement). By 1831, the Society was leading the country in the manufacturing of silk.[42] A steamboat, the *William Penn*, had been built for the Society at Pittsburgh. It was used to transport the Harmonists from Harmony to Economy and was later used for a time to market their products. The Harmonists' industries prospered sufficiently to prompt a writer in the *Allegheny Democrat* in 1829 to declare that Economy was becoming a monopoly and had the power to "regulate the trade in our market."[43] If there was such a danger it was short lived, for a problem soon arose, once again in the theological area, which profoundly affected the Harmonist industries and created a situation from which the Society would never fully recover.

Rapp had preached the Second Coming of Christ since the first meetings in Württemberg. The concept of Adam as having originally been a dual being, borrowed from the seventeenth-century German mystic, Jakob Böhme, and Rapp's interpretation of Revelation as found in the Berleburg Bible[44] were all bound together in a deep millenial hope. One can, therefore, imagine the impact on Rapp of a letter which arrived at Economy, 24 September 1829. Mailed from Frankfurt-on-the-Main and dated 14 July 1827, it stated that "Count Leon, Archduke Maximilian of the Stem of Judah and the Root of David"[45] would be coming to Economy.

Rapp and the other Harmonists had almost two years to contemplate the arrival of the self-proclaimed Messiah because Count Leon did not reach Pittsburgh until the fall of 1831. His entry into Economy was a colorful one. Two of his party which consisted of some forty followers were sent ahead to announce his arrival. Rapp called the community to the church and, as was the tradition for special occasions, the band was stationed in the church-tower balcony. Years later, Jonathan Lenz, who played French horn in the band, gave his account of the event.

But this one did not come like the Saviour riding on an ass, but in a carriage of four with a suite of courtiers in gala attire and livery, the Count himself wearing a full uniform with epaulets and sword. Says I to myself: 'Play what you will, I'm going downstairs to see the things that are to happen.' Well the Count enters the church, is escorted to the pulpit by Father Rapp, all eyes are upon him and we are all expectancy. But instead of doing any justice whatever to the occasion, he states that he is too full of emotion for utterance. Thereupon Father Rapp did the talking; his speech was not effected by any emotion. . . .[46]

Intense religious discussions were held between the Count and Father Rapp. They also conferred on the subject of the "Philosopher's Stone," a "stone" which Rapp and the Count and many of their contemporaries believed could be made if secret formulas of alchemy were carried out under specific spiritual circumstances and conditions. If discovered, the stone would enable the possessor to change base metals into gold. Rapp had been trying for years to discover the correct formula. The Count, on the other hand, created no small excitement by proclaiming that he already had the stone in his possession. This claim was obviously advanced to gain the support of Rapp's followers and ultimately of the community and its financial resources.

But differences between the two were also developing over more practical matters and a number of the Harmonists were finding the Count's arguments increasingly appealing. In the minds of some, Rapp had recently been particularly irritable and dictatorial and had occasionally shown favoritism toward some of the members. Above all, the rule of celibacy was causing problems and the Count, by opposing the rule, gained followers among the more liberal members in the Society.[47]

Within a few months a schism had developed and had reached irreversible proportions. By 6 March 1832, a document of eight articles outlining a division of property was drawn up. The dissenting group, totaling 358 persons, was to leave the Society with the Count as their new leader. They were to receive $105,000 as their share of the accumulated wealth, less $1,817, the hotel bill which Frederick Rapp levied on the Count and his party for food and lodging during their visit. The financial loss to the Society was great, but the most grievous loss was the loss of many skilled artisans and workers with which the Harmonists had operated their industries.

The dissenters, with their new wealth and a leader who supposedly could manufacture gold, established the town of Phillipsburg (now Rochester), not far from Economy. The satisfaction which they may have felt, however, was not to endure for long. To their dismay they found that the Count did not possess the Philosopher's Stone nor the leadership necessary to keep the group together. A year and a half after the schism, the Phillipsburg community dissolved amid much bitterness. To avoid a court case, the Count and a few followers secretly sailed down the Ohio and Mississippi and attempted to establish a new community in Louisiana. This venture ended abruptly when the Count took ill and died 29 August 1834. Some of his followers later successfully established a community called Germantown in the Red River Valley of northern Louisiana.

At Economy, in the meantime, demands for Harmonist products increased, but because of a lack of laborers many of these could not be met. The woolen factory, Frederick's favorite of the industries, mysteriously caught fire in November 1833, and burned to the ground. Arson was suspected. The strain of the schism, and now the fire weighed heavily upon Frederick, who had been in ill health for some time. Despite a trip to Philadelphia to see a doctor, he died 24 June 1834. With his death, the Society lost the strongest mind in its business complex.

Upon Frederick Rapp's death, George Rapp was made head of temporal affairs. A document giving him power to transact business for the Society was drafted and signed by the members on 5 July 1834. Two members, R. L. Baker and Jacob Henrici, were appointed to assist Rapp in "external" affairs. Business was conducted much as it had been under Frederick, at least to the degree that it was possible to replace him.

George Rapp was seventy-seven years of age in 1836 and, in October of that year, he called the congregation to the church and had Henrici read a revision of the Articles of Agreement which he had written. In this version, article six, the controversial article which provided for the restoration of property brought in by members in case they decided to leave, was deleted and a thorough explanation of complete community of property was given. A total of 391 persons signed the new agreement which made Rapp the undisputed head of all matters pertaining to the Society. Rapp felt that finally they were a truly Christian congregation in the primitive sense, and he began to preach heavily on the coming of the millenium. No new members were taken in and applicants were firmly discouraged.

Rapp believed that when the millenium began, Jerusalem would be rebuilt and, since money would be needed to reconstruct the temple, a church fund to be used for this purpose was begun. The goal was $500,000. Romelius Baker, in a court case in 1852, related his part in achieving this goal:

At the time the $85,000 was brought from Philadelphia (1836 or 1837), Elijah Lemmix was with me. . . . We brought it in boxes. Also in October, 1838, $110,000 in gold sovereigns was brought from the bank of the United States. . . . Mr. Rapp wanted foreign gold . . . time was given for the bank to procure it. . . . The $110,000 was transported in kegs, by canal partly . . . partly by wagon, to Pittsburgh and by water to Economy. The money was in four kegs . . . packed in with dye-wood chipped. . . . Either in 1841 or 1842, I brought the third time, specie from Philadelphia . . . about $50,000. In 1843 another $35,000 from Philadelphia. On one occasion . . . I had coin in bags which I had taken to George Cochran's warehouse, and there packed in a barrel with other things, I believe I filled in the vacant space with oats.[48]

By 16 June 1846, there was $510,000 on hand at Economy. It was reportedly kept behind a large stone in the foundation wall of the Great House where Rapp lived.[49] His preaching during the next year became pleading and impatient. On 7 August 1847, Father Rapp died. One of the elders who was by his bedside reported his last words:

> If I did not so fully believe that the Lord has designed me to place our Society before his presence in the land of Canaan, I would consider this my last.[50]

Necessitated by Rapp's death, new articles were again drafted in 1847. A board of elders was established and trustees were appointed to conduct business. Membership decreased steadily and nonmember laborers were hired to do the work. Primarily under Henrici's leadership, the Society began to invest its money in outside commercial ventures. Among these were the Saw Mill Run Coal Mines and Railroad; a six-mile railroad connecting with the Pittsburgh-Fort Wayne-and-Chicago railway at Darlington; the entire town of New Brighton; and a six-thousand acre tract of land with oil and timber opposite Tidioute.[51] For another twenty years, the financial empire endured. But, as numerous letters in the archives at Economy Village show, applicants for membership were firmly discouraged and no appreciable numbers of members were taken in after the schism of 1832. The Harmonie Spirit remained surprisingly strong in the older members who remained in the Society, but their dwindling number clearly indicated that the Harmony Society was dying a slow but certain death.

RETIREMENT AND DISSOLUTION

"The Society is now comprised of principally elderly men, many of which are retired from active business . . ." reads a real estate advertisement printed to sell Harmonist property in 1864.[52] Ten years later Economy was a peaceful but dying community. "Once it was a busy place, for it had cotton, silk, and woolen factories, a brewery, and other industries; but the most important of these have now ceased"[53] wrote Charles Nordhoff in 1874. "At present Economy is inhabited by . . . 110 persons—most of whom are aged, and none, I think under 40. There are 25 or 30 children adopted by the Society or apprenticed to it, and an equal number belonging to hired laborers," continued Nordhoff. But the millenial hope was still there and when William Hinds visited Economy a few years later he quoted one Harmonist as saying, "We believe that God has called us and given us the truth, and we will wait on him till the end. . . ."[54]

The end came after a series of bitter law suits brought against the Society by former members and heirs of former members. The terminating financial struggle as related by one of the last trustees, John S. Duss, follows below. It is a highly subjective account and, as Dr. Karl J. R. Arndt has conclusively proven, the procedures followed by Duss at the time of the dissolution were ethically questionable to say the least.[55] Our judgments, however, shall be limited to Duss's music and its influence on the Society during its last years. Since this was considerable, it is appropriate that his description of the closing events follow here:

> How through the natural transition from doing everything themselves, through depletion in their numbers and the introduction of hired help, there came about a condition diametrically opposed to the original system; and how through this and their endless contributions to charity—far beyond the point of wisdom—I found, after being elected to the office of Junior Trustee, upon the death of Jonathan Lenz early in 1893, that the Harmony Society, far from being wealthy, was virtually in a state of bankruptcy (there was due to banks alone the sum of $1,500,000, and almost no available security with which to begin the liquidation of this enormous indebtedness) and our dear old members were directly in line for the poor house; how through an agonizing struggle against enemies within and without the Society, and ten years of vexations, wearisome litigation, by the aid of a kind providence (my splendid legal advisors and friends in financial matters are not forgotten) we won the various lawsuits instituted and paid the Society's debt. . . . I resigned my trusteeship in 1903, withdrew from the Society, and devoted myself exclusively to music. Upon resigning my Trusteeship, Mrs. Duss was chosen my successor. The Society, more and more depleted in numbers, was formally dissolved in 1906.[56]

Duss and his wife moved to New Smyrna, Florida, shortly after the Society was dissolved. Later, as the result of an Escheat Case filed by the state of Pennsylvania, approximately six acres of the village on which stood the buildings of central importance to the Harmony Society, were restored and are presently maintained as an historic site under the auspices of the Pennsylvania Historical and Museum Commission. Here extant artifacts of the Society's many industries and crafts are displayed. Here, also, a vast collection of letters and accounts which reveal the daily experiences of George Rapp and his associates, covering more than one hundred years, are preserved. In the archives there are the remaining books of a once magnificent library. They also contain a collection of manuscript and printed music which reflects a broad cultural interest and thriving vocal and instrumental musical activity throughout the history of the Society (see appendix D). It is to this rich musical legacy and the people who formed it, that we now turn our attention.

1.   Arthur Eugene Bestor, Jr., *Backwoods Utopias. The Sectarian and Owenite Phases of Communitarian Socialism in America, 1663-1829* (Philadelphia: University of Pennsylvania Press, 1950), pp. 235-43.

2.   E. B. O'Calloghan, ed., *Documents Relative to the Colonial History of the State of New York.* 11 vols. (Albany: 1856-61). See "A Report of 1684," 3:346. Quoted in Bestor, *Op. cit.*, p. 27.

3. Bestor, *Op. Cit.*, p. 28.

4. William Robertson, *The History of the Reign of the Emperor Charles the Fifth*. 2 vols., (Philadelphia: 1856, 1890) 1: 400-403.

5. Albert Edward Bailey, *The Gospel in Hymns* (New York: Charles Scribner's Sons, 1950), p. 308.

6. Ibid., p. 322.

7. John Julian, *Dictionary of Hymnology*. 2 vols. (New York: Dover Publications, 1957), 1st ed., 1892, 2: 1071-72.

8. Karl J. R. Arndt, *George Rapp's Harmony Society: 1785-1847* (Philadelphia: University of Pennsylvania Press, 1965), p. 17.

9. Ibid., p. 15.

10. John A. Bole, *The Harmony Society: A Chapter in German American Culture History* (Philadelphia: American Germanica Press, 1904), p. 37.

11. See Arndt, *Op. Cit.*, pp. 15-49. At an investigation in 1803, Rapp gave the exact figures of his congregation as 228. He said he did not include "those who were still in a state of fermentation."

12. Arndt, *op. cit.*, gives the full text on pp. 35-40.

13. Rapp was not alone in his millenarian views. The official name of the Shakers was the Millenial Church. The Oneida Society believed that the millenium had begun with the fall of Jerusalem in A.D. 70. The Holy Alliance of 1815, drafted by Tsar Alexander of Russia, and signed by all European rulers except the prince regent of England, the pope, and the sultan of the Ottoman empire, showed the influence of millenium thinking in the highest political offices.

14. Copies of Herder's works are extant in the archives of Economy Village, Ambridge, Pennsylvania.

15. Frederick Klees, *The Pennsylvania Dutch* (New York: Macmillan Company, 1952), pp. 137-46.

16. Sandar Farkas, *Útazás Észak, Amerikaban* (Kolozsvarott: 1834). Quoted in Arndt, *Op. Cit.*, p. 458. Farkas was a Hungarian official who visited Economy in 1832. Arndt, (p. 49) says there were three others who came with Rapp: Rapp's son, Johannes, who was a licensed surveyer; Doctor P. F. C. Haller; and Doctor Johann Christoph Mueller. John Duss, in *George Rapp and His Associates, an Address delivered by J. S. Duss of New Smyrna, Florida, June 6, 1914. New Harmony, Indiana*, (Printed by Hollenbeck Press, Indianapolis), mentions only Johannes and Doctor Haller.

17. Arndt, *Op. Cit.*, p. 56.

18. Haller and Gloss split from Rapp shortly after their arrival and founded their own communities. They took some of Rapp's followers with them and there were, as a result, not as many people to build Harmony in Butler County as Rapp had anticipated.

19. Ibid., p. 106.

20. *The Harmony Society in Pennsylvania*. Federal Writer's Project. WPA Beaver County, Pennsylvania (Philadelphia: William Penn Association of Philadelphia, 1937), p. 10.

21. Sexual and marriage customs were a problem in most communal groups. Many societies practiced celibacy. When William Owen visited Ann Lee's Shakers in New York, he told them of his father's plan to form a new society. They asked if marriage would be forbidden. When he replied, "No," they said "then you can't agree; there will be continual quarrels" (*The Diary of William Owen from November 10, 1824, to April 20, 1825*. Ed. Joel W. Hiatt. [Indianapolis, 1906]. See p. 15).

22. Aaron Williams, D. D., *Harmony Society at Economy, Pennsylvania; Founded by George Rapp* (Pittsburgh, 1866), p. 101.

23. From 1803 to 1813 there were 262 births in the Harmony Society. From 1814 to 1824 there were 69, and from 1825 to 1830 there were 25. See the membership file, Old Economy Museum, Ambridge, Pennsylvania.

24. See "Hildegard Mutschler" and "Conrad Feucht" (Arndt, *Op. Cit.*, pp. 425-432).

25. Accounts, 26 May 1814.

26. Accounts, October 1814.

27. Letter from Frederick Haymaker, 19 November 1814. The respite was temporary and the following death rates indicate that the Indiana climate never did fully agree with the Harmonists: 1818—nineteen deaths; 1819—fifteen deaths; 1822—twenty-five deaths; 1823—twenty deaths. For details on the general health of the Society, see: John W. Larner, Jr., "Nails and Sundrie Medicines" (Master's Thesis, University of Pittsburgh, 1961).

28. Owen, *Op. cit.* pp. 81-83.

29.   Letter from David Love, Springfield, 30 December 1817.

30.   Letter from Alexander Philips, 17 July 1818.

31.   *Harmony Society in Pa.*, p. 12.

32.   See Accounts, 12 November 1818; 26 May 1819; 9 September 1819.

33.   Accounts, August, September 1819.

34.   Arndt, *Op. cit.*, pp. 193, 198, 199. Nothing was stated in these agreements about the return of property (Art. 6). Most of the people coming in at this time were quite poor.

35.   This letter accompanied a bill for goods ordered, among which was a large supply of medicines.

36.   Accounts, 6 April 1820. Letter from Abishai Way.

37.   The Harmonists were antislavery and bought the freedom of the Bores Stag family whom Sandar Farkas met on his visit to Economy in 1831.

38.   *Harmony Society in Pa.*, p. 14.

39.   Bestor, *Op. cit.*, p. 62.

40.   Owen, *Op. cit.*, p. 92.

41.   Duss, *Op. cit.*, pp. 24-25.

42.   Arndt, *Op. cit.*, p. 392.

43.   Quoted in Duss, *Op. cit.*, p. 32.

44.   The Berleburg translation of the Bible was born out of the mystical movement of the early eighteenth century. It was used by the Ephrata Mystics, the Dunkers, and by the Mennonites in Pennsylvania.

45.   His real name was Bernhard Müller. According to the most likely story about him, he was the illegitimate son of a German nobleman and a peasant girl and was born about 1787. His career ascended from tailor's apprentice to Catholic priest; from there to Protestant clergyman and finally to self-proclaimed Messiah. The latter role got him into great difficulty from London to Frankfurt, and finally made him decide to "sell his estate and sail for America." Arndt, *Op. cit.*, pp. 462-67, gives a well-researched account of his origin and activities.

46.   Quoted in Duss, *Op. cit.*, p. 35.

47.   A comprehensive account of Leon's role in this schism is given in the June 1972 issue of the *Harmonie Herald*, the newsletter of the Harmonie Associates, Daniel B. Reibel, ed., Ambridge, Pennsylvania.

48.   Joshua Nachtrieb v. Romelius L. Baker and Society. Circuit Court of the United States, Beaver County, 3 August 1852. Docket book, pp. 26, 29, 33, 36.

49.   This cubicle, with the stone which enclosed it, can still be seen at Economy Village, Ambridge, Pennsylvania.

50.   Arndt, *Op. cit.*, p. 577.

51.   Williams, *Op. cit.*, p. 94.

52.   Leavitt and Honnewell, Real Estate Brochure (Boston: 1864), p. 12.

53.   Charles Nordhoff, *The Communistic Societies of the United States* (New York: Schocken Books, 1966), p. 64.

54.   William Hinds, *American Communities* (New York: Corinth Books, 1961, first printed Oneida, N.Y., 1878), p. 19.

55.   Karl J. R. Arndt, *George Rapp's Successors and Material Heirs* (Cranbury, N. J.: Fairleigh Dickinson Press, 1971), part 3. Dr. Arndt, through his research and study of hundreds of documents relative to the Society's final years, many of which are reproduced in his book, leaves little doubt that the Duss takeover of the Society was planned over a long period of time and was motivated more by selfish ambition than concern for the welfare of the aging Harmonists.

56.   Duss, *Op. cit.*, pp. 41-42. Jacob Henrici died on Christmas Day, 1892. The last surviving members of the Society were Susie Duss and Franz Gillman. Gillman died in 1921. Before his death he turned over "all his belongings" to Susie Duss in return for care and maintenance. In this way the Dusses became the sole possessors of all that remained of the Harmonist fortune.

2

The Music of the Harmony Society:
1805-1825

The music of the Harmonists seems to have developed and expanded, like its industries, in proportion to the size of the streams and rivers which flowed by the Society's lands. The Butler County settlement was made on the banks of the Connoquenessing Creek, a small, wandering stream which formed two of the borders of the Society's property. Comparing the Connoquenessing Creek to the Wabash River in Indiana, and both of these to the Ohio River near Pittsburgh, suggests how the Society's music expanded from 1805 to 1825.

The frequency and extent of the performance of instrumental music at Harmony on the Connoquenessing Creek (1805-1814) remains somewhat a matter of conjecture because there are so few of the Society's music manuscripts extant which clearly date from that time. Some idea of the size of the orchestra and its repertoire can be gotten, however, by determining which of the musical members of the Society might have been present then, and by examining those part-books which contain music in a simpler style than that performed when resources were at their peak some twenty years later. In addition, the travel account of John Melish, who visited Harmony in Butler County in 1811, gives firsthand information both on the size and instrumentation of the orchestra and on the pieces performed at this time. Melish and a physician-companion, Dr. Cleaver, set out from Pittsburgh for Harmony on the Connoquenessing on Monday, 20 August 1811. They arrived there mid-afternoon of the same day and were cordially greeted and given a tour of the community. On the evening of the second day of their visit, they attended a worship service in the church. After the service, the musicians assembled and Melish gives this account of an impromptu concert given in his honor.

The various instruments—three violins and a bass, a clarionet, a flute, and two french horns—were then assembled before the pulpit, and on these the band of musicians entertained us with a great variety of airs. Most were of the solemn kind, and some of them accompanied by vocal music.[1]

This first Harmonist orchestra was modest in size compared to contemporary European ones, but Pittsburgh, the community closest to the Harmonist settlement, had nothing comparable until 1819 when William Evens organized a "band" in conjunction with his Allegheny Musical Society, a choral organization begun sometime after 1811.[2] But, by 1819 the Harmonist orchestra was one of the most prominent musical organizations outside the cities of the eastern seaboard, a distinction achieved largely through the efforts of Johann Christoph Mueller, the Society's physician, schoolteacher, printer, botanist, museum curator, and music director.

Christoph Mueller was born 15 May 1777, in Heimerdingen in the district of Leonberg, Württemberg.[3] Little is known of his background or education except that he had some university training in the disciplines related to the practice of medicine. Mueller had come under the spell of Rapp's preaching in Württemberg and migrated to America with him, either arriving with the survey group in 1803 or with Rapp's followers shortly thereafter. That Rapp would have wanted Mueller with the investigative party is understandable for he was one of the few Harmonists who spoke English and his education and quiet personality commanded respect from persons of all social and cultural backgrounds. Under Mueller's direction, the instrumentalists of the Society were early organized into an ensemble. Although none was allowed to treat music as more than an avocation, the opportunity to study an instrument was open to those who were inclined to do so. Music was taught according to an apprentice system, just as were the trades and crafts, with the more experienced practitioners teaching the beginners.

The Melish account suggests that some of the pieces played by the early Harmonist orchestra may have been hymns or chorales "of the solemn kind." The contents of the various part-books support this (as we shall see in the following chapter on Harmonist hymnody) but under Mueller's direction a secular repertory was also being compiled which, by 1830, totalled more than 300 selections (see Appendix B). These pieces were arranged from printed sources—keyboard copies for the most part—which were purchased from Johnston and Stockton, a piano and music store in Pittsburgh, and from George Willig's music store in Philadelphia.

A typical example of the secular music which Mueller arranged for the orchestra is "Hail Columbia," sometimes called "The President's March" (see Appendix A, ex. 1). This piece appears as the first item in the secular repertory and its frequent appearance in concerts in Pittsburgh at this time attests to its popularity outside as well as within the Society. For example, the "Pittsburgh Harmonic Society" gave a concert at Foster's Ferry House on the Allegheny River 4 July 1818, and the first piece on the program was "Hail Columbia." Foster's Ferry House was owned by William Foster, the father of Stephen and Morrison Foster. The latter, in his book *My Brother Stephen*, states: "At the age of seven he [Stephen] accidently took up a flageolet in the music store of Smith and Mellor, in Pittsburgh, and in a few minutes he had so mastered its stops and sounds that he played "Hail Columbia" in perfect time and accent."[4]

Records at Economy indicate that at one time there was also a clarinet book, now lost, which contained this piece. It is interesting to note that this setting (Ex. 1, Appendix A) does not include a part for violoncello, horn, or trumpet, and the extant clarinet book does not contain this arrangement. Later part-books, most of which date about 1825, have a more elaborate setting of the piece, with a horn fanfare inserted after measure eight of the second strain.

Keyboard accompaniments were an integral part of most festival vocal pieces and hymn settings and were eventually written for the pieces in the orchestra's secular repertoire. Melish, however, makes no mention of a keyboard instrument in the church or in any other building in the community at the time of his visit. It is not likely that there was a pianoforte in the Society in 1811, but a bill from Bosler & Company (Pittsburgh) dated 2 July 1814, suggests that by that time there was one and that it apparently was in need of repair, as the following items on the bill show:

5 forte piano strings @ .50	$2.50
2 rolls of brass strings	$1.50
2 rolls of steel strings	$1.25

Where the instrument came from is not known. Pianofortes were being built in Pittsburgh at this time by Charles Rosenbaum who advertised his instruments for sale "for $250 to $350" and offered "to contract for the building of grand pianos for those who desired them."[5] The Harmonists became quite interested in Rosenbaum's pianos but letters in the archives at Economy indicate that they did not purchase one while the Society was located at Harmony on the Connoquenessing.[6]

The acquisition of a piano for the Society would certainly have been the concern both of Dr. Mueller and of Frederick Rapp. But there were other keyboard players among the membership in addition to these two men, the most proficient probably being Frederick Eckensperger who had joined the Society in 1805. Born in 1779, Eckensperger served the Society as a school teacher and hosteler until his death in 1849. He composed both keyboard and vocal pieces, and a "Presto" (see Appendix A, ex. 2) attributed to him was a favorite of the Society.

The flute was a popular instrument among the Harmonists, and there is considerable music for it in the early manuscripts.[7] There is evidence that George Rapp himself played a "Flute in F" or "Tierce flute," an instrument which became obsolete early in the nineteenth century.[8] The flute pieces in the Harmonist manuscripts are generally short dances and marches by well-known composers of the late eighteenth century. Typical of these are pieces by J. Vanhall found in a manuscript part-book owned by Mueller and inscribed "Leichte Trio für Violine oder Flöte" (Easy Trios for Violin or Flute). The first entry is dated 1803.[9] A flute part-book belonging to a Harmonist musician, Jacob Schreiber, contains marches and waltzes, all of which are anonymous and undated but which obviously belong to the early period.[10]

Mueller did most of the arranging and, therefore, the orchestral and keyboard scores are in his hand. There are a few scores which are dated before 1825, but it is difficult to say how many of these were written before 1814. The individual part-books were sometimes copied by the players. Generally, the hymn tunes were entered in a group at the beginning of a part-book; the book was then inverted and secular entries made. It is not unusual for the two portions of a book to be for different instruments since not all instruments used for orchestral music were used to support hymn singing. Also, some Harmonist musicians played more than one instrument, and entries for two different instruments in the same book for one musician are common. Like all Harmonist property, part-books were turned over to another member if the original owner died or withdrew from the Society. A given book may, therefore, contain entries made over as many as sixty or seventy years, which obviously makes dating books and pieces difficult.

Although there are large musical works included in printed sources extant at Economy Village which could have been available for performance during the Butler County years, there are no records to indicate if or when they were played. A series of six quintets for flute, 2 violins, alto and violoncello by Joseph Haydn[11] (published by Simrock), string quartets by Pleyel[12] (published by J. Andre), and pieces for small ensembles by Bruno Held, von Weber, and Mozart, are among the printed works in the collection which could have been brought to America by musical members of the Society. But it is not likely that these were performed during the early period because neither the instruments nor the players required to perform them were available in the Society at that time.

Watermarks on extant music manuscripts indicate that paper used to copy music was purchased from the same Pittsburgh merchants—the Holdship Company, and Patterson Brothers—throughout most of the Society's early history.[13] European watermarks do not necessarily indicate an early piece since new members arrived from Europe in a steady stream through the 1820s. Many of these brought with them books, Bibles, and hymnals which were quite old then, some printed early in the eighteenth century. It is reasonable to assume that they also brought music with them.

Considering these things, and that the Butler County years were relatively difficult ones when most of the Harmonists' resources were needed to assure physical survival, it seems safe to assume that during this time instrumental music was limited to simple marches, dances, and hymn tunes, and that these were played by small ensembles.

THE ORCHESTRA ON THE WABASH

The move to the Wabash River site in Indiana Territory took place in 1814-15. A surveying group began there in August of 1814 and the Society was moved from Butler County during the winter of 1814 and the spring of 1815. The orchestra showed no appreciable growth during this time, the sole musical purchase recorded being that of two "octave flutes" from the Abishai Way Company on 29 December 1814.[14]

At the very time when the greatest effort was required to build a new community, the Society was weakened by fever and ague resulting from the change in climate. Acquiring medicine in sufficient quantities and caring for the sick filled Dr. Mueller's days, and when medical needs were met he had to concern himself with the school.[15]

Education was taken seriously in the Society and the children were required to attend school until they reached fourteen. At that time they were apprenticed to craftsmen in the various industries in the Society. School hours were held in the forenoon, the afternoon being devoted to mild labor. In the Harmonist philosophy of education, this work experience was as important as the German, English, writing, and arithmetic taught in the classroom.

Singing and the fundamentals of music were also taught. Students were given a music book containing exercises which the instructor selected from printed sources or devised himself. The lessons were numbered and proceeded from the study of scale degree names and intervals to writing and singing in two, then three, and finally four parts.[16]

The students who studied instruments used well-known method books. August Eberhard Mueller's *Elementar Buch für Clavier Spieler*,[17] F. Kauer's *Kurzgefasste Clavier Schule*,[18] and C. P. E. Bach's *Versuch über die wahre Art das Clavier zu spielen*[19] were favored. Kasper Kummer's *Flötenschule*[20] received some use, as did Leopold Mozart's *Violinschule*.[21] Generally, the time from 1815 to 1822 was one of intensive and methodical music study and the proficiency of the orchestra in the late 1820s was the result of the teaching effort expended during this time.

In 1816, Mueller began to compose songs, four of which became very popular among the membership. "Durch zerfallne Kirchenfenster" (Through

284127

LIBRARY
MURRAY STATE UNIVERSITY

Fallen Church Windows) (Appendix A, ex. 3) and "Es blüht ein Blümlein," (There Blooms a Flower) (Appendix A, ex. 4) were written on 24 July and 31 July, respectively. "Herr, führe mich mit Engels-Treue" (Lord, Lead Me . . . .) (Appendix A, ex. 5), and "Die Menschenlieb," (Charity) (Appendix A, ex. 6) were both composed 2 February 1817. All were used extensively as hymn tunes, and their position in the instrumental part-books is of some aid in dating the pieces which precede and follow them.

In 1817 the instrumental music program of the Society was greatly expanded. The industries were flourishing, a steam engine had been purchased and there was economic growth and prosperity. In April, an interesting cargo of materials was purchased from Abishai Way and shipped to Harmonie, Indiana. It consisted of "1 box of drugs and glass weighing 56 lbs.," and ". . . 1 box a piana forty, 379 lbs."[22]

This piano appears to have been purchased from the Pittsburgh piano manufacturer, Rosenbaum. Its arrival at Harmonie, Indiana, must have created considerable excitement. The following excerpts from two letters written by Frederick Rapp to David Shields, one of the Society's agents, show that the purchase had been considered almost a year before the instrument arrived.

August 1, 1816
. . . Our Doctor Miller says that he hath tryed Mr. Rosenbaums forte pianno, and found [it] very good and if you can get them examined by some of your friend, I am no ways in great haste but which to get a good one. . . .[23]

January 6, 1817
. . . I received not long since a Letter from M. C. Rossenbaum of Pitts informing that he has a forte piano ready for me, expecting an answer whether I would have it. I shall write him to day that I want him not to send it before Spring, as it is danger to forward at this Season of year. . . .[24]

In August of the same year, seven wagon loads of supplies for the Society were purchased in Philadelphia at a total cost of $10,616.12. Among the purchases were the following made of the Allyn Bacon Company:

1 pair of horns	$30.00
1 pair of bassoons	$30.00
1 packing case	$ .75
2 octave flutes	$ 4.00

Also purchased on the same trip were a copy of "Lamp's Thorough Bass" and "one Piano-Forte Tutor." These were bought from George Blake's Music Store in Philadelphia.

There were frequent purchases of violin strings, music books—usually in dozen lots—and more piano strings, indicating that the instrumentalists were busy and that music was taking on increasing importance. "Rousseau's Dream," a piece found in a conductor's score-book dated 1819, shows the instrumentation of the orchestra during this intermediate period and in addition, gives some indication of Mueller's skill at orchestration (see Appendix A, ex. 7).

Preparation of the *Harmonisches-Gesangbuch* of 1820, the Society's first printed hymnbook, must have occupied Mueller's time in 1819, although the book proved less than satisfactory. Still, the orchestra rehearsed, and it played not only for Society functions, but for the neighbors in the surrounding area as well. On 19 October 1822, the Harmonists gave a dinner and concert for their neighbors, and the orchestra received favorable mention in the *Niles Register* and *Indiana Gazette*. The scope of the musical resources—musicians and instruments—then available can be seen from the following list given in a conductor's score belonging to Dr. Mueller. It contains the names of some of the musicians active in the Society between the years 1822 and 1828.[25]

Verzeichniss der Musicanten, Sänger und Sängerinen nach ihrer Ordnung bei Singstücken. (A list of the instrumentalists and singers according to the parts which they perform.)

1. Musicanten
     Violino Primo—J. Ch. Müller
     Violino Secondo—Jonathan Wagner
     Viola—Burghard Schnabel
     Cornoes—Jonathan Lentz, Christian Wohlgemuth
     Violoncello—Wallrath Weingärtner
     Fagot—Daniel Schreiber

2. Sänger und Sängerin
   a. Soprano 1
       Felix Wolf, Sylvester Gayer, Gertrude Rapp, Hildegard Mutschler, Sibilla Henger, Sibilla Hurlebaus, Helena Reichert, Mensueta Schmid.
   b. Soprano 2, wie Alto
       Killinger, Christ. Knodel, Stahl, Lemox, Endris, Logina [Henger], and Paulina [Speitel]
   c. Tenore
       Adam Schreiber, Bamesberger, Elias Speitel, Christian Knodel.
   d. Basso
       Henrici, Feucht, Wolfert, J. Bauer.

This list gives the names of those musicians who were part of an oratorio or cantata performing group rather than the full orchestra. The bugles, clarinets, and trumpets are not listed, nor are the flutes. Further, some known instrumentalists, such as Speitel and Henrici, are listed as singers and some are listed as both. Since Henrici's name is on the list, it must have been added after 1826, the year of his arrival. Some names are crossed off in pencil, indicating that the list was altered over the six-year period which it represents. It is, nevertheless, a good indication of the performance potential in 1822. Manuscript sources indicate that several performers were versatile. Lentz, Schnabel, Henrici, and Mueller, to mention a few, played more than one instrument, and it is reasonable to assume that performances at this time were of a good quality.

The musicians on the preceding list, with the exception of Mueller, Weingärtner, and Speitel, were in their late teens and early twenties in 1822. Some of them, including Jonathan Lenz, Gertrude Rapp, Helena Reichert, Mensueta Schmid, and Sibilla Hurlebaus, were born in the Society, several of them in 1806 and 1807, the time when celibacy was being adopted. Mueller must have felt considerable attachment to them for he had probably been present at their births and had served them as physician and school master all their lives.[26]

Other names on the list deserve notice here. Both Conrad Feucht and Hildegard Mutschler, who ran away and were married in 1829, are in this group. They returned to Economy about 1836 and, as though to show their contempt for the rule of celibacy, had three children while living within the Society. Conrad, through the apprentice system, became a physician to the Society and was highly respected. One of the children, Benjamin, also became a doctor. For a time, he served as a bandmaster in the Society.

Musically, the list creates some difficulty. At least two of the names in the Soprano 1 section are men. Felix Wolf (b. 1805) and Sylvester Gayer (b. 1801) were beyond the age when male voices change. At least two second sopranos were also men: Christian Knodel, who is listed twice, and William Killinger.[27] The music which they performed does not suggest any peculiar performance practice, such as having the tune in the tenor as was done in early American fuguing tunes and hymn settings. Also, there is no reason to believe that these were "tenors" for the tenors are listed under a separate heading.[28]

Two other instruments, the "Klappenhörner," are conspicuous by their absence from Mueller's list. In 1821, the Society had sent two members to Germany to collect money resulting from inheritances and the sale of property formerly belonging to Society members. When they returned in 1823, they brought with them "choice varieties of grapes from the Rhineland, many books, a small telescope, a new kind of musical instrument called the Jubel Horn, a camera obscura, and astronomical charts."[29]

Just what a "Jubel Horn" is is not clear, but it is possible that the instrument referred to was one of the keyed bugles which so impressed the Duke of Saxe-Weimar Eisenach when he visited Economy in 1826.[30] This instrument had been invented by an Irishman, Joseph Halliday, in 1810, and was later called the Royal Kent bugle. It was a chromatic instrument and was generally built in C in England and in B flat on the Continent. It permitted rapid playing with little effort, although to play it in tune demanded a good musician.[31]

It is likely that the bugles were acquired in Europe by the two Society agents at Frederick Rapp's request. It is strange that this instrument, with an exclusively military background, should have appealed to the Harmonists who regularly paid impressive fines to avoid participation in the militia.[32]

The orchestra was looked upon with favor by George Rapp, and there is no doubt that he encouraged Mueller's musical efforts.[33] A letter written by Rapp in April, 1823, states:

> At 11 o'clock we went rowing in the boats . . . you can easily picture what a fine echo the French Horns and the music otherwise made in the corners and curves in the Wabash—you would scarcely believe it. . . .[34]

The acquisition of another instrument, a pipe organ which was to be installed in the "cruciform church," was planned in 1823.[35] A description of the building (see plate 3) which was to house the instrument was written by William Herbert of London on 6 February 1823:

> They are erecting a noble church, the roof of which is supported in the interiour by a great number of stately columns . . . the kinds of wood made use of for this purpose are . . . black walnut, cherry, and sassafras. Nothing . . . can exceed the grandeur of the joinery, and the masonry and brick-work seem to be of the first order. The form of this church is that of a cross . . . the sides of which, inclining towards the top, are terminated by a square gallery, in the center of which is a small silvered globe . . . I can scarcely imagine myself to be in the wilds of Indiana, on the borders of the Wabash, while passing through the long and resounding aisles and surveying the stately colonnades of this church.[36]

Earlier, a church bell had been purchased in Liverpool, England, and shipped to New Orleans aboard the *Richard George Finlater*, ". . . in account and at the risk of Fred. Rapp," and to Harmonie, Indiana, via riverboat.[37] The cost of the bell was £ 153.7, no small expense.

Along with the bell, consideration of a pipe organ for the church was seemingly consistent with the Rapps' religious views at this time. On 28 April 1823, Phillip Bachmann, an organ builder in Lititz, Pennsylvania, sent a letter addressed to Frederick Rapp and a list of specifications for an instrument for the Harmonist church.

> Pursuant to our conversation I shall forward to you specifications for a new organ for your church. According to the size of your church and school, I have found that no organ will give adequate service than one having at least 30 stops with 2 manuals and pedals.

Bachmann's stop list includes twelve stops on the Great, eleven on the Swell, and seven on the Pedal, the total consisting of 1,696 pipes. There are no reeds "since the best are affected by the weather and are never in tune. . . ." The cost of the instrument was to be $7,000 at the factory.[38]

He then goes on to suggest that Rapp consider an additional six ranks which would result in an instrument equal in size to the largest organ in the United States, "the same being located in the Catholic Church in Baltimore, which cost $12,000 without installation. . . ." Bachmann concludes, "you may depend upon the most skillful workmanship and best obtainable material. I am not new in the business. I have learned in Germany and have earned my bread in this kind of work for thirty-one years. Altogether I have made thirty-two larger and smaller organs. I hope for a favorable answer." There is every reason to believe that Bachmann was as skilled and experienced as he said because he was a son-in-law of the noted organ builder Tannenberg. Regrettably, the installation never took place, for little more than a year later, 11 May 1824, property for a new settlement was purchased on the Ohio River just beyond Pittsburgh. The Harmonists were preparing to move again.

During this last year on the Wabash, however, some revealing observations concerning the social function of music among the Harmonists were recorded in the diary of William Owen, the son of Robert Owen, the English socialist-industrialist who purchased the Indiana property from the Rapps in 1825. William Owen arrived at Harmony 16 December 1824, and kept notes on activities there through April, 1825.

Sunday, December 19, 1824

. . . We dined at 11 and at 1/2 past 12 we were summoned to church by the band playing different airs. . . . At 5 o'clock in the evening it was still light. We returned to tea with Mr. Rapp, [Frederick][39] or rather to an elegant supper composed of all sorts of meats, cakes, etc. Afterwards, in an adjoining room, music commenced and we heard a concert of vocal and instrumental music until 9 o'clock. There were 12 or 14 singers and a pianoforte, 2 violins and 2 flutes, and a bass. Gertrude Rapp sang and played. During the concert wine, fruit, etc., were passed about.

Sunday, January 2, 1825

At 6 [P.M.] we went by invitation to Mr. Rapp's, where we supped and dined and afterwards assisted at a concert composed of the same performers as that we attended a fortnight ago.

Sunday, January 16, 1825

No sermon in church, owing to Mr. Rapp's absence. The principle observable occupation of the Harmonians was music, which they carried on in small parties in different parts of the village.

By the time of the January 16 entry, the Owens had been at Harmony for one month. It is curious that Owen did not mention Dr. Mueller in the preceding account. It is possible that Mueller was away during the early part of Owen's visit for he traveled about tending to the medical needs of neighbors outside the Society as well as looking after the health of the membership.[40] Owen's entries reflect boredom but, after 19 January, when he apparently met Mueller, they show renewed enthusiasm. Mueller was then engaged in printing and astronomy as well as in music.

January 19, 1825

We visited Mr. Rapp and Dr. Mueller . . . afterward we noted down a few Scottish airs.

January 21, 1825

. . . called on Mrs. Rapp and Miss Gertrude, who sang "Auld Lang Syne" to us. Dr. Mueller came in and assisted.

January 22, 1825

. . . in the evening . . . we had a little music.

January 24, 1825

. . . in the evening, made music, and astronomised and wrote.

February 14, 1825

. . . we practiced music a little.

February 16, 1825

After tea Dr. Mueller came in, also several performers on different instruments came in and a number of female singers, whereupon a concert commenced which lasted until half past nine . . . .

Most social music-making took place on Sundays, as the above excerpts show, but was not confined to Sundays alone. Indeed, the vast quantity of music manuscripts, hymnals and pedagogical items at Economy, representing only a portion of what was once the Society's music library, is proof that music occupied much of the leisure time of the Harmonists. Hours were spent not only practicing and performing, but also composing and copying parts for singers and instrumentalists.

There is no record of dancing of any kind within the Harmony Society. Waltzes, quadrilles, minuets, and other dance forms are well represented in the instrumental repertoire, and in the hymn tunes as well, but the only record of actual dancing in Owen's diary describes that done at a home near the Society in Indiana.

I led off with Mrs. Carter in a country dance. Afterwards in the course of the evening, we danced a Kentucky reel, but except that, only country dances.[41]

By late March 1825, most of the Harmonists were at Economy,[42] their new home near Pittsburgh. The departures of various groups of the membership from Harmony are described by Owen who mentions that the band played as the boats left. The steamboat *Ploughboy* and the Harmonists' own steamboat, *William Penn*, were used to transport goods and personnel to the new site.[43] It was a colorful and emotional time and Owen watched with interest although he was somewhat surprised at "all the kissing that took place . . . from man to man, instead of as is customary in England . . . among man and wife and between females among themselves."[44] While surprising to Owen, this display of affection was another manifestation of the intense community spirit or "Harmonie Geist" which held the Society together. This spirit is apparent in the instrumental pieces written by Dr. Mueller in 1830 and in pieces composed for the Society by the Pittsburgh attorney Charles von Bonnhorst and the composer-publisher W. C. Peters between 1826 and 1833. It is most apparent, however, in the vocal music, for here texts written by Society members reveal the principles which were at the heart of this peculiar brotherhood.

HARMONIST VOCAL MUSIC

The vocal music which was performed by the Harmonists before 1825, besides the extensive hymn repertoire, consisted of anthem-like pieces called "odes" which were composed by members and friends of the Society for festival observances.[45] These festivals consisted of traditional Christian holy days as well as those peculiar to the Society.

The festivals carried over from the church year were Christmas, Easter, and Pentecost. The Harmonist festivals added to these were Harmoniefest, observed on February 15, to commemorate the signing of the articles of association which formally established the Society on that date in 1805; Erntefest (Harvest Festival), observed during the early part of August; and the Liebesmahl (Lovefeast), the Harmonists' own version of the Lord's Supper which was observed in late October. Each of these had theological and communal peculiarities which were often reflected in the texts of the songs written for these occasions.

Harmoniefest, the day most peculiar to the Society, was described by William Owen who, in 1825, recorded the observance as taking place on February 17:[46]

> This day the Harmonians celebrated the anniversary of their union into a Society. They began with music between 5 and 6 o'clock and at 9 they went to church. At 12 they dined and remained together with a short interval until near five o'clock, and at 6 they supped and remained together until after 9 o'clock. What they were engaged in we did not learn as they kept it to themselves, but they seemed to think they had passed the day agreeably, and from many expressions they made use of, I should conclude that the meeting, from some cause or other, had tended to strengthen the bond of union subsisting among them. Part of the day was probably

employed in getting a knowledge of the state of their affairs. They have now been united 20 years. They transacted no business at the store but many persons arrived on business and were disappointed as they had not given any notice of the intended holiday before. This the Americans thought they should have done. But they seemed to wish to throw a veil of secrecy over all their proceedings. Before breaking up at five o'clock, they marched out of the church in closed ranks preceded by their music, all singing. They halted before Mr. Rapp's house and sang a piece of music and dispersed.

This day became the official time for new members to be taken into the Society. It began with a band concert, usually from the tower of the church after the Society moved to Economy, and throughout the day every effort was made to emphasize those principles which made the Harmony Society different from the world outside.

The festivities usually included the performance of one or more odes, such as "Wem tönet heut der Feier-Klang" (For Whom the Festive Sounds this Day?) composed by Mueller for the Harmoniefest of 1822 (see Appendix A, ex. 8). The phrase lengths of this piece are irregular, and the general structure of the music is determined largely by the text and the antiphonal performance procedure (Mägdlein-girls; tutti-all; and Knaben-boys). In this respect the music of the Harmonist odes resembles the music of the Seventh Day Baptists of Ephrata, Pennsylvania, which contains intricate singing in alternation. Harmonically, however, Mueller's piece is limited to tonic, subdominant, and dominant chords with an occasional super tonic, usually in major. Rarely did he use augmented or diminished chords and, while he used passing tones occasionally, his melodies are largely comprised of triadic patterns. The high range of the piece probably reflects a low tuning of the instruments rather than unusual range on the part of the singers. Despite these limitations, the performance—with men, women, and children seated in different parts of the church, as was the Harmonist custom—must have been appealing and even stunning to the average Indiana frontiersman.

"Seyd beglückt" (Be Blessed), an ode composed by Mueller 2-4 May 1823, shows considerable expansion over the preceding piece (see Appendix A, ex. 9). There are soli for bass and tenor as well as sections designated for "Mägd.," "Knabe," and "Tutti." In addition, it has a brief recitative section in which the metre changes from 6/8 to Common time.

The Harmoniefest also appears to have included a memorial service with music to be performed at the cemetery. Some manuscript hymnbooks contain a piece called "Wie Seelig lässt sich sterben" (How blessed are they that die [in the Lord]) which is designated as "Kirchhof Lied aufs Harmoniefest 1818." (Cemetery song for Harmoniefest 1818).[47]

Prior to 1833, festival music was comprised of two or more odes like the preceding, which were alternated with hymns sung by the congregation and with instrumental pieces. The following list of music performed at Christmas in 1817 shows the impressive quantity of music which was prepared for festive occasions.

Schmükt das Fest
In des Ostens fernem Lande (Aria)
Empor zu Gott mein Lobegesang
Sehet wie die klären Sterne
Wie schön bist du Freundliche Stille
Schweight ihr ernsten Glocken (Christnacht)
Sey uns gegrüsst (Choral)
O du holder süsser Knabe (Aria)
Senke dich (Aria)
O Nacht, und du O feyerliche Stille (Aria)
Wie wird des Grabes

After 1833, when instrumental resources declined, the number of festival odes decreased and the quantity of hymns used during festival observances increased.

The penultimate item on the above list, "O Nacht, und du O feyerliche Stille," was composed by Frederick Eckensperger, the Society's hosteler. (See Appendix A, ex. 10). This piece reflects a greater concern for harmony and voice-leading than that displayed in the Mueller pieces. The quarter-note triplets create rhythmic variety and, with the flute descant, make this piece more interesting than the preceding ones.

The instrumentalists played the odes, although most hymn and ode entries appear primarily in the books for bassoon, flute, strings, and keyboard. There are few ode or hymn entries in the extant brass books. Keyboard sources, however, have favorite hymns scored in several keys, indicating an effort to accommodate voices in various ranges and, possibly, transposing instruments.

The Liebesmahl (Love Feast) of the Harmonists was similar in some ways to the Communion observances of the Amish and Moravians.[48] The Harmonists did not observe a fixed "Bet und Fasttag" (Prayer and Fast Day) prior to Communion as did the Amish, but the time prior to the service was of a devotional character and all quarrels and misunderstandings were to be resolved before the members participated in the Lord's Supper. Fast and prayer days were not uncommon in the Harmony Society, but they appear to have been reserved for times of communal and personal crises.[49] Odes which alternated singing groups, recitatives, and tutti, as well as hymns which stress the sacrificial aspect of the traditional Christian Communion service, were an important part of the Liebesmahl festivities.

Music in the Harmony Society, both instrumental and vocal, was not confined to festivals or to one group of performers. There were a number of vocal ensembles in the Society, as Owen's diary indicates.

Friday, December 17, 1824
As they dine at 11, we returned to Mr. Rapp's house and dined with him and his
granddaughter, Gertrude, a very pretty, innocent young girl of 15 or 16, who after
dinner played some airs tolerably well on the piano-forte and sang a few German
songs along with 3 other girls also very good looking. . . .

This quartet of girls, comprised of Gertrude Rapp, soprano; Sibilla Hurlebaus, alto; Logina Hingerin, tenor (!); and Sibilla Hingerin, bass (!), were
close friends and sang together for many years. Several sets of part-books
used by them are extant in the collection.[50]

On the same day, 17 December 1824, Owen and his father visited the
Harmonist cotton mill which was powered by oxen walking on an inclined
plane. A heavy rain came up and they were obliged to remain inside the mill
which ceased operating until the shower was over.

While we waited till the shower was over, the women in the room formed a circle
and sang songs to us of their own accord. The words are usually about friendship
and harmony and the music is their own. Those who work together learn to sing
with each other, thus forming a number of small singing parties. . . .

These songs of "friendship and harmony" were probably two pieces which
were favorites of the Society, "Harmonie, du Bruderstadt," the text of which
was written by George Rapp and "Freut euch ihr Kinder," a piece written by
Frederick Rapp. (See Appendix C, nos. 85 and 70).

Owen found the Harmonists' singing entertaining, and he was impressed
by their lack of "bashfulness or false modesty."[51] He says on one occasion,
however, that "almost all the females [sing] with a nasal twang."[52]

In addition to the simpler vocal music, manuscript and printed copies of
oratorios and cantatas by prominent eighteenth-century composers are in the
collection at Economy Village. Two of these are *Abraham auf Moriah*, an oratorio by J. H. Rolle,[53] and *Die Hirten bey der Krippe*, by D. G. Turk.[54] It was
assumed that these works had been given to the Harmonists by the Moravians with whom they occasionally communicated. Early in 1974, Daniel B.
Reibel, curator of Economy Village, discovered a letter which leaves no doubt
as to the origin of the works. Addressed to R. L. Baker and dated 26 November 1838, it states: "I sent last Friday morning a package addressed to you
containing a collection of German music in manuscript . . . this collection
came into my possession several years since through a distinguished Lutheran clergyman of New York, the Reverend Frederick Christian Schaeffer,
whose father brought it from Germany." The author of the letter, a certain
Titus W. Powers of New Brighton, thought that the pieces might "afford
some entertainment to the choir of your Society as well as to your friends
generally." The letter gives the titles of five other eighteenth-century works
which clearly could not have been performed by the Harmonists before 1838.

In addition, the fine state of preservation of the manuscripts, the quality of the music, and the instrumentation—especially the presence of oboes, instruments not used by the Harmonists—indicates that these pieces were never performed in the Society although both instrumental and vocal music expanded to grand proportions at Economy, the third and final home of the Harmony Society.

1. John Melish, *Travels in the United States of America in the Years 1806-1811.* 2 vols. (Philadelphia, 1812), 2:73. Through examination of music manuscripts at Old Economy, it is possible to tentatively identify three musicians in this group. One of the violinists could have been Johann Christoph Mueller, who also played the flute and pianoforte. The bass could have been Wallrath Weingärtner who came from Glöttbach in Württemberg and brought considerable wealth to the Society. The flute could have been played by Jacob Schreiber, whose father, a wealthy German-American farmer with a family of nine children, had joined the Society in 1806. See Appendix D, IM 2.25; IM 2.8-3; and IM 2.26.

2. Edward Gladstone Baynham, "The Early Development of Music in Pittsburgh." (Ph.D. diss. University of Pittsburgh, 1944), p. 45.

3. Some sources give the year 1779 as the year of Mueller's birth. A marker in the Old Beaver Cemetery, Beaver, Pennsylvania, where Mueller is buried, gives the year of his birth as 1777.

4. (Indianapolis: 1932), p. 31.

5. *Pittsburgh Mercury*, 8 June 1814.

6. John Duss comments that some members of the Society made their own instruments. The bill from Bosler & Co. may have some relationship to his remark: "One of the young men even made a piano, which was later sold, but Frederick saw to it that several handsome pianos and organs were purchased." John Duss, *The Harmonists: A Personal History.* (Harrisburg: The Telegraph Press, 1943), p. 65.

7. See Appendix D, IM 2.10; IM 2.11; IM 2.12; and IM 2.22.

8. Rapp's hymn tune book (IM 2.41) has entries marked "Flute in F."

9. Appendix D, IM 2.22.

10. Appendix D, IM 2.26.

11. Appendix D, IP 2.3.

12. Appendix D, IP 2.6.

13. Holdship's watermark consisted of his name in block letters with an anchor design. Patterson's consisted of his name in block letters.

14. "Octave Flute" was the term given to the piccolo during the eighteenth century. Whether these are transverse instruments or Blockflöte is not clear, but the price paid—$3 each—would suggest the latter.

15. Mueller got the school under way in Indiana by ordering a large supply of "Primers, United States Spelling Books, Pencils, German and English Testaments, Paper of different kinds, and Watts' Hymns" from R. Patterson in Pittsburgh and D. Billmeyer of Philadelphia. See Accounts of February 3, 1815; March 1, 1815; and May 8, 1815. Book titles which frequently appear on invoices are "Pilgrims Progress," "The Life of Washington," "Scott's Lessons," "Manners and Customs," and "The American War."

16. See Appendix D, TM.1, TM.4, and TM.8. These books contain considerable material from Knecht's *Elementarwerk der Harmonie* (TP.11).

17. A. E. Mueller (1767-1817) based this method upon Löhlein's *Pianoforte-Schule*, a two-volume work published in 1765 and 1781.

18. This appears to be comprised of selected exercises from Kauer's *Kurzgefasste Generalbass-Schule für Anfänger*, published in 1800. See TM.6.

19. Appendix D, TP.9.

20. Appendix D, TP.14.

21. Appendix D, TP.8.

22.   This piano probably inspired Frederick Rapp to make himself a keyboard score-book of the "Aria und Gesänge der Harmonie" (see HM 2.28). Many of the entries in the book are dated 1816 and 1817.

23.   Economy Village Archives, Correspondence Book 2, p. 96.

24.   Ibid., p. 109.

25.   Appendix D, VM 3.4.

26.   Mueller and his wife, Joanna, had two children (1806 and 1808), but both died in infancy.

27.   There were other Killingers in the Society, but they did not arrive until 1829.

28.   Ugly rumors regarding the alleged practice of castration were circulated by enemies of the Society from time to time (see Arndt, *Op. cit.*, pp. 339, 543, 609). This listing of the male voices probably has some musical explanation because Felix Wolf's name is also on a tenor part book in the collection (see HM 2.17-5).

29.   John Duss, *The Harmonists: A Personal History* (Harrisburg: The Telegraph Press, 1943), p. 53. Also see Owen, *Op. cit.*, p. 54.

30.   Bernhard, Duke of Saxe-Weimar Eisenach, *Travels through North America during the Years 1825 and 1826*. 2 vols. (Philadelphia: Carey, Lea & Carey, 1828), 2:166.

31.   The Kent bugle was considered a novelty in Pittsburgh as late as 1831. In February, the publisher-composer W. C. Peters announced a public concert: "Mr. Peters will give a concert on Wednesday evening next, the 16th at Mr. Bond's Concert Hall on Penn Street. Tickets may be obtained in the principle book stores. The qualifications of this gentleman as a musician are already too well known and admired to require comment from us. Mr. Burns is engaged to perform some solos on the Kent Bugle, which alone would be a treat of no ordinary value." Quoted in Evelyn Foster Morneweck, *Chronicles of Stephen Foster's Family*, 2 vols. (Pittsburgh, 1944), 1:82.

32.   Fines paid on this account in April and May, 1815, totaled $657.87. A receipt signed by Samuel Power, Brigade Inspector of 2nd Brigade,16th Division, Penna. Militia reads: ". . . Recd of John Baker . . . for refusin [*sic*] to march to Erie when ordered by Major Genl. David Mead."

33.   Mueller was a prominent figure in the Society. It is interesting to note that his signature is the third one (George and Frederick's being first and second) on the "Jefferson Petition," a request regarding the purchase of land which the Harmonists submitted to the United States government in 1805.

34.   Quoted in Arndt, *Op. cit.*, p. 246.

35.   There were two Harmonist churches in Indiana. One was a frame building and the other was made of brick and built in a cruciform design.

36.   The letter was published in 1825 under the title: "A Visit to the Colony of Harmony in Indiana, in the United States of America." Quoted in Arndt., p. 284.

37.   Accounts, 4 May 1818.

38.   Two other letters from Bachmann are extant in the Archives. They are dated 28 April and 30 May 1823. The second of these appears to be the last communication which Bachmann had with the Society, and there is indication that there was disagreement as to where and how the instrument was to have been placed in the church.

39.   George Rapp was then at Economy with a building crew of approximately one hundred workers. The Owens had stopped there enroute to Indiana. The horn and bugle players were at Economy with Rapp.

40.   The Harmonist Store Record Book of 1814-1825 shows income for various services rendered outside the Society. The total recorded earned by Dr. Mueller in 1814 is $1353.00, an impressive figure considering his many duties within the Society as well.

41.   Owen, *Op. cit.*, p. 119.

42.   Mueller was one of the last to leave. As late as Monday, 28 March 1825, he was still working with the printing press. Owen says he "corrected the press" for him (ibid., p. 131).

43.   On the trip of 18 March, one of the Harmonist children fell from the *William Penn* and was drowned. This event is pathetically recorded in Sabine Hartmann's Ms hymnbook, Appendix D, pM.9-2.

44.   Owen, *Op. cit.*, p. 122.

45.   Ode texts were printed in *Feurige Kohlen* (1826) and *Eine Kleine Sammlung Harmonischer Lieder* (1824), two books of verse printed by the Society on their own press.

46.   It is unlikely that Owen made a mistake in the date but rather that, owing to the impending move and the absence of some of the members, the observance had been postponed two days.

47.   See pM. 3-1, p. 332, and pM. 5-1, p. 197.

48. Frederick Klees, *The Pennsylvania Dutch* (New York: Macmillan Co., 1952), p. 101.

49. The cover of John Schreiber's manuscript hymnbook (Appendix D, pM. 3-1) is inscribed: "Fast und Bet Tag an January 25th, 1820."

50. The part-books are so inscribed. Since those who worked together sang together, a full SATB grouping of voices was not always possible, making it necessary for some of the men to sing "soprano" and "alto," and some of the women "tenor" and "bass."

51. Owen, *Op. cit.*, p. 89, 28 December 1824.

52. *Ibid.*, p. 78, 19 December 1824. Owen's opinion was shared by one Johann Schmidt who left the Society on the Wabash and found employment as a school teacher in Montgomery County, Ohio. Following an unhappy marriage which ended tragically, he tried to return to the Society as a teacher. Apparently possessing some ability, he volunteered to teach singing, but commented that this would be difficult because in Harmonie "they all sing, but they all sing wrong." See also Arndt, *op. cit.*, pp. 420-21.

53. Barry S. Brook, *The Breitkopf Thematic Catalogue 1762-1787* (New York: Dover Publications, 1966), p. 668. The work is listed under "Geistliche Gedichte," published 1779-80. See also Appendix D, IM 3.13.

54. *Ibid.*, p. 841. The work is listed under "Deutsche Oratoria," published 1785-1787. See also Appendix D, IM 3.14.

3

Harmonist Hymnody

The followers of George Rapp formed themselves into a congregation while still in Württemberg, and worship patterns were established there long before the Harmony Society was formed in America in 1805. The services were simple, consisting of prayer, scripture reading, preaching, and hymn singing.

The hymns sung by the congregation were not distinctively Harmonist at this time. The term "Die Harmonie" probably had not yet been chosen as a name for the congregation and, at this formative period, there was little need for a sectarian hymnody. The many printed hymn collections available to them met their needs and suited even the most pietistic tastes.

Among these printed books were the numerous editions of Gerhard Teersteegen's *Geistliches Blumen-Gärtlein inniger Seelen*,[1] the first edition of which appeared in 1729. It consisted of three parts, the first two containing religious poetry and scripture and the third consisting of Teersteegen's hymns. This was a very popular hymnbook among German pietists and remained in print for more than one hundred years. American editions of the book were made by Christoph Saur of Germantown.

Gerhard Teersteegen (1697-1769) was originally a member of the Reformed church, but his mystical leanings caused him to withdraw from it and become the leader of a group of Separatists. He read Catholic predecessors such as Tauler and Eckhart and visited groups of mystics in north Germany and Holland. His hymn texts were printed in editions which contained only tune names, as well as in editions with the tunes notated.

Equally popular as his hymns was his declaration of faith which was printed in the *Geistliches Blumen-Gärtlein*. This "Erklärung," or confession, reportedly written shortly before his death, was known by many pietists and was copied onto the covers of Bibles and psalters by the Harmonists. Possibly inspired by Teersteegen's example, the Harmonists also composed statements of faith which they recorded in their printed and manuscript hymnals and in their Bibles.[2] The esteem in which they held Teersteegen is demonstrated by the following verse found inside the cover of David Lenz's copy of the 1794 edition of the book: "Es lebe Teersteegen und seyn Geist uns zu Gottes Wortt anweisst-Hallelujah!" (Long live Teersteegen, and his spirit direct us to the word of God-Hallelujah.)

Several other hymnbooks were favorites of the Harmonists; many of these are extant at Economy. Two deserve attention here because, unlike the Teersteegen books which eventually fell into disuse, these had a lasting influence on the hymnody of the Harmonists. The *Davidisches Psalterspiel oder sammlung von Alten und Neuen auserlesenen Geistlichen Gesängen* (Büdingen, 1775), a less pietistic collection than Teersteegen's, was equally popular among the Harmonists. Like numerous other German hymnbooks, this one was eventually printed in America.[3] A thoroughly Protestant collection, its contents were organized under fifty-five topics, most of which pertained to the life of Christ and the church year.

The importance of the *Davidisches Psalterspiel* to the Harmonists is indicated by their curious practice of cutting the title page from their copies and, in some cases, writing "Harmonisches Gesangbuch" on the flyleaf. Even after the *Harmonisches Gesangbuch* of 1820 replaced other printed hymnbooks, some Harmonists clung tenaciously to their *Psalterspiel*. Extant copies show that some were used as late as 1860[4] and, when Henrici prepared his accompaniment book for the 1827 *Harmonisches Gesangbuch*, he found it necessary to include a cross reference code relating some of the hymns of the Harmonist book to their respective numbers in the *Psalterspiel* and *Württembergisches Gesangbuch* (Stuttgart: 1770) (see plate 2 and Appendix D, HM 2.29).[5]

As with the *Psalterspiel*, the *Württembergisches Gesangbuch* was personalized by the Harmonists. Most editions contained 368 pages consisting of 393 hymns; a "Kurze Gebete" (short prayers); a section called "Evangelien, Episteln, und Texte"; a "Collecte"; and an Index. In most of the copies at Economy, the "Kurze Gebete" was cut out, usually with great care so that it is difficult to tell at first glance that the pages are missing, because the Harmonists were generally opposed to "written-out" prayers. Title pages were also frequently removed, probably to eliminate any association to other denominations and churches.

These books, along with a few others of lesser prominence, were used during the Society's formative years. An extreme sectarian spirit eventually arose in the Society which led to the creation of a distinctively Harmonist hymnody. Consequently, these earlier collections fell into disuse and, despite their former popularity, relatively few of their texts were retained in the Harmonist printings. Their musical influence, however, was great because the

tunes in these books, which the Harmonists sang, later were used to sing
Harmonist-composed texts.

Among the earliest hymns composed by Rapp's followers were the "travel songs" or departure hymns. Written when the congregation was anticipating the day of departure from Europe, the texts show how deep was the religious fervor which drove them to leave Württemberg. One such song was
called "Travel Song of the Zionists going to the Land Silva [Pennsylvania]."
The text emphasized that God was about to destroy Europe and establish His
kingdom in America. Another, "Up Brothers, the time has come to leave for
North America, the Promised Land," praised God for freeing them from
"Babel," and compared the congregation to a bride being led to North America where she would be prepared for her eventual marriage to Christ the bride-
groom. Many of the doctrinal and theological principles upon which the Harmony Society was founded and by which it was governed appear in these
hymn texts.[6]

The travel and departure hymns had little purpose after the Society settled in America, but the printed psalters and hymnbooks continued in use
and were purchased in quantity until 1815. In addition to these, members of
the Harmony Society began handwritten hymnbooks as early as 1811. These
books, containing hymn texts and religious poetry to be read as well as sung,
were objects of personal artistic expression and were among the few personal
possessions which the Harmonists were able to claim. Most were pocket-size,
bound in boards and leather, and contained title pages with the possessor's
name drawn in fraktur. They are informative books because they were frequently used to record births and deaths. The year in which a book was begun
is generally written on the title page. Walrath Weingärtner's book (plate 4),
in addition to hymn texts, even contains directions for making dyes of various colors.

Despite the presence of title pages, it is difficult to establish a reliable
chronology of the contents of the manuscript hymnbooks because some contain hymns in as many as five different hands, indicating that the books were
passed from member to member, with each owner adding texts. Tabulating
the contents of these books is also difficult because, in addition to containing
hymn texts and religious prose, some served as penmanship, arithmetic, and
grammar exercise books.

The manuscript book bearing the earliest date is that belonging to Jo-
hann Dietrich Knodel (pM.1) which is inscribed: "Ein aus schreib buch von
Johann Dietrich Knodel. In Heittlingen ist gebohren 16 Mertz, Anno 1781.
Das aus schreib buch hab ich kauft im Jahr 1801." (Writing book of Johann
Dietrich Knodel, born in Heittlingen, March 16, 1781. I bought this book in

the year 1801.) The songs of Johann Christoph Mueller, written in 1816, appear early in this rather small collection, however, indicating that not all of its contents are from the earliest period.

A more distinctive and reliable example of early Harmonist hymnody is a book which belonged to Elizabeth Schnepper. Her book (pM.2-1) was begun in 1811; Mueller's songs appear toward the end of the collection, indicating that the contents were likely entered in the order of introduction. The study which follows is largely based upon the contents of this book. Elizabeth Schnepper's book contains one of the earliest hymn texts written by a Harmonist, George Rapp's "Kinder seyd nun alle munter" (Children All be Wakeful Now) composed in 1806. It is the longest text in the Harmonist repertory, having twenty-four stanzas, and was inspired by the United States government's response to the "Jefferson Petition," a request for land submitted to the government by the Harmonists in 1805. The bill upon which the request depended was defeated by one vote, and Rapp wrote the hymn to give encouragement to the Society which was then not too happily located in Butler County, Pennsylvania. A single sheet found in the music collection at Old Economy bears the text to the hymn and the following note:

> Dieses lied hat Vater Rapp 1806 geschrieben, als er in Washington war, oder um ein Stücken Land beim Congress für sein Gemein anhielt, hat aber sie kein bekommen. Auch schrieb er einen brief mit diesen Lied, in welchem er am ende sagte: "Die Liebe halte euch warm: und der Friede Gottes sei mit euch." (This song was written by Father Rapp in 1806 while he was in Washington attempting to get Congress to give him a piece of land for his congregation, but he was unable to get it. He then wrote a letter with this song, at the end of which he says: "May love keep you warm, and the Peace of God be with you.")

This hymn remained a favorite and was printed in the hymnbooks of 1820 and 1827. The first stanza is given below:

> Kinder seyd nun alle munter, weil der innere Liebes-Zunder, Freunde Jesu wieder paart: Sonnen-Blicke, Lichtes-Strahlen, lassen Geistes-Funken fahren, auf die Paradieses Saat.[7]
> (Children be cheerful while the friends of Jesus are united by love's inner spark. Sun glances and light rays allow the Spirit's sparks to stream upon the seed-fields of Paradise.)

The tune used to sing this text was "O wie selig sind die Seelen," (Appendix C, no. 155), a tune which the Society had sung from the *Psalterspiel* and the *Württembergisches Gesangbuch*. As a text, "O wie selig" was dropped, a fate shared by many traditional texts between 1806 and 1827, but its tune was retained and used to sing Harmonist texts. Another example was the text and tune "Wachet auf, ruf' uns die Stimme." The text was dropped but the tune was retained and was used to sing a Harmonist text called "Harmonie, du Auserkohrene" (Harmonie, Thou Chosen One), among others.

To give a more complete picture of the contents of the manuscript hymnbooks, three lists of hymns are given below. They are based upon a representative group of hymns which were popular in the manuscript collections. The first list gives the first lines of hymns which were carried over with their tunes from printed sources. The second list consists of new poetry which was sung to tunes originating in printed sources. The third is comprised of those hymns which contain new poetry and new music, the music being either Harmonist-composed or originating in folk or popular music sources.

THE HYMNS OF THE HARMONIST'S
MANUSCRIPT HYMNBOOKS

1. Hymns and Tunes borrowed from Printed Sources

First Line	*Appendix C,*	*Tune No.*
Der Herr ist in den Höhen (Tune: Nun Lob, Mein Seel)		138
(The Lord is in the Heights)		
Endlich, endlich, muss es doch		61
(At Last, At Last . . .)		
Erwacht zum neuen Leben (Tune: Wie soll ich dich empfangen)		63
(Awake to a New Life)		
Freude, schöner Götter-Funken		*
(Joy, Beautiful Divine Spark)		
Hoch über Erd und Welt und Zeit		t4
(High above Earth and World and Time)		
In diesen heil'gen Hallen		109
(In these Hallowed Halls)		
Willkommen O seliger Abend		216
(Welcome O blessed Evening)		

2. Harmonist-Composed Hymn Texts with Hymn
Tunes borrowed from Printed Sources

Willkommen frühe Morgen-Sonn (Tune: Mein Gott das Herz)		127
(Welcome early Morning Sun)		
Der schöne Maienmond begann (Tune: Mein Gott das Herz)		127
(The Lovely Month of May Begins)		
Empor zu Gott mein Lobgesang (Tune: Gelobet seyst du Jesu)		75
(Up to God, My Song of Praise)		
Harmonie, du Bruderstadt (Tune: Schwing dich auf zu deinem G.)		169
(Harmonie, City of Brotherhood)		
Hier stund Sophia (Tune: Alle Menschen müssen sterben)		5
(Here Stood Sophia)		
Ihr Sonne kan euch nicht (Tune: O Gott, du frommer G.)		147
(Your Sons Know you Not) [?]		
Schöne grünet die Au (Tune: God Save the King)		162
(The lovely Meadows Greening)		

3. Harmonist-Composed Hymns and Tunes

Bundt sind schon die Wälder		17
(The Woods are already Brightly Colored)		

Wie sanft, wie ruhig fühl ich hier   213
  (How peaceful, how restful I feel here)

These hymns are a dramatic departure from traditional hymnody, even contrasting with the most pietistic texts of the *Blumen-Gärtlein* and *Psalterspiel* because they show the impact of rationalism in the hymnbooks and liturgies which appeared in the German churches between 1757 and 1817.[8] Under the influence of rationalism, the older hymns were adapted to current tastes by putting them into common, sometimes unusual, language. Rhyming was curious or even ignored; and metre became irregular, often approaching prose. The dignity of man, the duty of self-improvement, the nurture of the body and the care of animals and flowers—all traits of rationalism—can be found in many Harmonist hymns of this period. Behind all of this, at least to the Harmonists, was the confidence in man's restoration to his state before the fall.[9]

Rationalist poetry served especially well to express the religious philosophy of a communal society like that of the Harmonists. A few specific examples will show the pattern which they followed in the development of their sectarian hymns. "In diesen heil'gen Hallen" (In these Hallowed Halls), one of the seven hymns taken from printed sources (see list 1, above), was a great favorite of the Harmonists. The "sacred halls" were symbols of the cloistered life which they led and which protected them from the vindictiveness of the world outside. The source of both the text and the music was not in traditional hymnody. Both are taken from Act 2 of Mozart's opera, *Die Zauberfloete.*

In diesen heil'gen Hallen, kennt man die Rache nicht, und ist ein Mensch gefallen, führt Liebe ihn zur pflicht; dann wandelt er an Freundes Hand, vergnügt und froh ins bessre Land. (In these hallowed halls, vengeance is unknown; And if one man falls, loved ones through duty aid; then he walks with a friend's hand, content and happy in the better land.)

The great German poets Goethe, Schiller, Wieland, and Lessing had little sympathy with evangelical religion, but their poetry was adapted by the Harmonists whenever it proved useful. Schiller's "Freude, schöner Götter-Funken" appears in most manuscript hymnbooks although it was not included in any of the printed ones. The problem appears to have been a musical one. A setting by J. F. Reichart (1752-1814) attained some popularity in Europe, but the Harmonists used another tune, the source of which has not been found. One manuscript copy bears the note: "Nicht gut gesungen!" (not sung well).[10] The text eventually fell into disuse, and the appearance of the Beethoven melody came too late to revive it in the Society.

Traditional hymn tunes such as "Mein Gott das Herz" (c. 1667), "Gelobet seyst du Jesu" (c. 1524), "Schwing dich auf zu deinem Gott" (c. 1653), "Alle Menschen müssen sterben" (c. 1687), and "O Gott, du frommer Gott" (c. 1648) were used to sing texts such as "Harmonie, du Bruderstadt" and others which pertained to nature and brotherhood (see list 2 above). The identity of the original was sometimes lost through association with a new text. The tune "God Save the King," for example, was used to sing the text "Schöne grünet die Au," and became known by the latter title.[11] The original texts of all of the above tunes were dropped from use.

By far the greater part of the hymnody of the manuscript books was written by members of the Harmony Society. Except for Christoph Mueller, however, authorship is generally difficult to determine. Where authorship cannot be ascertained through signed manuscripts, the subject of the texts sometimes gives a clue as to authorship because the hymnody of the Society appears to have been the domain primarily of three men: George and Frederick Rapp, and Johann Christoph Mueller.

The elder Rapp's texts generally concern brotherhood and often specifically "Die Harmonie." There are no records to substantiate that he wrote the text "Harmonie, du Bruderstadt," but it is generally ascribed to him. This text was first sung to a traditional hymn tune, "Schwing dich auf zu deinem Gott," but later was sung to a melody which the Harmonists named after the text—"Harmonie, du Bruderstadt." This latter tune (Appendix C, no. 85) is generally ascribed to Rapp, but was, in fact, written by J. Adam Hiller and is found in G. W. Fink's *Musikalischer Hausschatz der Deutschen*, a collection of one thousand German religious, patriotic, folk, and popular songs, printed in Leipzig in 1842.[12] There is no proof that George Rapp wrote any music and his texts usually make use of a firmly established hymn or folk tune.

The hymns of Frederick Rapp also concern brotherhood, but they are generally more cheerful than George Rapp's. The tune and text "Freut euch ihr Kinder," are attributed to Frederick, although his own keyboard collection (HM 2.28) does not give the author or composer for this text and tune. Frederick was very active in the music of the Society, however, and it is quite likely that he wrote both the tune and text of this hymn.

Mueller's hymns and hymn tunes are dated and autographed in various sources. The following were written by him (see Appendix A, exs. 3-6): "Durch zerfallne Kirchenfenster" (24 July 1816); "Es blüht ein Blümlein" (31 July, 1816); "Herr, führe mich" (2 February 1817); "Die Menschenlieb" (2 February 1817). Other hymns are ascribed to Mueller, but these are the only ones which he, himself, claimed to have written.[13]

A man of deep faith, Mueller was nonetheless influenced by rationalistic thinking. His many professions—physician, teacher, botanist—and hobbies reflect the interests of a man caught up in the concerns of the Age of the Enlightenment. The preceding hymns are early creations of his and show an obsession for flowers, the joys of rural living, charity, and in "Durch zerfallne Kirchenfenster," mystical preoccupation with death. The effect of his interest in astronomy and classic symbolism will be seen in the texts which he compiled for the 1820 *Harmonisches Gesangbuch*.

The manuscript hymbooks contain the hymns most often used by the Harmonists from about 1811 to 1820. These books were not replaced completely, however, with the 1820 printing, and Mueller found that some of the texts and tunes which he omitted in 1820 had to be included again in the 1827 printing. The music used to sing the manuscript hymns was drawn primarily from German folk sources. Country dances, waltzes, and marches are well represented in the Harmonist repertory (see Appendix C). According to Henrici, various members sang folk and hymn tunes to Mueller, who wrote them down as accurately as he was able and matched them with appropriate texts. This often resulted in irregular rhythms and phrases and the final tune sometimes bore little resemblance to its original form. This mattered little to the Harmonists, and the body of sectarian hymns grew to the point where compiling them by hand became impractical. Thus, in 1820, a printer was sought for the first *Harmonisches Gesangbuch*.

THE HARMONISCHES GESANGBUCH OF 1820

In May of 1826, when Bernhard, Duke of Saxe-Weimar Eisenach, visited Economy, the *Harmonisches Gesangbuch*, printed for the Society in 1820, was in use. It caught his attention and he commented upon it in his *Travels through North America*.

> They have a peculiar hymn-book, containing many hymns from the Württemberg Psalm-book, and others written by the elder Rapp. The latter are truly in prose, but Rapp is very fond of psalmody. . . .[14]

Arndt's *A Documentary History of the Indiana Decade of the Harmony Society 1814-1824*, contains letters relative to the printing of the book. The printer, Heinrich Ebner, on one occasion complained of the ". . . extremely erroneous manner . . . of the writing of the book. . . ."[15] There were other interesting circumstances surrounding its printing, and Duke Bernhard had good reason to describe it as a "peculiar hymn-book" (see Plate 5).

The 1820 *Harmonisches Gesangbuch* was printed in two sections. The first has on the title page, "Allentown: Lecha Caunty, im Staat Pennsylvanien, Gedruckt bey Heinrich Ebner, 1820." It contains two hundred pages consisting of a main section of one hundred ninety-six hymns and an "Anhang" (supplement) of fifty-eight more. The "Vorrede" states that "everything in books and poetry which admonishes and edifies is material which can be used to become familiar with the name of the Lord." Further, that the mind should

be concerned "next to morality and religion, with nature," and that the poetry contained in this book reflects "feeling, consideration, education, and
experience." The last paragraph states that the supplement is for use by
young people "to sing and to use with music because in developing the minds
of youth, music is useful and necessary" (nützlich und nöthig).

The hymns in Heinrich Ebner's printing are entered under thirty-three
topical divisions followed by the supplement. ("Herman" refers to a second
supplement to be discussed below.)

	Topical Division	Ebner	Herman
I	(On the Works of Creation) Von den Werken der Schöpfung	4	0
II	(Festival Songs) Fest-Lieder	5	2
III	(On the Hereafter and Judgment) Von der Zukunft zum Gericht	2	4
IV	(On the Incarnation of Christ) Von der Menschwerdung Christi	11	5
V	(On the Passion and Death of Christ) Vom Leiden und Tod Christi	15	1
VI	(On the Resurrection) Von der Auferstehung	2	0
VII	(On Man's Misery and Destruction) Vom menschlichen Elende und Verderben	3	0
VIII	(Penitence and Funeral Songs) Buss und Leichen Lieder	5	1
IX	(On Faith) Vom Glauben	8	2
X	(On the Spiritual Battle and Victory) Vom geistlichen Kampf und Sieg	4	4
XI	(On Renouncing Self and the World) Von der Verleugnung seiner selbst und der Welt	6	6
XII	(On Longing toward God) Von dem Verlangen nach Gott	7	5
XIII	(On the Love of Christ) Von der Liebe zu Christo	8	12
XIV	(On Brotherhood) Von der Bruder-Liebe	11	3
XV	(On the Imitation of Christ) Von der Nachfolge Jesu	4	0
XVI	(On the Conversion of the Heart) Von der Uebergabe des Herzens	2	6
XVII	(On Peace and Rest of the Soul) Vom Frieden und Ruhe der Seelen	7	3
XVIII	(On True Wisdom) Von der wahren Weisheit	9	13

XIX	(On the High Nobility of Mankind)		
	Vom hohen Adel des Menschen	5	4
XX	(On the Kingdom of God)		
	Vom Reich Gottes	8	6
XXI	(On the Hope of Zion)		
	Von der Hoffnung Zions	12	10
XXII	(On Heaven and Heavenly Jerusalem)		
	Vom Himmel und Himmlischen Jerusalem	8	0
XXIII	(On Virtue)		
	Von der Tugend	6	1
XXIV	(Comfort and Consolation Songs)		
	Trost Lieder	8	4
XXV	(Nature and Mercy)		
	Natur und Gnade	4	1
XXVI	(About Sadness)		
	Ueber Wehmuth	3	2
XXVII	(On Friendship)		
	Von Freundschaft	6	0
XXVIII	(Devotion and Prayer Songs)		
	Andachts-Lieder	7	2
XXIX	(Fate [Destiny])		
	Schicksal	7	0
XXX	(Spring Songs)		
	Frühlings-Lieder	2	8
XXXI	(Fall and Winter)		
	Spätjahr und Winter	2	0
XXXII	(On Freedom)		
	Von der Freyheit	4	0
XXXIII	(On Zion's Complaint) [Not in Table of Contents]		
	Vom Klagen Zions	1	9
	(Supplement)		
	Anhang	58	0

Of the 254 texts contained in the Ebner printing, more than one hundred are not found in the manuscript hymnals and, presumably, were unfamiliar to most of the Harmonists when the book first appeared. These new texts were probably compiled by George Rapp and Dr. Mueller and are present in only one earlier source, a manuscript hymnbook which appears to have been the model used for the printing (Appendix D, pM. 8-4) and which belonged to Mueller. It has an index and topical divisions ("Inhalts-Verzeichniss") just like the printed book and, with the exception of a few texts, contains the hymns printed by Ebner.

As can be seen, the number of texts in the supplement is considerably greater than in any of the topical divisions. Many of these texts are found in the manuscript hymnbooks and the new ones which were added to this section are in the style of the earlier ones, generally being about nature and brotherhood. Consequently, it can be assumed that the hymns in the "Anhang" saw the greatest use. The following is an example of the texts which were added:

Der Apfel-Baum prangt schön und weiss auf zart begrasster Haide: Der Wonne-Ruf des schönen Mays weckt uns zur sanften Freude. (The apple tree shines fair and white on the delicately grassy moor; the enraptured call of lovely May wakes us to tender joy.) (Anhang: No. 224, stanza 1)

It is a nature hymn with some allusion to the joys of communal living; the rhyme scheme is typical of many of the Harmonist texts.

It should not be inferred from this that the Rapps or Mueller did not have a sound Christian theological base. On the contrary, their Christian fervor was intense and mystical, but nature provided useful symbols to express their beliefs as in the following translation of an excerpt from stanza 1, hymn number 33.

> As the flowers unfold themselves to
> the warm sun's rays, And the
> glistening dew forms on the breath
> of the mouth of Spring;
> Each morning shines fairer, each
> midday dearer,
> So to me more important everyday is
> the Saviour-Reconciler.

Hymns were an important tool for teaching Harmonist principles. Many, like the text below, emphasized a common goal and the power of faith in overcoming all forms of corruption.

> In the town nothing rotten [Corruption]
> can be ground [milled];
> Here nothing grows with barren blade
> While the blessed troop
> Labors together toward the goal.
> (No. 118, stanza 1)

"Was ist dieses für ein Feuer" is another text with a strong Harmonist doctrinal message. It gives more than a passing allusion to celibacy and the need to control the lusts of the flesh. It is listed under topical division XIX (On the High Nobility of Man).

> What is this which breaks out in passion like
> a fire in you
> Is the flesh so dear that you lust so;
> Are you the bride of man, he who acquaints
> you with lust?

In Henrici's hymn accompaniment book this tune and text are crossed out. John Duss, in his usual fashion, wrote the following comment below the manuscript.

> The above [i.e., crossed out text] indicates a dislike on the part of Henrici or some other Harmonist regarding the salacious words. In all of my years this hymn never was used.

There is no doubt that religious fervor declined in the later years, especially under Duss' trusteeship, but this text was very popular in the early years and was included in the 1820 and 1827 printings as well as in the manuscript hymnals.

Poetic license was sometimes carried to extremes, as in the following example.

> . . . und Aurora's Rosenfinger, zeigt die Pfort zu Salems Shimmer. (. . . and Aurora's rosy finger shows the way to Salem's lustre.)
> (Anhang: No. 200)

Aurora, goddess of the dawn, is one of several classic symbols which came to the Harmonists through the mystic Jacob Boehme. She was generally painted by artists as heralding the day, charging across the sky in a horse-drawn chariot, surrounded by angels and cherubs. To the Harmonists, Aurora symbolized the dawn of a new day for mankind which would be ushered in by "Die Harmonie."

Flora was the goddess of flowers and spring. The first text which alludes to her is No. 261 in the second supplement, the first stanza of which is translated below:

> O fairest of Roses bedecked with Pearls,
> Blessed with sultry thorns of charm
> From whom streams the Sun reddened in fire,
> O Flora, beloved, to us you stay dear.

By far the most popular of the goddesses was Sophia, the Spirit of Wisdom who was interpreted by the Harmonists as the formative and controlling power of the universe. Sophia symbolized Heavenly Wisdom and the Harmonist poets mentioned her often. Most texts referring to Sophia are found in division XVIII, "Von der wahren Weisheit" (On True Wisdom) from which the examples below are taken:

> O Sophia, theure Holde, deren Anblick mich entzückt.
> (O Sophia, Precious darling, whose appearance delights me.)
> (No. 106, stanza 1)

Als Sophiens Schönheit glüthe, als im Paradies sie stund.
(As Sophia's beauty glowed, as in Paradise she stood.)
No. 108, stanza 3)

Hier stund Sophia, die Lüfte haben heilig sie berührt.
(Here stood Sophia, the air touched her sacredly.)
No. 111, stanza 1)

Sophia, ich kann's nicht lassen, mein Herz brennt mit süsser Gluth.
(Sophia, I cannot leave it, my heart burns with sweetness.)
(No. 113, stanza 1)

The name Sophia was not confined to the hymns in the section on wisdom, however, as the following taken from division XXIII (On Virtue) indicates:

Im stillen Thal da stund voll Reizen, mir Sophia im Mondenschein;
(In the still valley there stood, full of charm, my Sophia in the moonlight.)
(No. 152, stanza 1)

Among all the melodies in Zahn's[16] collection, there is none with the name Sophia in its title. Nor are there any texts in Knapp's collection[17] which include this name. The *Davidisches Psalterspiel* contains one text which uses the name Sophia in its title, and, immediately following the name, in parenthesis, is given "O Weisheit" (O Wisdom). The compiler, obviously, felt it necessary to offer a substitute term indicating the limited use of the symbol at that time (1775).

While, undoubtedly, an improvement over the manuscript hymnbooks, the Ebner printing had its failings. Many of the texts were printed with omissions which must have made performance awkward. For example in the selections below, the words in parentheses were omitted by the printer.

Edle (Heil'ge) Freundschafts (No. 83)
Still und heilig ist das (Tiefe) Dunkel (No. 6)
Salems Töchter (kommt) gegangen (No. 26)

In one case, a text was printed twice with only one word alteration. "Wann die Sinnen-Götter flattern auf und ab," No. 98, was changed to "Wann die Sinnen-Hüter flattern auf und ab" and printed as No. 186. The first means "gods of the senses" and the second "mind's keeper," hardly sufficient reason to print the six-stanza text twice. Whether the second printing resulted from an error in the first cannot be determined because the text is not in any of the manuscript sources.

The Ebner printing also had musical difficulties. Most printed hymnbooks and psalters which did not contain music gave the name of the tune to which a text was to be sung. Even when tune names were given, uniformity in performance was sometimes difficult to achieve because most tunes had several variants. The variant which a given person might know depended upon where he came from. In a group such as the Harmony Society, this was an important consideration. It is therefore surprising to find so many texts without tune names in the Ebner printing. Of the 254 texts, only eighty-two have tune names given with the texts.

Further, in most hymnbooks without music, when a tune name is not given, one of three terms may be used to indicate what melody is to be used. "Eigene Melodie" is used to indicate that the text has its own tune, that is, that the tune to be used has the same name as the text. "In bekannter Melodie" means that the text is to be sung to a well-known melody which is generally associated with that text. "In voriger Melodie" appears only occasionally, meaning that the text is to be sung to the tune which was used to sing the preceding text. All of these directions appear in the Harmonist manuscript hymnbooks, but none are given in Ebner's printing of the 1820 *Harmonisches Gesangbuch*.

Even among the tune names given, there was sometimes great confusion. For example, the *text* "Willkommen frühe Morgen-Sonn" (No. 204 in the Anhang) is to be sung to the tune "Mein Gott das Herz," while the *tune* "Willkommen frühe Morgen-Sonn" is matched with the text "Der Apfel-Baum prangt schön und weiss" (No. 224). The text "Willkommen frühe Morgen-Sonn" was dropped from use by 1827, no doubt as a result of the confusion, and not until considerably later did Henrici get the original tune and text together again (see HM 2.29, No. 186).

A "Zweyter Anhang," or second supplement, was printed soon after Ebner's was completed. This second supplement, which was bound to Ebner's printing permitting the use of both in one volume, was not printed by Ebner, but by Johann Herman[18] of Lancaster, Ohio. Herman printed a newspaper called the *Ohio Adler* (*Ohio Eagle*) to which the Society subscribed. His Zweyter Anhang differs in several respects from the Ebner printing, suggesting that the features described above were of some concern to the Society.

Heinrich Ebner's title page, along with the hymns which he printed, continued to be used, and Herman's name appears only on the final page of the Zweyter Anhang. There is no date given on this page, but accounts at Economy for 18 February 1822, show that Johann Herman was paid "170 in gold for printing books" and it is, therefore, probable that his Zweyter Anhang was printed sometime in 1821.

The Zweyter Anhang consists of 96 pages with 117 texts. The pagination and hymn entry numbers were made consecutive to the Anhang of Ebner's printing with which it was bound. The Ebner printing remained unchanged except that the indexes were eliminated and a new alphabetical index, listing the first lines of both printings, was included. A "Register nach den Haupt-Materien" (Index of the Main Material), listing the first lines of the texts under their respective topics, was also added. The topical index, however, did not include any of the texts of the Anhang of the Ebner printing, even though these texts were given in the alphabetical index.

In the Zweyter Anhang, the title of the last entry on each page is given at the top of the page, but there appears to be no particular reason for the order of the entries. (The number of hymn texts which were added in the Zweyter Anhang in each of the thirty-three topics is shown on page 47 in the column under the heading "Herman.")

Discovering the sources of the texts of the Zweyter Anhang, as in the case of other Harmonist hymn collections, is largely a matter of chance because texts can rarely be found by searching first-line indexes of printed sources. For example, five texts were taken from a printed source, Petrus Wulffing's *Ronsdorffs Silberne Trompeten oder Kirchen-Buch* (Mülheim am Rhein, 1761) which contained both texts and tunes in notation. Most are very long paraphrases of psalms, one having one hundred and sixteen stanzas. The texts borrowed by the Harmonists from this collection and the ways in which they were adapted are illustrated below.

"Gott, es dürstet meine Seele" (God, my Soul Thirsts), No. 310 in the 1820 *Harmonisches Gesangbuch*, was adapted from a ten-stanza paraphrase of Psalm 30 which is found on page 372 of the *Silberne Trompeten*. The first eight stanzas were adopted with a slight change in stanza six. The sixth stanza in the *Silberne Trompeten* reads: "Drum gedenk dann an die meinen" (Think upon these as you deem fitting, [let thine ears be attentive]). The Harmonists changed this to: "Vater! drum denk an die meinen" (Father, think upon these as you deem fitting).

"Herr, das Jahr ist angefangen" (Lord, the Year is begun), No. 312 in the 1820 *Harmonisches Gesangbuch*, was adapted from a thirty-eight stanza text found on page 548 of the *Silberne Trompeten*. Stanza 24 was altered from "Zwar das Jahr ist angefangen" (Indeed the Year is begun) to the line given above and was made stanza one in the Harmonist's version. The other stanzas used were 26, 10, 31, 35, and 36, in that order. One additional stanza was added by the Harmonists, either from another source or Harmonist-composed.

"Der Herr lässt nun die Seinen wissen" (The Lord grants them His Wisdom), No. 313 in the 1820 *Harmonisches Gesangbuch*, was taken from page 714 of the *Silberne Trompeten* where the text has 116 stanzas. Stanza 96 became the first stanza in the Harmonist version and the others added were 111 through 116.

"Denk des Volks das du erwählet" (Think on the People you have chosen), No. 316 in the 1820 *Harmonisches Gesangbuch*, was taken from page 474 of the *Silberne Trompeten* where the text has 90 stanzas. Stanza 27 become the first stanza in the Harmonist printing with the others added being 30, 31, 32, and 36. Three other stanzas were taken from another source or were Harmonist-composed.

"Ach Herr Jesu! wie verachtet" (Ah, Lord Jesus! How Despised), No. 323 in the 1820 *Harmonisches Gesangbuch*, was taken from page 477 of the *Silberne Trompeten* where the original has 90 stanzas (a continuation of No. 96, above). Stanza 37 became the Harmonists' first stanza with others added being 38, 39, 40, 41, and 44. Two other stanzas were taken from another source or were Harmonist-composed. The original first line, "So bist du O Gott verachtet," was changed to the line given above.

The texts borrowed from the *Silberne Trompeten* were sung to tunes already in use among the Harmonists, such as "Wann die Ström," "O welch' angenehme Freude," "Gott, der du alle Welt," "Auf du Priesterlich's," and "O Durchbrecher aller Bande." Although the *Silberne Trompeten* contained music, it had no musical influence on the hymnody of the Harmony Society.

In addition to these, nine texts which had been used in the manuscript hymnbooks, but which had not been printed in the Ebner collection, were now added. These were:

> *Ich will dir, O König singen (No. 274)*
> *Mein Geist soll in die Tiefe schauen (No. 275)*
> *Schaut mein Hoffnungs Blick (No. 305)*
> *Schöne grünet die Au (No. 318).*
> *Wer unter denen Unterdrückten (No. 320)*
> *Unsre Tage sind gehüllt (No. 321)*
> *Wann die Engel Gottes schweben (No. 327)*
> *Wann ich schau durch die Hülle (No. 365)*
> *Was willst du die Schöpfungen lehren (No. 367)*

There is more than a slight suggestion that some texts and tunes of the 1820 *Harmonisches Gesangbuch* are traditional items which were so severely altered that the original forms are barely recognizable. For example, "Geh hin in deine stille Kammer" (Go into your quiet Chamber), No. 74, resembles a text with the title "Geh hin in deine Kammer" given by Knapp (No. 3359). A tune "Geh hin in deine Kammer" to which the Harmonist tune bears some resemblance is listed by Zahn (No. 3772) who gives the source as *Dretzel's Choralbuch* of 1731. Another text, "Lass mich bey der Liebe Schwören" (Let me swear by love), No. 75, is similar to a text in Knapp. "Lass mich meine Zunge zahmen" (Let me Tame my Tongue), No. 2181.

Possibly more significant than the addition of new texts was the attention given to the tunes in the Herman printing. All but six of the 117 texts of the Zweyter Anhang have tune names given with the texts, and the term "Eigene Melodie" is used wherever applicable. Twenty-eight tunes were added in

this section, raising the total number of tunes in the 1820 *Gesangbuch* to 193
A list of the tunes and the frequency of their use in both sections of the 1820
Gesangbuch, as well as in the Harmonist printings of 1824, 1826, and 1827,
appears on pages 55-59. An asterisk under "Appendix C" indicates that a tune
probably existed by this title but has not been found. Most alternate titles appear only in the 1827 printing and many tunes have been associated with
texts of the 1820 book only through their appearance together in the 1827
book and manuscript sources.

As the list shows, twelve tunes were used to sing approximately one-
third of all the texts. The tune used most often is Christoph Mueller's
"Durch zerfallne Kirchenfenster" which appears sixteen times. This tune
and the tunes "Dein gedenk ich holder," "Alles lebt und schwebt," "Gott
will ich soll in meiner Jugend," and "Herr führe mich," the latter being
another tune by Mueller, are in the folk-song style which characterizes the
remainder of the tune repertory.

THE TUNES OF THE *HARMONISCHES GESANGBUCH* OF 1820
IN ORDER OF APPEARANCE

Title	Ebner	Herman	1824	1826	1827	Appendix C
Als todt und schweigend	1				1	8
Wo sprudelt deine heil'ge Q.	1				1	222
Auf, du priesterlich's geschl.	4	7			11	12
Hoch ueber Sonnen stund der	1					*
In diesen heil'gen Hallen	1				1	109
Heilig sei dein Name	4				2	87
O Gott, du frommer Gott/oder						
Der frohe Tag bricht an	2	4			21	147
Befiehl du deine Wege/oder						
O Haupt voll Blut/oder						
Herzlich thut mich Verl.	8				7	13
Gott will ich soll in meiner	2	4	1		5	83
Dein gendenk ich holder	9	4			14	26
Gelobet seyst du Jesu	2				3	75
Sehet wie die klären Sterne	1				1	173
Schweigt ihr ernsten Glocken	1				1	168
O du holder, suesser Knabe	1				1	141
Hirten aus den goldnen Zeit.	1				1	93
Senke dich von Purper-Wolk.	1				1	175
O Nacht, und o du feierliche	1				1	149
In des Ostens fernem Lande	1				1	108
Die Wahrheit ist das Nächst.	2	2			6	45
Was soll deine Schoenheit k.	3				8	201
Allein Gott in der Höh/oder						
Ich schau im Geist	8	1			16	4
Herr, führe mich	2	3			7	88

Golgatha, meiner Andacht	1		1	77
Der am Kreutz ist meine L.	2	1	7	28
O Durchbrecher aller Bande/oder				
Werde munter mein Gemüthe	4	5	4	142
Alle Menschen mussen sterben	8	2		5
Die Menschenlieb/oder				
Die Wahre Treu	2		6	41
O wie verderblich	1		1	156
Wie die Blumen sich entf.	1			*
Höher als der Wall der W.	1		1	95
Verliebtes Lustspiel	5	5	10	191
Auferstehen! ja Auferstehen	1			*
Juda zittert	1			*
Schwing dich auf mein Geist	1		1	170
Ferne in der Einsamkeit/oder				
Liebster Jesu, wir sind h.	1			*
Durch zerfalle Kirchen f.	12	4	21	56
Des Lebens letze Stunde	1		1	38
In froher Eintracht sind w.	3	1	10	111
Geheimnissvoll, O Herr	1	3	3	73
Hoch über Erd und Welt	1		1	94
Jesus, meine zuversicht	2		1	115
Wer nur den lieben Gott	3		1	206
Gott sei dank/oder				
O der alles hät verl./				
oder Jesu, komm doch h.	2	2	16	82
Du reine süsse Liebes-Gluth	1			*
O du allerschönste Liebe	1		1	140
Endlich, endlich	1		2	61
In den Höhen, in den Tief.	1		1	107
Nur Wahrheit kann mein H.	1			139
Welt und Eitelkeiten	1			203
Wie sanft, wie ruhig	1			213
Meines Herzens Jesu	2		1	129
Ursprung aller Seligk.	1			189
Gottes Wahrheit triumph.	1			80
Staub, den Gott gebiltet	1		1	183
Kinder, sucht euch schon	1		1	117
So entzückt vom Gotter-Kusse	1			*
Schön ist mein Geliebter	1		1	163
Geh hin in deine stille K.	1		1	74
Lass mich bei der Liebe	1		1	121
Schönster, du kannst mich n.	1		2	167
Vater, deine Gunst	1		1	190
Ich hör von goldnen Saiten	1		2	100
Edle Freundschafts-Sympath.	1		1	26
Das alter bringet dir Verdr.	1			19
Brüder, liebt was gut und s.	1			16
Harmonie du Bruderstadt	2		4	85

Alles lebt und schwebt	2	4	8	7
Was ist dieses für ein Feuer	3	1	9	199
O wer wills mit mir wagen	1		1	154
Seele was ist schöners	1			172
O wie selig	3	2	13	155
Wann die Sinnen-Götter	2			*
Wenn mein Geist	1			204
O Sophia, mein Licht	1		1	151
Mir blüht ein Paradies	1		1	130
Gott ist getreu/oder				
So fuhrst du doch/oder				
O Sophia, beim f./oder				
So bricht mit macht	1	2	9	81
Hier stund Sophia	1	4	6	90
Erwacht zum neuen L.	5		5	63
Sophia, ich kanns nicht l.	1			181
Preiss sey Dir Herr	1		1	157
Edle Tugend	1			57
Sey mir tausendmal	2			177
Hinauf mein Geist	1		1	92
O ernste Nacht	1		1	143
Lasst mich allein	1		1	120
Schmücke dich, o lieb.	1		1	160
Wer weiss wie nahe	1	1	3	207
Herr Jesu Christ, mein/oder				
Nach dir, O Herr	2		7	89
Was kann meinem Geiste	1			*
Die Trübsals Zeit	1		1	43
Stille Ahndung	1		1	185
Auf, Christenmensch/oder				
Mir nach! Spricht Christ.	1	1	3	11
Oft kommt ein Lichtes	1		1	146
Was mein Gott will	1	1		200
Der ewig glänzend	1			*
Schwing dich auf zu deinem	1	1		169
Es blüht ein Blümlein	1		1	64
Im stillen Thal	1		1	104
Am stillen Pfad	1		1	9
Kennst du das Land	1			116
Wo ist die Jugend-Zeit	1		1	218
O süsse Ruh	1			152
Die ihr am Abend	1		1	40
Preisst den Herrn in allen s.	1			158
Ehrerbietigkeit meinen g.	1		1	58
Der Fluren Grün	1			30
Im vertrauten Kreiss/oder				
Schmückt das Fest	2		2	105
O seelige Stunden	2	2	3	150
Heil'ge Freundschaft	1		1	86

Freut euch ihr Kinder	2		2	70
Die ernstlich Nacht	1			39
Du meine Seele singe	2			52
Der Greiss des Silber-Haars	1		2	31
Nenne nicht das Schicksal	1			*
Du armes Herz	1			*
Nun lob mein Seel	1		2	138
Alles ist an Gottes seg./oder				6
Ach was soll ich Sünder	1			
Ist dann hienieden nichts von	1		1	112
Schaut liebe Freunde	1			*
Trübe aus westlichem Duft.	1			188
Den Weisen wird allhier	1	2	1	36
Drey Worte nenn ich Inhalt.	2		1	48
Wie prächtig von bunten	1		1	211
Klagt mit mir	1			118
Wann der Lenz in allen Thal.	1			193
In dem wölbend grunen	1	2	7	106
Mein Gott das Herz	2			127
Welche Symphonien	1			202
Schön so frühe meine Schwest.	1			165
Wann Weisheit schön	1			197
Es färbet sich	1		1	65
Für mich bestrahlt die S.	1			72
Wie Herrlich grünet und blühet	1			210
Muss ich jetz die Schönheit	1			131
Ich geh in Wald	1		1	99
Schön blühet und duftet	1			161
Bunt sind schon die Wäld.	1		1	17
Der junge Sommer weicht	1			32
Täuscht mich der süsse/oder				
Auf meinen Liebe Gott	1		1	186
Dort wo sanfte Milde	1		1	47
Wir gehen ins frei	1		1	217
Wann des Nebels Grauer	1			194
Schönster meiner Flur	1			166
Es ist gewährt das sehnende	1	1	1	66
Willkommen frühe Morgen S.	1	1	1	215
Hüll in deinem Schatten-M.	1		1	96
Lösst ab vom Stamm	1		1	123
In duftigen Schatten	1		1	110
Sollt ich meinem Gott	1			180
Nun liebster Salomon	1	2	3	137
So glücklich so vergnügt	1			179
Du meine Seele liebt	1		1	52
Jesu, meine Freude	1		1	114
Jesu hilf siegen	1		1	113
Wo ist wohl der Schönste	1			219
Reiss loss mein armer Geist	1			159

Warum flieht der leichte Schl.	1				*
Kommt schauet an den Blick	1	1			119
Gott der du alle Welten träg.	1	2	1	7	78
Gott, der du auf dem e'wgen	1	1		3	79
Steh still mein Geist	1				184
Du ruhige Stille	1				55
Mein edler Freund	1			1	125
Ich fühle dass in mir	1			1	98
O Harmonie, voll Töne	1			1	148
Ach wie voll Drang		1		1	3
Urania, vor allen Schonen		1		1	*
Der liebliche Lenz		1		1	33
Der Weisheit holder Perl.		1		1	37
Mein Geist soll in die T.		1		1	126
Die Nacht, die Heilige		1		1	42
Wo blüht in einem Thal.		1			*
Zeuch mich/oder					
Liebe die du mich		1		3	223
Denk ich oft an die verg.		1		1	27
Sulamith versüsste		1			*
Wie reizend schön ist nun		1			212
Wie heimlich blühet hier		1			*
Wenn die Ström der		1			*
O welch angenehme Freude		1		1	153
Jesus Christus ist der Temp.		1			*
Schöne grünet die Au		1		1	162
Zion klagt mit Angst		3		2	177
Wie die Engel Gottes		1			195
Wie gross ist des Allmächt.		1			209
Der Frühling ist im L.		1			*
Natur ist wieder heiter nun		1			132
Christus der ist mein L.		1		1	18
So tritt hervor		1		1	182
Ich denke dein		1		1	97
O Bräutigam		1			*
Die Tugend wird durchs		1		1	44
Das Klaggeschrei		1		1	21
Halleluja, Lob Preiss/oder					
Wie Schön leuchtet der M.		2		3	84

A confusing feature of chorale tunes, both within and outside the Society, is that some were known by several names. For example, "Befiehl du deine Wege" (Command your Way) was also known as "O Haupt voll Blut und Wunden" (O Head wounded and Bleeding), and "Herzlich thut mich verlangen" (My Heart is Longing). Originally, these tunes were not the same, as a comparison of Zahn's sources shows (Zahn 5459; 5485; 5385a). Hassler's well-known tune, however, was eventually associated with all three titles.

Again, the title by which a given member of the Harmony Society may have known a melody would have depended upon his background. In such a closed group, however, it is unusual that one tune name was not soon agreed upon. Even Mueller gave a second title to his tune, "Die Menschenlieb," the alternate being "Die wahre Treu," the first line of another text which was also sung to this tune. Despite the familiarity of these melodies to some members, the frequency with which this was done must have confused the less attentive when they were sung in the religious services.

The Harmonists sang most of the hymns of the 1820 *Gesangbuch* unaccompanied and in unison. Some of the manuscript books indicate that a few of these texts were to be performed "mit Begleitung des Claviers" or "mit besonderer Music" but, in the church services before 1830, accompaniments were not common. The only instrumental part-books which contain a significant number of hymns are those for flute and bassoon, but, even here, there are no indications that these instruments were used with any regularity in the church. Another distinguishing feature of Harmonist hymn singing was that they did not need to "line out" their hymns. That is, a leader did not sing each line ahead of the congregation,[19] a necessity in many American churches well into the nineteenth century. A contemporary account indicates that this procedure was unnecessary among the Harmonists

> as every individual had a book, the page and number, and the first line of the hymn was sufficient to be given out; as after that, all could proceed without having lines repeated. . . .[20]

One other performance feature favored by the Harmonists which would have attracted a visitor's attention was the use of antiphonal groups in the singing of some of their hymns. A typical example of this is "Des Lebens letze Stund" (Life's Final Hour) (Appendix C, No. 38) which begins in common metre, either by a soloist or solo group, with the last line going into 3/4 time and being designated "alle" (some manuscript sources use the term "tutti"). This kind of performance was particularly favored for ceremonial occasions such as the Liebesmahl (Lord's Supper) and at funeral services held at the cemetery. Dated hymn leaflets printed on the Harmonist press also show that occasionally readings were alternated with singing. While designations for antiphonal singing are most prevalent in the manuscript hymnbooks, they are also found in the 1820 *Gesangbuch*, both in Ebner's section and in Herman's Zweyter Anhang.

The Harmonists made use of Ebner's 1820 printing and Herman's somewhat later Zweyter Anhang until 1826, even though the shortcomings of the Ebner portion were considerable. This fact, along with the cultural growth which the Society experienced during the mid-1820s, and especially Doctor Mueller's interest in printing, led to the creation of a second *Harmonisches Gesangbuch* in 1827.

HARMONIST PRINTING AND THE GESANGBUCH OF 1827

Early in 1824, or possibly late in 1823 (exact records are wanting), the Harmony Society acquired a printing press, and Dr. Mueller was put in charge of its operation. This press was to print George Rapp's *Gedanken über die Bestimmung des Menschen* (Thoughts on the Destiny of Man), a philosophical treatise based largely upon Herder's *Ideen zur Philosophie der Geschichte der Menschheit* [Outlines of a Philosophy of the History of Man] 4 vols., 1784-1791).

Mueller printed the German edition of Rapp's work between July and December of 1824. Before doing this he acquainted himself with the mechanics of the press by printing an experimental collection called *Eine kleine Sammlung Harmonischer Lieder als die erste Probe der anfangenden Druckerey anzusehen* (A Little Collection of Songs as a first attempt at the Beginning of Printing, Harmonie, Indiana: 1824). He began work on it in March and completed it late in July 1824.[21] It contains eighty-four texts, most of which are in prose, which express the religious fervor of the Society in highly emotional, sometimes passionate, language. It also contains texts of odes sung at various Harmonist festivals. These frequently have directions for performance by antiphonal speaking and singing choruses and soloists, and are usually inscribed "mit musik gesetz"[22] (set to music). The music for these texts is found in the manuscript sources and is similar to the ode settings described earlier. The majority of the texts, however, were intended for reading only.

All of the texts of the *kleine Sammlung* were written by members of the Society and the names of the authors, while not given in the printed version, are written in the manuscript hymnbooks which contain these texts. [23] The collection begins with a section consisting of a group of three unnumbered texts which are to be sung to traditional hymn tunes. The tunes used are: "Gott will, ich soll in meiner Jugend"; "Du Perlen-Volk sing' Gott"; and "Gott, du der alle Welten trägest" (Appendix C, nos. 83, 54, 78).

This section is followed by eighty-two numbered texts in prose and verse. Only five of these are designated to be sung to hymn tunes. The tunes with their text numbers are: "Valet will ich dir geben" (No. 28); "Ein Blümlein auf der Wiese spross" (No. 65); "Willkommen O seeliger Abend" (No. 79); "Es reizet die Menschen" (No. 81); and "Schön ist zwar die ganze Welt" (No. 82).

Apparently Mueller made only a few complete copies of this collection and, as the title indicates, it was meant to be an experiment in printing rather than a practical tool.[24] Nevertheless, it did serve a purpose beyond giving Mueller the experience of printing because seventy-eight of its eighty-four texts were used in a volume which he printed after he finished Rapp's work. The title page of this new collection reads: *Feurige Kohlen der aufsteigenden Liebesflammen im Lustspiel der Weisheit* [Fiery Coals, the Ascending flames of Love in the Play of Wisdom] (Oekonomie, 1826).

The *Feurige Kohlen* contains a total of 361 texts. Some copies at Economy have the original *kleine Sammlung* pages bound with the new printing and, in these, the numbering of the texts is as follows: 1 to 266; 1 to 78; 352 to 361. The copies which do not contain the old printing are numbered consecutively from 1 through 361 and, as the above numbers show, there are seven texts in these books which are missing in those containing the old printings. The binding of the old printing texts with the new probably explains why there are so few copies of the *kleine Sammlung* extant.

Of the 361 *Feurige Kohlen* texts, only five were sung to hymn tunes. The tunes with their text numbers are: "Gott, der du alle Welt." (No. 53); "Hier stund Sophia" (No. 57); "Gott, der du auf dem Ewigen" (No. 75); "Valet will ich dir geben" (No. 295); and "Ein Blümlein auf der Wiese" (No. 333).

The preceding two books are relatively insignificant as far as Harmonist hymnody is concerned, but they prepared Mueller for the crowning achievement of his compiling and printing career, the *Harmonisches Gesangbuch* of 1827. The title page of this book was similar to that of the 1820 book but the contents and organization were quite different.

More than fifty tunes and texts which had been printed in 1820 were not included in this book. Conversely, approximately 290 texts and more than sixty tunes were added. The most remarkable feature of the book, however, was the order in which the 518 texts which the book contains were printed. They are arranged, not within topical sections as was the 1820 *Gesangbuch*, but in alphabetical order of first lines.[25] This relatively uncommon format, which made the book easy to use, indicates even less concern for traditional liturgical observances than was previously exhibited. The book does contain a topical index, but the divisions are reduced from the thirty-three of the 1820 printing to twenty-nine.

The topical index shows considerable change over the previous book. There is more emphasis upon Christ and a Trinitarian theology. The topic "Vom Himmel und Himmelischen Jerusalem" (On Heaven and Heavenly Jerusalem) which appeared in 1820 was changed to "Die Kirche Christi und Ihre Herrlichkeit" (The Church of Christ and Its Magnificence). The headings "Von dem hohen Adel des Menschen" (On the high Nobility of Man) and "Vom Menschlichen Elende und Verderben" (On Man's Misery and Corruption) were dropped, indicating a decrease in the humanistic emphasis. Most significantly, a new topical division, "Lob und Dank Lieder," (Praise and Thanks Songs) is added. This section contains nineteen hymns of praise, all but two of which had not been used previously. Much of the nature symbolism remains, but there is a noticeable change in emphasis, at least in these categories in which the hymns were placed.

An interesting example of the Harmonists' extrareligious interests in the late 1820s is seen in their adoption of a relatively large number of hymn texts from another communal Society, the Seventh Day Baptists of Ephrata, Pennsylvania. Founded in 1732 by Johann Conrad Beissel, a German Pietist who in 1720 had migrated to America, the Ephrata colony was probably the most austere and ascetic of all the communal societies. Beissel, who was born at Eberbach in the Palatinate, had assimilated the intense spirit of pietism which surrounded him during his youth. He had communication with the founders and followers of other sects, such as the Inspirationists who founded the Amana Society, and the disciples of Jacob Böhme who in 1694 had established the society called "The Woman in the Wilderness" near Germantown, Pennsylvania.

In America, Beissel associated himself with the Dunkers in the Germantown area and conducted the singing at their evangelistic meetings. Their hymnal was the *Davidisches Psalterspiel der Kinder Zion*, the hymns of which they sang in unison. Beissel broke away from the Dunkers in 1727, became an evangelist in his own right, and in 1732 established his own colony. He prepared his own hymnal, the *Göttliche Liebes und Lobes Gethöne*, which was printed for him by Benjamin Franklin in 1730. It was enlarged and reprinted by Franklin in 1732 and again in 1736.

Other hymn collections compiled by Beissel followed these. The *Zionitischer Weyrauchs-Hügel oder Myrrhen-Berg*, which contained 792 texts, was printed for him by Christopher Sauer in 1739. In these books, Beissel utilized traditional tunes for his texts. In later collections, however, he composed music in which he incorporated antiphonal singing, and he trained his singers to a high degree of perfection in producing this particular vocal effect which he greatly admired.

Although lacking formal musical training, Beissel developed an intricate theory of harmony which he employed in arranging his hymn settings. He also wrote a short treatise on singing and included it in his hymnbook, *Das Gesäng der einsamen und verlassenen Turtel-Taube*, which was printed in 1747. In this peculiar preface, Beissel attributes good singing to "angelic and heavenly life," "celestial virginity," and "care of the body," the last of which he says consists of a strict diet which forbids the eating of almost all foods except wheat, especially buckwheat, as well as the drinking of all beverages except well water.[26]

Beissel's *Turtel-Taube* contained only texts and was the first book to be printed by the Ephrata brotherhood on their own press. The music for the texts of the *Turtel-Taube* and other collections of the Ephrata colony is contained in various manuscript books which were made by members of Beissel's community. The best-known of these is the *Paradisisches Wunder-Spiel* which consists of music, presumably arranged by Beissel, in four- and five-part vocal scores. Each page of this collection, in addition to containing music, was illuminated with colored drawings of flowers, birds, and scenes depicting scriptural passages. Another Ephrata music source is a manuscript hymnbook containing approximately four hundred chorale melodies, most of which are set in four-part vocal score. Although extremely rare today, a number of copies of both sources were made by the Ephrata colony during the second half of the eighteenth century.[27]

The *Wunder-Spiel* was compiled for use by the choirs at Ephrata which Beissel trained in a special singing school. The hymnbook, on the other hand, was compiled for the use of the "House Fathers" who were the married members of the Ephrata community. The music of the hymnbook is in a simpler style than that of the *Wunder-Spiel* which has indications for intricate antiphonal singing. Further, examination of the copy of the 1754 *Wunder-Spiel* shows that none of its contents were borrowed by the Harmonists, and it is doubtful that any of them ever saw a copy of this work. However, forty-three texts used by the Harmonists in their *Gesangbuch* of 1827 are found in the hymnbook of the Ephrata House Fathers. The titles of these hymns, along with the tunes used by the Harmonists to sing them, are given below.

Title	*Tune in HG 1827*
Auf du ganze Zions-Heerde	Wachet auf
Auf du keusches Jungfrau'n-Heer	Mache dich mein Geist
Auf ihr Gäste	Auf du priesterliches
Auf schmucke dich	Wie schön ist unsers K.
Der bittre Kelch und Myrrhen	Eigene Melodie
Der frohe Tag bricht an	Eigene Melodie
Die Flammen der Liebe	Ach alles was Himmel
Die klugen Jungfrau'n sind erwacht	Wie schon ist unsers K.
Die starke Bewegung	Ihr Kinder des Höchsten
Die Weisheit ist mein bester	Herr Jesu Christ mein
Ein Herz, das Gott	In froher Eintracht
Freu' dich, Zion Gottes Stadt	Eigene Melodie/oder
	O der alles hät
	verloren
Fried' und Freud' sei in den Thoren	O wie selig
Gott ein Herrscher aller Heiden	Wachet auf
Gottes Wohnung ist sehr schön	Ach was sind wir ohne Jesus
Gute Nacht, o Welt	Seelen-Bräutigam
Herz der Liebe	Eigene Melodie
Ich lauf' den schmalen Himmels-Weg	Die Menschenlieb
Ich sehe die Pflanzen im Para.	Ach alles was H.
Ich sehe mit Freuden	Ach alles was H.
Ich stehe gepflanzet	Ach alles was H.
Ihr Bürger des Himmels	Ach alles was H.
Ihr Gäste macht euch bereit	Wer ist der Braut
Kommt ihr Glaubens-Kämpfer	Eigene Melodie
Lobsinget, lobsinget	Ach alles was Himmel

Mein Herz ist plötzlich
Mein Seel soll Gott lobsingen
Muss ich schon oft traurig gehn
Nun gehen die Geister
O auserwählte Schaar
O himmlische Wollust
O Jesu meiner seelen Lust
O Jesu reine Lebens-Quelle
O mein Täublein reiner Liebe
O! Was für verborgne Kräfte
O was wird das sein
Perl aller keusch verliebten
   Seelen
Wann Gott sein Zion lösen
Wann Zion wird entbunden
Wenn die Liebe aufgezehrt
Zion geht schwarz umher
Zion hat im Geist vernommen
Zion werde hoch erfreut

Es glänzet der Christ
Nun lob mein Seel
Entfernet euch
Es glänzet der Christ.
Mein Jesu, der du mich
Ach alles was Himmel
Mein Herzens Jesu
In froher Eintracht
Wo ist wohl ein süssern
Frölich lasst uns
Seelen-Bräutigam
Gott der du alle Welten
   trägest
In froher Eintracht
Wie schön ist unsers
O der alles hät verloren
O Gott du frommer G.
Wachet auf
Mache dich mein Geist

As the list shows, these texts were sung by the Harmonists to traditional chorale melodies rather than to the tunes found in the Ephrata hymnbook. Further, none of these texts are found in the Harmonist manuscript hymn-books, clearly indicating that the Ephrata influence was felt only during the time of the compilation of the *Gesangbuch* of 1827. The lack of any permanent influence of these texts among the Harmonists is shown by the fact that Henrici's accompaniment book (HM 2.29) contains only three of them; the remainder are either dropped entirely or are simply included as a number in his cross reference index. Finally, three of the Ephrata texts designated to be sung "In eigener Melodie"—"Freu' dich, Zion Gottes Stadt," "Herz der Liebe," and "Kommt ihr Glaubens-Kämpfer"—are not to be found in any music manuscript sources at Economy. This indicates that the source which the Harmonist compiler used was either exclusively a textual one or, if it did contain music, the music was of no interest to him.

In the 1827 printing, 261 texts, more than one-half the contents of the book, were sung to tunes which had been used in the *Württembergisches Gesangbuch*, the *Davidisches Psalterspiel*, and the *Geistlichen Liedern*. In comparison, the 1820 printing matched only 122 of its 371 texts with traditional tunes. In preparing keyboard accompaniments for traditional tunes, Mueller relied heavily upon Justin Heinrich Knecht's *Vollständiges Württembergisches Choralbuch*[28] (Stuttgart, 1816), a collection of 267 chorale harmonizations set in four parts with texts and a figured bass. It contained most of the chorale tunes used in the 1827 Gesangbuch. The following list gives the tunes added, the frequency with which they were used, and the source from which the Harmonists probably got the tune. The location of the tunes in Appendix C is also shown.

TUNES ADDED 1827

Title	Times Used	Source	Appendix C, No.
Ach alles was Himmel	30	Württ.	1
Ach ja, mehr als zu gern	1		*
Lobe den Herrn	1	Württ.	122
Frölich lässt uns Gott Lobs.	3	Württ.	71
Wachet auf, ruft uns die Stimme	5	Württ.	192
Mache dich, mein Geist	4	Württ.	124
Wie schön ist unsers König.	11	Ps.	214
Entfernet euch	14	Württ.	62
Nicht bloss für diese U.	1		134
Wo ist wohl ein süsser L.	4	Ps.	220
Wann mein Stündlein vor.	1	Ps.	196
Das laufen macht mich matt/oder Ich weiss nicht wie mir ist	2		25
Der bittre Kelch	2		29
Der Glaubens-Grund ruht auf	1		20
Ach treib aus meiner Seel	1		*
O Welt, du bist voll Trug.	2		34
Die Braut geht aus und ein	1		*
O Ewigkeit, du Freuden-Wort	3	Ps.	144
Ihr Kinder des Höchsten/oder Es glänzet der Christ.	6	Geist.L.	102
Die Welt hat ihre Gunst	1		46
Ein Blümlein auf der Wiese	2		60
Du meiner Augen Licht	1	Ps.	51
Du miterwählte Schaar/oder Mein Herz sich innig freut	3		53
Du Perlen-Volk sing Gott	1		54
Es kostet viel	1	Ps.	67
Freu dich Zion Gottes Stadt	1		*
Ehre sei jetzo mit Freud	1	Ps.	*
Bei der Weisheit	3		15
Meine Seele sehnet sich	1	Geist.L.	172
Ach was sind wir ohne Jesu	1	Württ.	2
Seelen-Bräutigam	2	Württ.	171
Herz der Liebe	1		*
Freude, Freude aller wir	3		69
Himmels Lust ist bewusst	1		91
Wer ist der Braut	3		205
Ihr Jungfrau'n wacht/oder Herr ich bin dein	2		101
Sey Lob und Ehr dem H.	1	Württ.	176
Ihr Töchter Zions kommt herbey	1	Ps.	*
Kommt ihr Glaubens-Kämpf.	1		*
Mein Geist ist liebevoll	1		*
Nennt mich eine Blume	1		133

Nun freut euch ihr lieben	1		136
Nun Seele auf	1		*
Die sanfte Bewegung	1	Ps.	*
Mein Jesu, der du mich zum L.	1	Ps.	*
Eil doch heran	1	Ps.	59
Was Gott thut	1	Württ.	198
Triumph, Triumph des Herrn	1	Ps.	187
Nur frisch hinein	1	Ps.	*
Womit soll ich dich wohl l.	1	Ps.	221
Nun da Schnee und Eis	1		135
Im Lenz ist nun gebor.	1		103
Seht, Gespielen	1		174
Wie des Lenzes milde	1		208
O Freunde wie blühet	1		145
An einem feierlichen Morgen	1		10
Der schöne Maienmond	1		35
Willkommen, o seeliger Abend	1		216
Du hoher schwarzer Tannenwald	1		50
Mein Hoffnungs-Anker liegt	1		128
Es reizet die Menschen	1		68
Schön ist zwar die ganze Welt	1		164
Bei Brüdern welche Treu	1		14

These hymnbooks were, of course, dependent upon earlier musical sources for their tunes. A representative list of sources from which they drew, along with some of the tunes which the Harmonists used which originated in these sources, is given below.

Appendix C, No.

Etlich Christlich Lider Lobgesang und Psalm
(Wittenberg, 1524)

    Sey Lob und Ehr dem Höchsten gut/oder   176
        Es ist das Heil uns kommen her

Hymnodus sacer (Leipzig, 1625)

    Herr Jesu Christ, meins Lebens Licht   89

Praxis Pietatis Melica (Berlin: Johann Crüger,
1st ed. 1648, 44th ed. 1736)

    O Gott, du frommer Gott (1648)   147
    O Ewigkeit du Donnerwort (1653)   144
    Erwacht zum neuen Leben (1653)   63
    Schwing dich auf zu deinem Gott (1653)   169
    Jesu meine Freude (1653)   114
    Jesus, meiner Zufersicht (1653)   115

Stralsund Gesangbuch (1665)

    Lobe den Herrn   122

Nürnberg Gesangbuch (1690)

    Was Gott thut ist wohl getan   198

Darmstadt Gesangbuch (1698)

Ach alles was Himmel	1
Entfernet euch	62
Ehre sei jetzo mit Freud	*
Seelen-Bräutigam	171
Alle Menschen müssen sterben	5
Zeuch mich	223

Geistreiches Gesangbuch, den Kern Alter und Neuer Lieder
(Halle: Johann Anastasio Freylinghausen, 1st ed. 1704, 19th ed. 1759)

Ihr Kinder des Höchstens (1704)	102
Du meiner Augen Licht (1704)	51
Es kostet viel (1704)	67
O Durchbrecher aller Bande (1704)	142
Gott sei dank (1705)	82
Seele was ist schöners (1704)	172
O wie seelig (1710)	155

Numerous chorale books which were printed after these contain variants of the tunes which appeared in these early sources. The chorale tunes used by the Harmonists invariably were drawn from the more recent sources and, as has already been noted, the original melodies were sometimes obscured and confused with others because of the variants which evolved. Nevertheless, two of the early sources in particular deserve attention here.

Johann Crüger's *Praxis Pietatis Melica* constitutes the mainstream of Lutheran hymnody in the latter half of the seventeenth century. Crüger is best known for his settings of the texts of Paul Gerhardt, a poet whose hymns are generally the only ones equated with those of Martin Luther. There are no copies of Crüger's *Praxis Pietatis* in the collection at Economy, but the influence of his melodies can be seen in the list above. "O Gott, du frommer Gott," for example, was used twenty-one times in the 1827 *Gesangbuch*.

The only collection dating from the eighteenth century which equalled Crüger's was Freylinghausen's. A copy of the eighth edition of his *Geistreiches Gesangbuch* is in the collection at Economy. The musical settings in this book consist of soprano and bass lines with figures. The number of tunes in the Harmonist hymn repertory which originally appeared in Freylinghausen's book indicates the importance of this collection in German hymnody.

Among the tunes in the nonchorale category which were added in 1827 are the four given below:

Nun da Schnee und Eis	Appendix C, No. 135
Der Greiss des Silber-Haares	Appendix C, No. 31
Seht Gespielen	Appendix C, No. 174
Wie des Lenzes milde Lüfte	Appendix C, No. 208

These tunes, with their texts, were used extensively in the manuscript hymn-books, but had not been included in the 1820 printing. Their absence from the 1820 *Gesangbuch* probably proved awkward and they were included in the closing section of the 1827 printing, "Songs for Youth and Music."

One tune from a popular music source is of interest. "Bei Brüdern welche Treu Beweisen" which appears as No. 514 in the 1827 printing is found in most manuscript hymnbooks. The text was sung to a popular song called "Song to the memory of Mozart." The original, which was set for two voices and piano accompaniment, was written by a certain D. Thompson and published by G. Willig of Philadelphia. Thompson's first line reads, "If e'er when solemn stillness reign, our wakeful eyes a vigil keep." The copy which Dr. Mueller used to make a keyboard version for the Harmonist hymn text has written on it in his hand: "Bei Brüdern welche Treu Beweisen—in D# zu setzen" (see Appendix C, no. 14).

In conclusion, Martin Luther's translation of the Bible was widely used by the Harmonists, but his hymn, "Ein' Feste Burg," was not used in the manuscript or printed hymnals of the Society. Another curiosity is that there is not a single piece by J. S. Bach in the entire Harmonist music collection. Finally, a curious deletion was made in the 1827 *Gesangbuch*. The tune "Alle Menschen müssen Sterben" which was used ten times in the 1820 *Gesang-buch* was dropped from use in 1827. Was the objection to it a musical one? It seems unlikely that it was, for Henrici included it in his accompaniment book (HM 2.29). The most plausible reason appears to be that George Rapp, who was convinced that he would live to bring his holy Society into the presence of Christ, objected to the title, "All men must die."

---

1. Copies of the following editions are extant at Economy: 1756, 1766, 1769, 1779, 1786, 1794, and 1834.

2. A typical Harmonist statement of this kind is that of Augusta Beysser, contained in her copy of *Der Cöthnischen Lieder* (Esslingen, 1756), another popular hymnal among the Harmonists: "Dort ist ein jedes Seufzerlein, An unser Kron ein Edelstein. Das ganze Leben Christi war Leiden und Aufopferung, und wir suchen nur Ruhe und Freude." (There each sigh is a diamond in our crown. The entire life of Christ was suffering and sacrifice, and we seek only rest and joy.)

3. A version was printed by Billmeyer of Germantaun in 1797 and another by Schaeffer and Maund of Baltimore in 1816. See Appendix D, pP. 40 and pP. 55.

4. A copy belonging to Sibilla Hurlebaus is inscribed "1850" and another belonging to Christoph Leicht, "1860."

5. See Appendix D, pP.16; 19-21; 24-28; 30, 34; 41; 46; 54; 58.

6. For further discussion of "departure hymns" see Arndt, *Op. cit.*, pp. 58-59.

7. John Duss, *The Harmonists*, p. 26, suggests that the word "paart" refers to the re-pairing of the two sexes into one bi-une being. A strong movement toward celibacy was beginning in the Society at this time.

8. Julian, *Op. cit.*, p. 417.

9.   A letter from George Rapp to Frederick Rapp, dated 8 April 1824, reads in part: "Most religious people busy themselves with conditions after death; as for us there stands here before our eyes, a great structure to which all ages have contributed; now it is our turn to take an active part in this building of mankind until the Lord will come again to distribute the reward. That is our first duty, rather than dreaming about eternity."

10.   pM.8-3, p. 70.

11.   This tune also appears in some instrumental part-books with the title "God Save Great Washington." See IM 2.8-2, p. 10.

12.   See HP 2.23, p. 174. This is a third edition printed in 1862.

13.   See TM.5.

14.   Eisenach, *op. cit.*, 2:165.

15.   Arndt, *A Documentary History of the Indiana Decade of the Harmony Society 1814-1824* (Indianapolis: 1975) I, 782. Heinrich Ebner (b. Düsseldorf, Germany, 1783; d. Allentown, Pa., 1850) arrived in Philadelphia from Germany aboard the *Orland* 3 August 1806. From 1812 to 1815, in partnership with J. Ehrenfried, he published a newspaper in Allentown called the *Friedens-Bote*. Although opposed to the War of 1812, Ehrenfried was drafted and marched under Marcus Hook. Ebner continued the paper alone until 1821 when he formed a partnership with Friedrich G. Rütz. The paper was sold in 1831 and Ebner appears to have operated a bookstore in Allentown from then until his death in 1850. See *Proceedings of the Lehigh County Historical Society*, Allentown (1947), 16:210.

16.   Johannes Zahn, *Die Melodien der Deutschen Evangelischen Kirchenlieder aus den Quellen geschöpft und mitgeteilt.* 6 vols. (Gütersloh: C. Bertelsman, 1889).

17.   Albert Knapp, *Evangelischer Liederschatz für Kirche und Haus.* 2 vols. (Stuttgart und Tübingen: J. G. Cotta'schen Buchhandlung, 1837).

18.   Johann Herman came to Lancaster, Ohio, in 1816 from Chambersburg, Pa. He was a practical printer and bought "Der Deutsche Ohio Adler," the first German newspaper in Ohio, from his brother-in-law Edward Schaeffer, who had established it in 1807. The office was located on the west side of Columbus St., on the corner of the first alley north of Wheeling St. A respected citizen, he was visited by the Duke of Saxe-Weimar in 1825. He died in 1833. See C. M. L. Wiseman, *Centennial History of Lancaster, Ohio* (Lancaster, Ohio, 1898), p. 98.

19.   John Duss refers to a group of singers active in the church after 1880 as "Vorsänger." Their function, as he describes it, was clearly that of leading singers.

20.   J. S. Buckingham, *The Eastern and Western States of America.* 2 vols. (London: Fisher, Son & Co., 1842), 2:222.

21.   Mueller dated some of the pages. The earliest date given is 17 March 1824, and the latest is 26 July 1824.

22.   No. 53, "Einsetzung des Ewigen Königes Jesu auf dem Berge Zion" (The Establishment of the Eternal King Jesus on Mount Zion), is divided into "Erster Chor," "Zweyter Chor," "Dritter Chor," "Alle Chor," and "Bass Solo."

23.   See Appendix D, pM.4-7; pM.10-1, 2, 3; pM.12-2, 3. Many of these texts were written some years before they were printed.

24.   There are no copies of the *Kleine Sammlung* extant at Economy. The above is based upon examination of a copy contained in the Darlington Library, Cathedral of Learning, University of Pittsburgh.

25.   A recent compilation which follows this arrangement is *The Worshipbook, Services and Hymns* (Phila.: Geneva Press, 1972).

26.   James Ernst, *Ephrata, A History* (Allentown: Schlechter's Press, 1963), p. 241. Posthumously edited by John Joseph Stoudt.

27.   In searching for sources of Harmonist music and texts, photo-copies of the three Ephrata items given above were examined. The photo-copies used are contained in the private library of Theodore M. Finney of Pittsburgh, Pennsylvania. Finney's photo-copy of the *Paradisisches Wunder-Spiel* is of an original dated 1754 and his hymnbook photo-copy is of an original found in the Archives of the Moravian Church in Lititz, Pennsylvania. According to an attached note signed by Abraham Reincke Beck and dated January 1908, the original hymnbook was given to an anonymous Moravian pastor by Peter Miller who was Conrad Beissel's successor as superintendent of the Ephrata colony.

28.   HP 2.1.

4

Music During the Golden Age of the Harmony Society: 1825-1832

A GERMAN COURT ORCHESTRA ON THE BANKS OF THE OHIO

The prosperity which the Society enjoyed at Economy near Pittsburgh between 1825 and 1832 was reflected in its increased emphasis upon the arts. A two-story Feast Hall was built which, along with a large dining and meeting room (Saal), a schoolroom, a museum, and a printing shop, contained a room set aside solely for the orchestra. Paintings, statuary, stuffed animals for the museum, and an extensive library were acquired. The grounds were planted in gardens and were carefully maintained.[1] In manufacturing, Economy was an example of a community caught up in the excitement and multiplicity of the Industrial Revolution. Culturally, however, it was much like an eighteenth-century German court, with a fine resident orchestra, which now presented several concerts each month, and which gradually attracted the attention of some of the most prominent musicians in Pittsburgh. One of these was the Pittsburgh attorney and musical dilettante, Charles von Bonnhorst (see plate 6).

Charles von Bonnhorst was born in Prussia in 1776, served as an officer in the artillery corps of the Prussian army, and took part in the battle of Jena in 1806. Shortly after 1806 he came to America. He spent a short time in Philadelphia, then settled near Pittsburgh where he engaged in sheep raising in Mifflin Township. He later moved into the city, became an Alderman, studied law, and was admitted to the Bar Association of Allegheny County.[2] His skill as an attorney and his ability to speak both German and English made him a valuable aid to the Harmony Society as well as to the other German immigrants in Pittsburgh.

Bonnhorst was a skilled violinist and wrote more than fifty instrumental pieces for the Economy orchestra (see Appendix B, Nos. 192-240). All are short pieces, waltzes, quadrilles, polonaises, and marches, such as his "Jackson's March" which he presented to the Society in July, 1826[3]

[Appendix A, ex. 11]. Before writing the pieces he inquired at Economy about the performance skills of the Harmonist instrumentalists. In a letter to Frederick Rapp dated 6 April 1826, Bonnhorst stated that he wished to compose "several beautiful pieces" for the orchestra and for that reason he wanted to know which kinds of instruments they had and in which keys they played best. In reply Dr. Mueller wrote:

> We have 2 clarinets, 2 violins, 1 violoncello, 2 flutes, 2 piccolo flutes, 2 regular French horns, and 2 trumpets [Flügelhorner], 2 bassoons, 1 large drum. Our musicians play well in C major, G major, and D major. In B flat major and A major they cannot play clean [rein]. The instruments play best together in C major. N.B. Our violinists are not practiced to play higher than d^3 (3 gestrichenes d) and the flute players go up to g^3 (3 gestrichenes g).

Bonnhorst's pieces expanded the orchestra's repertory from 192 to 240 entries. In addition to instrumental pieces, he also wrote a tune for a favorite Harmonist text, "Heilig sey dein Nam" (Holy be Thy Name), (see Appendix A, ex. 12), which was used during the various Harmonist festivals.

Bonnhorst's interest in the Harmonist orchestra at this time may have been prompted in part by the forthcoming visit of an important and prominent German nobleman, Bernhard, Duke of Saxe-Weimar Eisenach. When Bonnhorst wrote to Frederick offering to write pieces for the Harmonist orchestra he may have been anticipating the duke's visit and the efforts which the Harmonist musicians would undoubtedly exert to entertain such a famous German visitor.

In any case, Bonnhorst and Charles Volz,[4] a Pittsburgh merchant who lived on the east side of Wood Street between Front and Second streets and who was also active in Pittsburgh musical life, were the first to greet Duke Bernhard when he arrived in Pittsburgh 17 May 1826. Duke Bernhard, as his published travel account shows, was the most musically discriminating visitor to tour Economy in the 1820s. He was brought to the village on May 18 by Bonnhorst and Volz. Part of his account of the event follows:

> In approaching Economy . . . we came to a newly-built house, at which stood three men with horns, who began to blow upon our arrival. . . . We spent the evening with Mr. Rapp. He collected the musical members of the Society, and entertained us with music. Miss Gertrude played upon the piano, and three of the girls sang; the other instruments were violins, a violoncello and two flutes. The music was really not so good as we had heard in the preceding autumn at Bethlehem; but gave us much entertainment. Mr. Bonnhorst also delighted us with his fine performance on the violin. The music was principally directed by a German physician named Mueller, who belongs to the community, and also has charge of the school.[5]

Duke Bernhard heard the musicians again a short time later and remarked: "We had an excellent dinner in Mr. Rapp's house, and the musical members of the Society took the opportunity to play their best in front of it. The band consisted of twelve musicians, and performed very well, among them were two who played bugles. . . ."[6]

Dr. Mueller began to show more discrimination in selecting music, probably because of the sophisticated audiences which the Society was now entertaining. A memorandum notebook prepared for a purchasing trip to Philadelphia in 1826 has the following entry:

> Für music—2 doz. G or bass strings for the small violin; 2 setts [sic] strings for the violoncello or Bass Violin; Music sacred for the church or marches, should be in partitur, that is, set in 4 or 7 voices by Masters, or else none.

Instruments continued to be a matter of concern to Frederick Rapp, as well as to Dr. Mueller. A letter of 22 May 1826, written by him to one Abraham Ziegler at Harmony reads: "It is some time since you promised to send over . . . the forte piano I bought from Mr. Kilken. . . ." Nor had Frederick given up hope of procuring a pipe organ for the church he was planning for Economy. On 18 September 1827, he wrote to the Society's agent, J. Solms, in Philadelphia:

> When I come to your city this winter I will have to contract for an organ with from 12 to 15 stops. I wish you to select the best master for the building of one for us. . . .[7]

Not all the Harmonists' instruments had the most recently improved mechanisms, but some were contemporary enough to be the only ones of their kind in the Pittsburgh area. Charles Volz, who sold musical instruments to the Society from time to time, wrote a letter to Frederick Rapp on 17 July 1827 requesting permission to borrow the Society's B clarinet because he was to appear in a concert in Pittsburgh: "Sie würden uns sehr verbunden eine B clarinette mit einem A stücke für unser Conzert zu leihen."[8] The German "B" designates B-flat, and Volz is referring to a clarinet developed by Baumann in Paris during the early nineteenth century which had square keys, including extendable long keys for use with an extra joint which could lower the pitch to "A."[9]

Because of Mueller's efforts and the encouragement of the Rapps, the orchestra approached classical instrumentation. Mueller probably felt that an orchestra should play overtures and symphonies as well as short dances and marches. He also recognized that the help and leadership of a professional musician was needed. How Mueller won the Rapps to his way of thinking is a mystery. Equally remarkable is the fact that the musician they hired eventually became one of the most prominent music publishers in America during the nineteenth century.

William Cummings Peters was the oldest of three sons of William Smalling Peters who emigrated from Modbury, Devonshire, England, around 1820 (see plate 7). Information regarding the activities of the family is meager and often contradictory. "Old Man Peters," and his sons William Cummings, John, and Henry J., were all musicians who through various partnerships established important music stores and publishing houses in many of the major cities along the Ohio and Mississippi rivers.[10] This family, along with sixteen associates from England and the United States—some also musicians—founded the famed Peters Colony which settled Dallas County, Texas. The planning of this important movement in American colonization may have been done in the music store which W. C. Peters established in Cincinnati, Ohio, in the early 1840s. Some of the inspiration for the venture may indeed have grown out of the association which William Cummings Peters had with the veteran colonizers, the Harmonists, between the years 1827 and 1831.[11]

Most sources agree that William Cummings Peters was born in Modbury, Devonshire, England, March 10, 1805 and that he migrated to America with his parents. His exact whereabouts during the early 1820s is not definitely known; some sources say that the family first moved to Canada where the father supposedly was a bandmaster;[12] another maintains that the family moved to Texas around 1823, although this appears unlikely. Descendants of the Peters family were living in Blairsville, Pennsylvania, in 1907 and a reliable source states that at least a portion of the family may have moved there around 1825. The extant records which concern the elder Peters further confuse the issue, for some mention him as residing in Pittsburgh while others place his residence in Louisville and refer to him as the "Kentuckian who formed the Peters Colony." Whatever the true circumstances and chronology of events, William Cummings Peters, the oldest and most prominent son of W. S. Peters, arrived in Pittsburgh probably as early as 1825, certainly no later than 1827, and was earning his living by teaching music and presenting concerts, being proficient on the flute, violin, and piano.

Peters began his association with the Harmonists no later than 1827. A march composed by him appears in a violin part-book and is dated 12 August 1827. Like Bonnhorst's, his first compositions for the Harmonist orchestra were short pieces such as his "Economie Walz" and "Economie Quickstep" (Appendix A, nos. 13 and 14). From August 1827 to March 1828 he appears to have been closely associated with the Harmonists and composed an ode "O schöne Harmonie" (Appendix A, no. 15) which was probably performed at the Harmoniefest of 15 February 1828. Musically, the work is superior to the other odes in the collection, most of which had been composed by Dr. Mueller. The text, consisting of eleven stanzas, was probably written by Mueller and praises the virtues of "Die Harmonie," emphasizing in particular the protection which the Society offers from the storms of the outside world. Peters achieves musical variety by alternating solos and duets with the chorus on the various stanzas and separating these by brief instrumental "symphonies." The closing stanza is a rousing chorus with abundant rhythmic motion, especially in the bass line, and must have evoked an enthusiastic response from the Harmonists.

At about this time larger, more ambitious works were added to the orchestra's repertory. Peters, apparently at Mueller's direction, began arranging for the Harmonists overtures by leading European composers. The letter below was written on the score to an arrangement of J. P. Martini's "Overture to Henry IV."

Dear Sir
    Please excuse me for not having written this within the time specified (which was 4 or 5 weeks) as my time is much occupied with other matters that I have written the greater part of this after 11 o'clock at night. The last part in 2/4 time I have not arranged as it does not altogether belong to the Overture, it being played after the commencement of the 1st act. I have some trios for 2 violins and violincello [sic] which I will give you a copy of when I come down which will be next Sunday or Sunday a week. Please copy this by the time I come.
    Yours,
        W. C. Peters[13]

This letter and others indicate that while Peters did not stay at Economy for any long periods, he did make regular visits there to direct rehearsals and teach the musicians the arrangements. Transportation from Pittsburgh to Economy via riverboat was relatively dependable and regular at that time. Letters and manuscripts, incidentally, do not show Peters to be the unscrupulous man which some biographers of Stephen Foster have made him out to be.[14] At Economy he was respected and admired and there are fanfares in the part-books which were played to greet him when he came to visit, usually on Sunday afternoons. There are no records which indicate that Peters was paid by the Society, but the quantity of work which he did for the Harmonists and the fact that he was making his living by teaching and performing suggests that he was hired by the Society as an arranger-composer and teacher.

Some sources speculate that Peters left Pittsburgh and went to Louisville in 1829. Whether or not this was the case he increased the orchestra's repertory between 1828-1830 by approximately sixty selections. The new pieces included: *Sinfonia I* (Sterkel); *Sinfonia II* (Pleyel); Overture *Tancredi* (Rossini);[15] Overture *Enterprise* (Clifton); Overture to *Figaro* (Mozart); and other pieces by Gyrowetz, Handel, Ware, Latour, and Fuchs. Many of these were arranged to fit the Harmonist instrumentation by W. C. Peters (see Appendix B, nos. 242-320). Very few printed copies of large instrumental forms—symphonies and quartets—are extant in the Economy archives. A "Grande Sinfonie," Op. 6 by Gyrowetz (published by Simrock) and several quartets by Haydn and Pleyel, however, are representative of what was once at least a modest collection of published large-form pieces by major European composers. The overtures appear to have been, without exception, arranged from keyboard scores published in America. The following overtures exist in keyboard copies, some bearing the signature of W. C. Peters, and are bound in one volume:[16]

Mozart: Overture to *The Marriage of Figaro* (Phila.: G. Willig)
Arne: Overture to *Artaxerxes* (New York: Riley)
Clifton: Overture to *The Enterprise* (Phila.: Willig)
Ware: Overture to *The Enchanted Harp* (Phila.: Willig)
Martini: Overture to *Henry the IV* (Phila.: Willig)
Weber: Overture to *Der Freischütz* (Phila.: Klemm)
Rossini: Overture to *La Gazza Ladra* (Phila.: Willig)

The Sterkel *Sinfonia I*, is scored for two violins, two clarinets, two bugles, two flutes, three horns, trumpet, bass, and drums. It appears in a volume entitled *Partitur Buch für die Music-Bande Oeconomie, angefangen im December, 1828.*[17] The second entry is *Sinfonia II*, by Pleyel, which has the same instrumentation as the Sterkel piece but adds two bassoons.

Bassoon parts occur in music prior to this, but it appears that two new bassoons were purchased, or the old ones were repaired, in 1828. An instrumental part-book contains the following note written inside the front cover: "Bassoon bekommen den 26 April, 1828."[18] Two months earlier, probably in preparation for the Harmoniefest, the following items were purchased from Charles Volz:[19]

2	violins and mahogany case	$60.00
2	extra bows	2.00
1	tenor and bow	15.00
1	violoncello preceptor	3.00

Chamber music played at this time can be identified with certainty because the manuscripts are dated. J. Vanhall's works were favorites, as is indicated by a volume entitled *Trois faciles pour deux violons et violoncelle par J. Vanhall, Oeconomie, August 21, 1828.*[20]

CONCERTS AT ECONOMY WITH J. C. MUELLER, MUSIC CRITIC

Important political and business figures visited Economy more frequently during the late 1820s and Mueller, as the result of Peters' tutelage, began more and more to feel the presence of a sophisticated audience. Rapp must have noticed the frequent inclusion on these programs (printed by Mueller) of sinfonias, overtures, and cantatas by European masters and the less frequent performances of the short, rhythmic marches which the less-educated in the Society enjoyed most. Both men loved music, but a clash in philosophies regarding its use was developing. Rapp believed in true "Gebrauchsmusik" (music for use). Music was to be enjoyed by all—played as the harvest crews entered the fields; from the church tower to call the congregation to the church; in the factories to relieve the tedium of labor; and in recreational gatherings, indoors and out, while fruit and wine were passed around. Mueller's early musical efforts were compatible with this philosophy. Although he was a religious mystic he felt the need to grow artistically and intellectually, and it was this philosophy which in a few short years was to bring, for him and many of the musicians, this idyllic setting to a bizarre and unfortunate end.

In the spring of 1828, Mueller's growing musical self-consciousness led him to begin a critical record of the concerts presented by the Harmonist musicians. Inscribed "Memorandum Buch des Music Bandes der Oekonomie, Angefangen im Märtz, 1828" (Memorandum book of the Music Band of the Economy, begun in March, 1828), the book contains the programs of concerts given at Economy from 9 March 1828 to 23 November 1831[21] (see plate 10). In addition to the titles of the pieces performed, Mueller included critical comments, in German and Latin, on the quality of the performances as well as notes on who attended the concerts. Mueller's notes provide valuable information about the impressive concerts presented by the Harmonist musicians during these years. Between the lines, however, one can see developing the disagreement and dissention which culminated in the schism in 1832.

Mueller's record begins with a concert presented Sunday, 9 March 1828, the program of which appears below:

1. No. 8 Der Harmonie March
2. No. 120 March of Stuttgart
3. No. 272 Overture to Enterprise
4. No. 267 Latour's Overture
5. No. 215, Walz 21 of von Bonnhorst in Es
6. Funny Walz
7. On Request, Calif's Overture
8. No. 229 Quadrille 34 of von Bonnhorst as finishing piece
Gesungen Wurde
106 Who, who can express
    Dein Leben Herr zeigt uns die Pforte

The concert began with two short pieces familiar to the Harmonists.[22] These were followed by two overtures arranged by Peters. Two more short pieces, one by Bonnhorst, were played and then, apparently by request, another overture. Another piece by Bonnhorst was played "as a finishing piece." Most concerts were closed with vocal music, usually of a sacred nature as in this case, "Thy Life, Lord, Shows us the Way." It is significant that Bonnhorst's pieces, most of them written in 1826, remained an important part of the orchestra's repertory. When the schism finally occurred, Bonnhorst sided with the Rapps, but it must have saddened him to see the bitterness develop and divide the Society.

The second concert listed in Mueller's record was played 23 March 1828, two weeks after the date of the first. W. C. Peters attended, and the eighth selection on the concert was listed as "Concerto on the Clarinette by Mr. W. C. Peters als Abschieds Symphonie" ("Concerto on the Clarinet as a farewell symphony." See No. 293 in Appendix B). In January of this year Mueller had requested George and Frederick Rapp to retain the services of Mr. Peters for three more months to allow him time to develop the Harmonist orchestra to the point where it could continue independently. The program, unlike the first, began with the Overture to *Figaro* and also included pieces by a "violin quartet," a "metal Band," and a "Flute Quartet." These ensembles played works by Pleyel, Vogler, and Weber. The vocal pieces on the program consisted of a "Te Deum" by Knecht, and Haydn's "The Creation" which was sung by "the singers and the machine company." Mueller's entry is unclear but seems to suggest that the women and girls (Sängerin) and the machine company (probably men) combined to perform the work. It was an ambitious program, undoubtedly planned to bid Mr. Peters a proper farewell.

It was on the third concert, presented Easter Day 6 April 1828 that Mueller began to grade the performances. Using a mixture of Latin and German terms—"male" poor; "bene" good; "Mangelhaft" unsatisfactory—he appraised the quality of the performances of the pieces. To these he added remarks describing precisely what went well or poorly. The Easter concert began with the "Overture of Bagdad." Following the title Mueller wrote, "Male, Male." Other pieces on the program are graded "bene" and "Mangelhaft," and Mueller comments further: "this concert was severely criticized. It was claimed that the pieces were too wild, so it turned out badly." As did the first two concerts, this one closed with several pieces of sacred vocal music.

On the next concert, the orchestra played better and Mueller commented: "In the concert of April 20 we had a visit from Mr. Peters and several of his friends. For that reason, among others, the following [additional pieces] were played." The extra pieces consisted of an overture, two short pieces from the early repertory, and a waltz by Charles von Bonnhorst.

The next three concerts included more pieces from the old repertory and Mueller's ratings for these are all favorable. On the Pentecost program of 5

May he wrote: "This concert was performed very well and was completely satisfactory."

W. C. Peters was back again for the concert of 6 July and brought with him a noted medical doctor and geologist, Dr. Gerard Troost. The following week the harvest festival was celebrated and the guest of honor was Thomas B. Robertson, the third governor of Louisiana. On 20 July the concert was played in the Saal (Feast Hall) and the Passavant family, founders of the town of Zelienople, Pa., and formerly one of the most respected families of Frankfurt a/M was present.

These concerts are representative of those given in 1828. W. C. Peters visited with Dr. Troost again on 17 August and Mueller commented: "Because of the presence of a good and lively important personage everything went well." On October 26 he writes: "We had many neighbors in the audience. Since every musician always showed himself willing and industrious in learning and practicing, the Lord blessed this, so that all went well." The final concert recorded for the year was that given Christmas Day. All of the pieces were from the early repertory. Mueller comments: "It was more a solemn festive meditation combined with singing than a concert, so it was beautiful and pleasant." Peters attended only two of the twenty-two concerts which the orchestra gave in 1829, those of May 17 and August 9. (He may have been in Louisville during this year and perhaps returned for occasional visits.)

Mueller, nevertheless, continued to upgrade the repertory. He began the year by giving the musicians several weeks to practice some pieces, among which were *Sinfonie I*, by Sterkel; *Quatour I* by Hoffman; and the accompaniments to various vocal selections including excerpts from Haydn's *The Creation*. It should be noted here that the European masterworks which the Harmonists arranged and performed were composed, for the most part, before 1800. The following list contains some of the names and dates of the composers represented in the Harmonist repertory:

W. A. Mozart (1756-1791)
G. J. Vogler (1749-1814)
I. Pleyel (1757-1831)
C. M. von Weber (1786-1826)
J. Sterkel (1750-1817)
J. H. Knecht (1752-1817)
J. Haydn (1732-1809)
G. Rossini (1792-1868)
J. B. Wanhal (1739-1813)
N. Jomeli (1714-1774)

More names could be added but these are sufficient to show that the musical tastes of the Harmonists were firmly rooted in the eighteenth-century classical style.

Mueller presented the first concert for the year 1829 on 26 January. He began with Sterkel's *Sinfonie I*, one of the few complete four-movement symphonies in the orchestra's repertory. Of the performance Mueller wrote: "Everything was played in time but the mood of the symphony was not completely clean. Also a certain lack was felt which I would be unable to name."

Following this concert he again gave the musicians practice assignments and a concert was not played until 15 February, Harmoniefest. Most of the assigned pieces, with the exception of Pleyel's *Symphony in D*, were Harmonist odes and short marches from the early years. On festive occasions, especially the Harmoniefest, pieces from the earlier repertory formed the larger part of the orchestra's programs. On this occasion "Harmonie du Bruderstadt" (Harmony thou town of Brethren); "Hail Columbia"; Pleyel's "Menuet," among others, were played. The weather apparently was bad and Mueller states that the music because of the cold and rain did not sound well. He adds, "the festival was most solemn, elevated, spirited, blessed and without noise— music thereby quite incidental."

If somewhat unenthusiastic over the music of the Harmoniefest, Mueller appeared encouraged by the next concert, given 5 April. He included the following comment in his criticism of the concert.

> A music lover in Economy wrote the following about the last concert: "Artistic, expressive and beautiful was the music and the singing of the concert on the evening of the 5th of the month in the large hall in Economy; the audience was numerous and never inspired with so much attention; for the presentation of the cantate of Cherubini made everyone all ear. The gentle beginning of 3 solos, the mighty chorus accompanied by instruments which followed, and the many changes and fugues tastefully interwoven, which alternately rose from a swansong-like melancholy tone to the most joyous trio and in this way drew heart and ear upward, moved the entire Society, and with admiration for the art and industry and the continuous persistence of our musicians, often under unhappy circumstances, old and young applauded them most sincerely."

The piece described in these glowing terms was the first performance at Economy of the secular cantata *La Primavera* by Luigi Cherubini. Mueller, working from a keyboard version published by Probst of Leipzig, had arranged the piece for two horns, strings, and voices.[23] The same program also included W. C. Peters' arrangement of Martini's Overture to *Henry IV*.

The orchestra played again Easter Day, 19 April. Here Mueller inserts a strange and somewhat cryptic comment, indicating that all may not have been harmonious at Economy. "Everything went fairly well and tolerably for a good ear—but *discordia* could not hide itself, both in the beat and in playing, which however will be brought in order by *veritate*." Mueller often wrote short notes in Latin, French, and German—probably just for practice—but here the Latin suggests reference other than to music.

The program for the Pfingstfest (Pentecost) celebration of 7 June 1829 illustrates how the Harmonists mixed secular and sacred music in the religious observances (see plate 8). Printed on the Harmonist press by Mueller, it has three divisions; two during the day and one in the evening. "V.M." and "N.M." are abbreviations for "Vormittag" (before noon) and "Nachmittag" (after noon). Two pieces comprise each of the first two divisions, and these were probably played at different locations throughout the festivities, possibly in the Feast Hall, in the church, or at the cemetery. The evening program was a full-length concert, included choral music and, considering the time of year, may have been held outdoors. Mueller had mixed feelings about the concert: "This festive evening as usual was more inspired entertainment than a concert. It would not only take far more perfect masters, but also more intelligent brethren than we are to express such high spiritual and prophetic feelings with the voices of our throats and our instruments."

The summer and fall of 1829 were uneasy times at Economy. Several incidents occurred causing irritation and even suspicion among the members. On 25 June Conrad Feucht and Hildegard Mutschler, two members of the chorus, ran away and were married. Hildegard had assisted Father Rapp in the garden and greenhouse and Duke Bernhard, who saw her there, described her as "a very beautiful girl." Frederick Rapp, on the other hand, thought her immoral and dishonest. All records indicate that she was a seductive, sexy, and clever girl, and this incident along with her earlier reputation should have provoked severe condemnation from Father Rapp. Instead, he strangely defended her giving rise to unsavory speculation. Frederick, especially, was deeply wounded by Father Rapp's attitude and stated so in a long letter written to him 2 September 1829.[24] Secondly, Count Leon's letter, in which he announced himself to be the Messiah, arrived at Economy September 24, at a time when the Society was impatiently waiting for the coming of the millennial dawn. Rapp's authority was being questioned and threatened. On the program for the 9 August concert, Mueller adds a cryptic note which reflects this impatience: "We hope that the day may approach, who likes to wander in the night!" Despite the presence of "Herrn Peters" (Master Peters) at this concert, Mueller continues, "It was extremely oppressive . . . which dampened the concert to some degree."

In his later concerts Mueller expresses his growing dissatisfaction and depression. On 30 August, one piece was "accompanied most miserably." September 13, Mueller notes that "everything went quite well except my flute, which several times failed to play the high notes. The cause of this is unknown to me since this never happened to me before." The concert of 4 October was played without Mueller who "lay sick from a contusion and could not attend the practice sessions, whereupon the musicians chose the pieces." Then on the following concert "several instruments stumbled and one of the important voices failed almost entirely. And finally in No. 9 (*Magic Flute March*) several musicians during half the time looked for the piece while the others played even though everyone knew in advance what was to be played. This notice is purposely added here, so that at another time such mistakes may be avoided."

The crises gradually subsided and the orchestra and Mueller seem to have recovered their confidence. The November and December concerts contain favorable comments and the final concert for the year has the comment: "Both the musical numbers and especially the odes were executed with feeling to the enjoyment of all."

In 1830 Dr. Mueller increased his musical efforts. A concert given in January pleased him. This was followed by the Harmoniefest, held 14–15 February which marked the Society's twenty-fifth anniversary and included music played in the church, in the Saal, and from the tower of the Church. Many of the pieces from the early repertory, and hymns, including one of the oldest Harmonist hymns "Mein Hoffnungs-Anker liegt" (My Hope's Anchor Rests), were included. Mueller's comments now clearly show how he was increasingly being torn by his love for the simplicity and peace of "Die Harmonie," and his growing musical aspirations. "The festival was, to be sure, very much blessed by the general inner spiritual rest and divine peace which permeated almost everything—however, the green life-giving leaves of music were very sparing. Why?—God knows." Two weeks later Mueller programmed two new pieces of his own: "Freundschaft March," and "Die Magnolia" (see Appendix A, ex. 16). The performance of each was given his highest rating, "Optime." However, a flute "sonata" on the program, presumably played by Mueller, is rated "Male, Male," and a part of the commentary on the program is cut out of the book. Other pages which follow also have portions of the comments cut away. Whether this was Mueller's doing or someone else's following the schism remains unknown.

In March another piece by Mueller, his "Viola Walz" was played in a concert given in the Saal. Mueller makes no mention of it in his notes but he does make some curious remarks concerning the pieces which precede it. "No. 1 (Graham's March) is a rather one-sided march. No. 2 (Overture Enterprise) always good when played well. No. 3 (Chorus: At the Graveside) beautiful and artistic but only connoisseurs know the graces. No. 4 (Symphonie by Gyrowetz) the same. No. 5 (Chorus: Haydn's Swansong) excellent but only for connoisseurs. No. 6 (Di Tanti Palpiti) Excellent."

Pentecost was celebrated on 30 May and Mueller comments: "It was a blessed festival. The music was not poor, but scarcely one piece was played perfectly well!" The program has the standard divisions: Morning, Afternoon, and Evening. In the evening one of the pieces performed was "In diesen heiligen Hallen" (In these Hallowed Halls) from Mozart's *The Magic Flute*, a piece which the Harmonists loved and which had deep meaning for them.

In addition to new music, an additional instrument—a double bass—was added to the orchestra in 1830. In November 1824, the Society had had the opportunity to acquire a bass but apparently turned it down.

> . . . Mr. Holloman at Vandalia [Ill.] was informed that our people did not want the large Bas violine at no price, since it is so bulksome to transport. . . .[25]

On 2 November 1830 W. C. Peters wrote a letter to Gertrude Rapp which indicated that he had added a contra-bass part to his arrangement for the Economy orchestra. It also reveals his fine personal relationship with the Society.

> Miss G.
> With this you will receive Haydn's Waltz arranged for the Band— I will begin to arrange Gazza Ladra directly and will send it down the first opportunity. The Doctor will perceive that I have put a contra-bass part——
> "Ich bin sehr verbunden *ehrin* (I have forgotten how to spell the last word) for your handsome present to my little son. Mrs. P. desires me to thank you for her present. Meanwhile, I remain your friend.
> W. C. Peters[26]

There are no records to establish when a double bass was purchased, but from a letter written to Miss Rapp one month earlier, it appears that one was acquired sometime in 1830: "Please tell Dr. Miller that I am preparing some rules and directions for the Contra Bass for him, and when finished I will immediately send it him."[27]

Peters' remark, "I . . . will send it down" suggests that he was then back in Pittsburgh. In the following month (December) he placed the following advertisement in a Pittsburgh paper.

NOTICE
The subscriber has removed his "Musical Repository to No. 19 Market Street where he has for sale two splendid Piano Fortes from the Manufactory of Loud and Brothers. The subscribers will always keep a supply on hand and will also furnish pianos on order. Old pianos received in exchange at fair price.

W. C. Peters, Professor of Music.

The pieces sent down by Peters were not played in the remaining months of 1830. Mueller apparently was unable to direct the music in September and October and Jacob Henrici, who played the piano and violin, and who was later to rise to great prominence in the Society, took charge of the concerts of 5 and 26 September. Henrici's comments are given in the memorandum book, indicating that Mueller's record was not a private one, and they reflect the respect in which Mueller was held. For some reason, unexplained by Mueller, there were no concerts given during the month of October. Was Mueller away from the village? Whatever the circumstances, W. C. Peters knew of his periodic despondency and his fluctuating attitude toward music. In a letter to Gertrude Rapp in October 1830, Peters remarks: "Tell him [Dr. Mueller] if he gives up music I shall skin him alive, stuff him, and put him in the *Museum*."

Gertrude was the daughter of Father Rapp's son, John, who had died while the Society was in Butler County. While she was not spared the labors of other women in the Society, the education which she received was unequaled. Her French, German, and English grammar books are extant. She learned mathematics, painting, and music. Mueller made more manuscript music books for her than he did for himself[28] (see plate 11). Printed keyboard music was purchased for her and copies contain notes such as "Gertrude vorzugleich zu lernen," in Mueller's hand.[29] It appears that while other girls and women sang at Economy, Gertrude was the only female who was taught to play an instrument. If George Rapp led the life of a German duke, Gertrude, at least in education, led a life not unlike that of a princess, and her chief mentor through the years was Johann Christoph Mueller.

Henrici and Gertrude became close friends and delighted in playing four-hand piano arrangements. When Mueller returned for the concert of 28 November four pieces on the program were listed as having piano accompaniments. One of them, Vanhal's "Allegro," was arranged for four hands and was played by Gertrude and Henrici, according to Mueller, "by special command." Mueller states that the performance was "poor." Mueller's relationship with Henrici and Gertrude, however, appears to have been cordial. On the final concert of 1830 given on Christmas Day, Mueller remarks that "all went well because He for whom this festival was celebrated was with us," but he continues, "our Henrici was sick with typhoid fever."

1831: THE "ROYAL" PIED PIPER ARRIVES

The year 1831 was the final one in the Harmonists' golden age of music. On the first concert of the year, Mueller programmed his arrangement of Handel's Water Music. He remarks that the performance was "bene." Gertrude played some "waltzes" on the same program, and Mueller notes that they, too, were good.

The Harmoniefest concert of 1831, the last under Mueller, was memorable. Mueller writes:

> Today the 26th Harmonie Festival was celebrated. In the morning at 6 o'clock the wind instruments announced the festival from the church tower. In the church we played number 39 (*March of Howard*) and out of the church number 143 (Pleyel's *Menuetto*). In the hall before the meal the *March of Friendship* was played—and on

the piano with 1 flute and 1 violin [Mueller and Henrici?] Köhler's *Rondo*—and Haydn's song of thanks *Thou art the One to whom Honor and Fame Belong* was sung. And at night we sang *We greet you, Oh Day* (!). Outside the church: *The Magnolia Waltz* and the *Viola Waltz*, the latter moderate. There was not much ceremony to the festival, but it was powerful and satisfactory, assuring the mercy of the Lord!

Interestingly, three pieces by Mueller—"Magnolia Waltz," "Viola Waltz," and the "March of Friendship"—were on the program.

On 16 February, the day following the Harmoniefest, W. C. Peters gave a concert at Bond's Concert Hall in Pittsburgh. A Mr. Burns also appeared on the program and performed some solos on the Kent bugle. Earlier, Peters had composed a piece which has created some excitement among scholars of early American music, a "Symphony in D" (see Appendix A, ex. 17). According to part-books at Economy it was composed for the Harmonist orchestra on 1 February 1831 and may have been the first symphony composed west of the Alleghenies. Mueller's Memorandum Buch shows that it was first played Sunday evening, 27 March. The Harmonists apparently did not attach particular importance to the performance and Mueller made no note of it except "bene" was placed beside the title. He did comment upon his own despondency. "In consideration of the difficulty of the pieces, the concert turned out fairly well, but all in all nothing is more to be criticized than my despondency (cowardice) on the violin, especially in somewhat difficult passages." Peters was not mentioned and apparently was not present for the performance.

Distinguished visitors continued to receive mention in Mueller's notebook. On 13 June 1831, George Wolf, governor of Pennsylvania 1829-1835, along with a "Mr. Beelen" and W. C. Peters visited Economy. The concert that evening included a cantata, *Liebet den Ewigen*, by J. G. Schade, a skilled European composer-oboist who played in the Gotha Court orchestra.[30] The piece was not "arranged" but performed from the printed copy published by Johann André (Offenbach a/M) and must have been well received because this was its third performance for the year.

From this time on, Mueller's notes reflect trouble and dissention. No concerts were played in July 1831, because the field work required "almost all craftsmen from time to time . . . to leave their shops to work out in the fields. Much of this was due to the moisture, the hay and fruit harvests—not to mention other excuses." Mueller gives the impression that these may have been excuses put forth to keep the musicians from performing. During this month Lewis David von Schweinitz, the great-grandson of the Moravian leader Count Zinzendorff, visited Economy and said he sensed trouble in the Society. Rapp reportedly told him that "obedience in America does not outlast the second generation."[31]

A concert was finally given 21 August. W. C. Peters was present along with the Pittsburgh dealer in musical instruments, C. L. Volz "and many strangers." Mueller remarks: "The weather was extremely sultry and moist so that the string instruments could scarcely be used. Although Mr. Peters was present, he did not touch an instrument."

The harvest festival was celebrated three days later, on 24 August, and another new piece by W. C. Peters, "March of Pittsburgh," was on the program. No concert was given again for an entire month and Mueller writes: "On September 19, 1831, the music room without my knowledge was locked up, and when I made enquiry, I was told that music shall cease entirely for an entire month—then, however, it would continue—then with double zeal. J. C. Mr." In October, however, Mueller postponed a concert scheduled for the thirtieth because "the weather was very unfavorable with rain. . . ." Both the cancellation and the earlier order—which must have come from Father Rapp—were probably related to Count Leon's entry into Economy. As reported by Jonathan Lenz, the self-proclaimed Messiah entered the village with considerable pomp and with a retinue of forty followers while the Harmonist wind band played from the church tower (see plates 9 and 13). Among the forty were some excellent musicians and it is significant that the next concert which Mueller describes was not given by the Harmonists but by the count's men.

> On the 23rd of October of this year [1831] I had the pleasure of hearing a little concert in Father's house, where several quintets were played, namely Mr. Ziegwolf played the violin, as accompaniment Mr. Ziegwolf, Jr., the violincello, Mr. Rupp the clarinet, Mr. August Hausser the flute, and Mr. Carl Hausser the horn. To say it without flattery, everything was played with taste, finesse and feeling.

Many in the Count's retinue were educated, musically sophisticated people. The Haussers (Heuser) of Frankfurt-on-the-Main were from a prominent and wealthy family which had been knighted for its outstanding service to the German empire.[32] Apparently they did not treat the Harmonist musicians condescendingly, and a concert was played 6 November in which musicians from both the Count's retinue and the Harmonist orchestra participated. All of the pieces on the program were from the Harmonist repertory. Mueller described the concert:

> On Sunday evening November 6, a concert was given. Messrs. Carl and August Hausser and Mr. Rupp participated with violins and flute. Mueller, Gertrude and Henrici each played a piece on the piano. Each poorly enough. Mr. Count Leon and retinue were present. The practice went much better than the concert itself.

Because the count's musicians were superior to the Harmonists, Mueller may have felt intimidated. This was Mueller's final concert at Economy and ironically, the closing piece on the program was his own "Friendship March."

Following this entry there are four empty pages in Mueller's book, then four pages of records of purchases of musical supplies. Six more empty pages follow and then a record of some pieces practiced, but there are no more concerts listed and presumably none were played. The final entry in the book is somewhat confusing although its ultimate significance is clear enough:

> Economy Nov. 23.8.1831
> When Mr. Peters took his parting leave from this etc. When all musical practice was at a Stand and stoped [sic]
>
> J.C.M.

Mueller was greatly impressed by the Count's cultural tastes and at least at the beginning, with his religious views as well. He eventually joined the 358 dissenters who, under the Count's leadership, seceded from the Society and built the town of Phillipsburg (Rochester) in 1832, although he appears to have been the last to sign the document of separation. But by July of 1833, Mueller was thoroughly disenchanted with the Count and accused him of being a charlatan. He threatened the count with a law suit which was to begin 1 September 1833, but a day before the trial, the Count and a few followers who remained loyal to him sailed down the Ohio and Mississippi rivers, eventually settling at Grand Ecore, Louisiana. Here the climate proved unhealthy for them and many, including the Count, died. Back in Phillipsburg, the other seceders divided the property and went their separate ways.

Mueller became extremely bitter toward the Rapps over the next decade. The arbitration committee which supervised the division of property during the 1832 schism had deprived him of all medical and musical instruments. A letter from Mueller to Trustee Romelius Baker dated 21 February 1833 reads in part:

> Have I not with all my services in the musical line and otherwise, earned my violin and my flute which you took from me? . . . Furthermore, I have not taken along a single book or anything which was not mine. The very careful Fritz cared busily that several books which I had used from the museum were returned, but it did not occur to him to return to me those that I had purchased in Germany, and which contained my name. In the apothecary shop is my dictionary, also purchased in Germany . . . besides other volumes. . . . Another book, a precious remembrance of my grandfather's is also with you. . . . As when I was with you I served the Lord, and the brethren, so is my heart inclined today and thus comes solace and peace, and in this sense and spirit I greet heartily all those that will accept it. . . .

The good will which Mueller extended was apparently not reciprocated even by Gertrude for whom he copied a keyboard method book as late as February 1832 and inscribed it "für seine Freundin, und ehmalige Schülerin-Gertrude Rapp."[33] Eleven years later, in 1843, he wrote the following on one of the pages of a keyboard method book which he had prepared for one of his students, Thalia Bentel:

Arien und Gesaenge, componirt von J. C. M. in Harmonie am Wabbash und Oeconomie, unter der despotischen Herrschaft, (the greatest monopolist I ever knew) viz. George Rapp and his adobted [sic] son Fredk. Reichert. Yet, the Lord seeth the Heart![34] (See plate 12)

W. C. Peters, in the meantime, unaware of the difficulties at Economy, continued his career. In 1831 he became a partner in the music store of John H. Mellor and W. D. Smith at 9 Fifth Avenue in Pittsburgh. About this time he was engaged as a music teacher by the family of Stephen Foster, who was to have a profound effect upon his career some ten years later. By 1832 he was again back in Louisville where city directories list him as "Professor of Music" and in 1838 as the proprietor of a "Piano and Music Store." He continued to live in Louisville where in 1843 his store address was on the south side of Main street between Third and Fourth Streets and his residence on the east side of First Street between Chestnut and Prather Streets.[35] He established a branch store in Cincinnati in 1839 and apparently moved there around 1845. He also established a branch store in Baltimore in 1849 and began to issue his music magazine the "Baltimore Olio," in 1850.

Possibly as early as 1842, Peters began his career as a publisher. With his brother Henry J. and others he eventually controlled a veritable dynasty of music publishing houses. His most notable publishing achievements took place in 1848 when he released some of Stephen Foster's most popular songs: *Uncle Ned*, *Stay Summer Breath*, *Susanna Don't You Cry* and *Away Down South*, among others. He had already published Foster's *There's a Good Time Coming* in 1846, and copyrighted *Lou'siana Belle* in 1847. He reportedly made $10,000 from *O Susanna* alone, although all records indicate that Peters dealt fairly and, considering the circumstances, even generously with Foster. Publishing music was a business gamble which Foster clearly understood and he had, in fact, given copies of *O Susanna*, *Lou'siana Belle*, and *Uncle Ned* to "several persons before . . . Mr. Peters."[36] The career of Peters and his publications warrants a volume in itself. He was noted as the choir director at St. Peter's Cathedral in Cincinnati. He had three sons who eventually assisted him in his business, the final location of which was in the old Pike's Opera House. Charles Cist, in his book *Cincinnati in 1851*, gives an impressive account of the Peters publishing establishment.

W. C. Peters and Sons, Melodeon Building, are publishers of various approved works of instruction . . . of which they are the authors, or hold the copyrights. They also issue the newest and most popular music; of which their catalog presents a variety of solos, duets . . . to the extent of 1600 pieces, 60 of which have been published during the last 6 months. Their stock of engraved copper and zinc plates cost upward of $30,000 and they have paid out during the past year $3,000 for copyrights. . . . They employ 30 hands; value of product $50,000; raw material 25 per cent. Since first established as W. C. Peters, they have sold 1000 of A. H. Gale and Co. pianos and upward of 2000 of those of Nunns and Clark of N.Y.[37]

Peters' career and his enormous collection of publishing plates were tragically swept away when Pike's Opera House was destroyed by fire 22 March 1866. The curtain had just fallen on *A Midsummer Night's Dream* when the fire broke out. The total loss was estimated at 1¾ million dollars but the eventual loss to the cause of American music was beyond calculation. Peters died of apparent heart failure just one month and one day after the fire, 20 April 1866.[38]

There is no evidence at Economy which indicates that anyone was aware of or interested in the career of W. C. Peters after the schism in 1832. He in turn, seemed unaware of how completely the schism had depleted the orchestra because on 20 March 1833, he scored a "Favorite German Waltz," for orchestra and dedicated it to the "Economy Musical Society."[39] The instrumentation consists of a full string section including contra-bass, two bassoons, bugle, flute, two clarinets, two horns, trumpet, and timpani. The full score is in Peters' hand and is extant at Economy, but the piece was not copied into the part-books indicating that it was probably never played.

Among the musicians who left Economy as a result of the schism at about this time were Dr. Mueller (first violin and flute), Jonathan Wagner (second violin), Burghard Schnabel (viola), and Christian Knodel (second violin). By 1847 only Lenz (horn), Wolgemuth (horn), and Weingärtner (cello) remained of Mueller's original list of instrumentalists. The orchestra continued to play under the direction of the remaining members, principally Jacob Henrici, but the golden age of music in the Harmony Society had come to a close amid much strife and bitterness. Mueller eventually established himself as a physician in Bridgewater, an area near Beaver, Pennsylvania, not far from Economy. A history of Beaver County, published in 1904, states: "About 60 years ago Bridgewater was a thriving business center. An old subscription list gives us the names of many prominent residents then carrying on its business."[40] Among the names in the list is that of "Doctor J. C. Mueller."

Mueller died in the fall of 1845. His "Last Will and Testament" was registered in the Beaver County courthouse, 5 November 1845:

I direct that my body be decently interred in the burying ground in the Borough of Beaver according to the rites of professing Christians, and that my funeral take place in the evening at as late an hour as possible in the day so that those in attendance be enable to return to their respective place of abode before dark, and that my grave be so prepared as to be two feet deeper than the usual depth of graves dug in that grave yard. . . .

His estate was left to his brother John with the provision that he would care for his widow as long as she would live. He also made donations to the Methodist Episcopal and the Baptist Sabbath Schools of Bridgewater for the purchase of "such books as the schools may need." There are no records at Economy which indicate that anyone there acknowledged the passing of their former beloved physician, school teacher, and music director.

1.   A letter of 30 July 1827, from Thomas Brown, a land surveyor from Scotland, requests that his son be taken "into your Germanic Family Village." A postscript to the letter requests a "free ticket to your local museum and garden." See Accounts, 27 July 1827.

2.   *The Twentieth Century Bench and Bar Association of Pennsylvania.* 2 vols. (H. C. Cooper, Jr., and Bros. and Co., 1903), 2:822.

3.   See IM 2.8-3, No. 197. The manuscript bears the inscription in Mueller's hand: "Nous avons reçu la musique de Monsieur Charles v. Bonnhorst en mois juillet 1826." This piece was also published by Blake of Philadelphia in 1829. See KP 1.22.

4.   Charles Volz had a music store on Wood Street as early as 1814. He began selling pianos in 1818. He was one of the performers in the concert given at Foster's Ferry House, 4 July 1818.

5.   Eisenach, *op. cit.*, 2:160-64.

6.   Ibid., p. 166.

7.   Correspondence Book: 1825-1828, (Economy Archives) p. 258.

8.   Accounts, 17 July 1827.

9.   See Anthony Baines, *European and American Musical Instruments* (New York, 1966), p. 112, entry 626.

10.   For a thorough account of the Peters family as publishers see Ernst C. Krohn, *Music Publishing in the Middle Western States Before the Civil War* (Detroit Studies in Music Bibliography, 1972).

11.   A fascinating account of the Peters Colony and the Peters family is given in S. V. Connor, *The Peters Colony of Texas* (Austin, 1959).

12.   Baynham, in his Ph.D. dissertation "The Early Development of Music in Pittsburgh" (University of Pittsburgh, 1944) states that "William Snelling Peters" and his family first moved to Canada, then to Blairsville and that W. C. Peters was a music teacher for some time in Troy, New York. Baynham says his information is based upon notes found in a family Bible owned by a daughter of W. C. Peters, Mrs. C. E. Corcoran, who in 1902, was living in Kansas City, Kansas. Other works which contain information on Peters are *Appleton's Cyclopedia of American Biography* (New York, 1888); *Dictionary of American Biography* (New York, 1934); and Morneweck, *op. cit.*

13.   Appendix D, IM 3.5.

14.   Harvey B. Gaul, in his *Minstrel of the Alleghenies* (Pittsburgh, 1934), page 28, describes Peters as "a man who followed the piano trade down the river. He . . . made enough out of Foster's works to open another office in Louisville. There he sat spiderwise in his advertised 'emporium' waiting for inquisitive little flies like Stephen to walk into his clutches. . . ."
Gaul's assertion, in addition to being untrue, suffers from chronological error. Peters opened his store in Louisville as early as 1838, and was already registered there as a "Professor of Music" in the directories of 1832 and 1836. He did not begin publishing until around 1842. Foster's songs were not published until 1846, by which time Peters was in Cincinnati.

15.   In this score Peters added the note: "The Dr. will be careful the trumpet and horns play their part correctly."

16.   See Appendix D, IM3.4; IM3.5, IM3.8 and accounts, 30 January 1828 and 17 March 1828.

17.   Appendix D, IM3.4.

18.   Appendix D, IM2.8-1.

19.   Accounts, February 1828.

20.   Appendix D, IM 2.22. See also IM3.3.

21.   For a translation of this document see Karl J. R. Arndt and Richard D. Wetzel, "Harmonist Music and Pittsburgh Musicians in Early Economy," *The Western Pennsylvania Historical Magazine*, 54:2, 3, 4, 1971.

22.   The numbers just to the left of the titles show the position of the pieces in the orchestra's numbered repertory. Some of Mueller's program numbers, however, sometimes disagree with those of Appendix B—which is based upon the order of pieces given in his own violin part book, IM2.8-3. When new instruments were added to the orchestra Mueller often reorchestrated some of the pieces, a practice which created confusion in the numbering. In one score (IM3.8) Mueller wrote the following over *Russian March No. 101*: "Muss in diese nummer stehen bleiben" (Must stay in this number).

23.   See Appendix D, VP 3.12.

24.   A translation of the text is given in Arndt, *op. cit.*, pp. 429-31.

25.   Letter of 3 November 1824.

26.   Accounts, 2 November 1830. The Bass-Geigen part-book (IM 2.8-4) belonged to Jonathan Lentz, who also played horn.

27.   Accounts, 13 October 1830.

28.   Mueller was very fond of Gertrude. Duss states in his "Memoirs" (uncataloged manuscripts in the Archives of Old Economy) that Henrici told him that the two were in love and once tried to elope. That Henrici would repeat such a tale is unlikely. There was great disparity in the ages of the two, and Dr. Mueller was already married.

29.   See KP1.24.

30.   Robert Eitner, *Quellen Lexikon*, 10 vols. (Leipzig: Breitkopf & Härtel, 1898-1904), vol. 8, p. 464.

31.   Quoted in Arndt, *op. cit.*, p. 445.

32.   The document of elevation to knighthood was found in an old trunk in Hot Springs, Arkansas, by Dr. Karl J. R. Arndt. Some of the count's followers settled there after the Rochester, Pennsylvania settlement failed.

33.   Appendix D, TM.3.

34.   Appendix D, TM.5, Aria No. 1.

35.   *Louisville City Directory, 1843-1844* (Louisville, 1844), p. 117.

36.   From a letter by Stephen Foster to Wm. E. Millett, 25 May 1849. Cited in Morneweck, *op. cit.*, 1:357.

37.   Charles Cist, *Cincinnati in 1851* (Cincinnati: Wm. H. Moore and Co., 1851), p. 222.

38.   Obituary notices are found in the *Cincinnati Daily Gazette*, Saturday, 21 April 1866 and the *Cincinnati Commercial*, Sunday, 22 April.

39.   Appendix D, IM3.6.

40.   The Reverend Joseph H. Bauman, *A History of Beaver County, Pennsylvania* (New York: 1904), 2 vols., vol. II, p. 773.

5

Music Under Jacob Henrici: 1833-1892

THE SOUND OF HARMONIUMS AND A FADING TRADITION

Jacob Henrici[1] walked into Economy in 1826 (see plate 16). This was an easi-er time for the now prosperous Society and, as Henrici rose to the highest position in the Society, some members periodically reminded him that he en-joyed benefits for which he had not labored. While this was true in some re-spects, it was also important to realize that Henrici virtually gave his life to the Harmony Society.

Born 15 January 1804, at Grosskarlbach in Rhenish Bavaria, Henrici attended the government schools and then took a two-year course in the teachers' seminary at Kaiserslautern where he finished in 1822. He taught at a Protestant school for boys at Speier 1822-1824. During this time, he read of the Harmony Society and became deeply interested in George Rapp's teachings. In 1825, he persuaded his parents to migrate to America with him.

His interest in the Society intensified after meeting with George Rapp, and he urged his parents to join the Harmonists with him. They refused, but despite their opposition,[2] he became a member of the Society and was ap-pointed a teacher in the school at Economy.

Henrici was a violinist, pianist, singer, and composer. The responsibil-ity for the Society's music fell upon him after the schism and, in his own way, he attempted to keep the established traditions alive. On 4 July 1833, a celebration was held at Economy to attempt to gain back some of the spirit lost during the schism and to show good will toward America. Carl Volz read the Declaration of Independence, Charles von Bonnhorst spoke, and the band played from the church-tower balcony. Despite these efforts, the orchestra, like the Society, declined, and there was little added to the instrumental or vocal repertory under Henrici's leadership.

Festival programs of the 1830s contain more hymns than do earlier ones.

A comparison of the printed programs for the Harmoniefeste of 1830 and 1833 shows considerable variety of trios, duets, and choruses in the odes of the first and almost none in the second. The text of the ode for 1833 reflects an attempt to revive a fading spirit: "Auf Harmonie, sei guten Muths, und hänge nicht dem Erden Leben nach!" (Up Harmonie, be of good courage, and don't cling to earthly life.) Odes written by Henrici were performed into the 1850s, but often both the texts and music were reworkings of earlier efforts.

Music direction under Henrici is characterized by keyboard pieces which were usually played on two pianos by Henrici and Gertrude Rapp. There are indications that the orchestra now required this kind of reinforcement. Whereas instructions were given earlier for the purchase of music in "four or seven parts," a memorandum book from this period states "this book [a compilation by Lowell Mason] is preferred to the other . . . provided it is arranged to be accompanied by the piano. If that is not the case, it is not wanted at all."[3]

Pianos were always important in the Society. A postscript to a letter from W. C. Peters to Gertrude Rapp, dated 13 October 1830, states: "I am glad to hear you have purchased a piano of Mr. Nunns make, as I believe they are the best and cheapest instruments. . . ."[4] This piano remained in use for many years and is still at Economy. The instruments favored by Henrici and Gertrude, however, were the square grands with reed attachments made by Nunns & Clark between 1833 and 1858. These instruments contained a pedal which, when depressed, activated a series of reeds creating the effect of a harmonium. Two of these instruments were purchased and placed in the sitting room of the Great House, the room where visitors were entertained and where music was played after church services on Sundays. Eventually two were also placed in the church.[5]

Henrici's musical interests were primarily in hymnody, and he generally wrote his hymn scores in a numeral notation.[6] His contributions as a Harmonist composer are characterized by his settings of the Ten Commandments, the Apostles' Creed, and his hymn text and tune "Hilf Herr, ein neues Jahr bricht an" (Help, Lord, A New Year is Begun.) (Appendix A, exs. 18, 19, 20).

There are no records which tell anything of Henrici's skill as a violinist. In 1833, he made copies of a collection of duets for two violins, by N. B. Challoner, which had been published by Klemm of Philadelphia.[7] This is the only manuscript extant which indicates that he played the violin. Another instrument apparently played by Henrici was the bass trombone. A manuscript part-book inscribed "Bass Posaune, Economie, 24 Merz, 1835, Economy, Pennsylvania—Jacob Henrici," contains hymns and sacred pieces as well as short marches and dances from the earlier secular series.[8]

Next to the schism, Frederick Rapp's death in 1834 was the single factor most closely related to the state of music in the Society in the late 1830s and 1840s. When Frederick wrote to J. Solms, the Society's agent in Philadelphia, telling him to find an organ builder who could make an instrument for the church, Solms approached no less than four builders who submitted specifications to Rapp. The builders were James Hall, Loud and Brothers, Thomas Hall, and E. N. Schur.[9] Together they submitted specifications for thirteen different instruments. None materialized, and the dream of having a pipe organ in the church died with Frederick, although reed organs were purchased and used from time to time.

On 20 February 1844, Charles von Bonnhorst died. In 1846, Charles Volz was killed by a falling building which had been partially destroyed by the Great Pittsburgh Fire of 1845.[10] Both had been close friends of the Society and had encouraged its musical projects. Violin strings, clarinet reeds and other music items were purchased throughout the 1840s from John Mellor and W. P. Baum, both of Pittsburgh,[11] but orchestral music was fast becoming an occasional event in the Harmony Society.

After George Rapp's death in 1847, Henrici became a trustee, with even less time to devote to music. But the Society's reputation as an outstanding musical institution was widespread, and musicians who had heard of its earlier glories wrote letters of inquiry regarding membership in the Society. One such person was H. F. Albrecht who played viola and second clarinet in the famous Germania orchestra which toured America from 1848 to 1854. This orchestra consisted of twenty-five young men who, weary of the European patronage system, formed a purely democratic musical organization. No member was to aspire to personal or financial superiority over the others, regardless of his position or prominence in the orchestra. A constitution was drawn up, each member signed it, and the motto "One for All, and All for One," was adopted. Ardent idealists, they felt that democracy was "the most complete principle of human society" and their ambition was to travel to the United States "in order to further in the hearts of this politically free people the love of the fine art of music through performances of masterpieces of the greatest German composers as Bach, Haydn, Mozart, Beethoven, Spohr, Schubert, Mendelssohn, Schumann; also Liszt, Berlioz, and Wagner."[12] They dazzled audiences with their precision and on at least one occasion, when their music was lost in traveling, played a concert from memory, placing other printed sheets on the stands in order to conceal the fact from the audience. In six years they gave more than 900 performances and made an immeasurable contribution to the future development of orchestras in America. But the noble venture was a financial failure, largely because the average American at the time responded to their music somewhat like the St. Louis woman who, after hearing them play Beethoven's *Second Symphony* remarked: "Well, ain't that funny music?"

How Albrecht first heard of The Harmonists is not known but he was a social idealist with communal interests and investigated other communal colonies in America as well. He may have visited Economy on one of the three occasions that the Germania orchestra played in Pittsburgh.[13] In October 1854, the year in which the orchestra disbanded, Henrici wrote to Albrecht who was then in Chicago, giving him a detailed explanation of the Harmony Society. In any case, Albrecht did not join the Harmonists and shortly thereafter married and settled in Philadelphia. Albrecht had a magnificent collection of music and books on music, and he became well known in music circles in Philadelphia. He eventually decided to return to Germany and bought a small property in his native town, Grevesmuehlen, Mecklenburg, and booked passage on the steamer *Schiller* for himself, his wife, and their three children. Tragically, the ill-fated vessel went down in the Atlantic and he and his family were drowned.[14]

Whether the decision not to join the Harmonists was Albrecht's or whether the Harmonists turned down his application is not known because Albrecht's letters to Henrici, if there were any, have not been found. It could have been either or both, because persons interested in membership in the Society then were generally discouraged by Henrici, Baker, or Lenz.[15] At the same time, musical possibilities were limited at Economy then and would have appealed little to Albrecht.

BRASS BANDS AND SINGING CLASSES 1850-1888

Henrici shared the financial responsibilities of the Society with another trustee, R. L. Baker, until the latter's death in 1868, at which time Jonathan Lenz was appointed to fill the vacancy. Since the time of George Rapp's death, however, he had also been the spiritual leader of the Society and prepared sermons for both Sunday and mid-week services.[16] The orchestra was left to itself and the minister-historian, Aaron Williams, who visited the Society remarked: "the old musicians of the band have relinquished their labor (except at religious festivals) to younger and less skillful hands. . . ."[17]

Among the younger generation of the 1850s and 1860s were the Feucht brothers, Benjamin and Henry. They were the sons of Conrad and Hildegard Feucht who had been the center of controversy in 1829, and both played the cornet. Benjamin (see plate 17) later became a doctor and Henry an attorney. The extent of their musical activity is not clear, but from manuscript music dating 1860-1865, it appears that instrumental music under the Feuchts' leadership was exclusively for wind instruments and consisted of waltzes, polkas and marches. It was just after the Feuchts left in 1865 that the orchestra was permanently and, according to the story told by John Duss, violently dissolved.

When he [Benjamin] and his brother Henry, in 1865, left the Society to take unto themselves wives, the cornet chairs were left vacant. Rivalry arose as to who should be the leader. . . . Mostly composed of young fellows, the band at all times had its rivalries. . . . When for one reason or another it became apparent that the band would not be able to play at the ensuing Harvest Home, the old men of the erstwhile orchestra were coaxed or bullied into action by the women. . . . In any case, the orchestra performed so nobly that many said that they preferred the orchestra to the band. But lusty young bucks of the band decided to nip this sentiment in the bud. One night, a little later, some of them entered the music room and smashed to pieces the double basses, 'cellos, and bassoons.[18]

For the next few years, vocal music surpassed instrumental music in importance. Singing classes were organized and held weekly with Henrici and Gertrude Rapp presiding from the two pianos with reed attachments. Rumors of romantic connections between the two arose, primarily as a result of their musical associations, but Henrici's temperament was hardly conducive to such a relationship. According to Duss, the following incident transpired during a singing class:

Gertrude made a slight mistake. Henrici stopped the singing and vigorously criticized Gertrude. When the passage was repeated she made the same mistake. Quick as a flash, Henrici rose from the piano, walked to Gertrude and boxed her ears.[19]

Compilations by Lowell Mason, Thomas Hastings, Ira Woodbury, and Horace Waters are well represented in the Harmonist vocal repertory of this period. Some of these books, and those of many lesser-known compilers, were published to meet the needs and tastes of the American singing societies and classes which were springing up even in the most remote areas of the country. Many were printed in shape notes, that is, with a particular shape given to the note of each scale degree, supposedly to make sight reading easier. One collection printed in shape notes which was popular among German Americans was H. C. Eyer's *Die Union Choral Harmonie* (Philadelphia: 1839).[20] A copy of this compilation is in the collection at Economy, but it is doubtful that the Harmonists used it to any appreciable extent.

"Lowell Mason's Music Charts,"[21] two series of graded sight-singing exercises which were printed on a large sheet for classroom use were used in the Economy school. T. Heim's *Siona, Sammlung von drei und vierstimmigen Volksgesangen für Knaben, Mädchen und Frauen* (Philadelphia, n.d.); C. J. Heppe's *Gesänge für Sonntag Schulen* (Philadelphia, 1866); and *Die Kleine Missionsharfe* (Philadelphia, n.d.); are a few of the many German counterparts to the English oblong singing books which were printed in America and were purchased in large quantities by the Harmonists for use in the school.

GEORGE KIRSCHBAUM'S MAENNERCHOR

Among the later Harmonist singing organizations was the Maennerchor, formed around 1877, which was comprised primarily of men employed by the Society and was directed by a colorful figure, George Kirschbaum. Once again, it appeared that the Society would be blessed by the efforts of a vigorous man who, like Frederick Rapp, Jacob Henrici, and Jonathan Lenz, possessed the gift for musical as well as business leadership.

Kirschbaum was born 3 April 1849 in Württemberg and received the usual grade school education. Exactly when he came to America is not clear but he appears to have become associated with the Harmonists in the 1860s, working for the Society as a hired hand. In 1868 he left the Society's employ and went to California. For about ten years he was a migrant. In 1877 he applied for readmittance to the Society and records indicate that the Maennerchor was formed at about the time of his return.

Despite objections to his character, which was considered too worldly by some, he was admitted to membership during the Harmoniefest of 1879. Because leadership abilities were sorely needed, he was probably groomed for high office in the Society, possibly to become senior trustee upon Henrici's death. He was unmarried, took the religious tenets of the Society seriously, and appealed to the young people. Beyond this, he possessed vigor and vitality which advancing age was diminishing in Henrici, Lenz, and Gertrude Rapp.[22]

Kirschbaum devoted considerable time and effort to the Maennerchor. Manuscript part-books containing arrangements of pieces by Beethoven, Mozart, Abt, Heim, and others, were begun in October 1877. Some of the names of the singers found in extant part-books are those of Bernhard Kweifel, Fritz Gebbhard, Peter Schwab, John Miller, Markes Knabel, F. Jackson, Jacob Stadelmann, and Gottlieb Riethmueller, among others, although all the part-books appear to have been copied by the same hand. The pieces were copied from printed books (see Appendix D, HP 2.56;66;67;68;69) although some printed books were bought in multiple copies, such as Ernst Hauschild's *Maennerchöre* (a collection compiled for use in the Evangelical Mission School at Basel), of which twenty-seven copies are extant in the Economy archives.

Kirschbaum also directed a "Gemischter Chor" (Mixed Chorus) which, judging from the number of books purchased for the group, consisted of about twenty-four voices. It was a musically active group and criticisms of its performances are positive and flattering. New life was being infused into the Society and it looked as though the transition into the twentieth century would be made under competent and congenial leadership. But in 1889 and 1890 the course of Harmonist history was altered by bizarre and tragic circumstances, as the following hurried but pathetic letter by Jonathan Lenz, dated 3 January 1890 shows.

... Since my time is so much in demand I will only briefly and in a hurry report to you what sort of fates have come over us. At the close of the old year [29 December 1889] our dear sister Gertraud was called away by death. At her funeral very many people, not only those who live with us but also many strangers, were present. By all the song was sung

"Who knows how near my death?"
[Wer weiss, wie nahe mir mein Ende]

and Kirschbaum, with his singing society also sang a beautiful song, but no one would have believed that today on the third, they would sing the same for him, for a terrible fate overcame him.

When yesterday morning the gas pressure went down, he and the man who usually takes care of the gas went into the gas reservoir (near the saw mill) and they had a lantern with them, they opened the jet too much, and the container filled quickly with gas, and Kirschbaum stood in flames from head to foot and in a minute he was burned to death.[23]

But the choir would soon sing their funeral hymns again amid the unmarked graves of the Harmonist cemetery. On 22nd January, Jonathan Lenz, the gentle Harmonist of exemplary morality and character, joined his departed brethren in the communion of death. And on 28 July, Ernst Woelfel, who had been selected to replace him, died of a stroke. Dr. Karl J. R. Arndt, the leading Harmonist historian, appropriately entitled his chapter dealing with these circumstances "1890—the Year of Crisis." Indeed, had these men, especially Kirschbaum, lived another ten years, our concluding chapters on the musical career of John S. Duss would read differently.

Despite Kirschbaum's death, the male chorus of hired hands remained strong to the very end of the Society and then became the nucleus of a community Männerchor which is still active in Ambridge. A set of books dated 1892-1898 contains some of the pieces found in the 1877 copies, as well as additional selections by a favorite composer of the Harmonists, Hans Naegeli (1773-1836). Participants in this later group were A. Berger, J. Werner, Jacob Boxx, W. J. Armer, Fritz Gerhard, Fred Riethmueller, William Mattes, Gus Krueger, Gottlob Betz, and P. W. Strawle. They sang from printed collections by Ernst Hauschild, Wilhelm Hartman, Reinhard Schmelz and C. Wonnberger,[24] collections which contained religious songs, as well as patriotic and secular pieces and which were distinctly separate from the Harmonist hymn repertoire.

JACOB ROHR'S SILVER CORNET BAND

Instrumental music floundered until another outside musician was hired to teach and direct the players. This time the man whom they hired, Jacob Rohr, was a bandmaster in the military style.

Born in Alsace-Lorraine in 1827, Rohr served in the Franco-Prussian War of 1870-71, a war which had aroused great patriotic feelings at Economy.

Sometime after the war ended, he migrated to America and established himself as a music teacher in Pittsburgh. The date of his arrival is uncertain, but he is listed in a city directory of 1877-78 as a musician residing at 17 Congress Street. According to John Duss, who played under his direction, Rohr was a combination of "German thoroughness and French finesse."[25]

Rohr played and taught the cornet and alto horn and became director of the 18th Regiment Infantry Band in Pittsburgh. By 1878 he was working as a music teacher at Economy. John Duss says he was so successful that not only was a band organized but a second band, consisting of young boys and affectionately called the "cheese band," was formed.[26]

Rohr was a prolific arranger and composer. He arranged overtures, waltzes, and marches by Strauss, Verdi, Hamm, Suppe, Labitsky, and other composers for the "Economy Cornet Band," as the group was then known.[27] A letter dated 9 March 1885, and addressed to "Messrs. Henrici and Lenz" indicates the band's popularity under Rohr's direction.

> We desire very much to have your band come down some evening next week and favor us with one of your excellent entertainments at our Loan Exhibition [Beaver Falls] for the benefit of our Band. Please arrange so that you can come and notify us what evening we can expect you. . . .[28]

The letter is signed by the members of the "Entertainment Committee."

There are few records which show that Rohr purchased music for the Economy Cornet Band. He appears to have arranged most of the repertoire himself. There are occasional instrumental repairs, but no instrument purchases recorded through the year 1886.[29]

In 1887, Henrici took special interest in the band. He wanted the Harvest Home Celebration, the eighty-third in the Society's history, to be an outstanding one. Why this particular one was so important is not clear, although his religious inclinations were following an unusual bent at this time and may have had some bearing upon the occasion. Preparations began early in the year with the purchase of new instruments for the band. In May, the following purchases were made from Henry Ditson of Philadelphia:

1	E flat Alto	$30.00
1	B flat valve Trombone	$32.00
1	B flat Baritone	$40.00
1	E flat Tuba	$58.00
1	Solo B flat Cornet	$90.00

In July, two other instruments were purchased from Ditson:

1	E flat Alto	$50.00
1	B flat Trombone-Bass	$45.00

All of the preceding were silverplated at extra cost, and the band thereafter was known as the "Silver Cornet Band."[30]

For the Harvest Home celebration, Henrici also purchased a "Sohmer grand piano with 2 stools" from J. M. Hoffman and Company of Pittsburgh. The instrument cost $600.00.[31] About the same time, a bill shows a purchase made by "Prof. Rohr" of a cane, "mounted and engraved" from John Heckel, Jr., a jeweler in Pittsburgh, which he probably used as a bandmaster's baton.

In April 1887 another letter concerning the band was sent to Henrici and Lenz.

> Gentlemen:
> The Young Men's Library Association of the borough [New Brighton] intends to give an exposition in the Opera House next month, beginning the 12th. In addition to the display of goods of our several merchants, entertainments will be given every night. We address this communication to you to request an evening's entertainment from your admirable band. There seems to be a universal desire expressed on the part of our music loving people to hear your musicians, and we are not ignorant of the fact that the people of your band at the Exhibition in 1884 contributed in no small degree to our success at that time. We hope you will find it convenient to favor us with your band on some one of the evenings of the 16, 17, or 18 of May . . . the exact date to be fixed by you.
> H. C. Cuthbertson, Press.[32]

The band continued to grow in proficiency and popularity and by 6 September 1889 the instrumentation was as follows:

Piccolo
E flat Clarinet
1 B flat Clarinet
2 B flat Clarinet
1 B flat Cornet
2 B flat Cornet
3 B flat Cornet
Solo Alto
1 E flat Alto
2 E flat Alto
1 B flat Trombone
2 B flat Trombone
Baritone
B flat Bass
1 E flat Bass
2 E flat Tuba
Drums[33]

Rohr continued teaching at Economy at least until the turn of the century and, possibly, to the time of the dissolution of the Society. *The Pittsburgh*

Music Directory of 1894-95 gives his address as "Economy, Pa." There is no indication, however, that he ever considered membership in the Society. Jacob Rohr died 28 June 1906, the year in which the Harmony Society was dissolved. He was seventy-nine at the time of his death and was residing at the home of his daughter and only child, Mrs. Philip d'Ivernois of 403 Park Street, Knoxville, (Pittsburgh).[34] His obituary states that he had served the Harmony Society as music master for twenty-six years and was known as one of the "oldest musicians in Western Pennsylvania."[35]

From all indications, Jacob Rohr was a competent musician who served the Society faithfully without distorting the purposes established for the band by the Harmonist Trustees. Long before Rohr's death, however, there was, standing in the wings, a man of great cunning, with musical ambitions such as the Harmonists had never envisioned for one of their membership. He was waiting for his moment to take over the baton. It came Christmas Day, 1892, when Jacob Henrici, the strongest link with the Society's past, died. The greatest obstacle in the way of the musical ambitions of John S. Duss was gone and the strangest, almost incredible, musical episode in the Harmony Society's history was about to begin.

1. W. C. Peters addressed notes on the scores which he sent to Economy to Dr. Mueller and Henrici, spelling the latter "Henreke." This gives some clue as to how the name may have been pronounced at that time. Later German letters, however, spell it "Henrizi."

2. John Duss, in *The Harmonists: A Personal History*, pp. 102-6 states that this caused a permanent breach between Henrici and his parents. According to Duss, when Henrici's mother died in Pittsburgh, Henrici did not attend the funeral saying, "Let the dead bury their dead." Duss generally speaks of Henrici as an impulsive and sometimes harsh person, an impression not shared by other Harmonists and historians.

3. Memorandum book belonging to R. L. Baker, dated 1835, and found among the manuscripts in the music collection.

4. See page 83 where other portions of the letter are quoted. Robert and William Nunns were English piano builders who came to New York in 1821. They worked together until 1833 when Robert combined with John Clark as Nunns, Clark & Co., continuing until 1858. William worked alone until 1839 when he combined with the Fischers. William was also the teacher of William Steinway. See Waldo Selden Pratt and Charles N. Boyd, *American Supplement to Grove's Dictionary of Music and Musicians* (New York, Macmillan Co., 1934), page 19. Also see Plate 15.

5. The instruments used in the church are now located in the Feast Hall at Economy.

6. Day and Beal, who published *The One-Line Psalmist* (Boston, 1848), presented this system as their exclusive patent. Actually, it was in use in Germany some years before their publication appeared. See the author's "Some Music Notation Systems in Early American Hymn-Tune Books," *Keystone Folklore Quarterly*, Winter Issue, 1967, pp. 247-60.

7. Appendix D, IM 2.32 (1 and 2).

8. Appendix D, IM 2.31.

9. Accounts, April 1828. The addresses of these builders are not given, but, since Solms was working in Philadelphia, it is likely that they all were from the Philadelphia area.

10. Throughout its history and especially during the trusteeship of Henrici, the Harmony Society made generous contributions to charities and to needy persons. On 12 May 1845 William Howard, mayor of Pittsburgh, wrote to George Rapp thanking him for "liberal contributions to sufferers of the late awful fire in our city. . . ."

11.   Accounts, 20 February and 22 September 1846.

12.   H. F. Albrecht, *Schizzen aus dem Leben der Musik-Gesellschaft Germania* [Germania Musical Society] Philadelphia, 1869. See also H. Earle Johnson, "The Germania Musical Society," *The Musical Quarterly* 39 (1953):75.

13.   See Frederick Louis Ritter, *Music in America* (New York: Charles Scribner & Sons, 1883), p. 322.

14.   Ibid., p. 326. Albrecht's library was purchased by J. W. Drexel of Philadelphia.

15.   Most letters requesting consideration for membership received the reply: "Wir haben so viel Leute als wir aufheben können." (We have all the people we can support.)

16.   According to Duss, *op. cit.*, p. 228, there were some who thought Henrici to be a wearisome preacher. During a Wednesday evening service, one of the "Vorsaenger," Louis Pfeil, apparently could stand the preaching no longer and said to Henrici: "This is no longer to be endured the way you blatter. . . ."

17.   Williams, *op. cit.*, p. 70.

18.   Duss, *op. cit.*, p. 159.

19.   Ibid., p. 111. Duss is prone to exaggeration and chronological error, but the incident probably transpired somewhat in the manner described.

20.   Appendix D, HP 2.6.

21.   Appendix D, TP. 30 and TP. 31.

22.   See Karl J. R. Arndt, *George Rapp's Successors and Material Heirs: 1847-1916* (Fairleigh Dickinson Press, 1971), pp. 159-161.

23.   Quoted in ibid., p. 159.

24.   See Appendix D, HP 2.66; HP 2.67; HP 2.69; HP 2.77; and HP 2.80.

25.   Duss, *op. cit.*, p. 159.

26.   Ibid.

27.   See Appendix D, IM2.51-52; 58-59; 61-62; 66, 68, 80, and 85.

28.   Accounts, 9 March 1885. Requests of this kind were invariably for "benefits."

29.   Accounts, 15 April 1885, contains a bill from J. H. Rotthoy, manufacturer and dealer in Musical Instruments, 13 Chestnut Street, Allegheny City. The bill, in the amount of $6.00, is for the repair of two clarinets.

30.   See accounts of 27 May 1887, and 8 July 1887. John Duss, who provides some colorful accounts of music in the Harmony Society, is unfortunately often confused chronologically. His *Personal History* leads one to believe that instruments were purchased for the band around 1869. He also states that Rohr taught him the cornet when he, Duss, was nine. Both statements conflict with records in the archives at Old Economy. Rohr, being a veteran of the Franco-Prussian War, could not have been in America before 1872, at which time Duss would have been twelve. Also, there are no records of instrument purchases between 1860 and 1890 except those given above.

31.   See Accounts, 20 June 1887. This instrument is now in St. John's Lutheran Church, Ambridge, the church built by the Harmony Society in 1828.

32.   Accounts, 29 April 1887.

33.   The list occurs in a bill showing the purchase of music stands for the Silver Cornet Band. See Accounts, 6 September 1889.

34.   Philip d'Ivernois, Rohr's son-in-law, was a clarinettist and played in Duss's Economy Band.

35.   *Pittsburgh Gazette*, Friday, 29 June 1906.

6

The Last Fanfare: John S. Duss

Of all the personalities which appear prominently in the history of the Harmony Society, none is more colorful, or more controversial, than John S. Duss. Born 22 February 1860 to parents who had emigrated from Württemberg, throughout his entire life he vacillated between the seclusion and protection of the Society and the aggressive free enterprise of the commercial world.

John's parents, Johann and Caroline Duss, were married at the communistic settlement at Zoar, Ohio.[1] At the time of John's birth, they were living in Cincinnati where Johann was employed by a brewery and for which he was then in New Orleans on business. He was still there when the Civil War broke out and was conscripted into the Confederate Army.

Not wanting to fight against the North, Johann feigned illness until the Battle of Bull Run, at which time he escaped and joined the Union army. Since he would be considered a deserter if captured, he decided to change his name to John Rutz, and under this name he served as a private in Company H, 75th Pennsylvania volunteers.

While waiting for the war to end, Mrs. Duss and her son stayed with the Zoarites for a short time, and then with some friends near the Ohio settlement. Finally, through the recommendation of these same friends who knew some of the Harmonists, they moved to Economy in March 1862. Young John never saw his father who was wounded at the Battle of Gettysburg, 3 July 1863 and died in a Baltimore hospital shortly thereafter.[2]

John S. Duss' education began in the school at Economy and continued there until 1868, at which time his mother received a widow's pension from the government. With this money, she decided to leave Economy and moved with her son to Strassburg, Ohio, near Zoar. After a short time there, she became dissatisfied and returned to the Harmony Society. John's education was resumed there and continued until 1873 when he was granted admission to the Phillipsburg Soldiers' Orphan School at Monaca, Pennsylvania.

Duss attended classes at Monaca and also lived there while the school was in session. He spent his summers at Economy where his mother was working as a housekeeper and nurse. He was graduated from the Orphan School in 1876 and returned to Economy where he was put to work caring for the orchard. He also played alto horn and snare drum in the Economy cornet band which was then under the direction of Jacob Rohr. Shortly after Duss returned to Economy, his mother became restless and decided to return to Germany.

The visit to Germany was brief and disappointing (Duss was "horrified by the brazen nudity of statues scattered everywhere")[3] and they soon returned to Economy. There Duss went to work in the various industries of the Society, became a tailor's apprentice, and resumed playing in the band.

> In the band after my return from Phillipsburg, I first occupied the chair of B flat Cornet, to which I gave serious study, but was soon promoted to that of E flat Cornet which in that day was the ranking instrument. At the same time I acquired proficiency on the clarinet. By the time of the Harvest Festival concert in 1878, I had not only played a difficult solo on the E flat Cornet but had progressed far enough to play the leading part of a clarinet duet with Chris Loeffler. This varied training on different instruments and in different types of music . . . played an important part in the preparation for my short but brilliant professional musical career of later years in New York and throughout the country.[4]

The Economy school was conducted both in German and English and, in 1878, Duss was appointed as teacher to the German classes. The English classes were conducted by Miss Kate Creese, whose sister, Susanna, was later to become Duss' wife. The teaching assignment was of short duration because Henrici and Duss had conflicting viewpoints on a number of issues. Duss states that after a Sunday concert Professor Rohr invited him to accompany the Great Western Band on a concert tour. When Duss asked Henrici's permission, the latter replied: "No! Absolutely no! You cannot go. Also you are too sentimental toward a young lady."[5] Duss decided to leave Economy and go to college.

In September 1879 he enrolled at Mount Union College, Mount Union, Ohio. During his second and final year there, he lived with the Lane family who owned a music store in Alliance, Ohio. Duss says he tutored the youngest of the four Lane sons, Bert, and helped James and Charles, who played the violin and piano respectively, to demonstrate instruments to prospective buyers. He also practiced the cornet.

> Every day I shut myself in a large closet to study tone production, sometimes for hours. The result was such that it led critics to proclaim that the beauty of my

cornet tone was equalled only by one artist, Matthew Arbuckle, the famous church cornetist of New York.[6]

Upon leaving Mt. Union College, Duss accepted employment as a teacher at the Kansas Reform School at Topeka. He began his work there in the Spring of 1882. By early summer he had had enough of "horse and cattle thieves, train wreckers, . . . robbers . . . men posing as boys, having been spared from the penitentiary by their parents attesting that they were only sixteen years of age."[7] In relating his experiences at Topeka, Duss tells how he impressed the boys with his feats of physical strength. By the time he left he was, in fact, close to physical and mental collapse.

In July of the same summer, he and Susanna Creese were married. They moved into a wing of the Lane mansion near Mount Union, Ohio, and Duss began selling reed organs for the Lane music store. It wasn't quite the fun it had been when the Lane boys were at home and, after a few months, he decided to leave Ohio and try his hand at homesteading.

My mother's ready cash would start us on the way. . . . After consultation with my wife, and in spite of flattering offers from the musical stage, I decided to cast our future with the West.[8]

Duss planned to raise cattle, but did not have sufficient money to stock a ranch. Consequently, he worked for some time as an assistant to his wife's brother, Mitchell, who operated photo galleries at Burr Oak and Mankato, Kansas. At the same time, he used the studio waiting rooms to display parlor organs for the Kansas Organ Company, for which he became a sales representative. In addition, the merchants of Burr Oak hired him to direct a community band. The arrangement lasted about a year and a half, and, in the spring of 1884, Duss says "planning and scheming, my wife and I . . . decided to migrate to . . . South Central Nebraska.[9]

With their daughter, Vera, who had been born in August of 1883, they moved to land near Red Cloud, Nebraska, in May of 1884. Here Duss began raising cattle, but barely succeeded in making ends meet. With the "monetary assistance of Mother Creese" (Susanna's mother) he tried raising hogs, which proved more successful. He reportedly began to prosper, built a new house, organized a "Literary Society," and considered entering local politics.[10] But a letter from his mother in the summer of 1888 stating that Henrici was seeking a teacher for the school, prompted him to abandon these "successes" in Nebraska and return to Economy.

When Duss resumed teaching at Economy, he introduced changes in the curriculum and other activities which drew sharp criticism. Daily marching drills, which he felt improved the posture of the students, were looked upon as unnecessary militarism by the members. Other problems within the Society, however, soon superceded these. In the fall of 1889 there were only twenty-five members in the Harmony Society, ten men and fifteen women. It was decided that some new members should be taken in, but disagreement developed regarding these new members. Sharp differences developed, especially between the Feuchts, who wished to become members again, and John Duss and his wife. The quick succession of deaths (Gertrude Rapp, G. Kirschbaum, E. Woelfel, J. Lenz, J. Wirth) created a panic as to who would govern after Henrici. Kirschbaum and Wirth had only recently been elected members of the board of elders, and while Lenz was deeply mourned, to many, the most severe blow was the unexpected loss of George Kirschbaum who was being groomed to replace Henrici as the Society's leader. A desperate effort to fill the vacancies followed. Duss and three others (not the Feuchts) were taken into membership on 24 January 1890, a noteworthy event in that new members were generally taken in during the Harmoniefest on 15 February. At the next Harmoniefest, 15 February 1890, the Feuchts, Susanna Duss, and thirteen others were admitted to membership, raising the total to forty-four, twenty men and twenty-four women.

The new membership was far from being of one mind; differences developed over clothing styles, religious interpretations, and the state of the Society's industries. The first two of these were of secondary importance, however, because this sudden growth in membership was not the result of interest in the Society's religious principles. Most of the membership knew the Society was dying and, if dissolved, its assets would be divided among the remaining members. A power play between two factions developed— one headed by Duss and the other by the Feuchts. The Feuchts, however, were no match for Duss, who carefully manipulated the remaining members, particularly the older ones. After Ernst Woelfel's death 28 July 1890, Duss was elected junior trustee. A year and half later, Christmas Day, 1892, Jacob Henrici died, and Duss was elected senior trustee becoming the chief spokesman for what remained of the Harmony Society.

From then until 1906, the membership declined again. Older members died, and one by one, remaining ones, including the Feuchts, were given financial settlements as they resigned their memberships. Susanna Duss was chosen to be the successor to John Duss when he, himself, resigned in 1903 to devote himself "exclusively to music" and pursue what he later described as his "short but brilliant" career as a professional musician. Under Susie Duss' trusteeship, the Society was dissolved in 1906, and she and the other remaining member, the elderly Franz Gilman, moved to Florida. Duss joined them there in 1907 after his musical career had ended.[11]

THE "SHORT BUT BRILLIANT" CAREER BEGINS

Prior to Henrici's death, the band was under the direction of Jacob

Rohr. During this time, Duss says he "served in various musical capacities—as cornetist, writer, composer, and after the death of Gertrude Rapp, as church organist."[12] After Henrici's death in 1892, Duss had a freer hand and took over the leadership of the band although Rohr remained in the Society's employ:

> In 1893 I began improving the personnel of the band. To the local groups I added select professional talent from Pittsburgh, Beaver Falls, and other sections. Local members rehearsed three times weekly. At rehearsals of special music the entire group had to be on hand. Sunday afternoon concerts became a regular feature. For these concerts I designed and had built a pavilion which from the standpoint of acoustics was superior to any similar structure. At times I not only conducted the band, but appeared as cornet soloist. Newspapers gradually sounded more and more the excellence of the band as well as of my interpolated explanatory remarks in reference to important numbers on the program. They praised my conducting and vaunted my ability as a cornetist. . . . I came to be regarded as . . . musician-in-chief of a most musical Western Pennsylvania community.[13]

Just at the time Duss was discovering the Society's "towering debts and financial losses,"[14] he enlarged the band with professionals and began to publish his compositions. Three pieces, "Liberty Chimes March," "Life's Voyage Waltz," and "The Limited Express March" were published in 1894 by William C. Ott and Company of Beaver Falls, Pennsylvania. The first, "Liberty Chimes March,"[15] was arranged by the publisher, William C. Ott, and the second, "Life's Voyage Waltz,"[16] was arranged by a prominent Pittsburgh-area musician, Henry Neubauer.

There are printed programs extant for concerts played by the Economy Band in 1894. Three were played at Economy: Harvest Home, 12 August; a general concert 28 October; a Thanksgiving Concert on 29 November; and one at Knauff's Opera Hall, Zelienople, Pennsylvania, 30 August. The program for the Harvest Home concert bears a footnote: "*Liberty Chimes March* is in process of publication and should be available in two weeks. . . ." The Thanksgiving concert included a guest performer, Abram Kaprachevsky, a violinist.

The band continued to be built up throughout 1895 and Duss commented:

> We were making retrenchments of every kind . . . only the Economy Band grew in size and importance. . . . I issued a decree that during my band rehearsals I was not to be disturbed by any caller, be he president or potentate.[17]

Duss began to take engagements for the band throughout southwestern Pennsylvania. In 1895 they also participated in the "G. A. R. National Encampment at Louisville."[18] Duss says: "we caused a furore and were entertained by the great Henry Watterson, editor of the *Courier-Journal.*"[19] For the occasion, he wrote his "March G. A. R. in Dixie" (see Appendix A, ex. 21).[20] In the same year, he wrote a piece called "The Brownies-Dance Characteristic" (arranged by Henry Neubauer) and a cornet solo called "Diana Polonaise." All three were published by W. C. Ott and Company of Beaver Falls.

In addition to the above, five concerts were played at Economy. The New Year's Day concert featured guest soloists Edith Fry, soprano; Abram Karpachevsky, violin; Sgr. G. Bolli, baritone; and Alice Ott, accompanist. On the same program, Duss and Philip D'Ivernois, the clarinettist-organist and son-in-law of Jacob Rohr, played solos. Other concerts were played on 14 April (Easter concert), and 2 June, at which the guest soloists were the "Noss Family Saxophone Quartet," and on Thanksgiving and Christmas Days. At least two concerts were also given in Pittsburgh that year—one at the Music Hall, 19 July and another on 23 July, the place of the latter not recorded on the program. While very few records at Old Economy tell anything of the money spent on the band and its activities between 1893 and 1906, some extant notes indicate that some of the musicians were paid.[21]

The following year, 1896, the band traveled to St. Paul, Minnesota, for the G. A. R. National Encampment, and Duss wrote a march called "The Great Northwest" for the occasion (Appendix A, ex. 22). In the same year the John Church Company of Cincinnati, Ohio, published Duss' "Pittsburgh Dispatch March."[22] A manuscript copy bears the inscription: "Composed November, 1896, by J. S. Duss. Arranged for piano by Gus Mueller."[23] The keyboard version was published, but Mueller's name is not on the copy.

Duss was appointed sole trustee of the Harmony Society in 1897, the same year in which a band version of his "Life's Voyage" was published by W. C. Ott. The arrangement, again, was made by Henry Neubauer.[24] During this year, concerts were played at Economy on New Year's Day; Easter (18 April); and Whitsuntide (6 June). A concert was also played at Zoar, Ohio, on 30 May in honor of the Zoar Society. The program for this concert is the only one extant which gives the names of the members of the Economy Band (see plate 14). They are listed as follows:

J. S. Duss, director and cornet soloist
William C. Ott, solo cornet
William Fritsch, solo cornet
Paul Straube, B♭ cornet
J. S. Duss, Jr., B♭ cornet
Gottlieb Flneckign, B♭ cornet [sic]
Herman Heideger, E♭ cornet
Elmer Stoffel, piccolo
Frank Thuma, oboe
William Wahrhaus, E♭ clarionet
PH D'Ivernois, clarionet soloist
Otto Straube, B♭ clarionet

PLATE 1. George Rapp (1757-1847), Founder of the Harmony Society. ". . . I am a Prophet and am Called to be One."

Photograph courtesy of Daniel B. Reibel

PLATE 2. A Page from Jacob Henrici's Hymn Accompaniment Book. The letters and numbers between the staves refer to the location of the hymns in various collections which the Harmonists were using simultaneously.

PLATE 3. A Contemporary Sketch of the Harmonist Church in Indiana.

PLATE 4.   Examples of Harmonist Manuscript Hymnals.

Harmonisches

GesangBuch.

Theils

Von andern Authoren,

Theils neu verfaßt.

Zum Gebrauch von Singen und Musik

für

Alte und Junge.

Nach Geschmak und Umständen zu wählen gewidmet.

∞∞∞

Allentown,
Lecha County, im Staat Pennsylvanien.
Gedruckt bey Heinrich Ebner.
1820.

PLATE 5.   Title Page of the Harmonist's Hymnbook, 1820.

PLATE 6. Charles von Bonnhorst (1776-1884). Soldier, Barrister, Violinist-Composer, and friend of the Harmonists.

PLATE 7. William Cummings Peters (1805-1866). Composer and Publisher.

Courtesy of Stephen Foster Memorial Museum.
Pittsburgh, Pennsylvania.

XXX.

Musicalien auf das Pfingstfest,
Juni, 7. 1829.

1. V.M. Wogende Flur.   Nr. 32.
March 1 v. Bonh.   Nr. 192.
2 N.M. Der Tugend-March.   54.
Friedens-March.   Nr. 28.
       Abends.
1 March von Hanover Nr. 292.
2. Der Traum mit Variat. N. 291
3. Cantate : Komm Heil. Geist,
4 Sonatina.   Nr 258.
5. Cantate : Who, who can expr.
6. Der sæusselnde Schwung.
7. Choral : Halleluia, Lob, Preis.
8. Geweihte Flammen. Nr. 250.
9. Beetho.en's Menuet. Nr. 114.

PLATE 8.   Program for Pentecost Concert, 7 June, 1829.

PLATE 9.   Jonathan Lenz (1807-1890). Harmonist Musician and Trustee.

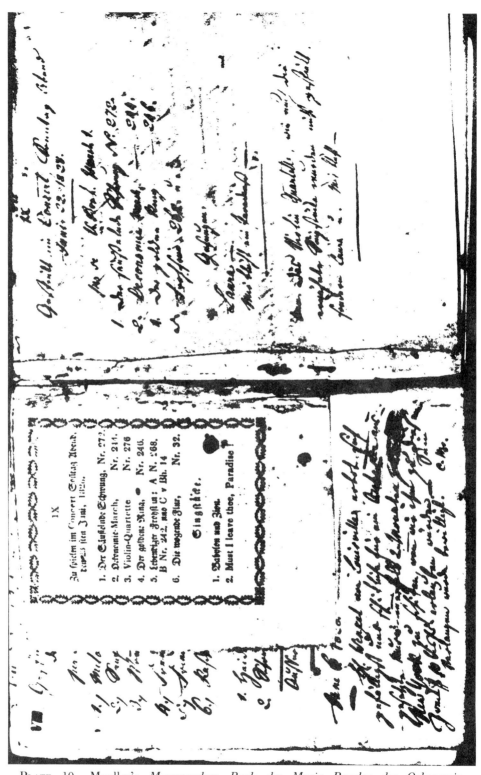

PLATE 10. Mueller's *Memorandum Buch des Music Bandes der Oekonomie*, showing the entry for the concert played 23 June, 1828.

Credit: Photograph by Karl J. R. Arndt

PLATE 11.   Title Page from Gertrude Rapp's
Keyboard Accompaniment Book.

PLATE 12.   A Copy of Dr. Mueller's Hymn "Durch
Zerfallne Kirchen Fenster." Copied in 1843, it
bears a bitter denunciation of the Rapps. The note
at the bottom states: "This was the first piece
which I composed."

Plate 13.   Count Leon.

Credit: Photograph by Karl J. R. Arndt

PLATE 14.   The Economy Band c. 1897.

PLATE 15.   Harmonist Musical Instruments. Left, one of a pair of horns purchased in 1817. Right, a piano from the early Economy years.

PLATE 16. Jacob Henrici (1804-1892). School Teacher, Musician-Composer, and Harmonist Trustee.

PLATE 17. Dr. Benjamin Feucht (1834-1898). Medical Doctor and Musician.

PLATE 18. Nahan Franko (1861-1930). Violinist-Composer and Conductor of the Metropolitan Opera House Orchestra.

Credit: Photo Courtesy New York Public Library

PLATE 19. John S. Duss (1860-1951). Homesteader, Harmonist Trustee, Bandmaster-Conductor, Composer.

PLATE 20. Robert E. Johnston, New York Publicity Agent.

Credit: Photo Courtesy New York Public Library

DUSS

<small>AND HIS</small> — **Incomparable BAND**

THE ST. NICHOLAS

66th STREET AND COLUMBUS AVE.,

Beginning

To-morrow Night, May 26

and every evening thereafter at 8.15.

PEERLESS

RE-EMINENTLY OPULAR;

RONOUNCED ECULIARLY ROGRESSIVE;

REDOMINANTLY OWERFUL AND RACTICALLY ERFECT.

THE ST. NICHOLAS on humid nights will be **20** degrees cooler than outside, as it will be artificially cooled by tons of ice.

FLOWER GIRLS will give bouquets to each lady.

PINAUD will furnish cologne fountains free.

THE FIFTH AVENUE COACH CO. will run stages direct to the St. Nicholas from 66th St. and Fifth Ave., free for DUSS CONCERT patrons.

PABST with the coolest and finest beer in America serves the thirsty.

HEALY the Restauranteur, supplies the hungry—AND

DUSS WITH HIS GREAT BAND, can and will delight all those attending.

R. E. JOHNSTON,

Lessee of THE ST. NICHOLAS, and Manager

DUSS AND HIS BAND.

Gilmore

Day

BY

DUSS

And His Band

At *Forest Park Highlands*

Tuesday, July 2, 1907

<small>PRESS A. R. FLEMING PRINTING CO., ST. LOUIS</small>

PLATE 22. Duss and His Idol. From the "Gilmore Day" Program 2 July 1907 (Page 1).

PLATE 21. Excerpt from Metropolitan Opera House program, 25 May 1902.

To Morrow Night

Monday Eve., May 26

First of the Summer Nights' Band Carnivals by America's Greatest Bandmaster

DUSS
AIDED BY NOTED SOLOISTS

AT THE ST. NICHOLAS, COLUMBUS AVE. AND 66th ST.

Monday Evening's Programme

PART I.

1—OVERTURE, "Raymond"..................THOMAS
2—MENUETTE, "Pautins Vivants,".....LEONCAVALLE
3—CHARACTERISTIC MARCH, "The Trolley," DUSS
4—FANTASY ON SCOTCH AIRS.............GODFREY
"The Campbells are Coming," "The White Cockade," "The Braes of Auchterarden," "Strathspey," "Annie Laurie," "Within a Mile of Edinboro," "Bonnie Blue," "Blue Bells of Scotland," "Tullochgorom," and incidental variations galore.

PART II.

5—EXCERPTS from "Tannhauser,"..........WAGNER
6—INTERMEZZO, "Love's Dream after the Ball."
....CZIBULKA

7—CORNET SOLO, "Whirlwind Polka,"..........LEVY
MR. BOHUMIR KRYL.
8—WALTZ, "On the Beautiful Blue Danube,"...STRAUSS

PART III.

9—OVERTURE, "Midsummer Nights Dream,"
..................................MENDELSSOHN
10—INTERMEZZO, "Flirtation,"................STECK
11—TWO DANCES from "Casse Noisette" (The
Nutcracker,"......................TSCHAIKOWSKY
a) "Danse de la Fee Dragee."
b) "Danse Russe Trepak."
12—MARCH, Op. 82, "Buelow,".............F. V. BLON

Management, - R. E. JOHNSTON

General Admission, 50c.

Free Stages from Fifth Avenue and 66th Street to The St. Nicholas

PLATE 23. Excerpt from Metropolitan Opera House program, 25 May 1902.

SOLOISTS AND COMPOSERS OF THE DUSS BAND.

1. Luigi Sperandei, Horn Soloist and composer. 2. Nicholas Sirignano, Petit Clarinet Soloist. 3. P. C. Funaro, Euphonium. 4. Alfredo Ravel, Flute. 5. Bert Wright, Cornetist and composer. 6. Vincent Ragone, Saxophonist and composer. 7. Harry Carlson, Trombone. 8. Frank Campbel, Trumpeter and composer. 9. Gavino Napolitano, Tuba. 10. Samuel Eranson, Solo Clarinet. 11. Richard McCann, Solo Cornet. 12. Charles Fisher, Xylophone. 13. R. Boninsegni, Oboe soloist and composer. 14. Peter Weber, String Bass. 15. J. J. Scull, Saxophonist and composer. 16. Frank Hurtt, Trumpeter and composer.

PLATE 24.   The "Gilmore Day" Program, July 2, 1907 (Page 4).

K. R. Wagner, B♭ clarionet
John Stoffel, B♭ clarionet
Carl Nusser, bassoon
Christian Kroll, baritone
Gottlieb Kuttule, tenor
Karl Rye, tenor
Walter Javens, trombone
J. Merriman, trombone
Fritz Reithmueller, B♭ bass
Gustav Schumacher, E♭ tuba
J. Ablatti, E♭ tuba
Gottlieb Nagel, BB♭ contra bass
George Leppig, }
Jacob Bass, } Horns
Fritz Kroll, }
H. Thumm, }
Fritz Knoedler }
William Gibson } Percussion
James Grey }
C. Bruff }

Up to this time, the band had been billed as the "Economy Band." Its communications were handled by one of the players, K. R. Wagner, and the printed programs were sometimes used to promote Economy products, such as the "Economy Boneset Cordial," a home remedy medicine. The program for the Zoar concert was the first to suggest a change in emphasis, listing the band as "Duss' Economy Band," the name by which it was known for approximately two years. Finally, the Economy name was dropped entirely and the name used was "Duss' Band."

W. C. Ott and Company published two more Duss pieces in 1898, "The Cross and Crown March Song and Two Step,"[25] and "The Shot and Shell March and Two Step."[26] The second of these was dedicated to Rear Admiral George Dewey, "the Hero of Manila." Duss also wrote a funeral march "Durch Kampf zum Sieg" (Through Battle to Victory) in February, 1898, "as a memorial to the members past and present of the Harmony Society."[27]

On Memorial Day, 1899, the Economy Band was the featured attraction for the festivities held at Schenley Park in Pittsburgh. Duss says: "for the occasion I composed a piece called *America Up to Date* . . . the crowd put up such a noisy demonstration so that it had to be repeated four times."[28] If Duss had ever looked upon the band under his leadership as a Harmonist organization, he soon ceased to do so:

The return of the Tenth Regiment from the Philippines to Pittsburgh on August 28, 1899, was another occasion that called my band to the attention of thousands. . . .[29]

The band played continuously from 10:00 A.M. until late in the afternoon. President McKinley was on hand to welcome the returning troops and when the Guenther Band, another instrumental group, missed its cue, Duss had his band do an "impromptu" performance of "Hail to the Chief."[30]

Two days later the band played at Beaver, Pennsylvania, for the reception given in honor of returning Company B. Duss wrote a march entitled "The Fighting Tenth"[31] for the occasion. Toward the end of the summer, he also wrote "Jordan's Riffles, a Rag-Time Two Step."[32] The instrumental parts are stamped "Gus. Mueller, arrg. of Music, Allegheny, Pa." and are dated 8 September 1899.

Mueller, Neubauer, and two other Pittsburgh-area arrangers, Otto Merz and W. A. Metzner, along with the publisher Ott, wrote most of Duss' arrangements. An examination of Duss' publications shows that all but one of those printed before 1902 were published by "Wm. C. Ott and Co.," of Beaver Falls, Pennsylvania. The last Duss piece to be printed by this company was "The Trolley Song March"[33] (1901) which was "dedicated to W. L. Mellon, President of the Monongahela Street Railway Company."

William C. Ott played solo cornet in the Economy Band. (His name is directly below Duss' on the 1897 program.) No extant records tell how young Ott became established in the publishing business, but there are numerous letters addressed to "W. C. Ott and Co." among Duss' uncataloged papers at Economy which indicate that Duss had an active hand in the business of this "company." These letters, which are actually orders for music published by W. C. Ott, have notes written on them in Duss' hand stating that the requested pieces were sent.[34] A letter written to Duss on 20 November 1902, suggests that Ott's publishing company was, in fact, financed by Duss.

> You may remember having had some correspondence with Mr. R. T. Townsend regarding *Blue Eyes*, published by Wm. C. Ott and Co., the assets of which firm we understand are in your hand. . . .[35]

An advertising flyer for this company shows that all of its publications except four were pieces written by John Duss.

Early in 1900, Duss says he merged the Great Western Band, presumably the largest band in the Pittsburgh area, with his own.

> Under the new banner our first important appearance was at a place where I had successfully weathered many a suit at law, namely the Court House at Beaver. In these congenial surroundings we were a brilliant spot throughout the four day Beaver County Centennial Celebration . . . the Reverend Doctor J. S. Ramsey . . . concluded his remarks by presenting me a handsomely wrought medal—the first I received for my musical accomplishments . . . my acceptance speech sounded inadequate, so I set the band to work on the Beaver County Centennial March which I had composed for the Occasion.[36]

The piece is inscribed "*Festival March*, written expressively [*sic*] for and in honor of the Beaver County Centennial held at Beaver, Pennsylvania, June 19th to 22nd, 1900." Duss had it copyrighted and printed in 1903, but the name of the publisher is not on the copy.[37]

Numerous concerts by "Duss' Economy Band" were given at various Pittsburgh-area parks throughout the summers of 1900 and 1901. Those parks most frequently played were Kennywood Park, Calhoun Park, and the Oakwood Park where a concert given on 30 June 1901, also featured a chorus of "80 vocal artists of the Second Presbyterian Church, Pittsburgh." With the band, they gave a rendition of *The Holy City* by Adam.

Almost ten years had now passed since Henrici's death. In that time nine more members of the Society had died, including Duss' strongest opponent, Benjamin Feucht. Only eight remained: one man of seventy-seven, and five women ages eighty, seventy-seven, fifty-eight, fifty-four, and forty-seven, in addition to Duss and his wife Susie. Others had left the Society and were paid an average of $5,000 to resign their memberships and claims on its assets. Duss, through his attorneys, had laid the groundwork for the Society's dissolution and time and these attorneys would eventually declare the Dusses its last surviving heirs.

It would at this juncture in Duss' career be interesting to know how much of the Society's funds had been spent upon his musical pursuits since Henrici's death. Unfortunately, no such record, or the documents necessary to create one, exist. However, receipts hurriedly scratched on fragments of paper—which somehow escaped Duss' later purge of the Economy archives—and Duss' own comments in his autobiographical writings make possible a partial reconstruction of the extent and cost of his musical activities to this date.

1. After 1893 Duss added "professionals" to the Economy Band, which consisted of thirty musicians in addition to Duss and his son, John, Jr. None appears to have been a member of the Society. The payroll for the band was approximately $160 for each concert. According to Duss, the band rehearsed three times and played at least one concert each week. Were the "professionals" paid for the rehearsals as well as the concerts? Probably, but the cost of the concerts alone must have exceeded $8,000 per year, or about $65,000 from 1893 to 1901.

2. Under the name of William Ott, a cornet player in his band, Duss in 1894 established a publishing house in Beaver Falls. He later moved it to 225 Fourth Avenue in Pittsburgh. No less than fifteen pieces and arrangements were published during this period. Ott, Neubauer, Metzner, and Mueller, Pittsburgh musicians who arranged the pieces, were presumably paid for their work. No records

exist to establish the costs of printing or the other costs of maintaining the publishing firm.

3. Band publicity and administrative details, which in the late 1890s demanded considerable attention, were handled by K. R. Wagner, a curious figure who, while not a member of the Society, served as secretary to the Harmony Board and who thereby was privy to all of the Society's business affairs at that time (!). How much and how he was paid for his services is not known.

4. Several professional soloists were featured on most programs. They were paid about $15 per concert. This would have cost from $1500 to $2,000 annually or approximately $16,000 over the period under consideration.

5. The band traveled to Louisville, Ky., in 1895; St. Paul, Minn., 1896; Zoar, Ohio, 1897; and Buffalo, N.Y., in 1898. Duss presumably paid the costs of transportation and room and board for the band on trips like these. The cost must have been in the thousands of dollars. There were numerous shorter trips as well.

6. According to a receipt dated 9 February 1901, the uniforms worn by the band cost $15 each. Whether or not Duss purchased these is not known.

7. A special pavilion was built for the band at Economy. The cost is unknown.

8. Only a few bills for music survive, but the repertory played under Duss was not the one played under Rohr.

9. Printed programs for each concert cost approximately $2.50, according to a receipt dated 27 May 1893 from Ferguson Co., Pittsburgh. The annual expenditure would have exceeded $100.

10. In addition to the above, records of assorted musical expenditures not related to the band have been found.

> May 1895—a violin for Duss from Charles F. Albert, of Philadelphia, $195.00
>
> 15 January 1901—The Mehan School of Vocal Art, Detroit, Mich., Tuition for Vera Duss, $40.00
>
> 21 January 1901—Anna Ebling, Bellevue, Pa., Piano lessons for Vera Duss, $22.14

This sketch is not meant to be definitive but to suggest the scope of Duss' musical investments before 1902. The band was now clearly a "business" like many others during this era, and presumably there was some income realized from performances. There are, however, no records available to confirm whether the band earned or lost money. Either way, it was of little importance to Duss whose consuming passion was to become a famous bandmaster. Cost was not considered because he and Susie were gradually becoming heir to a fortune which would make such small expenditures seem trifling. Duss, with the aid of clever lawyers, was transferring into cash and bonds, the Society's railroads, factories, banks, oil and gas wells, lumber and brick yards and other industries. Above all, land which the Society owned was becoming very important to one of the largest steel fabricating corporations in the world—the American Bridge Company (hence the name "Ambridge" eventually replaced that of Economy). The total Harmonist fortune can only be guessed at, although Dr. Karl J. R. Arndt's comment, based upon years of research "there were millions of dollars, which means billions in terms of our current devaluated currency, in spite of all the denials made. . . ." is a useful guide. Duss could pursue his musical career with little or no regard for cost. It is not surprising, therefore, that he now turned to the lights of an infinitely larger and brighter stage.

THE CALL OF BROADWAY

In 1902, Duss was catapulted to national fame through the work of a clever publicity agent, R. E. Johnston, of New York City (see plates 19, 20). How the two met is not clear, but early in December 1901, Johnston made a trip to Economy. "Apparently the word of our Band's excelling musicianship had reached New York. . . . I quickly arranged an impromptu concert," writes Duss.[38] It isn't likely, however, that this alone brought Johnston to Economy. He may have heard of Duss' financial as well as his musical resources through a mutual acquaintance, or perhaps Duss sought a New York agent. In any case, when Johnston returned to New York, the following items were agreed to or discussed and Johnston presumably was given sufficient funds to begin their implementation:

1. Johnston was to be the agent for Duss and his band, probably for one year.
2. The Metropolitan Opera House was to be leased for an initial concert, to be follbwed by a summer concert series at St. Nicholas and Madison Square gardens. A tour was to take place in the fall.
3. An extensive publicity campaign with a practically unlimited budget was to be initiated immediately upon Johnston's return to New York.

Some details of the preceding may not have been completely settled when Johnston left Economy, but this visit marked the beginning of a musical spending spree for which it would be difficult to find a parallel at that time.

Back in New York, Johnston began generating publicity the magnitude of which must have amazed even Duss. A printer, C. B. Bradford, was hired to assist him and from an office in the St. James Building at Broadway and Twenty-sixth Streets, they bombarded New York with sensational notices and articles for the six months prior to the arrival of Duss and his band. Articles were run in the *Musical Courier* praising Duss as a "magnetic and forceful conductor," and the band was described as "a sensational surprise; in fact a revelation."[39] Johnston epitomized Duss as the "do-it-yourself American." An article in the *Musical Courier* of 22 January 1902, states:

> He [Duss] has become one of those striking phenomena—this business man, philanthropic, [*sic*] financier, economist, interesting himself in literature, and at the same time conducting and rehearsing a concert band . . . the first Duss Band concert will take place in New York at the Metropolitan House, Sunday Evening, May 25.

The band was now to be known as "Duss' Band." Duss says he submitted the matter "to the remaining members [of the Harmony Society] and they voted in the affirmative"[40] that he should appear in a limited number of concerts during the coming summer. He retained some of his "local boys" whom he rehearsed every night through the winter months, and upon reaching New York, combined them with "professional musicians gathered from the four winds."[41]

The repertory which Duss rehearsed consisted of overtures by Wagner, Mendelssohn, Tchaikowsky, Liszt, Glinka, Rossini, Delibes, Ponchielli; a liberal number of waltzes and marches by Strauss, Sousa and Duss; and numerous medleys, pastiches and other programmatic works by these and lesser-known composers. The larger works—the overtures and opera excerpts in particular—were, of course, transcriptions for band of works originally conceived for orchestra. Some of these were adequate representations of the originals—as far as it was possible for clarinets and other winds to approximate string textures—and some were not. In either case, the musicians of Duss' band had been rehearsing pieces from the standard available literature for concert bands, they were presumably the best "local boys" which money could buy, and the effect which they produced should have been pleasing if not outstanding. Reviews of their first concerts, unfortunately, indicate that their efforts were not completely satisfactory. This was due partly, if not completely, to some bad judgment on the conductor's part.

The band was scheduled to play its first concert in New York City on 25 May. Quite appropriately, Duss scheduled some off-Broadway concerts enroute. Reviews of these concerts, if favorable, could have influenced the band's reception at the Metropolitan Opera House which at best was not an especially appropriate place for a band to present a concert. The two concerts played at Rochester, New York on 22 and 23 May were, therefore, important ones. But Duss had developed some personal idiosyncracies which frequently interfered with the band's efforts:

> I made it a practice whenever we gave a concert to introduce to the audience the more important numbers . . . the innovation gradually became a habit and led to

. . . short speeches or sermonettes on matters outside the realm of music . . . patriotism, statesmanship—and topics of the day . . . all of which caught on . . . I became known as the "talking conductor."[42]

The review of the Rochester concerts which appeared in the Rochester *Herald* was, unfortunately, a devastating one, indicating that Duss' personality had completely obscured the efforts of the band.

> Rochester has had its fair share of band concerts; it has a band or two of its own, but not one of the local directors has any pretension to shine as a buffoon. So when Mr. Duss began his chatter about this, that and the other thing last Thursday evening it came as a surprise. Rochester music lovers are not accustomed to have a leader of a band or orchestra come on the stage after the intermission and remark: "It's raining outside." That is not what they paid a dollar at the box office to have him do. But the man who has paid his money to listen to a concert is more or less at the mercy of the man who gives the concert. Mr. Duss should remember that when he feels that he is about to have a fit of talking.
>
> It is understood that the Duss Band is to give a series of concerts in New York this summer. If Mr. Duss undertakes to occupy his programme time with replies to all his New York critics the chances are that he won't have time to play any music at all—that is, if the New York press condescends to take him seriously. Last evening, with only one critic to engage his irate attention, Mr. Duss talked at such a rate that he omitted the final number on the programme. Eccentricity is sometimes pardonable, but rarely when it is studied.

The second of the two Rochester concerts was given on Friday, 23 May. This gave Duss two days to get the band into New York City and prepare for the Sunday evening concert at the Metropolitan. The original band of thirty was increased to sixty shortly after Duss's arrival. Was it during these two days that he combined his "local boys" with "professional musicians gathered from the four winds"? The review in the *New York Herald* of the Opera House concert suggests that Duss may have expanded the ensemble too quickly: "Millionaire Makes His Debut With Band. Duss, Owner of the Town of Economy, is Original, and His Musicians Make lots of Noise." The critic found the band poorly balanced, having too many bass instruments with the result "more noise than music." In addition, the reviewer criticized Duss's programming, specifically one of his own compositions, "The Battle of Manila in a Nutshell," the fifth selection of the twelve on the program. Before and following it the band played Rossini, Beethoven, Schubert, Tchaikowsky, Wagner, among others, and it was clearly inconsistent with the rest of the program. Little wonder that the critic remarked: "It will do—for its kind." The same critic suggested that Duss might rival Sousa "as a poseur and advertiser, if in no other way," and he further criticized his "bad habit of talking to the audience without rhyme or reason."

Inherent in this review was a message to Duss which required several years and thousands of dollars for him to grasp: the Metropolitan Opera House audiences were not fond of his kind of music, regardless of cost. But Duss had difficulty recognizing the incongruity in a printed program which had Met director Maurice Grau's name on the cover; names like Cornelius Vanderbilt, J. P. Morgan, and John J. Astor, among the list of boxholders; and contained a concert by Duss' "Peerless pre-eminently popular; Pronounced peculiarly progressive; Predominantly powerful and practically perfect" band (see plate 21).

After the Opera House concert, the band appeared at the St. Nicholas, a rink on Columbus Avenue and Sixty-sixth St. Here the sixty musicians, reportedly the highest paid band musicians in New York, along with Duss and approximately 140 other employees, presented entertainment which attracted thousands. The interior of the building was lavishly decorated and through the use of tons of ice was made fifteen to twenty degrees cooler than the temperature outside. Beer and food and a drink called "Duss' Lemonade" were sold and flowers and perfume were given to the ladies who attended these "Summer Night Band Carnivals by America's Greatest Bandmaster." (see plate 23).

In the meantime, Johnston and his printer assistant, Bradford, did their best to promote the concerts and increase Duss' reputation. They spent no less than $100,000 on publicity during the 1902 season and printed stationery with Duss' picture in the letterhead design. On this, notices about Duss and his band were sent every day to not only the New York papers but to the newspapers in the towns which the band was to visit during its fall tour. In many of these towns the reporters, with little critical judgment of their own, later used these notices as the bases for their own reviews.

Johnston, however, did not confine publicity to the newspapers. A single piece of advertising material which, in the opinion of C. B. Bradford, stood out above the rest was a booklet containing photographs of Duss and press notices taken from various newspapers which was prepared for distribution at the summer concerts.[43] They printed three hundred-thousand copies; it provoked the following response from a reporter for the *Pittsburgh Dispatch*:

> An edition deluxe of "Band Leader Duss" the crowning achievement of a wonderful press agent has made its appearance. The book is bound in a sort of snuff-yellow-wallpaper with a hole cut in the front cover to let the countenance of the bandmaster beam through. Within, scattered through a score of pages of press notices, are twenty-three pictures of Duss, leading one to the inevitable conclusion that he has a Kodak concealed in every horn in his band. There is Duss in repose, in action, in contemplation, in joy, as in Mendelssohn's "Spring Song," riding with the Valkyries, in what Sentimental Tommy called "the attitude of all geniuses about to have their photographs taken," and as "the hatred killer." But the picture of Duss seraphic is easily the best. It shows a two-thirds figure in

profile, the left hand holding the baton and the score of "Palm Branches," the right hand supporting the raised chin. The eyes have a look as far away as Economy. On the rear cover is an Economized doric pillar, adorned with a wreath of laurel and bearing the one word "Duss."[44]

But Duss and his advertising team did not limit themselves to printed material. Two giants and a midget, dressed in colorful costumes bearing the name "Duss," distributed literature in the streets and at the concerts. Periodically, they managed to have themselves arrested for "disorderly conduct"—the midget would "assault" one of the giants—and the arrest and subsequent appearance in court were carried in the papers. The giants were also arrested on one occasion for forcing their way into the theatre of William Hammerstein where "Signor Vermicelli Creatore," a conductor-competitor of Duss' who was noted for his "gymnastic gyrations," was appearing.[45] When they were jailed, agent Johnston soon appeared to supply the bond money for their release.

On his concerts Duss was especially fond of conducting patriotic airs, and he delighted in brassy performances of the national anthem which brought the audiences to their feet. In addition, for each concert he tried to provide some nonmusical novelty:

DUSS WILL OPEN WINE ON CONCERT ANNIVERSARY

Versatile Bandmaster Will Offer as Souvenirs Vintage of
Economy, Pa., Bottled in Small Vials

Duss the bandmaster, gives his 100th New York concert on the evening of September 1. Upon this occasion Duss will open wine—wine for all his patrons. Out in Economy, Pa., where Duss comes from, the Economites have a winery, and Duss is going to bottle a lot of it in small vials and hand it out to all comers on the night mentioned.[46]

Another favorite ploy of Duss' was to invite the show girls from theatres on Broadway to his concerts in the hope that they would add interest to the proceedings at the St. Nicholas:

On June 15 Duss added interest to his show by issuing a special invitation to Lulu Glaser and members of the "Dolly Vaden" comic opera then running in New York. She came with most of her company, and Duss played airs from the comic opera to honor them. On June 18 Duss and his band marched up Broadway to attend the matinee of "Show Girl" and on the next Sunday all 50 of the "Show Girl" girls were his guests at Nicholas Garden. Next he invited the company of "King Dodo," and he continued this kind of advertising through the summer.[47]

Less original and more contrived were the awards and gifts sent by well-wishers and admirers which Johnston would present to Duss during the

course of an evening. The most spectacular of these occurred on the night of
the last program of the season at St. Nicholas. A description of the event appeared in the *Pittsburgh Leader*:

> John S. Duss, bandmaster and Economite, has been made the recipient of one of
> the handsomest and most costly medals a musician has worn. It is a gift from the
> men of his band, and was presented at the close of the Duss season at St. Nicholas
> garden. A heroic figure of an American eagle surmounts the bar from which de-
> pends the base of the medal, and on which are Caesar's memorable words, "Veni,
> Vidi, Vici—I came, I saw, I conquered." . . . Heavy gold chains attach to ends of
> laurel branches between which is an embossed lyre flanked by trumpets, with two
> American flags supporting a shield on which are the figures "1902." The medal is
> massive gold and enamel, studded with diamonds and other precious stones, and is
> really a very artistic and showy jewel.[48]

Amid all the advertising stunts, awards, and other gimmicks, the band
often received secondary attention—unfortunate because there are indications that it was a fine band. According to Mr. Leon Prevost, a well-known
Pittsburgh cornetist who had been flugelhorn soloist with the Duss Band and
returned to Pittsburgh to play in a theatre orchestra, the band was "far superior to Sousa's." "You may judge what sort of band Duss has when I tell you
that the clarinet soloist of the Metropolitan Opera Company's orchestra is on
the second stand with Duss and Sousa's solo clarinet is on the third stand."[49]

To Duss, however, getting his own image before the public was most important. Even so, he was not ungenerous with his musicians. They were very
well paid and individual performers were given some recognition. Beyond
this, they were occasionally treated to pleasure excursions at Duss's expense
and each evening were provided "beer and clams" free of charge at the St.
Nicholas. The atmosphere may not have been as sophisticated as some might
have desired but it was steady, remunerative employment.

In promoting the Duss image Johnston had done his work with imagina-
tion and nerve, so well, in fact, that Duss began to believe the sensational
publicity. Duss came to see himself as a musical prophet—an authority on all
styles of music—and reporters delighted in printing his sweeping, often non-
sensical generalizations, such as the following which appeared in the *New
York News*:

> Possibly I am particularly and peculiarly sensitive to Wagner's music because I
> was born a Wagnerian. I dreamed of Wagner's music before I had heard a strain of
> it, and when a lad of nine I for the first time had its glorious harmonies burst upon
> me, I exclaimed: "This is my music. This is the realization of my dream."[50]

To many New York reporters, Duss was a millionaire musical oddity
from the backwoods of Pennsylvania about whom they could write amusing,
tongue-in-cheek articles which entertained their readers. To others, spe-

cifically to a New York correspondent for the *Pittsburgh Dispatch*, he was arrogant and obnoxious:

Bandmaster Duss and Gotham Critics

It seems that the spectacular Mr. Duss from Economy is taking himself too seriously. Good-natured New York goes to listen to his concerts in an old skating rink, and enjoys the music to the accompaniment of the opening of beer barrels and the shrill solicitations of Mr. Duss' flower girls to buy a "buttonin." The New York papers treated the new bandmaster extremely liberally, taking him on his face value, which he generously displays on the street corners in flaring colors and supported by an army of adjectives that would have brought the flush of envy to the cheek of a circus agent. . . . My dear Mr. Duss, in New York, you are not judged from the standpoint of high art. No beer garden entertainment is.[51]

Duss slowly became sensitive to this criticism, but his attempts to raise the level of his entertainment seemed doomed. Eugenia Mantelli, an Italian opera singer, cancelled her contract with him to join the Mascagni Italian Grand Opera Company. The managers of the opera company reportedly refused to hire her if she sang for Duss. The *New York Daily American* of 23 July 1902, carried the headline: "Mantelli Wouldn't Sing In Beer Garden." But the final blow came in a review of the band's last concert given at the Metropolitan Opera House after the fall tour of major cities in New York, Pennsylvania, Massachusetts, Maryland, and New Jersey. A critic for The *New York World* wrote in the 27 October issue:

Duss Lets Us Have a Real Good Look
Economite Bandmaster Far Overshadows Band
And He's Always in The Limelight

Ego was the chief characteristic of the Duss concert at the Metropolitan Opera House last night. First was this silently manifest in the lettered legend "Duss" which bespoke the simple vanity of the man, from the top of a rack of metal strips which served the purpose of church chimes.

Presently Duss began to exhibit himself. He came forward most consciously, then proceeded to direct with an evident desire to attract the attention of the audience to himself. To this end he indulged in various tricks which it might not be too severe to call "faky."

One thing he seemed to dearly love to do was to face the audience with his back to his band and manipulate his baton in a way to suggest the drum major.

When a horseshoe of flowers was ostentatiously handed over the footlights to him he squirmed and smiled and cast his eyes in a "Oh,-how-could-you-be-so-kind?" sort of way which reminded the spectator of an old maid receiving an unexpected proposal.

Later on he made a little speech to the audience with a few home-made gestures and two or three below-the-belt punches at the Queen's English. He was attempting to say that one of his singers had failed to put in appearance and to beg that her absence be condoned.

In this connection he took occasion to add that his other "lady singer," who had just sung, was not feeling very well herself; in fact, "she was hardly able to stand up!"

When the cornet soloist took a long blow at his horn, Duss pulled his watch to "time" the player on the Hold-Her Bill! note.

Throughout the evening Mr. Duss seemed bent on showing how capricious and amusing he could be.

The critic was so thoroughly incensed by Duss that the band's last efforts went unnoticed. At this point it isn't likely that Duss cared. In Boston during the recent tour he had received word that the United States Supreme Court had heard the famous case, *Schwarz et al.* v. *the Harmony Society*. This legal suit was now ten years old and had been brought against Duss and the Society by former members and their descendants who maintained that they were also legal heirs to the Society's assets. The Supreme Court filed against the plaintiffs. Duss and the few remaining members were now the uncontested heirs to the Harmonist millions. Duss dismissed his musicians and returned triumphantly to Economy.

DUSS' MOMENT WITH THE MET: "VENICE IN NEW YORK"

Back at Economy, Duss may have taken account of the losses he sustained in New York during the 1902 season. He denied that they exceeded $50,000, although he confided to a New York reporter: "I found the bill of fare expensive . . . to play here last year. . . . I have no regrets and no grudges against the stay-away audiences of my first season here, and it is not the memory of last year's business that causes me to writhe. . . ."[52]

Despite the losses (and they must have been very high) Duss and Johnston had already begun to plan for the 1903 season during the summer of 1902. In August an article appeared in a New York paper in which Johnston was quoted as saying that he (with Duss' money?) had obtained a lease on the Circle Auditorium which he would rebuild in which to present the finest plays and concerts.

> After the expiration of our present contract Mr. Duss will disband the Duss Band. He will return to Pittsburg [*sic*] to take up his business cares. But Duss will not be lost to the New York public. There will be a Duss symphony orchestra concert every Sunday night at the new theatre. In short, Mr. Duss will step out of the realm of a band leader into the higher and more exalted position of an orchestra leader. . . . Duss will leave Pittsburgh in a special car every Saturday night for New York for the Sunday orchestral concert, returning by the same manner after the close of the same.[53]

Another article in the *Daily America* of 14 August 1902, entitled "Duss threatens to Build a Theatre" supported Johnston's announcement, although the site for the construction of the proposed "Temple of Art," as Duss referred to it, was not given.

Duss clearly had no intention of retiring after one season in New York. Receipts and bills at Economy indicate that in November he was buying new music and clearing out the old music library. About this time he received a letter from an inmate at San Quentin requesting music to "keep their band going." Duss wrote on the letter: "Mailed him 11 discarded pieces—Dec. 3, 1902." Earlier in the year he had purchased the famed Innes Band library, reportedly valued at $40,000, and putting this material in order undoubtedly occupied much of his time during the winter months at Economy.

How Duss intended to use the Innes Band library is not clear. Perhaps he was seriously considering building his "Temple of Art" in which he could present concerts the year round and become recognized as more than a summertime bandmaster. There are no clues to suggest just when he drafted his plans for the following season but an event which must have influenced him was the announcement that Maurice Grau (1849-1907), the manager and director of the New York Metropolitan House since 1893, was to retire after the 1902-03 opera season. This meant that the Metropolitan's board of directors would decide upon a new manager early in the new year.

To comprehend the significance of this event and its subsequent effect upon Duss one must know the state of the Opera House orchestra as well as the Philharmonic society at the turn of the century. The Met's early life was plagued by financial and performance difficulties. Reviews of productions during the late 1880s and 1890s often contained passages such as "the instrumentalists made a sad mess of the orchestral score," and "a dazzling feat of vocalization [ended] to the discordant scrapings of a half dozen fiddlers."[54] The Metropolitan debut of Lillian Nordica (1857-1914), who later became closely associated with John Duss, was made in *Les Huguenots*, 18 December 1891. Her singing was well received, but a viola obbligato was one of the "most discomforting performances ever heard in the Opera House."[55]

In addition to performance difficulties, selecting a repertory within the performers' capabilities which was acceptable to American audiences was a continual problem. In 1895-96, Grau solved this problem for a time by emphasizing German opera, a move which was received with approval by the large German population then living in New York. Nordica, for one, rose to fame in the operas of Wagner and the repertory became somewhat solidified and gradually expanded during Grau's tenure. Even as late as 1901-02, however, the instrumentalists were having difficulty and during a performance of *Das Rheingold* the orchestra reportedly "warbled through the score in uncertain fashion."[56]

The Philharmonic orchestra had known some comfortable days but at this time it was no better than the orchestra at the Met. Under the excellent leadership of Theodore Thomas and Anton Seidl it had enjoyed vigorous growth and public support for almost two decades, reaching its zenith under Seidl, who died in 1898. In the next four years under Emil Paur, interest in the orchestra waned and in 1903, after one year as conductor, Walter Damrosch initiated a visiting conductor system. During this time the musicians were paid through a profit sharing plan in which they divided among themselves the gains and losses realized at the concerts. It was an unsatisfactory system and the players felt considerable financial insecurity during the several years in which the plan was in operation.

All of these circumstances affected the Met and had to be considered by those who were to select Maurice Grau's successor. In addition, the Opera House was sustained largely by an elite group of patrons and backers who expected to have their tastes catered to and who wanted to be granted the social recognition of the best boxes for their support. Factions developed among some of the patrons who had favorite candidates to suggest for Grau's replacement.

At the time of the announcement of Maurice Grau's retirement, John Duss had never directed, staged, or been particularly close to the production of an opera. His most intimate association with the form had been as the conductor of the overtures and medleys which his bands had played in transcriptions. Duss, nevertheless, came to feel that he was the man for the Metropolitan. In light of subsequent developments, it is interesting to conjecture how he reached this decision and more importantly, how he hoped to convince the Metropolitan board that he was the best of the long line of contenders for the position. Did Johnston suggest to him that in 1903 he might be able to hire the Met orchestra and thereby be in a position to bargain for the Opera House directorship?[57] Perhaps Duss himself concluded that this was a fateful point in his career and if he acquired the orchestra's support he might influence the Met board, or, if not that, be offered the position of permanent conductor of the Philharmonic society. In preparation for any eventuality he determined that during the coming season he would demonstrate that he was a power to be reckoned with in the world of orchestral music; that he could direct and manage opera singers; and that he knew something about sophisticated staging.

He began by hiring the entire Metropolitan Opera House orchestra for the 1903 season. Beyond this, two leading opera stars, Lillian Nordica and Edouard de Reszke, were contracted to sing a given number of performances. The season was to be divided into the usual sections: an early tour, a summer series, and a closing tour. Nordica and de Reszke were contracted for the tours and the first summer concert only, but Nahan Franko, the concert master (see plate 18), and the orchestra were employed by Duss for most of the six months extending from May to November.

The financial investment for 1903 was to be the largest of Duss' career. There were some sixty members in the orchestra and, although orchestra musicians were rarely paid more than fifty dollars per week, their payroll for approximately twenty-four weeks must have exceeded $70,000. Nahan Franko, in addition to being concertmaster, served as soloist and assistant conductor and would have to have been paid commensurately. Edouard de Reszke, the noted basso, and Lillian Nordica, one of the most versatile singers of her time, were both well established in their careers and were in the position to demand premium fees—Nordica was paid $1,500 (at least for the fall tour) and de Reszke $1,000 each performance. These fees, in addition to transportation costs and the rental and decoration costs for the building used for the summer concerts were to put the total figure in the hundreds of thousands of dollars. Did Duss plan all this to make a favorable impression upon the Met board? If so, it was a high stake to gamble and he must have eagerly awaited their decision. It came 13 February 1903: Heinrich Conried (1848-1909), for years a leading figure in the New York theatre world, was granted the directorship of the Opera House. He had won over his closest contender, Walter Damrosch, by one vote. Duss had never been given serious consideration.[58]

If Duss was disappointed, he did not show it and while the Met's board of directors had not taken him seriously, Conried, the new manager, apparently did. He agreed, through Johnston, to permit Duss to conduct sixteen Sunday night concerts in the Opera House during the 1903-04 opera season, an agreement he would later regret. The prospects for the 1903 season looked good for Duss and he now set out to accumulate the money to carry out these plans.

> For the continuance of my musical career, negotiations had been carried on as to the summer season of concerts at Madison Square Garden, New York. Toward the enterprise I had already entered into a written agreement with the other members of the Society permitting me to borrow five, ten, fifteen, or twenty thousand dollars (according to my need). . . .[59]

In New York, Johnston was getting off to a bad start. To promote the spring tour, he had cards printed showing himself pushing a wheelbarrow in which de Reszke, Nordica, Duss, and Nahan Franko were seated. Below the caricature was printed: "I push my business." De Reszke and Nordica threatened to cancel the tour if the cards were not destroyed. Johnston withdrew them but the disagreement was publicized in the papers and relations between the Duss-Johnston team and Nordica and de Reszke became strained. The tour, nevertheless, was carried out as scheduled and consisted of no less than forty-one concerts which were given in thirty major cities in the United States and Canada. A business staff of seven, along with the performers required the use of a sixty foot baggage car, two Pullman sleeping cars, one private car for night travel, and two additional regular coaches for day travel. The services of two hotels were also required for each day of the tour.

The first concert of the tour was given Wednesday evening, 29 April at the armory in Scranton, Pennsylvania. Duss did not wait for the audience to acclaim him among the great conductors. In an expensive souvenir program printed for the occasion, he declared himself equal to the best.

> John S. Duss has gained in one season that which many conductors have striven for years to attain—fame, success, and serious recognition in the musical world. . . . Duss has . . . a thorough knowledge of music, temperament, authority, accuracy of conception, magnetism and grace. . . . His genius is unquestioned; his ambition unbounded. He has become a factor in the musical world and is there to stay. Duss is the conductor of the century.
>
> The orchestra of the Metropolitan Opera House, of New York, is one of the most evenly balanced instrumental bodies in the world. Some years ago, when Anton Seidl was at its head, he insisted upon improvement in the brasses, and as a result the orchestra became famous for the richness and sonority of its horns and tubas. Later Emil Paur overhauled the woodwinds and more recently still Signor Mancinelli, with his Italian love for the beautiful in music, improved the strings. And now comes Duss, who readjusts each department, balancing the one with the others, weeding out here, adding there, and, with his keen musical insight, strengthening the entire body and making of it a rounded and perfectly balanced orchestra. . . . There are no orchestral players in the world who receive the salaries that are paid its members.

The last sentence above was intended more for the musicians than for the audience and it was repeated often in subsequent programs. If the musicians did not take Duss seriously as a conductor, and there is ample proof that violinist Franko's nod was watched more closely than Duss' baton, they did so as an employer, and even the best of them—Lillian Nordica included—did not criticize him to members of the press. There was an understanding on the matter between Duss and his musicians and it was clearly demonstrated early in the tour. The tenth and eleventh concerts of the series were played 7 May in the Agricultural Building in Atlanta, Georgia. To celebrate the occasion, members of Atlanta's society gave a reception for the performers, for Lillian Nordica and Eduard de Reszke in particular. Many people came to meet the famous diva and basso but neither appeared or bothered to explain why. The reason was that Director Duss had not been invited. Duss' shortcomings notwithstanding, his musicians observed their professional ethics more closely than Atlanta did its social etiquette.

Five days later, 12 May, Duss was conducting the orchestra at Convention Hall in Kansas City, Missouri. On the same day a curious meeting took place at Economy. Susie Duss called together the remaining three members of the Harmony Society (in addition to herself and John Duss). In the presence of attorneys and secretary K. R. Wagner, a document was read which contained the following:

> The undersigned member of the Harmony Society submits herewith his wish to withdraw from the membership in the Harmony Society herewith declaring that it

is his wish and intention to move away from Economy, and to receive a present from the Trustee of the Society, according to the custom of the Society. Economy, Pa., May 12, 1903.

John S. Duss

The "present" given to Duss consisted of 500 bonds, valued at $1,000 each. The move was another step toward complete dissolution of the Society which would leave Susie Duss the final heir to its wealth. Duss, in effect, was getting an enormous severance gift and would later share in all that was left to his wife, as well. It was a clever maneuver, but why was he doing it at this particular time? The most obvious reason seems to be that he needed money to complete the decorating of his summer concert hall—Madison Square Garden—where he planned to demonstrate to the world his spectacular gift for dramatic staging.[60]

Duss and his troupe completed their tour on May 29 with a concert at the armory in Hartford, Connecticut. They then returned to New York City and rested on May 30. On Sunday evening May 31, the summer season at Madison Square Garden opened with a concert which featured Duss and the Metropolitan orchestra, Edouard de Reszke and Lillian Nordica, and a chorus of 1,000 voices. Equally spectacular was the setting in which the concert was given. Through the use of elaborate props and staging effects, Duss transformed Madison Square Garden into a reproduction of the city of Venice!

> With an island "stage" for the orchestra, and a huge Venetian backdrop, I proposed to encircle the island with a canal, span it with bridges and float a number of gondolas manned by real Venetian boatmen. . . . Arthur Voegtlin painted the immense drop at the end of the garden . . . settings of the Doges Palace, Desdemona's House, and St. Mark's Cathedral were built, some to original size. Spanning the canal was a facsimile of the Ponte de Rialto . . . Tiffany Studios . . . loaned us $40,000 worth of decorative marble, sculpture, and fountains. A blue bunting sky with suspended electric stars and moving clouds produced cinematographically, added to the setting. . . .[61]

The cost of this set was estimated at from $75,000 to $100,000. A review of the concert appeared in the *New York Herald* of June 1.

> Mme. Nordica was the heroine of the opening of Mr. J. S. Duss' "Venice in New York" at Madison Square Garden last night. She made her entrance in a startlingly dramatic fashion in a gondola and after a superb rendition of the "Inflammatus" from Rossini's "Stabat Mater" thrilled the thousand auditors in the Garden by singing as an encore "The Star Spangled Banner." As the first notes of the national anthem rang out clear and true the great audience rose to its feet and joined with the trained voices of the Metropolitan Opera House chorus in the chorus of the song. At its conclusion the enthusiasm was intensified when Mme. Nordica made her exit through the Canal on a gondola. Her admirers on "The Island" and

in the audience cheered as she stepped from the boat and disappeared behind the scenes. De Reszke entered over the "Bridge of Sighs." It was a great night for Mr. J. S. Duss, the bandmaster from Economy, Pa. . . . . The Metropolitan Opera chorus gave a superb rendition of Handel's "Hallelujah Chorus" from the "Messiah" and other numbers on the programme were handled as only the Metropolitan Opera orchestra can handle them. At the end of the programme the audience joined enthusiastically with Mr. Duss in singing "America." . . . . Tonight the Metropolitan Orchestra will play, Mr. Duss will conduct, Mme. Maconda will sing, Mr. Franko will give a violin solo, and refreshments will be sold to those who wish them. Venice will then become Coney transferred to Manhattan.

After the opening night, however, the atmosphere changed and some concertgoers were puzzled as to the kind of entertainment offered.

New York is taking kindly to its Venice. Although the weather has been cool the crowds have been large. Some come in negligee and some come in evening dress. The reason of this is that New York hasn't solved the puzzle as to just what sort of entertainment it is stacking up against.

There are Italian trinkets for sale, and you can rap a round table with a cane and holler, "Hi, waiter, bring us four beers!" This makes it unconventional and roof gardeny. On the other hand, there is Max Hirsch and his bunch of grand-opera song birds and Nathan Franko and the rest of the Metropolitan Opera House Orchestra, and this means evening dress. So those who think most of rapping the tables and calling, "Hi, waiter!" come in blue serge and straw hats and Donegal homespuns and Panamas, while those who want to hear Maconda sing attend in low neck vests and opera hats.[62]

Some critics were less than amused by Duss' efforts. One in particular, F. N. R. Martinez, wrote a criticism of "Venice" which was remarkably incisive and got closer to what was motivating Duss than he knew. The title of the article was "P. T. Barnum's Mantle Falls on Leader Duss."

It is a mistake to suppose that Duss is an originator of the bold and undignified manner in which he advertises his musical stars and exploits their personalities. Many of those who view with astonishment the proceedings at the Madison Square last Sunday evening—the processional exit of Eduard de Reszke through the audience bowing to right and left like a conquering hero on his home-coming; the slow progress of Lillian Nordica in her gondola along the mimic canal, sitting in state, with tiara on head and blazing with diamonds like Cleopatra in her barge, or Louise Montague, of Forepaugh fame, on her triumphal chariot—were inclined to think that such things were never known before.

Old P. T. Barnum was the founder and promoter of this school of advertising. He has had imitators by the score, but no one ever equalled him in audacity and indifference to good taste.

Martinez then discussed Barnum's exploitation of Jenny Lind and the tricks of others such as Henri Herz, the pianist who at a concert in New Orleans presented a piece arranged for 114 hands to be played on nine pianos, and the "capers" of the violinist Ole Bull. But in the last paragraphs Martinez mentions the one figure who most influenced Duss from the time he picked up his first cornet, Patrick S. Gilmore (1829-1892).

> Jullien, the French conductor who came here in the early fifties was the originator of the monster band. But it was Gilmore who developed this idea to its limits. His musical jubilees, commencing with the one in Boston in 1876, were artistic absurdities, with their gerried ranks of trumpets and trombones, their aggregations of drums and tympani, their mobs of brawny red-shirted blacksmiths pounding on anvils, and their batteries of artillery accentuating with cannon-roars the strains of the National Anthem. . . . This year the man of the hour is Duss. He made Nordica and Edouard de Reszke step down from their pedestals and mingle with the many. He "Barnumized" two famous singers and made them do things that no other manager thought of. And he has done it in a way that marks him as an able disciple of the famous old showman. . . . Meanwhile he leads his band with a baton that is both complacent and complaisant, he sprints through a march and dawdles through a waltz, he reads scores in a way that indicates that all composers sound alike to him from Richard Wagner to A. Baldwin Sloane.[63]

Nordica and de Reszke sailed for Europe soon after the opening concert and lesser-known soloists took their places. Johnston, in the meantime, continued to bolster attendance through advertising stunts. One evening, as the story appeared in the newspapers, during the performance of Saint-Saëns' *Danse Macabre*, a young and lonesome Iowa girl was overcome by the music while riding in one of the gondolas. She fell headlong overboard into the canal. A gallant gentleman in full dress plunged to her rescue. The water was, in fact, only three feet deep and, in Duss' own words, "the stunt was engineered for fifty dollars by our efficacious press agent."[64]

In the newspapers, Duss became the frequent subject of caricatures and cartoons as more critics attacked his unorthodox conducting methods. The *Broadway Weekly* headlined an article with "Is Duss a Musician?" and asked some probing questions: "Is Mr. Duss a great musician because he happens to have a few millions of dollars at his disposal? Does the fact that he can lead his band with his back turned make him a great leader or platform buffoon? . . . we leave it to *Broadway Weekly* readers . . . who are . . . able to judge the qualities of a musician and differentiate him from the mere gallery-god."[65]

As the summer wore on, Duss' personality began to irritate even Johnston. One day, according to one of Johnston's secretaries, Duss came into the office in his usual voluble state. Johnston complained of the noise but Duss replied, "Why shouldn't I make all the noise I want to? I pay all the salaries." Their relationship cooled and, although they apparently completed the business they had mutually contracted, the partnership was dissolved soon after the close of the summer season at "Venice." As late as 1907, however, lawsuits were being filed against the two for materials used by them—but not paid for—when they were partners.[66]

The fall tour which followed the concerts at "Venice in New York" was arranged, not by Johnston, but by Loudon G. Charlton, a New York impressario who set out to create a more dignified, scholarly image of Duss. The tour took Duss, Lillian Nordica, and the orchestra to Indianapolis, Omaha, Denver, Salt Lake City, Tacoma, Seattle, Portland, Sacramento, San Francisco, Dallas, Galveston, Little Rock, and Washington, D.C. The tour also included a concert at the Lyceum Theatre in Beaver Falls, Pa., 9 November 1903 giving Duss the opportunity to conduct the Met orchestra in a concert very close to Economy.

Behind him, as well as ahead of him, however, was trouble in New York. To begin with, Duss had gone on tour without Edouard de Reszke who he said had not pleased the audiences on the spring tour. On this point, Duss may have been right, but Duss had hired him and de Reszke was suing him for breach of contract for $20,000 maintaining that Duss had promised him no less than twenty performances at $1,000 each. Johnston was named as a codefendant in the suit because he had been Duss' manager when the contract was signed. It was the one unpleasant relationship in de Reszke's extremely productive career, and it was further complicated by the fact that Lillian Nordica and he shared many historic moments at the Met, some of which had lasting influence upon the subsequent production of opera in America and in Europe. The case stirred up much controversy in New York and, considering his past career and the esteem in which de Reszke was held, it is not difficult to understand why.

The two Polish brothers Edouard de Reszke (1853-1917) and Jean (1850-1925), the noted tenor made their Met debuts in *Romeo et Juliette* during the 1891-92 season. It was the first time French was sung at the Met. In this production, Jean, who was probably the more outstanding of the two both as an actor and singer, was described as having sung agreeably but not possessing a "surprising organ." Edouard was acclaimed "a really great artist." Both devoted all their energies to opera, being diligent students of languages, particularly French and German. Jean became especially famous for his portrayal of Faust and Edouard for that of Mephistopheles.[67] During Grau's emphasis upon German opera beginning in the 1895-96 season, the de Reszkes joined with Lillian Nordica and rose to great fame in the roles of Tristan (Jean), Isolde (Nordica) and König Marke (Edouard). Edouard was called "stupendous" and Jean was paid the high compliment of "demonstrating that Wagner could be sung," no small achievement because there were many in America and in Europe who were convinced that it could not be.[68]

In 1903 Jean retired to Nice to teaching; he died in 1925. He had actually retired in 1901, refusing to sing rather than do it poorly, after he realized he was losing his vocal skill. Edouard was not as wise. He continued to sing after his breathing became labored and after Jean stopped singing in 1901, he was prone to laxity. In 1903, before signing with Duss, he had sung in *Tristan* in Chicago. It must have pained the critics to write, "The second act would have surpassed the first but for the very bad singing of Edouard de Reszke as König Marke. His phrasing was fragmentary, his intonation uncertain, his German often not to be understood."[69] He had actually sung his last full opera in New York on 31 March 1903. It is unfortunate that he signed with Duss and thereby made his final engagement in America such a dissatisfying and distasteful one.

While legal action awaited Duss in New York, bad publicity and unfavorable reviews trailed behind him. His speeches were again criticized; and the musicians were said to direct themselves, often rushing ahead of him on climaxes or coming in behind his beat. His whirling of the baton was found to be disconcerting and bewildering, and he was said to lack scholarship, having programmed too much popular music for an orchestral concert. Duss himself related some of the more embarrassing moments of the tour but blamed them on the musicians.

> At the matinee at Stanford University, Nahan Franko, gaping at an acquaintance in the audience during a critical moment in an involved Richard Strauss number, led the whole first violin section astray. . . .[70]

The next concert opened with Berlioz' *Roman Carnival Overture*, which Duss described:

> After a few vigorous opening measures comes a grand dramatic pause—and in this moment of tension, one of our trombonists, without rime or reason, gave forth a tremendous blast. This naturally upset the temperament of the others . . . the English Horn player missed his cue in the solo that follows. I sang frantically to bring the orchestra to a harmonious finish . . . at intermission I discovered that the boys . . . had paid visits to the Poodle Dog Inn and other such rendezvous of liquid refreshment. . . .[71]

The one consistently favorable response to Duss' concerts was the great acclaim for Lillian Nordica. Audiences universally loved her, although probably few knew that she was American, not European as her stage name suggested. Born Lillian Norton in Farmington, Maine, 12 December 1857, she achieved the most glamorous career of any singer of her time, having sung extensively in Europe and England before her Met debut. Like the de Reszke brothers, she was one of the first to demonstrate that opera singers had to develop versatility in languages if companies such as the Met were to acquire international repertories. Nordica achieved her greatest successes with the de Reszkes in Grau's productions of *Tristan*, but by 1903, although still in full command of her voice, she was approaching the twilight of her career. She sang her last Isolde at the Met in 1909, and then suffered a nervous breakdown. She did not sing again until 1913 when she attempted a world tour which she failed to complete, dying in Java, 10 May 1914, at the age of fifty-seven.[72]

Although providing an artistic treat for audiences, Duss' tours were of questionable value to Nordica's career. Considering her stature and Duss's reputation, it was at best a condescension on her part, although the salary he paid her exceeded what she was paid at the Met. But Lillian Nordica had an unusual background. Her career began as soloist with Patrick S. Gilmore's band with which she toured the United States, England, Ireland, and Western Europe. Because Gilmore was Duss' idol, this may have provided a bond even though they were miles apart artistically. Nordica was also impulsive. She had three bad marriages and wasted money on ill-conceived projects. But she had an especially unusual idea which may have found a sympathetic ear in Duss. Having studied with Cosima Wagner and taken part in the first *Lohengrin* at Bayreuth, she conceived the plan of founding a "Bayreuth-on-the-Hudson."[73] Did she see the possibility of the fulfillment of this dream in Duss' "Temple of Art?" If so, she must have soon believed that such a venture with him would be an artistic and financial disaster. After this tour, she was to sing only once more under Duss.

Back in New York Duss discovered that the opportunity which he had awaited with the greatest anticipation—the sixteen Sunday night concerts which he had gotten Conried to allow him at the Met—were to be cancelled. In his anxiety over his first opera season, (he was producing the first American performance of *Parsifal* against the wishes of Wagner's heirs who were suing him) Conried said he had imported too many foreign conductors and was forced to use them on the evening concerts originally reserved for Duss. Robert Johnston, who had been Duss' agent when the contract was made, sued Conried, but Conried would not honor the agreement and Duss did not conduct at the Met in 1903 or at any time thereafter.

Duss's most extravagant year was coming to a close. "Venice" and the western tour reportedly produced receipts of $20,000 but the expenditures reached $180,000.[74] Edouard de Reszke's suit would eventually cost $10,000 more. Duss was discovering that buying fame in the world of music could be very costly, but he had not yet learned that respect had to be earned.

THE LAST "VENICE" AND THE END OF DUSS' CAREER

Having resigned his membership in the Society, Duss now maintained an office in Carnegie Hall in New York City. From here he made plans for the 1904 season while Loudon Charlton, his new agent, set out to reshape the public image of conductor Duss. His picture was placed on the cover of an April issue of the *Musical Courier* and an accompanying article announced that the first concert of the season would be given 22 May at Madison Square Garden.

After praising Duss' "great ability as a musician and orchestral conductor," and "the noble educational work in which for several years he had been engaged," the writer of the article becomes defensive.

> With a devotion unparalleled, a sublime disregard of ignoble opposition and a magnanimous indifference to the stupid, oft times ill-mannered criticism of those who were either inadequately informed or basely influenced by rival conductors, Mr. Duss has faithfully and loyally tried to meet his responsibilities and carry out his mission, with the general result that his series of orchestral concerts have become historic for their supreme excellence, and the specific result that thousands upon thousands of music lovers have become broader, better and more enlightened in the truest phases of their nature for having enjoyed those opportunities in the direction of lofty musical cultivation afforded by Mr. Duss and his earnest coadjutors.

The tone of this advertisement is more sophisticated than Johnston's and, while it states that "the present Duss Symphony Orchestra is practically the same body of instrumentalists with which he has been identified since coming to New York," at no point is the name of the Metropolitan Opera House orchestra used.

In the 4 June issue of the *Evening Mail Illustrated*, however, a short article placed below a picture of Duss states:

> Good music, with cool and picturesque surroundings, makes very pleasant summer night entertainment, and that is what may be found in the representation of "Venice" at Madison Square Garden, where Mr. Duss is again conducting the Metropolitan Opera House Orchestra through a series of summer concerts. The picturesque arrangement of the Garden's interior is the same as last year, with the soft lights, the changing panoramic clouds, the canal and gondolas, and the addition of a glass sounding board has greatly improved the acoustic properties.

Sometime between the two dates, Duss received permission to use the Met orchestra. He had settled his dispute with Edouard de Reszke by giving him ten of the $1,000 bonds which he had received as a "present" when he resigned from the Harmony Society. The suit against Conried for breach of contract was not mentioned again and the opening night at Madison Square Garden featured Nordica, de Reszke, Nahan Franko and the Met orchestra in an all-Wagner program. The circumstances suggest that the program was the result of a compromise.

Apparently there was no spring tour in 1904, although for this season "Venice" was enlarged. The canal was made ten feet wider and many gondolas were added to the fleet. The opening program included performances by Lillian Nordica, Edouard de Reszke, and Nahan Franko. But after the opening night only Franko continued with Duss to the last concert, played on 31 July. It was Duss' shortest season in New York and some reviews indicate that interest in "Venice" and in Duss' programs decreased.

Loudon Charlton's publicity was not as dramatic as Johnston's. "Venice" (1904) was now portrayed as a place where lovers could hear their favorite songs and where broken marriages could be mended. The headline of one newspaper article reads: "Reconciliation Set to Music," "Duss and His Band, With Proper Stage Setting, Turn The Trick. Boston Couple Are Reunited." The article states that Duss had received a letter, written at the Waldorf by a Mrs. Alliston Browning, telling him that she and her husband, after being divorced, were reunited during a program at "Venice." They had separated ten years earlier because Mr. Browning had begun flirting with another woman in the audience of a Boston theatre where they had gone to hear a concert by Patrick S. Gilmore's band.[75] In Mrs. Browning's words, according to Duss, the reconciliation took place as follows:

> She was in the audience at the Garden yesterday, listening to the music and gazing pensively into the waters of the Grand Canal. Down the watery Pike came a gondola, and in the prow sat a man. He looked up, and his eyes met the eyes of Mrs. Browning. There was a flash of recognition. He waved a hand, she shook her handkerchief.

"In one minute and thirty seconds, the time it would take the man in the gondola to come ashore and make his way to the place where Mrs. Alliston Browning was sitting," says Duss, "the couple were together again. They made it all up after those ten years and had been married again and were going back to Boston to live happily ever afterward."[76]

The story provided some relief from the usual "Duss does everything" theme which had characterized much of the earlier publicity, but it seems more than coincidental that the couple, divided during a concert given by Patrick S. Gilmore and his band, should be reunited to the music of Duss, his successor and ardent admirer. At best, the story had a chronological flaw: if the couple had separated ten years earlier, the year would have been 1894, and by that time Gilmore had been dead for two years.

Duss also periodically conducted "request nights" which acquired a degree of popularity. One request letter, undated and written by an anonymous Pittsburgher, responded to one of Duss' own pieces:

Dear Sir,
    There are two requests that I wish to make: the first that you play the "Mar-

saileise" [sic] . . . the second . . . that you have the good taste to leave "America Up To Date" off your program.[77]

Despite these efforts, Duss' "Venice" lost its appeal and following the 31 July concert it was dismantled. Duss then finished the season by taking the orchestra to the Casino theatre where they played during the first week of August.

Duss did not conduct the Metropolitan Opera orchestra in 1905. Nahan Franko[78] was promoted from concertmaster to conductor that year and Duss' 1904 concert series, which was shorter than those preceding, was his last association with the Met orchestra. Printed programs for the 1904 concerts show that Franko was then getting more publicity than he had previously. He played a solo on most concerts, and his name was placed directly below Duss' in the same size print. In addition, he conducted the orchestra at Madison Square Garden in performances of his own compositions: "Polka-Française," on 15 June and 13 July, and "Gavotta-L'Americaine" on 4 July. Franko's ascendancy to the conductor's position may have left Duss without an orchestra for the 1905 summer season, but it is more likely that Duss began to feel that because of his waning popularity it was time to bring his career in New York to a close.

Duss' musical activities were minimal in 1905. One brief article states that Duss, after conducting the Metropolitan Opera House orchestra for two seasons and two tours, was "now considering a number of offers both abroad and in this country for the coming season"[79] but apparently these "offers" did not materialize. However, with a band consisting partly of musicians from the Pittsburgh area, he made an extensive tour in 1906. It began with a single concert at the Hippodrome in New York City, 20 May. On this concert Duss used both string and wind instruments. The strings played Schumann's "Träumerei" and then the Prelude from *Lohengrin* for an encore. The soloist on the program was one Effie Stewart who sang an excerpt from *Tannhäuser*. The concert was distinguished by the presence in the audience of John Philip Sousa, who reportedly "listened with the greatest attention."[80]

The tour then took the band to Rome and Utica, New York; then to Canada where they played from 5 June through 15 June in Montreal. After this followed concerts at Syracuse, the Manhattan Beach Theatre, the Arcade at Asbury Park, the Casino—among other places—and then a jaunt through Ohio, Minnesota, Illinois, terminating with a three-day engagement at Lexington, Kentucky in mid-September. Whereas soloists with the Metropolitan Opera orchestra had been singers and violinists, they were now brass players such as P. C. Funaro, euphonium, and Bert Brown, cornet. (See plates 22 and 24).

In 1907 Duss once again saw himself exclusively as a bandmaster rather than an orchestra conductor, and he forcefully maintained that bands were superior to orchestras.

> Why, they talk of the flexibility of an orchestra, the tonal effects it can produce. I can do a thousand things with a brass band which not even the finest symphony orchestras can produce. And all, too, without noise. [Was Duss recalling the review of his first concert at the Met?]
>
> That's the trouble with an orchestra! When it gets to a climax, when power is wanted, when big effects must be had, they let out the drums and smash away with the brass and get nothing but a devil of a racket. You see the violinists scraping away like this, and the double basses like this and the men a-pounding on the drums and you think that it's music all right, but it is all in the seeing. Close your eyes and there'll be no music. Only a terrible din.[81]

These remarks were made at the beginning of the 1907 tour in Cleveland. The tour extended through the midwest, and concluded with a twelve-day engagement at the Toronto Exhibition, 27 August through 6 September, the last appearance of "Duss' Band." Shortly after this, Duss was reportedly struck by a falling water tank which he maintained crippled his right arm and, except for occasional commemorative concerts at Economy, his musical career ended.

For the remainder of his life, he lived in retirement, alternately residing with his wife in Florida and in the Great House at Economy. He devoted himself to writing his autobiography and composing religious pieces, including a *Mass in Honor of St. Veronica* (1929, orchestrated by Otto Merz); and a series of anthems. The latter include "O Sacred Book" (1929); "O Salutaris" (1929); and "Psalm of Psalms" (1934). All were published by Volkwein Bros. of Pittsburgh. Duss' last published piece, "Florida, All Hail," was printed by Volkwein's in 1935.

Susie Duss died in Florida in 1946 and her body was cremated. John S. Duss, probably the most colorful and certainly the most uncharacteristic of all the Harmonists, died in 1951 at the age of ninety-one. He was buried, according to Harmonist tradition, in an unmarked grave in the Harmonist cemetery in Ambridge, Pennsylvania, with the ashes of his wife in an urn at his feet.

1.   The Zoar Society, like the Harmony Society, was comprised of Separatists from Württemberg, and was established in Tuscarawas County, Ohio, in 1817. Their Articles of Association resemble those of the Harmonists, and there is reason to believe that the Zoar Leader, Joseph Bäumler (Bimmler), and his followers may have originally been followers of George Rapp. See E. O. Randall, *History of the Zoar Society* (Columbus, 1904), pp. 13-14.

2.   The name of John Rutz appears on a memorial marker on the battlefield at Gettysburg, Pa. The Harmonists remained pacifists in this as in other wars, but they generously contributed clothing, medicine, and money to the Union cause. There was great anxiety at Economy because the "great

wealth" of the Society was widely discussed, and the Harmonists feared that the Confederate raider, General Morgan, would attempt to steal the supposed fortune.

3. Duss, *op. cit.*, p. 176.

4. Ibid., p. 182.

5. Ibid., p. 187. Duss makes frequent references to the Great Western Band and says that Jacob Rohr was the director of this Pittsburgh organization. Rohr's obituary, which lists the positions he had held during his lifetime, makes no mention of it. A program played by this band is contained in the *Anna McDonald Scrapbook*, a collection of newspaper clippings and music programs filed in the Music Division, Carnegie Library, Pittsburgh, and lists the conductor as "Prof. Weis."

6. Ibid., p. 191. Matthew Arbuckle was a cornetist with Patrick Gilmore's Band.

7. Ibid., p. 194.

8. Ibid., pp. 199-200.

9. Ibid., p. 202.

10. Ibid., p. 208. Duss, in fact, was not as successful as he reported. His mother had pleaded with Henrici to permit him to return to Economy. There can be little doubt that she was anticipating some changes in the Society's government and wanted John there when these changes took place.

11. Ibid., p. 360.

12. Ibid., p. 282.

13. Ibid., pp. 282-83.

14. Ibid., p. 281.

15. Appendix D, IP 2.33 and KP 1.100.

16. Appendix D, IM 2.53 and VP 1.55.

17. Ibid., p. 364.

18. Ibid., p. 372.

19. Ibid.

20. Appendix D, VP 1.59.

21. The account folder for 3 June 1895, has a receipt of payment to the Noss family quartet. That of 20 July has a receipt of payment to George Leppig for "music rendered June 2, 1895." The 23 July accounts contain a receipt from Leppig for payment for "two men at a concert given in Pittsburgh, July 19." That of 3 June 1900, has the following written on a piece of cardboard: "30 musicians paid $158.00."

22. Appendix D, KP 1.99.

23. Appendix D, KM 1.28. Gus Mueller was a well-known cornetist and arranger who lived in Allegheny (northside, Pittsburgh) and did considerable arranging for the band under Duss. He frequently appeared as a cornet soloist for the Duss band and with the Greater Pittsburgh Band, then being directed by K. F. W. Guenther.

24. Appendix D, IP 4.14.

25. Appendix D, VP 1.57.

26. Appendix D, VP 1.60.

27. Appendix D, IM 4.5.

28. Duss, *op. cit.*, p. 373. Duss is in error. The piece was copyrighted in 1897 by W. C. Ott & Co., and therefore was not composed "for the occasion."

29. Ibid.

30. Ibid.

31. Appendix D, VM 3.14.

32. Appendix D, IM 4.3.

33. Appendix D, VP 1.54.

34. See letters for 9 May 1895; 13 and 27 December 1900; 10 January, 26 January, 8 February, and 11 February 1901.

35. Accounts, 20 November 1902.

36. Duss, *op. cit.*, p. 374.

37. Appendix D, KP 1.103.

38. Duss, *op. cit.*, p. 374.

39. *The Musical Courier* (New York), December 11, 1901.

40. Duss, *op. cit.*, p. 375.

41. Ibid.

42. From "Duss' Memoirs," manuscripts in the Economy Archives. Topic XVI, p. 469.

43. See "Advertising Bandmaster Duss" in *Printer's Ink*, (New York) 27 August 1902, pp. 14-15.

44. *Pittsburgh Dispatch*, 18 August 1902.

45. See "Magistrate Frees The Duss Bandmen," in the Duss file, Music Division, New York Public Library, 14 August 1902.

46. Duss file, Music Division, New York Public Library, 14 August 1902.

47. Arndt, *Rapp's Successors*, p. 376.

48. *Pittsburg Leader*, 28 October 1902. It is amusing to note that a photograph of the medal appeared alongside this rather detailed description but was printed upside down.

49. Ibid.

50. 13 June 1902.

51. 21 June 1902.

52. "Frivolous Woman Takes a Gondola Ride with Duss," Duss file, Music Division, New York Public Library.

53. "Duss' New Theatre Will be Unique," Duss file, Music Division, New York Public Library, 18 August 1902.

54. Irving Kolodin, *The Story of the Metropolitan Opera, 1883-1950* (New York: 1953), p. 90.

55. Ibid., p. 119.

56. Ibid., p. 170.

57. Quaintance Eaton, *The Miracle of the Met* (New York: 1968), p. 141.

58. Ibid., p. 141.

59. From a typed manuscript entitled "Duss' Memoirs" in the Archives at Economy. See page 464 of "Chapter 12." This is a draft of what was later published as *The Harmonists, A Personal History*. Also see the Minutes of the Harmony Society, 17 April 1903. A "written agreement" or receipt indicating what amount was borrowed or paid back has not been found.

60. For the full text of the document referred to, see Arndt, *Rapp's Successors*, pp. 301-02. Duss placed 400 bonds in a trust fund in the Beaver County Trust Company, 19 August 1903, presumably keeping $100,000 for his musical enterprises.

61. Duss, *op. cit.*, p. 380.

62. Duss file, Music Division, New York Public Library, n.d.

63. F. N. R. Martinez, "P. T. Barnum's Mantle Falls on Leader Duss." Duss file, Music Collection, New York Public Library, n.d.

64. Duss, *op. cit.*, p. 382.

65. Duss file, Music Collection, New York Public Library.

66. "Bandmaster Duss Defines an Angel," *New York Telegraph*, 9 November 1907.

67. Kolodin, *Op. Cit.*, p. 118.

68. Ibid., pp. 133-34.

69. Clara Leiser, *Jean de Reszke and the Great Day of Opera* (New York, 1934), pp. 242-43.

70. Duss, *op. cit.*, p. 384.

71. Ibid., p. 385.

72. Kolodin, *op. cit.*, p. 246.

73. Henry Pleasants, *The Great Singers* (New York: Simon & Schuster, 1966), p. 267.

74. " 'I'm a Musician by Profession', says John S. Duss," Duss file, New York Public Library. The figures were given to a reporter by Robert Johnston.

75. As noted earlier, Patrick S. Gilmore (1829-1892) ushered in the age of the musical spectacular in America in Boston, Massachusetts, on 15 June 1869, with a fantastic rendition of the "Anvil Chorus" from Verdi's *Il Trovatore*. Featured were 100 Boston firemen who smashed away on as many anvils; a chorus of 10,000 voices solicited from church choirs all across America; and a 1,000 piece

orchestra which included a bass drum twenty-five feet high. The occasion was the National Peace Jubilee, a late but enthusiastic commemoration of the ending of the Civil War. It is interesting to note that Gilmore died in 1892, shortly before Duss became senior trustee in the Harmony Society and took full control of the band at Economy.

76. Duss file, New York Public Library, 15 June, 1904.

77. From a letter found among Duss' programs and manuscripts. See Appendix D, TP.54.

78. Kolodin, *op. cit.*, p. 196, states that Franko was not an especially inspiring conductor and the most notable aspect of his conducting career was the fact that he was the first native-born American to conduct an opera at the Met. Franko was born in New Orleans in 1861 and had been a student of Joachim in Berlin. He died at Amityville, New York, in 1930.

79. "Mr. J. S. Duss," Duss file, New York Public Library.

80. "Duss and his Band at the Hippodrome," *Musical America*, 26 May 1906.

81. W. E. Sage, "The Passing Show," The *Cleveland Leader*, 22 May 1907.

EPILOGUE

The Harmonists were one of the last German communal groups to settle in America and, by the time of their arrival, most German musical traditions, which the earlier groups had transplanted and nurtured here, were declining. The music performed by these earlier settlers had been kept alive through the work of diligent copyists who preserved the works of European masters as well as those composed by their own membership. By the beginning of the nineteenth century, however, much of this music was being replaced by popular music which was coming off the presses of music houses in Philadelphia, Boston, and New York.

The Harmonists did arrive in time to catch the fading glow of the Seventh Day Baptists who established their cloister at Ephrata in 1732 and to benefit from the experiences of the Moravians who settled in Bethlehem in 1740. They also communicated with Ann Lee's Shakers who built their first communities in New York in 1774. Since considerable speculation exists over the musical influence exerted upon the Harmonists by these groups, it is important that the extent of that influence be discussed.

The Harmonists' contact with the Shakers began early, but was probably greatest during the trusteeship of Jacob Henrici when both societies were in decline. A union of the two was proposed by the Shakers in 1856, but the Harmonists declined the proposal. Whatever their doctrinal differences, music would hardly have supplied a common meeting ground for the two groups.

The Shakers did not approve of instrumental music and their singing consisted of rhythmic vocal sounds produced on a neutral syllable, the purpose of the music being to supply a sound to which they could dance or "shake." Edward D. Andrews, an authority on the music of this sect, quotes an early Shaker treatise on music as stating: "as our Society does not practice singing . . . with several parts moving together, it will be

unnecessary to take much further notice of this branch of music."[1] Andrews states that after 1870 part-writing became prevalent among the
Shakers, but that nearly all early Shaker "songs" were wordless.[2] The music of the Shakers, then, was a purely unison vocal one and bore little
or no resemblance to the music of the Harmonists.

There was little instrumental music among the Seventh Day Baptists
of Ephrata, Pennsylvania, and any comparison between their music and
that of the Harmonists must be confined to the area of vocal music. The
Ephrata chorale books and the *Paradiesisches Wunder-Spiel* consisted of choral
music which was written to be performed unaccompanied. Two features of
the music in these sources are also found in the music of the Harmonists.
Both have irregular phrases which often depart from fixed metre and are set
off by fermatas at terminating points in the text, and both make extensive
use of antiphonal singing. Even in these common features, however, the
techniques employed are not identical, and the differences in the music of
the two groups far outnumber the similarities.

Conrad Beissel, the founder of the Ephrata cloister, early discarded
traditional hymn and psalm tunes. He replaced them with four- to seven-
part choral music of his own composition, written according to a system of
harmony which he invented himself.[3] A large number of Harmonist hymns,
on the other hand, were sung to traditional chorale and well-known
German folk melodies. In addition, most Harmonist hymn singing was done
in unison, and the Harmonist pieces which were sung in parts, the odes,
were seldom written for more than three voices. The voice parts indicated in
the extant odes are usually soprano, alto, and bass. Tenor parts are seldom
given, and many bass parts appear to have been added for a second or third
performance. Few odes show any attempt at contrapuntal writing or at
achieving a purely choral style, as in the Ephrata music, and the Harmonist
pieces are greatly dependent upon their accompaniment for cohesiveness
and support.

Finally, a distinctive feature of the music of the Ephrata cloister which
set it apart from that of the Harmonists was the way in which it was sung.
A contemporary report which describes this singing style, also developed by
Beissel, is quoted below.

> The whole is sung in the falsetto voice, the singers scarcely opening their
> mouths or moving their lips, which throws the voice up to the ceiling, which is
> not high, and the tones, which seem to be more than human, at least so far
> from common church singing, appear to be entering from above and hovering
> over the heads of the assembly.[4]

This singing technique, along with the peculiar rules of harmony followed by Beissel in composing, made the music of Ephrata unique, and
there is no evidence to suggest that the Harmonists attempted to imitate it.

The Unitas Fratrum, or United Brotherhood of the Moravians, was founded in the latter half of the fifteenth century in what is now Czechoslovakia. The interest which the members of this group had in music was manifested as early as 1501 when they issued the first printed hymnal to appear in the vernacular. They were driven underground by the Counter Reformation, but emerged again in Germany during the early eighteenth century. When they came to Pennsylvania in the 1740s, they brought with them a highly developed musical tradition, apparent to this day, in the extensive collection of manuscript and printed music preserved in the Moravian Archives at Bethlehem, Pennsylvania, and Winston-Salem, North Carolina.

Among the Moravians were skilled performers and composers who, by the year 1820, had composed more than one thousand sacred works alone, most being anthems and cantatas for soloists and mixed chorus with accompaniments for various string and wind ensembles and organ or piano. They also produced considerable instrumental music, however, such as the six quintets by Johann Frederick Peter (1746-1813) which are probably the earliest examples of chamber music written in America. John Antes (1740-1811), who admired the music of Haydn and met him in England; Peter Wolle (1792-?), who compiled the first Moravian tune book published in America; and Christian Latrobe (1759-1836) who wrote several impressive piano sonatas, were three of the many skilled and prolific composers in this sect.

The extent of contact made between the Moravians and the Harmonists is not fully known, but there is little doubt that some of the Harmonists knew about and greatly admired the Moravians. When Lewis David von Schweinitz, the great-grandson of Count Zinzendorf, visited Economy in 1831, Dr. Mueller, to Schweinitz' surprise, greeted him by name. On another occasion, Frederick Rapp "read for more than an hour an account of the Moravians"[5] in lieu of a Sunday sermon. The "General Economy," the name given to the communitarian system of the Moravians, may even have influenced the selection of the name given to the Harmonists' third community—Economy.

Despite these apparently common bonds, comparing the music of these two groups is a questionable procedure. It is true that both had flourishing instrumental music programs, but while that of the Moravians was staffed with highly skilled players, the other was comprised of self-taught amateurs who occasionally had the benefit of additional instruction and inspiration from a visiting tutor or performer. Also, the instrumental music repertory of the Moravians consisted of pieces by masters of the late Baroque and early Classical periods, such as C. P. E. Bach, D. G. Turk, and J. B. Wanhall, while that of the Harmonists contained primarily arrangements of works by master composers and was comprised principally of short dances, marches, and popular songs. Duke Bernhard's assessment of Harmonist music—"The music was really not so good as we had heard in the preceding autumn at Bethlehem, but gave us much entertainment"[6]—can be accepted as a definitive appraisal of the music of both groups.

One further difference between the music of these two communities becomes apparent in the vocal and choral repertories. The texts used by the Moravians are generally selections from scripture or are biblical paraphrases, while those of the Harmonists are often about "Die Harmonie" and its sectarian peculiarities. The Moravians were vigorous evangelists, probably without equal, and their texts were intended to have as wide appeal as possible. The Harmonists, on the contrary, rarely proselytized, and even discouraged outsiders who became interested in membership in the Society, and their texts were intended for a closed, sectarian audience.

Harmonist music, then, bears little resemblance to the music of the Shakers, the Ephrata cloister, or the Moravians. Of the three, it comes closest to that of the Moravians, but the disparity in style and form makes comparison difficult and even pointless. Further, the music of the Moravians, because of its universality, lends itself to comparative evaluation. Much Harmonist music, like the music of the Shakers and the Ephrata cloister, is so sectarian that it can only be evaluated by determining how effectively it fulfilled the purpose for which it was written.

The purpose of most Harmonist instrumental music was to entertain the players and those of the membership who cared to listen to its performance. Since musical tastes leaned strongly toward popular music of the day, large quantities of sheet music were purchased from the music houses of James Hewitt of Boston and New York; and from those of George Willig, J. G. Klemm, G. E. Blake, and Bacon and Company of Philadelphia. The interest of the Harmonists in this kind of music is well expressed by the following passage from a letter written by a Miss Mary Graf of Philadelphia, to Gertrude Rapp, 22 October 1832:

I have selected by your Uncle's desire some music for you. I hope my taste may agree with yours. They are from the newest operas. The music from the opera of "La Muette de Portici" is particularly admired, some of which you will find in the number. Rossini's music is highly spoken of. You have two or three pieces and some of Auber's who is the most liked now in Paris. I hope the day may come when I may hear you play them. Our city is quite lively. The theatres are full every night. Mr. Kemble and his daughter Fanny, an interesting young lady of 18, is now performing. We saw her last night and were delighted. She is so pretty, graceful, lively, and modest one cannot fail in being pleased. Your Uncle and my papa have gone to see her this evening. I expect they will get a good squeezing before they secure a seat. The street before the theatre is crowded long before the doors are open and it is almost impossible to gain a seat.

The large quantity of music of this kind in the Harmonist repertory shows that Miss Graf's taste not only agreed with Gertrude's, but with Dr. Mueller's as well. Even the more ambitious arrangements and compositions by W. C. Peters are notable for their entertainment value rather than their profundity. Peters's *Symphony in D*, for example, is largely a symphony in name only. The first movement, "Andante," is little more than a waltz in three strains (ABA) with a rather unimaginative cadenza for the first violin inserted between sections two and three. There is no development of the themes. Interest is created by having different instruments alternately assigned to the tune and some variety is achieved by having the strings alternate arco and pizzicato. The second and final movement, "Rondo," (ABCADA) closes with a thoroughly predictable "Presto" and the whole is a naive, though entertaining, piece. Dynamic and phrase markings are given in most of Peters' arrangements and compositions, however, indications rarely found in the other manuscript pieces of the instrumental repertory.

Among the Harmonist vocal music, the odes are the most sectarian and have little or no program value today. They were, however, greatly appreciated by the Society because they expressed the communal sentiments which bound the membership together. Mueller's "Wem tönet heut" and "Seyd beglückt" have obvious musical limitations and clearly are the work of an amateur composer. Musically, they compare poorly with Peters' "O schöne Harmonie" which has balanced phrases, pleasing melodies, and comparatively superior voice movement and harmonic interest.

There is indication, however, that the Society preferred the Mueller pieces to the one by Peters. The latter is extant only in keyboard score and a single viola part, whereas the Mueller pieces appear in numerous voice parts and keyboard scores and appear to have had frequent performances. They may have been favored because they utilized various age groups, possibly the entire congregation (Magd., Knaben, tutti), while "O schöne Harmonie" was obviously conceived as a program piece, is closer to the traditional cantata, and divided its eleven-stanza text among solo voices, duets, and chorus.

The hymn repertory of the Society also contains many items which, because of their sectarian texts, are limited in usefulness. Others, such as Mueller's "Herr, führe Mich" and "Die Menschenlieb"; Frederick Rapp's "Freut euch ihr Kinder"; and Henrici's "Hilf Herr, ein neues Jahr bricht an," are simple but charming pieces which have a broad appeal. Henrici's settings of *Die Zehn Gebote, Das Unser Vater,* (the Ten Commandments and Our Father), and *Das Apostolisches Glaubens-Bekenntnis* (the

Apostles' Creed) (Economy: 1891) are pedantic works, but his manuscript accompaniment book (HM 2.29) shows him to have been a sensitive and imaginative arranger with a good understanding of the basic rules of harmony.

In addition to the preceding, there were large nonsectarian works performed at Economy during the late 1820s which must be noted here if the musical activity of the Harmonists is to be seen in proper perspective. Luigi Cherubini's *Der Frühling* (La Primavera), a demanding cantata for four solo voices, was performed at Economy in 1829. A series of cantatas by J. G. Schade, set for soli and mixed chorus with accompaniment for strings, clarinets, and horns, and comparable works by Handel, Graun, Mozart and others were also performed.

In the middle of the nineteenth century, as we have seen, there was relatively little musical productivity at Economy beyond Henrici's hymns and the instrumental pieces of Benjamin Feucht. More significant were the later arrangements of Jacob Rohr, the Alsatian-born bandmaster. The most extensive musical activity at Economy after 1832, however, took place under the leadership of John S. Duss.

To fairly evaluate Duss' music and his part in the last two decades of the life of the Harmony Society, certain influences outside the Society and beyond his control must be considered. The continuance of a communitarian way of life became difficult after the Civil War because the United States experienced a rise in national consciousness and moved from an agricultural to an industrial economy. Communication and transportation facilities expanded and former economic and social limitations were greatly reduced. Duss' marches certainly reflect these facts ("America Up to Date," etc.). In addition, compulsory public school education and the emergence of a predominantly English-speaking society made survival difficult for foreign language enclaves and religious colonies. These influences probably would have made the Harmony Society obsolete under any leadership.

Still, under leadership dedicated to its religious principles, the Society had overcome great difficulties in the past. Frederick Rapp, Christoph Mueller, Jacob Henrici, and Jonathan Lenz, among others, were examples of personal character and ability which earned the Society a reputation for honesty, humility, and industry, as well as cultural awareness. John Duss, in comparison, did not possess these characteristics to the degree necessary to lead a colony of people dedicated to such a simple style of living. Nor was he able to accept personal anonymity in order to promote the welfare of the group. Indeed, there was little about John Duss which distinguished him as a Harmonist. Certainly his musical career was not compatible with Harmonist music traditions.

Music had always been encouraged within the Society, as the preceding history shows, but rarely were performances given by the band or orchestra outside the boundaries of the Society's villages. All members understood that music was to be limited to self-enlightenment and the enjoyment of the membership. For example, in September, 1863, Henrici wrote a letter to the Reverend W. G. Taylor of Beaver, in reply to the latter's request that the Economy Brass Band appear there for a benefit concert. This letter, given in part below, characterized the attitude which the Society had always had toward music.

> Were it not for so human an object . . . that is to relieve the condition of our suffering Brethren [victims of the War] and for which your concert is intended, we would have had to decline accepting your kind invitation as our Brass Band was not established for public use or show. . . .

Duss' attitude stands in direct conflict with the above as his own words to a reporter of the New York *Morning Telegraph*, 17 May 1904, indicate.

> If Andrew Carnegie took up a violin bow everyone would say it was a fad. My financiering was a hobby and music is my serious work. . . .

Trusteeship in the Society was "financiering" to Duss. To his predecessors, it had been a sacred calling inseparable from the religious tenets upon which the Society had been founded. When Duss became sole trustee, he was referred to as "President of the Harmony Board." Jacob Henrici, in contrast, through years of service had acquired the title "Father" Henrici.

Musically, Duss' contribution rests largely on his penchant for the spectacular, a characteristic repugnant to the Harmonists. His compositions are frequently derivative of the works of greater men—specifically John Philip Sousa. At the same time, his own opinion of his pieces reached egomaniacal proportions. A curious and ironic example of this is found in the *Harmonie Collection* compiled by Duss for the Centennial Celebration held at Economy in June, 1924. Supposedly representative of Harmonist compositions, it is largely a collection of his own pieces, including the "Gloria" from his *St. Veronica Mass*, a form most uncharacteristic of Harmonist musical tradition. It occupies fourteen of the twenty-five pages of music in the collection. The book also contains a "Centennial Ode," by Duss, the manuscript copy of which bears the note: "a majestic choral for band and chorus . . . [I] have a high opinion of it, even if it is my own composition."[7]

For the occasion, Duss also wrote new music for the hymn "O Come, All Ye Faithful" which he describes as "most stirring and joyful." The collection did include Henrici's "Das Unser Vater," but, apparently, not at Duss' insistence. The manuscript bears the note "As stated in my letter it [Henrici's piece] . . . is to go in for the purpose of Henrici's name. If the committee wants to save about $15 it can leave it out." The collection contains nothing written by Christoph Mueller.

In conclusion, Harmonist music, as it has been the subject of this book, must be defined as music compiled, composed, and arranged for performance by Harmonist musicians within the confines of the Society. The pieces by member musicians, such as Christoph Mueller, Frederick Rapp, and Frederick Eckensperger, and those by nonmembers W. C. Peters and Charles von Bonnhorst qualify as Harmonist music because they were written specifically for the Society. One march by John Duss, "Durch Kampf zum Sieg," approaches the above requirements. But the curious dedication which appears on the manuscript, "as a memorial to the members past and present of the Harmony Society," as well as his descriptive notes for the piece, indicate that to Duss the Society was already dead when he composed it in 1898. This piece, however, and all of Duss's other pieces—"March G. A. R.," "America Up-to-Date," etc.—were written to be played by professional musicians for audiences outside the Society. The titles of his pieces reflect the popular American spirit of the times but they do not reflect the spirit of the Harmony Society.

The final conclusion must be that Duss was never really a Harmonist at heart and his music was not intended to be Harmonist music. His position as a composer, conductor and performer must therefore be evaluated through comparison with the professionals with whom he associated and competed. Among these we mention John Philip Sousa, the bandmaster whom he thought he excelled; the violinist, composer and conductor, Nahan Franko; the singers who appeared on his programs—Lillian Nordica and Edouard de Reszke; and, considering his aspirations for the Metropolitan Opera House directorship, Maurice Grau and Heinrich Conried. Unlike these artists and impresarios, Duss attempted to buy his fame rather than earn it. His name was kept before the public in reviews, most of which were written by his agents, which say surprisingly little about music and a great deal about his wealth, eccentricities, and temperament. His concerts were publicized through stunts more appropriate for the promotion of a circus. Duss (he preferred to have it pronounced to rhyme with "deuce" or "puss" [?] after he arrived in New York) presented to the public a cartoon figure and then complained when the public refused to take him seriously.

To conclude, Duss was a self-trained nineteenth-century American village bandmaster. His marches are attractive, although not distinctive, pieces. Moderately gifted, he functioned well enough in this environment. When his ambitions drove him to seek national fame he became an oddity—thanks to the Harmonists' millions—a millionaire oddity. He bought agents, instrumentalists, singers—although some, such as Edouard de Reszke, came to regret their associations with him—but the flame of renown burned only so long as he fed it with the fuel of Harmonist money. When he stopped it went out, and not the faintest glow lingered on.

In contrast, the spirit of the Harmonists has steadily grown in influence. Thousands of men, women, and children annually visit the museums now maintained where they built their towns. Economy Village and Harmony, in Pennsylvania and New Harmony, Indiana, stand as reminders that diligence in labor and self-sacrifice for the common good are the strengths of any society. The respect and even awe in which their way of life is viewed today gives a prophetic ring to their hymn "Harmonie du Bruder-stadt":

> Harmonie, City of Brotherhood,
> Peace shall cover you.
> God will be with you early and late,
> and no enemy shall frighten you.
>
> When the time comes that you no longer can stand,
> God will be near his people:
> He will lift them up.

1. Edward D. Andrews, *The Gift to be Simple* (New York: 1940), p. 91.
2. Ibid.
3. Ernst, *op. cit.*, p. 243.
4. Quoted in ibid., p. 247.
5. Owen, *op. cit.*, p. 121.
6. Duke Bernhard, *op. cit.*, p. 164.
7. Appendix D, VM 3.15.

APPENDICES

Appendices A, B, and C which follow, contain examples of music composed and used by the Harmonists. Appendix D is a catalog of the musical items found in the Economy Archives at the time of the writing of this book. In the musical portions of the Appendixes, phrasing, articulation, and dynamic markings have been retained as found in the sources at Economy Village. In all of the appendixes the Harmonists' spelling and grammatical practices have also been retained. Where editorial remarks have been considered necessary for understanding, they have been enclosed in brackets.

When possible, a complete bibliographical description has been given for the entries in Appendix D. The description of a given item includes the name of the composer, author, or arranger; the title of the work; the publisher and date and place of publication; the number of volumes; and the dimensions of the item in centimeters. The number of pages contained is shown if the item itself was paginated. For items without pagination or with irregular pagination, the number of sheets contained is given. Names of owners, places and dates, and other notes found on a source are included in the description when considered relevant and informative. The catalog system was devised by bibliographers at Economy prior to the writing of this book.

APPENDIX A

Examples of Harmonist Music

HAIL COLUMBIA

Arranged by J. C. Mueller

PRESTO

Frederick Eckensperger

DURCH ZERFALLNE KIRCHEN FENSTER

J. C. Mueller

Durch zer- fall- ne Kir - chen Fen - ster
Grau - sig wan - deln die Ge - spen - ster

fällt so tief der Mon-den - schein:
ueb - er mo- dern - des Ge - bein.

Dump-fe Glock-en-

tö - ne schal -len, von dem ho - hen Thurm her -ab;

Und des Strau-ches Blät -ter wal - len, lis - pelnd auf be-

ES BLÜHT EIN BLÜMLEIN

J. C. Mueller

HERR FÜHRE MICH

J. C. Mueller

Herr, füh - re mich mit Eng - els - treu-e, durch
Ich fol - ge dir mit bang - er Scheu-e und

mei - ner Ju - gend bun - te Flur   Nun
seh auf dei - ne Win - ke nur.

folg' ich dir durch rau - he Lüf-te, mit

wun - dem Fuss auf Dor - nen nach; und

DIE MENSCHENLIEB

J. C. Mueller

Die Men- schen-lieb ist   Trieb und Sporn, zu je - der gu - ten
Sie räumt vom We-ge   je - den Dorn, dem sich ein Wan-drer

That,   Bleibt kalt nicht wie ein   Bild von Holz, bei Frem-dem Jam-mer
naht.

stehn,   wenn Selbst-sucht, Gold und A- del - stolz vor- bei auf Stel-zen

gehn.

ROUSSEAU'S DREAM

Arranged by J. C. Mueller

WEM TÖNET HEUT DER FEIER KLANG?

J. C. Mueller

Wem tö -net heut der Fei - er Klang? Wem rau - scht der

Hee-re hoch-ge- sang, gleich Nach- ti- gal- len schlag?

Jetzt hö-her und jetzt tief - er. Wen

SEYD BEGLÜCKT

J. C. Mueller

O NACHT! UND O DU FEIERLICHE STILLE

Frederick Eckensperger

fall ich hier in Staub vor dem, der mich ge - macht; von

die - sem un - tern Welt-ge - tüm - mel, hebt un - ser Herz nichts

JACKSON'S MARCH

Charles von Bonnhorst

HEILIG SEI DEIN NAM'

Charles von Bonnhorst

Arranged by William Cummings Peters

ECONOMIE WALTZ

W. C. Peters

Flute

Horn in C
Trpt. in C

Violin 1

Violin 2
Viola

Violoncello
Bassoon

ECONOMIE QUICKSTEP

W. C. Peters

O SCHÖNE HARMONIE

W. C. Peters

FREUNDSCHAFT MARCH

J. C. Mueller

SYMPHONY IN D

I. Andante

W. C. Peters

II. Rondo

DIE ZEHN GEBOTE

Jacob Henrici

DAS APOSTOLISCHE GLAUBENS-BEKENNTNIS

Jacob Henrici

Ich glau- be an Gott, den Va- ter, den all-

mäch-ti- gen Schöp-fer Him- mels und der Er- den,

und an Je- sum Chri- stum, Sei- nen ein- ge-

bor- nen Sohn, un- sern Herrn, der em-

pfan- gen ist vom hei - li - gen Gei- ste, ge-

HILF HERR, EIN NEUES JAHR BRIGHT AN

Jacob Henrici

Trio From The March "The G. A. R. In Dixie."

Dedicated to the G. A. R. National Encampment at Louisville, Ky., Sept. 1895.

by J. S. DUSS.

1 In Dixie, In Dixie, Fair
2 In Dixie, In Dixie, Where

land of cane and cotton; In Dixie, In Dixie, Where hearts are brave and
heroes fought and perished; In Dixie, In Dixie, Old Friendship starts a-

true; In Dixie, In Dixie, Old hatred is forgotten; And
new; In Dixie, In Dixie, Where mem'ries proud are cherished; Ken-

day and night, one banner bright, waves o'er the Gray and Blue.
tucky stands with loving hands and greets the Gray and Blue.

Copyright, 1895, by Wm. C. OTT & Co. Beaver Falls, Pa.

THE GREAT NORTH=WEST.

Dedicated to the 30th G. A. R. National Encampment at St. Paul, Minn. Sept. 1896.

by J. S. DUSS.

1 Hail, Hail, Min - ne - so - ta, Hail!
2 Shine, Shine, star of free - dom shine!

Boys in blue so tried and true are welcome one and all;...... then Hail, Hail,
Shine up-on a smiling land with peace and plen-ty blest;...... then Shine, Shine,

hearts that nev - er fail; beat in love and u - ni-y at fair St. Paul!
In thy light di - vine; Dear old Glo - ry floats above the Great North - West!

D.C.

Copyright 1896. by J. S. DUSS.

APPENDIX B

Melody Incipits of the Secular Instrumental Repertory from Dr. Mueller's "Violino Primo" Book (IM2.8-3)

No. 1 March Hail Columbia

No. 2 March von Eidenbenz

No. 3 March

No. 4 March von Mannheim

No. 5 March Wurtemberg

No. 6 Quadrille

No. 7 Angloise

No. 8 Harmonie March

No. 9 March

No. 10 March in Croaten

No. 11 Menuetto (alias No. 12)

No. 12 Allegro (alias No. 11)

No. 13 Pleyel's Variationen

No. 14 Bey Bruder

No. 15 March von Dresden

No. 16 Tyroler Waltz

No. 17 Waltz Epple

No. 18 March of Oestreich

No. 19 Preusisches Quadrille

No. 20 March de Bonaparte

No. 21 March of Augsburgh

No. 22 Mozart's Menuetto

No. 23 McLutt

No. 24 Allegro

No. 25 Menuetto Auberler

No. 26 Walzer Mozart (1)

No. 27 God Save Great Washington

No. 28 March

No. 29 Walz of Mozart (2)

No. 30 Pas Doublee [No entry]

No. 31 Walz

No. 32 March der Flur (w/Pas Doublee) v. Fuchs

No. 33 Walzer v. Mozart

No. 34 President Monroe's March

No. 35 Walz Mozart

No. 36 March of Hutton   Fuchs

No. 37 Pas Doublee

No. 38 Chicken Waltz   Mozart

No. 39 March of Howard

No. 40 March Fuchs

No. 41 Allegro

No. 42 Ney's March

No. 43 March Francois

No. 44 Allemande

No. 45 Walz Mozart

No. 46 Klage-Mensch   Fuchs

No. 47 Mozart's Favorite Walz

No. 48 Walz   Mozart

No. 49 Walz   Mozart

No. 50 Walz [No Entry]   Mozart

No. 51 Vivace

No. 52 Zauber Flauten March

No. 53 Presto Favorite

No. 54 Siege March (w/Pas Doublee)

No. 55 Hoffnung's March (w/Pas Doublee)

No. 56 Cornario (w/ Pas Doublee)

No. 57 Berliner Walz

No. 58 Jackson's March in G

No. 59 Allegro v. Lully

No. 60 Pas Doublee v. Lully

No. 61 Allegro

No. 62 Bonaparte's March

No. 63 March Demosthenes

No. 64 Andante Mozart [No entry]

No. 65 Wiener March

No. 66 Allegro

No. 67 March Der Oper

No. 68 Kriegs March

No. 69 March v. Nerwinde

No. 70 Air [No entry]

No. 71 Andantino Gratioso [No entry]

No. 72 Pas Doublee [No entry]

No. 73 General Bernadotes March [No entry]

No. 74 Maestoso

No. 75 Alexander Allegro

No. 76 Die Vogelfanger

No. 77 Sachsischer March

No. 78 Allegro Maestoso [No entry]

No. 79 Allegro

No. 80 Rondo

No. 81 Rondo Allegro [No entry]

No. 82 Augusta

No. 83 Emperor of Austria Walz

No. 84 Emperor of Russia Walz

No. 85 Walz Maria Louisa

No. 86 Swiss Walz

No. 87 Blake's Allegretto

No. 88 Menuetto   Haydn

No. 89 Menuetto   Haydn

No. 90 Allegretto

No. 91 Menuet   Holzbauer [No entry]

No. 92 Hungarian Walz

No. 93 Fanfare de la Victoria [No entry]

No. 94 Allegretto

No. 95 Menuetto [No entry]

No. 96 Rondo Vivace [No entry]

No. 97 Allegro [No entry]

No. 98 Nette's Walzer

No. 99 Bird Walz [No entry]

No. 100 Philadelphia Walz

No. 101 Russischer March

No. 102 Kunze's Allemande

No. 103 Walz

No. 104 Allemande by Kunze

No. 105 Walz Cyrus [No entry]

No. 106 Lycurgus Allemande

No. 107 Menuetto von Köhler

No. 108 March of Hamburg

No. 109 Parade March

No. 110 Wellington's March

No. 111 Jackson's March

No. 112 Moderato

No. 113 Gratiozo of Mozart

No. 114 Menuetto 1 (Beethoven)

No. 115 Menuetto 2 (Beethoven)

No. 116 Brittischer March

No. 117 National March

No. 118 Walz [No entry]

No. 119 Jones March, Quick Step

No. 120 Stuttgarter March v. Eidenbenz

No. 121 Menuet 1 v. Henkel

No. 122 Menuet 2 v. Henkel

No. 123 Menuet Yellow   Henkel [No entry]

No. 124 Menuetto 3 v. Henkel (Green Menuet)

No. 125 Hopps Walz [No entry]

No. 126 Violet Walz

No. 127 Menuetto Tempo

No. 128 March Consul of Bonaparte

No. 129 Wiener Walzer [No entry]

No. 130 Tempo di Menuet [No entry]

No. 131 Mozart's Menuet [No entry]

No. 132 Tyroler March

No. 133 Theater March

No. 134 March

No. 135 Anderson's March

No. 136 Graham's Grand March

No. 137 Orange March

No. 138 March of York

No. 139 Grandmaster's March [No entry]

No. 140 Blue's March [No entry]

No. 141 Monroe's March

No. 142 Mexican March [No entry]

No. 143 Pleyel's Menuetto

No. 144 Menuet v. B [No entry]

No. 145 Menuet v. B [No entry]

No. 146 Menuet v. B. [No entry]

No. 147 Battle Piece - Harold's Ruft

No. 148 Washington's March

No. 149 Haydn's March

No. 150 Companion's March

No. 151 Walzer Mozart [No Entry]

No. 152 Billings' Walz

No. 153 Russian Walz [No entry]

No. 154 Shives Walz

No. 155 Captain McDonald's Walz

No. 156 Comedy Walz

No. 157 Schlittage Walz

No. 158 Glocken Walz

No. 159 Ambos Walz

No. 160 Uhraufzieher

No. 161 [No entry]

No. 162 Gesang Walz

No. 163 Triangle Walz

No. 164 Ganse Walz

No. 165 Kukuck Walz [No entry]

No. 166 Walz 1 Steiner

No. 167 Rothe Rose

No. 168 Danischer Walz

No. 169 Rosen Hutchen

No. 170 Elster Walz

No. 171 The Barbier of Seville

No. 172 Wildes' Walz

No. 173 Junge Elster

No. 174 Redout Walz

No. 175 Coda aus dem Rosen

No. 176 Redout Deitscher

No. 177 Choeur des Chasseurs

No. 178 Waldman's Grand March

No. 179 Pittsburgh Angloise [No entry]

No. 180 Conquering Hero

No. 181 Regiment (w/Pas Doublee)

No. 182 Spring (Pas Doublee)

No. 183 Rural Felicity

No. 184 Steamboat

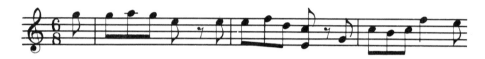

No. 185 Allegretto of Paris

No. 186 Duetto

No. 187 Holyoke

No. 188 London Air

No. 189 Pennsylvania

No. 190 Ohio

No. 191 Prague March

No. 191 Prague March

No. 192 March 1 by Charles von Bonnhorst

No. 193 March 2 Ch. von B.

No. 194 March 3 Ch. von B.

No. 195 March 4 Ch. von B.

No. 196 March 5

No. 197   Jackson's March (6th)

No. 196 [sic] Walz 1 Ch. von B.

No. 197 [sic] Walz 2   Ch. von B.

No. 199 Walz 4th Ch. von B.

No. 200 Walz 5th

No. 201 Walz 6th

No. 202 Walz 7th

No. 203 Walz 8th

No. 204 Walz 9th Ch. v. B.

No. 205 Walz 10th Ch. v. B.

No. 206 Walz 11th Ch. v. B.

No. 207 Walz 12th Ch. v. B.

No. 208 Walz 13th Ch. v. B.

No. 209 Walz 14th Ch. v. B.

No. 210 Walz 15th v. B.

No. 211 Walz 16th v. B.

No. 212 Walz 17th v. B.

No. 213 Walz 18th v. B.

No. 214 Walz 19th v. B.

No. 215 Walz 21 v. B.

No. 216 Walz 20 Mrs. Volz Wals v. B.

No. 217 Walz 22 v. B.

No. 218 Walzer 37 v. B.

No. 219 Walz 24 v. B.

No. 220 Quadrille 25th (by Ch. von B.)

No. 221 Quadrille 26th v. B.

No. 222 Quadrille 27th v. B.

No. 223 Quadrille 28th v. B.

No. 224 Quadrille 29th v. B.

No. 225 Quadrille 30th v. B.

No. 226 Quadrille 31st v. B.

No. 227 Quadrille 32nd v. B.

No. 228 Quadrille 33   v. B.

No. 229 Quadrille 34th v. B.

No. 230 Quadrille 35th v. B.

No. 231 Quadrille 36th v. B.

No. 232 Walz 38th v. B.

No. 233 Walz v. B. [No entry]

No. 234 Polonaise 1   Ch. v. B. [No entry]

No. 235 Polonaise 2 [No entry]

No. 236 Polonaise 3 [No entry]

No. 237 Polonaise 4 [No entry]

No. 238 Polonaise 5 Ch. v. B. [No entry]

No. 239 General Paschell's March Ch. v. B. [No entry]

No. 240 Jackson's March Ch. v. B. [No entry]

No. 241 March v. Blumenthal [No entry]

No. 242 Gavot   Arrn. Peters

No. 243 Lafayette's Quickstep

No. 244 March

No. 245 Hunter's Horn

No. 246 The Plain Gold Ring von Weber

No. 247 Latour's March

No. 248 Rondo

No. 249 Di Tanti Palpiti Rossini

No. 250 Calife's Overture

No. 251 (Alias 253)

No. 252 Irish Washerwoman

No. 253 Auld Lang Syne

No. 254 Aria with Variations

No. 255 Economie Walz (by W. C. Peters 1827)

No. 256 Economie Quickstep (W. C. Peters)

No. 257 Walz

No. 258 Sonatina   Vanhall

No. 259 Allegro by Rosini

No. 260 Overture to Artaxerxes (Dr. Arne)

No. 261 Deutscher Walzer

No. 262 Funny Walz

No. 263 Latour's Overture 1827

No. 264 Aria (1828)

No. 265 March Freischutz (Maria Weber)

No. 266 Rouseau's Dream

No. 267 Yanky Doodle

No. 268 Mehul's Overture

No. 268 [sic] Jomelli's Trio

No. 269 Overture to Enterprise

No. 270 Overture to Figaro by Mozart

No. 271 Overture to Henry 4th   Martini

No. 272 Overture (Kreitzer)

No. 273 Allegro

No. 274 Presto (alias 279)

No. 275 Thalia Polonaise (alias 280) Meyer

No. 276 Calliope

No. 277 Andante   Vanhall

No. 277 (1) Allegro

No. 278 Adagio   Vanhall

No. 278 Allegretto   Vanhall

No. 278

No. 279 Chorus Allegro (The Heaven's are Telling)
Beethoven

No. 280 Rauschender Stegel Schlag   Steibelt

No. 281 Nachtisch   Vanhall

No. 282 Sinfonia (Sterkel)

No. 283 Sinfonia   Pleyel

No. 284 Sinfonia (Pleyel)

No. 285 Walz

No. 286 Walz

No. 287 Preussischer Walz   W. C. Peters

No. 288 Polyminia March

No. 289 March in Tancreti

No. 290   Mozart's Military Walz

No. 291   Rousseau's Dream   (arr. W. C. Peters)

No. 292   Hanover March

No. 293   Concerto   (arrn. Peters)

No. 293 [sic] Overture   by Ware

No. 294   Walz by Woelf A

No. 294   Walz (by Woelf) B

No. 295 Sinfonia   Gyrowitz

No. 296 Overture "Messiah"   Handel

No. 297 Eccossis (5) v. Bonhart 1829

No. 289 Overture (Weber)

No. 299 Overture La Gazza Ladre (Rosini)

No. 300 Casino Walz (1830)

No. 305 sic   Viola Walz

No. 301   General Lafayette's Grand March   Meineke

No. 302   Copenhagen Walz

No. 303   Magnolia Walz   1830   Mueller

No. 304   Freundschaft March   Meuller

No. 305   Viola Walz   Mueller

No. 306   March of Dublin

No. 307   March of Edinburgh

No. 308 Lobelia

No. 310 [sic] Dr. Haydn's Walz

No. 311 Clifton's March

No. 309 [sic] Overture Tancredi   Rosini

No. 312 Handel's Water Music

No. 313 Symphonie   W. C. Peters

No. 314 Overture to Caravane

No. 315 Sonata v. Kotzwara (arrn. Peters)

No. 316 Overture of Haydn (arrn. Miki)

No. 317 Overture von Fodor (arrn. Miki)

No. 318 Melodien Walz von Mozart

No. 319 Pittsburgh March W. C. Peters

No. 320 Rosenwalzer

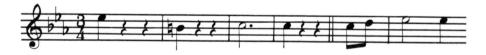

APPENDIX C

The Melodies of the Harmonist Hymnbooks
of 1820 and 1827

No. 29 Der bittre Kelch und Myrrhen

No. 30 Der Fluren Grün

No. 31 Der Greiss des Silber-Haares

No. 32 Der junge Sommer weicht

No. 33 Der lieblich Lenz

No. 34 Der Lillien-Zweig sich wieder

No. 35 Der schöne Maienmon't began

No. 36 Den Weisen wird allhier

No. 37 Der Weisheit holder Perlenschatz

No. 38 Des Lebens letze Stunde

No. 39 Die ernstlich Nacht

No. 40 Die ihr am Abend und am Morgen

No. 41 Die Menschenlieb

No. 42 Die Nacht! die Heilige

No. 85 Harmonie, du Bruderstadt

No. 86 Heil'ge Freundschaft

No. 87 Heilig Sey Dein Nam

No. 88 Herr, führe mich, mit Engelstreu

No. 89 Herr Jesu Christ, mein Lebens Licht

No. 90 Hier Stund Sophia

No. 91 Himmels Lust ist bewusst

No. 92 Hinauf, mein Geist

No. 93 Hirten aus den goldnen Zeiten

No. 94 Hoch über Erd und Welt und Zeit

No. 95 Höher als der Wall der Welten

No. 96 Hüll in deinen Schatten-Mantel

No. 97 Ich denke dein und halte deine Spuren

No. 98 Ich fühle dass in mir

No. 127 Mein Gott das Herz

No. 128 Mein Hoffnungs-Anker liegt

No. 129 Meines Herzens Jesu

No. 130 Mir blüht ein Paradies

No. 131 Muss ich jetz die Schönheit meiden

No. 132 Natur ist wieder heiter nun

No. 133 Nennt mich eine Blume

No. 134 Nicht blos für diese Unterwelt

No. 135 Nun da Schnee und Eis zerflossen

No. 136 Nun freut euch! ihr lieben Gespielen

No. 137 Nun liebster Salomon

No. 138 Nun lob mein Seel den Herren

No. 139 Nur Wahrheit kann mein Herz bestricken

No. 140 O du allerschönste Liebe

No. 169 Schwing dich auf zu deinem Gott

No. 170 Schwing dich mein Geist

No. 171 Seelen Bräutigam

No. 172 Seele was ist Schöners

No. 173 Sehet wie die Klaren Sterne

No. 174 Seht, Gespielen, seht die Flur!

No. 175 Senke dich von Purpur-Wolken

No. 176 Sey Lob und Ehr dem hochsten gut

No. 177 Sey mir tausendmal

No. 178 So bricht mit Macht

No. 179 So glücklich so vergnügt

No. 180 Sollt ich meinem Gott nicht singen

No. 181 Sophia ich kann's nicht lassen

No. 182 So tritt hervor

No. 197 Wann Weissheit schön den Garten zeigt

No. 198 Was Gott thut, das ist wohl gethan

No. 199 Was ist dieses für ein Feuer

No. 200 Was mein Gott will

No. 201 Was soll deine Schönheit krönen

No. 202 Welche Symphonien

No. 203 Welt und Eitelkeiten Brosen

No. 204 Wenn mein Geist vom Leib entfesselt

No. 205 Wer ist der Braut

No. 206 Wer nur den lieben Gott

No. 207 Wer weiss wie nahe

No. 208 Wie des Lenzes milde Lüfte

No. 209 Wie gross ist des Allmächtiger

No. 210 Wie herrlich grünet und blühet

APPENDIX D

A Catalog of the Music Collection
of
Economy Village, Ambridge, Pennsylvania

MUSIC CATALOG KEY

The contents of the collection have been cataloged with letters and numbers as shown below:

1st Letter:
H   Hymn
I   Instrumental
K   Keyboard
Ṗ   Psalter or Hymnbook with Texts and Melodies Notated
p   Psalter or Hymnbook with Texts and Melody Names Only
T   Theoretical, Pedagogical, and Historical Manuals, Treatises, and Periodicals
V   Vocal

2d Letter:
M   Manuscript
P   Printed

1st Number:
1   Solo
2   Ensemble Part*
3   Score
4   Score with Parts

2d Number:
Indicates the position of an item in a given category

*A third number indicates the position of an item in a family of parts. The third number is placed to the right of the first and second numbers and is separated from them by a dash.

Example: IM2.7-3 (Instrumental Manuscript, Ensemble Part, entry 7, part-book 3.

INSTRUMENTAL: PRINTED PARTS

IP2.1—Gyrowetz, A. Grande/Sinfonie/pour/2 Violins, Alto, Basse, 2 hautbois, 2 Cors,/et Basson/composée/par/A. Gyrowetz/ouvre 6/A. Offenbach sur le Main/chez Jean André [n.d.] [24.5 x 32.5 cm. 16 sheets. Alto missing.]

IP2.2—Beethoven, L. V. Première/Symphonie/ en Ut majeur/à Grand Orchestra/composée par/ L. van Beethoven, à Paris chez Richault, Editeur/ # 2272R [n.d.] [35 x 26.5 cm. 37 sheets.]

IP2.3—Haydn, F. J. Trois Quintours/pour la/ Flute, 2 Violins, Alto, Violoncelle/avec accompagn de Piano Forte ad libitum/arrangés des grandes Simphonies/composées pour les Concerts de Mr. Salomon/à Londres/par/Joseph Haydn/ Bonn et Cologne chez N. Simrock/ propriété de l'éditeur [n.d.] [Six quintets originally bound in sets of three.] 1. Sinfonia o Quintetto IX [Plate # 125. 35 x 26.8 cm. 15 sheets. Alto missing.] 2. Sinfonia o Quintetto X [Plate # 163. 35 x 26.8 cm. 17 sheets. Violin 1 incomplete.] 3. Sinfonia o Quintetto I [Plate # 163. 35 x 26.8 cm. 18 sheets.] 4. Sinfonia o Quintetto II [Plate # 163. 35 x 26.8 cm. 19 sheets.] 5. Sinfonia o Quintetto XIV [Plate # 1447. 35 x 26.8 cm. 16 sheets.] 6. Sinfonia o Quintetto XV [Plate # 1449 35 x 26.8 cm. 17 sheets.]

IP2.4—Weber, Carl Maria von/Küffner, J. Aufforderung Zum Tanze/als Walzer mit 2 trios bearbeitet und 2 galoppaden/von/J. Küffner/für/2 violinen, Floete, Clarinette und Bass obligat/2 Horn, 2 Trompeten und Pauken ad libitum./Eingerichtet von/G. Woetzel/Mainz und Paris/bei B. Schott's Sohnen, Antwerpen bei A. Schott [n.d.] [16.6 x 27.1 cm. 12 sheets]

IP2.5—Foreit, A. Introduction et Six Walses/ pour/Trompette à clefs (Klappen Trompete) Cor de Signal/à clefs (Klappenflügelhorn) 2 Violons, Flute, 2 Clarinettes/2 Cors, Trompette, Cornet de Postillon, Trombone, caisse/roulante, grande caisse, Timballes et Basse/ou/pour deux Violons, Flûte, Clarinette, et Basse/composées par /A. Foreit/Mayence/B. Schott [n.d.] [16.6 x 27.1 cm. 28 sheets.]

IP2.6—Pleyel, Ignace. Douze Quatuors/pour deux Violins, Alto & Violoncelle/dédiés/à Sa Majesté/ Le Roi de Prusse/ composés par/ Ignace Pleyel/A Offenbach aM/chez Jean André [n.d.] [Three quartets in each set, set 1 complete, set 2 missing 2nd violin and 'cello parts. 1. Quartets in B Flat Major, G Major, D Minor Plate # 1406. 24.5 x 34 cm. 25 sheets. 2. Quartets in C Major, A Major, E Flat Major Plate # 1407. 24.5 x 34 cm. 12 sheets.]

IP2.7—Griesbach, Charles. Fourteen / Military Divertimentos/for/Clarinets, Flutes, Horns, Bassoons,/Serpent & Trumpet/as performed before their Majesties/Selected from the works of the most esteemed composers, by Charles Griesbach/London/Printed by Clementi, Banger, Hyde, Gollard & Davis, 26 Cheapside. [n.d.] [Trumpet part-book. 17 x 25.4 cm. 6 pp.]

IP2.8—Anonymous. Neun Faschings Walzer/ für / 2 Violine, Basse, Flöt, Clar. u. Horn/ unter dem Nahmen/ Schlittage Walzer / bekant / B. Schott's Sohnen, Mainz [n.d.] Bound with: Six/ Walses Favorites/ composée par Steiner. . . . [Clarinet book. 16.8 x 24.9 cm. 14 pp.]

IP2.9—Anonymous. Vingt Quatre/ Walses/ Galoppades et Walses antrichiennes/ Laendler/ pour Flûte Seule. Cahier 6/ Mayence et Anvers/ chez les fils de B. Schott [n.d.] [Plate # 2828. 16.8 x 26 cm. 7 sheets. 2 copies.]

IP2.10—Faubel, B. XXIV/ Walses / Favorites/ Pour une Flûte/ Compossées/ par/ F. Faubel/ Mayence chez B. Schott fils [n.d.] [Plate # 1524. 17 x 27 cm. 13 sheets.]

IP2.11—Rossini, J. Ouverture/de l'Opera/La Gazza ladra7/à grand Orchestra/par J. Rossini/ chez Breitkopf & Härtel à Leipsic [n.d.] [Violino Primo part. 33.5 x 25 cm. 6 pp.]

IP2.12—Haydn, F. J. Violoncello zu Haydn Sonata, Opera 73 [No pub., n.d.] [Above written in ink. 25.5 x 33.5 cm. 2 sheets.]

IP2.13—Held, Bruno. 1st Cahier des Danses. [No pub., n.d.] [Parts for 2 violins, clarino 1 & 2, clarinetto 1,2, Flauto, Corno 1,2, Basso. Plate # 1523. 16.8 x 26.8 cm. 18 sheets.]

IP2.14—Rhein, L. Rondoletto/ pour le Piano/ avec accompagnement de Violon, Ad Libitum/ dédié à Mademoiselle/ Caroline Odart de Rilly/ par/ L. Rhein/ Oeuvre 22/ à Paris/ à Lyon/ chez Arnaud [n.d.] [Violin part. 26.8 x 35 cm. 2 sheets.]

IP2.15—Pleyel, Haydn, Mozart. Variations on "La Berger Silimene" from Mozart's 4th Book; Sonata, Op. 7, Pleyel; Sonata, Op. 73, J. Haydn; Marriage of Figaro Overture, Mozart [No pub., n.d.] [Violin parts. 26.5 x 35 cm. 9 sheets.]

IP2.16—Haydn, J. Trois/Quatuors/concertans/ pour/deux violons, viola & Violoncelle/composés/par J. Haydn/Ouvre 65/A Offenbach a/M, chez J. André [n.d.] [Viola parts to three quartets. Plate # 2885. 26 x 33.cm. 5 sheets.]

IP2.17—Kiesler, Eduard. 53tes Heft Blasemusik /Zigeunerleben/Ouverture/componirt und herausgegeben/von/Eduard Kiesler/Musiklehrer in Mehlby bei Kappeln (in Schleswig) [n.d.] [27 x 34.5 cm. 44 sheets. Band parts.]

IP2.18—Haines, Chauncey. Three Little Maids/ two step a la Japanese/The Whitney Warner Pub. Co., Detroit, Mich. Copyright 1903 [27 x 34.5 cm. 44 sheets. Band parts.]

IP2.19—Basler, H. R.-Mueller. After the 'Possum-Hunt March, Two Step and Cake Walk/

Arr. by Gus Mueller./Copyright 1900 by H. R. Basler, Pittsburgh, Pa. [17.5 x 13 cm. 53 sheets. Band parts.]

IP2.20—Alexander, J. I.(arr.) Funeral March "The Old Comrade."/Mace Gay, Brockton, Mass. [n.d.] [17.5 x 13 cm. 53 sheets. Band parts.]

IP2.21—Stanick-Herbtreise March No. 4; Abt-Annie Dear; Weissenborn-Polka "Turner"; Brooks-The Conscript's Prayer; Growe- Little Saucy Kate; Anon.-May Breeze; Lange-Liebeslieder [No pub., n.d. 27.5 x 17.5 cm. 6 sheets. Band parts. Incomplete.]

IP2.22—Guy, Harry P. Pearl of the Harem/ Oriental Rag Two Step/Willard Bryant, Detroit, Mich. [n.d.] [27.5 x 17 cm. 14 sheets. Band parts.]

IP2.23—Loraine, William. The Sultan/Turkish March/F.A. Mills, N.Y. [n.d.] [27.5 x 17.5 cm. 14 sheets.]

IP2.24—Kann, H. L.-Stephens. Army and Navy Autograph March/H. L. Kann/arr. by Jno. Stephens. Copyright 1899 John Shepp Music Co., Phila. [27.5 x 17.8 cm. 14 sheets. Band parts.]

IP2.25—Dett, Nathaniel-Smith After the Cake Walk/ Characteristic March/ two step/ Nathaniel Dett/ Arr. by Lee Orean Smith/ Vandersloot Music Co., Williamsport, Pa. and N.Y. [n.d.] [27.5 x 17 cm. 6 sheets. Band parts.]

IP2.26—Hirst, Charles R.-Beyer. The Comedy King/March & Two Step/by Charles R. Hirst/ Arr. by F. Beyer/Copyright 1900 by Charles K. Harris [No address] [18 x 27.4 cm. 13 sheets. Band parts.]

IP2.27—Chambers, W. P. Unser Heinrich Marsch/ W. Paris Chambers/ Copyright 1902 by W. Paris Chambers, N.Y. [27.5 x 18 cm. 16 sheets. Band parts.]

IP2.28—Theodor Hoch's/Sopran-Cornet-Quartets/Published by/Standard Music Co., (Grasmuk & Schott)/New York. Copyright 1884; Kreutzer- Das ist der Tag des Herrn; Lorenz-Die Heimkehr; Kreutzer-Die Kapelle; Otto-Das treu deutsche Herz; Lorenz- Im Frühling; Mason- Nearer my God to Thee; Kreutzer- Jägers Lust; Call- Die Sterne [27.5 x 18 cm. 16 sheets.]

IP2.29—Duss, J. S. The Cross and Crown March. Copyright 1898 by J. S. Duss. [13 x 17.5 cm. 65 sheets. Band parts. See VP1.57.]

IP2.30—Meacham, F. W. American Patrol/Carl Fischer, New York [n.d.] [32 x 23 cm. 33 sheets. Orchestra parts.]

IP2.31—Méditation/sur/le 1er Prelude de Piano/de/J. S. Bach/composée/par/Ch. Gounod/arrangée pour/Grand Orchestre par L. Stasny. Londres/Schott & Co./Mayence/B. Schott's Sohne/ Printed in Germany. [n.d.] [24 x 33 cm. 21 sheets.]

IP2.32—Wagner, A. Die Zauberlaterne Potpouri von A. Wagner/Lief. 60. [No pub., n.d. Stamp on copies: "Philadelphia, Harry Coleman." 20.3 x 26 cm. 52 sheets. Band parts.]

IP2.33—Duss, J. S. Liberty Chimes March/ Copyright 1894 and published by W. C. Ott, Beaver Falls, Pa. [Several sets of Band parts. 27 x 18 cm.]

IP2.34—Austin, B. P. "Adam" March./B. P. Austin/Copyright & published 1895 by Wm. C. Ott & Co., Beaver Falls, Pa. [18 x 27 cm. 15 sheets.]

IP2.35—Moskau-Aledo. Overture/The Night Wanderer/v. Moskau/arr. by M. F. Aledo/ Harry Coleman, Phila., Pa. [n.d.] [27.5 x 17.5 cm. 36 sheets. Band parts.]

IP2.36—Powell, W. C.-Lampe. The Gondolier/ Intermezzo/W. C. Powell/arr. by J. Bodewalt Lampe/Shapiro Remick & Co., New York [n.d.] [27 x 17 cm. 30 sheets. Band parts.]

IP2.37—Beethoven-Kneifel. Zwei Sätze/aus der Cis Moll (Mondschein) Sonate/Ludwig van Beethoven Op. 27 No.2/für Inftr-Musik bearb. v. K. Kneifel/Edition Louis Oertel, Hanover [n.d.] [34 x 27 cm. 41 sheets.]

IP2.38—Meyerbeer, G.-Tobani. Fackeltanz/G. Meyerbeer/arr. Theo. Moses-Tobani/Carl Fischer, New York [n.d.] [31 x 23 cm. 32 sheets. Orchestra Parts.]

IP2.39—Thomas, A.-Tobani. Raymond Overture/A. Thomas/arr. by Theo-Moses-Tobani/Carl Fischer, New York [n.d.] [31 x 23 cm. 32 sheets. Orchestra parts.]

IP2.40—Maurice, Louis-Hains. Cecilia/Waltzes/ Louis Maurice/arr. Chauncey Hains. Copyright 1903 by Whitney Warner Pub. Co., Detroit, Mich. [17.5 x 27 cm. 62 sheets. Band parts.]

IP2.41—Bennet, T.- Mitchell. Satisfied/arr. G. F. Mitchell. Victor Kremer Co., Chicago. [n.d.] [26 x 18 cm. 8 sheets. Band parts.]

IP2.42—Kiesler, Eduard. Vermischte Nachrichten/Potpourri/von/Eduard Kiesler. Druck von L. Handorff in Kiel. [n.d.] [35 x 27 cm. 19 sheets. Band parts.]

IP2.43—Kiesler, Eduard. Die Amazone. Ouverture/ von Eduard Kiesler/ Verlag von Ed. Kiesler, Musiklehrer in Mehlby/ Druck von L. Handorff in Kiel. [n.d.] [35 x 27 cm. 19 sheets. Band parts.]

IP2.44—Ripley, W. S. Serenade "Pleasant Dreams." [No pub., n.d.] [16 x 12 cm. 9 sheets. Band parts.]

IP2.45—Kielser, Eduard. 2te Lieferung Blasemusik/Frei bearbeitet u. herausgegeben von Eduard Kiesler, Musiklehrer in Mehlby/bei Kappeln/in Schleswig. [n.d.] F. Schubert- Am Meer F. Schubert-Die Taubenpost H. Berens- Gruss a.d.Nacht Beethoven- Lied Preyer- Lied Mendelssohn-Duet Romberg- Chor Mendelssohn- Duet F. Abt-Abenlied Abt- Ständchen Abt- Eine Mainennacht [Contained in 15 part books from the Economy Cornet Band. Ea. 25.3 x 20.3 cm.]

IP2.46—Kiesler, Eduard. 5te Lieferung (Marsch Heft). Herausgegeben von Eduard Kiesler/ Druck von Handorff in Kiel. [n.d.] [17 partbooks for Economy Cornet Band. 17.5 x 20.5 cm.]

IP2.47—Kiesler, Eduard. 22te Lieferung verlag von Ed. Kiesler in Mehlby/Kappeln [n.d.] [17 part-books from Economy Cornet Band. 17.5 x 20.5 cm.]

IP2.48—Samuels, E. A. [Publisher] Boston [n.d.] H. Prendiville-Adelia Waltzes; Fr. Zikoff-Approach of Spring; Gungl Patz- Artusklänge Walzer; T. Howard- Ashuelot Waltzes; H. Prendiville-Bella Waltzes; R. Smith- The Fairy Spell Goetz- Happy Memories Waltzes; Emmett- Souvenir Waltzes; Goetz-Andante & Waltzes; Keller-Beautiful Star Waltz; H. Prendiville- Andante & Waltz Cynthia; Keller- Echoes from the Forest; Waldteufel- Les Sirenes Waltzes; E. Brooks- Forest Songs; Keller- Forget me Not; E. Marie- Henrietta Valse; Fr. Webb- Lenore Waltz; T. Prosho-Lisette Waltz; Fr. Goetz- Lolo Waltz; F. Keller- Love of the Beautiful Waltz; J. Flockton-Mabel Waltz; T. Prosho- Mountain Echoes; J. M. Flockton- Moss Rose; T. Prosho- May Flowers; E. Samuels- Musette Waltzes; F. Goetz- Return of Spring; Wellman- Waltz Songs; F. Keller- Sweet Memories; T. Rollinson- Troop Waltz; F. Keller-Violet Waltz; H. Prendiville- When the Robins Nest Again; H. Prendiville- Popular Medley; E. Ramsdell- The Pretty Skater; Rummel- Waltzes of the Period; F. Goetz- Blanche Waltz; H. Prendiville- Sweet Alpine Roses; [Contained in 16 partbooks from the Economy Cornet Band. 17.5 x 25.5 cm.]

IP2.49—A Series of 23 part-folders from the orchestra of John Duss. Boards covered with buckram and each having in gold lettering "John S. Duss," name of instrument and section position. Folders extant are: 2 oboes, 3 clarinets, 2 horns, 2 basses, baritone sax., 2 violas, 1 cello, side drum, 2 faggotto, 2nd and 3rd trombone, violins 1 and 2, harp, tuba. Contents include: J. S. Duss-The Fair Debutante; F. V. Blon- Blumengeflüster; J. & J. Strauss- Pizzicato Polka; E. Gillet- Loin du Bal; M. Moszkowsky-Serenata; F. Bonnaud-Serenade Enfantine; P. Lacombe-Aubade Printanière; Delibes/Doppler- Intermezzo aus Naila; Anon.-Intermezzo et Valse; Anon.- Pizzacato & Cortège de Bacchus; Anon.- Under the Bamboo Tree; F. Chattaway (arr.)- Nancy Brown; E. Gillet- Entr' acte Gavotte; Mendelssohn/Lux- Frühlingslied; Duss- America Up to Date; Gautian- Le Secret; J. Knight- Rocked in the Cradle of the Deep; C. Dalbey- Patrol: the Blue and Grey; N. Moret-Hiawatha; D. Cruger- In Old Alabama; Meacham-

American Patrol; Schumann- Träumerei; Handel-Largo; Mascagni- Intermezzo Cavaleria Rusticana.

IP2.50—Anonymous. Marches, waltzes, polkas, schottisches, contained in 12 part-books of the Economy Cornet Band, c.1876. Printed and manuscript entries. 18 x 14 cm.

IP2.51—A series of 10 part-books of the Economy Silver Cornet Band, c. 1881. Marches in manuscript and printed by Brepsant, C. Faust, G. Southwell, D. McCosh, F. Linden, D. Boyer, Piefke, Stasny and Burk. 17.5 x 13.5 cm.

IP2.52—A series of 15 part-books for band, c. 1882-84. Anon. manuscript entries and two printed by C. Faust and Wellman/Ross. 13.5 x 16.5 cm.

IP2.53—A series of 31 part-books from "John Duss' Economy Cornet Band," c. 1896. Ea. 13 x 19 cm. Contents: Beethoven- Funeral March; Laurendeau- St. Louis Cadets; Brooks-American Medley; Wagner- Under the Double Eagle; Redfield- March Hammond; Ott- McCarthy's Mishaps; Duss- G.A.R. in Dixie; Duss-Limited Express; Laurendeau-Manfred March; Duss- International March; Sousa- King Cotton; Duss- Hail, Hail; Sousa- Stars and Stripes; Hall- Hamiltonian March; Anon.- March; Duss-America Up to Date; Mackel- Put Me Off at Buffalo; Hall- Tenth Reg. March; Sousa- El Capitan; Duss- Cross and Crown.

IP2.54—Wallace, J. A. Dolores/and The Pretty Bicycle Girl Waltz./Arranged for three mandolins and guitar./Published by Wm. C. Ott Co., Beaver Falls, Pa. [n.d.] [27 x 35.5 cm. 4 sheets.]

INSTRUMENTAL: PRINTED SCORES

IP3.1—Hewitt, J. [Pieces scored for flute, 2 clarinets, 2 horns, bugle, trumpet, bassoon, serpent or trombone. Covers and t.p. missing as well as other pp. 26.5 x 18.4 cm. 14 sheets.]

IP3.2—Jonas, E. Parisiana/Fantaisie Ouverture/ Evette et Schaeffer [n.d.] [25.8 x 33.8 cm. 21 pp. Concert band.]

IP3.3—Saint-Saëns, C. Danse Macabre/Poème Symphonique/ Arrangement pour Musique Militaire par E. Lointier chef de Musique au 8e d'Infanterie/Evette & Schaeffer/Paris [n.d.] [27 x 34.8 cm. 26 pp.]

IP3.4—Montanari, Angelo. Omaggio a Boito/ Mefistofele/Fantasia/G. Ricordi, Milano [n.d.] [23.4 x 30.4 cm. 64 pp. Concert band. Stamp on paper: "1899."]

IP3.5—Tirindelli, Giulio, Cristoforo Colombo/ di/A. Franchetti/composta da/Giulio Tirindelli/ Direttore della Banda Municipale de Treviso./G. Ricordi, Milano. [n.d.] [23 x 30.5 cm. 71 pp. Concert band. Stamp on paper: "1898."]

IP3.6—Massenet, J.-Chic, L. Le Cid/(Opera de J. Massenet)/Rhapsodie Mauresque/transcription par L.Chic./Evette & Schaeffer [n.d.] [34 x 26 cm. 21 pp. Concert Band.]

IP3.7—Lombard, Louis. La Derniere Priere de Sainte Cecile/pour orchestre/par Louis Lombard/ Chateau de Trevano/Lugano, Suisse [n.d.] [34 x 26.8 cm. 9 pp.]

IP3.8—Wettge, Gustave. Eliane/Ouverture/par Gustave Wettge/chef de Musique de la Garde Républicaine/Evette & Schaeffer [n.d.] [25.5 x 34 cm. 29 pp. Concert Band.]

IP3.9—Broutin, Clement. Le Suite Pour Orchestra/ par Clement Broutin/ No. 1 Pastorale, No. 2 Scherzo-Valse/Evette & Schaeffer [n.d.] [25 x 34 cm. 36 pp.]

IP3.10—Ponchielli, A. Original Orchestra Score/from Op: La Gioconda/By/A. Ponchielli. [No pub., n.d] [27 x 37.8 cm. Paginated from 718-791.]

IP3.11—Meyerbeer, G.-Belati, T. Gli Ugonotti/ Gran Scena e Duetto Finale: Stringe il perighio/ Instrumentazione de/Tito Belati Capo Musica nel 35 Reggto Fanteria/G. Ricordi, Milano. [n.d.] [30.3 x 23 cm. 56 pp.]

IP3.12—Lombard, Louis. Cubana/ (Caprice)/ pour orchestra 'Cordes et Harpe/ par/ Louis Lombard/ Transcription pour Musique Militaire/ Chateau de Trevano/ Lugano, Suisse. [n.d.] [27 x 34 cm. 17 pp.]

INSTRUMENTAL: PRINTED SCORES AND PARTS

IP4.1—Beyer, F. [arr.]. A Hot Combination/ Medley Overture/ arr. by F. Beyer Philadelphia/ J. W. Pepper [n.d.] [24 x 30.5 cm. 37 sheets. Orchestra.]

IP4.2—Sebek, G. The Alpine Post/Galop/Descriptive)/Copyright 1894 by Louis Vitak, Canton, O. [30.5 x 24 cm. 15 sheets.]

IP4.3—Duss, J.S. The "America Up to Date" March/Song two step/Published by Wm. C. Ott & Co., Beaver Falls, Pa. [n.d.] [27 x 18 cm. 15 pp. Band.]

IP4.4—Neubauer, Henry. Forest Club Quadrille/ Copyright and published 1895 by Wm. C. Ott & Co., Beaver Falls, Pa. [27 x 18 cm. 50 sheets. Orchestra.]

IP4.5—Duss-Neubauer. The Brownies Dance Characteristic/ J. S. Duss/ Arr. by Henry Neubauer/ Copyright and published 1895 by Wm. C. Ott Co., Beaver Falls, Pa. [27.5 x 18 cm. Band (17 pp.) and Orchestra (16 pp.)]

IP4.6—Adam, A.-André, E. Si J'Etais Roi/Overture (A.Adam)Arrangée pour Musique Militaire/ par Ernest Andre/Leduc [n.d.] [26.5 x 33 cm. 74 sheets.]

IP4.6—Eberle, W.H. Junior Republic March/ copyright 1897 by W.H. Eberle, Troy, N.Y. [27.5 x 18 cm. 12 sheets. Orchestra.]

IP4.8—Johns, Al. At a Garden Party/Two step/ F.A. Mills, N.Y. Copyright 1902. [17.8 x 27.5 cm. 11 sheets. Orchestra.]

IP4.9—Ringleben, Justus. Valse Marie/ Copyright F. A. Mills, 1902. [17.8 x 27.5 cm. 17 sheets. Orchestra.]

IP4.10—Sousa, J. Three Quotations/ A. The King of France with twenty-thousand men/ Marched up the hill, and then marched down again/ Copyright 1896 by the John Church Company, Cincinnati, New York, Chicago. [32 x 24 cm. 27 sheets. Orchestra.]

IP4.11—Nicolai, O. Merry Wives of Windsor/ Ouverture/O. Nicolai/arr. by Theo. Moses-Tobani/ Copyright 1893 by Carl Fischer, New York. [23 x 31 cm. 34 pp. Orchestra.]

IP4.12—Doda, Albano Seismit. La Caressante/ Valse Lente/F.A. Mills/N.Y. Copyright 1902. [18 x 27.5 cm. 11 sheets.]

IP4.13—Strauss, Joh. Wine, Woman and Song/ Waltz. Joh. Strauss Op. 333/Carl Fischer, N.Y., 1899. [27.5 x 18 cm. 29 sheets. Orchestra.]

IP4.14—Duss-Neubauer. Life's Voyage. Medley Overture arr. by Henry Neubauer/ Copyright by Wm. C. Ott & Co., Beaver Falls, Pa. [n.d.] [17.8 x 18 cm. 27 sheets.]

IP4.15—Edwards, Gus. Kitchy Coo/Cake Walk, March & Two Step/F.A. Mills, N.Y. [n.d.] [27 x 18 cm. 12 sheets.]

VOCAL: PRINTED SOLOS

VP1.1—Collection of songs bound in boards and leather with Economy grain. 25.4 x 34 cm. 35 sheets with 40 pp. music. Contents: Devereaux, L.- The Maltese Boatman's Song—Philadelphia, Willig. [n.d.]; Knight, Edward- Buy a Broom— New York, John J. Ricker. Copyright 1827.; Moore, Th.- My Heart and Lute—Philadelphia, Willig. [n.d.]; Clarke, W.- Lovely Rosabelle— Edinburg, J. Hamilton. [n.d.]; Phipps, J. B.- Here We Meet too Soon to Part—Philadelphia, Willig. [n.d.]; Bishop, H.-Row Gently Here—Philadelphia, Willig. [n.d.] Braham, Mr.- Is There a Heart that Never Lov'd?—Philadelphia, G. E. Blake. [n.d.]; Anon.- The Flower Girl/ as Sung by/ Madam Vestris Philadelphia, J. G. Klemm. [n.d.]; Moore & Bishop.- Go Then, 'Tis Vain— Philadelphia, Willig. [n.d.]; Clifton, A.- The Rejected Lover—Philadelphia, Willig. [n.d.]; Christiani, S.- The All of Life is Love—Philadelphia, Willig. [n.d.]; Bishop, H. R.- A Highland Laddie Heard of War—Philadelphia, Willig. [n.d.]; Moore (arr. Sir John Stevenson)- All That's Bright Must Fade—Philadelphia, Willig. [n.d.]; Moore/ Bishop.- Say, What Shall Be Our

Sport Today?—Philadelphia, Willig. [n.d.]; Gilfert, C.- Farewell—New York, J. Appel. [n.d.]; Paisello/ Bishop.- Oh! Maiden Fair—New York, Dubois & Stoddart. [n.d.]; Stevenson, Sir J. A.- I'll Watch for Thee From My Lonely Bower—Baltimore, Willig. [n.d.]

VP1.2—Collection of anon. songs and some from "Der Freyshütz." No publisher, n.d. 23.6 x 17.8 cm. 18 pp.

VP1.3—They Say, My Love is Dead!/ the celebrated/ Maniac Song/ from the First number of/ Linley's/ Scottish Melodies/ Philadelphia, G. E. Blake. [n.d.] [25 x 35 cm. 2 sheets.]

VP1.4—Zwölf Favorit Gesänge aus der Oper/ die Hochzeit des Figaro/ von Herrn/ W. A. Mozart/ in Heilbronn bei Anom. [n.d.] [24 x 30.2 cm. 60 pp.]

VP1.5—Selections from the Oratorio of the/ Creation/ composed by/ Haydn/ consisting of/ With Verdure Clad/ On Mighty Wings/ Most Beautiful Appear/ In Native Worth. Of Stars the Fairest/ Graceful Consort/ arranged for the/ voice and piano/ by/ B. Carr/ Phila., G. Willig. Copyright 1822. [25.5 x 26 cm. 37 pp. Written on cover: "Selections from the/ oratorio of the Creation/ composed by Haydn/ Harmonie, Ia., June 1823."]

VP1.6—A collection of songs bound in boards and leather. 33.5 x 25 cm. 155 pp. of music. In gold letters on spine: "Songs/ and/ Duets." Contents: Anon. arr.- Pleyel's Favorite German Hymn—Philadelphia, Willig. [n.d.]; Horn, C. E.- Cherry Ripe—New York, Dubois & Stodart. [n.d.]; Handel, G. F.- Lord Remember David—Philadelphia, Willig. [n.d.]; Moore/ O. Shaw- Mary's Tears—Providence, O. Shaw, performance date 1827; Handel, G. F.- Holy, Holy, Lord—Philadelphia, Willig. [n.d.]; Fowler, Miss.— My Native Land Goodnight—Philadelphia, G. E. Blake. [n.d.]; Parry, John- Sweet Home—Philadelphia, Willig. [n.d.]; Anon.- The Yellow Hair'd Laddie—Baltimore, Willig [n.d.]; Bishop, H. R.- Bid Me Discourse—Philadelphia, G. E. Blake. [n.d.]; Bayley, T. H.- I'd Be a Butterfly—New York, A. Fleetwood. [n.d.]; King, M. P.- Father Thy Word is Past—Philadelphia, Willig. [n.d.]; Mozart/ arr. Farrari- O Dolce Concento—Philadelphia, Willig. [n.d.]; Anon.- Our Way Across the Sea—Baltimore, John Cole. Copyright 1825; Cherubini, L.- La Primavera—Leipzig, chez H. A. Probst. [n.d.]; Moore/ arr. Stevenson, Sir John- O Come to Me—Philadelphia, Willig. [n.d.]; Moore/ Meincke- Oh Thou Who Dryest the Mourner's Tears—Baltimore, Willig. Copyright 1827; Braham, Mr.- The Bird Duet—New York, Dubois. [n.d.]; Boyde, Dr.- Together Let Us Range the Fields—Philadelphia, Klemm. [n.d.]; Devonshire, Duchess of- Sweet is the Vale—Philadelphia, John Aitken [n.d.]; Anon.- Sound the Loud Timbrel—New York, Geib. [n.d.]; Braham, Mr.- When Thy Bosom Heaves the Sigh—Philadelphia, Willig. [n.d.]; Moore/ Stevenson.- Hark! The Vesper Hymn is Stealing—Baltimore, Willig. [n.d.]; Clifton, A.- See the Leaves Around Us Falling—Philadelphia, Willig. [n.d.]; Heber, Dr.- From Greenland's Icy Mountains—Baltimore, Willig. [n.d.]; Anon.- Far, Far, O'er Hill and Dell—New York, T. Birch. [n.d.]; King, M.L.- Eve's Lamentation—New York, E. Riley. [n.d.]

VP1.7—A Collection of sheet music bound in boards and leather. 34 x 25.2 cm. 52 sheets.

Contents:

Handel.- Oh! Had I Jubal's Lyre—New York, Dubois. [n.d.]; Handel.- Angels Ever Bright and Fair—New York, Dubois. [n.d.]; Handel.- So Shall the Lute and Harp Awake—Philadelphia, Willig. [n.d.]; Anon.- Let the Bright Seraphim—New York, Firth and Hall. [n.d.]; Taylor, S.P.- That I May Dwell in the House of the Lord—New York, E. Riley. Copyright 1818.; Himmel/ Gardner.- Sound the Trumpets—Philadelphia, Willig. [n.d.]; Anon.- Thou Art, Oh God—[No pub., n.d.]; Taylor, J.B.- Thy Will Be Done—New York, W. Taylor. [n.d.]; Anon.- The Sky Lark—Boston, C. Bradlee. [n.d.]; Barnett, John.- The Light Guitar—Philadelphia, Klemm. [n.d.]; Fisher, Charles F.- Washington's March—Baltimore, Willig. 1830.; Hart, Joseph.- Tyrolese Peasant's Song—New York. J. Hewitt. [n.d.]; Rossini, G.- Green Hills of Tyrol—New York, J. Hewitt. [n.d.]; Smith, S. T.- Follow, Follow Over Mountain—Philadelphia, Klemm. [n.d.]; Horn, Charles E.- The Chimes of Zurich—New York, Hewitt. [n.d.]; Pons, Signior.- Mi Pizzica, Mi Stimola—New York, Bourne. Copyright 1830.; Willis, I.- A Feather—Philadelphia. R. H. Hobson. [n.d.]; Taylor, W.- Come Let Us Trip it Lightly, Love—New York, Firth & Hall. Copyright 1829.; Anon.- And Must We Part Forever?—London, J. Dale. [n.d.]; Mazzinghi.- See from Ocean Rising—Philadelphia, Willig. [n.d.]; Bishop, H. R.- In Happier Hours—New York, Dubois & Stodard. [n.d.]; Hodson, G.A.- The Arab Steed—Philadelphia, Klemm. [n.d.]; Mozart/ Peters.- The Memory of Joys that are Past—No publisher, [n.d.].

VP1.8—Der lte Psalm/ frei übersetzt/ von/ E.C. Eccard/ In Musick gesetzt für Sopran/ mit Begleitung des Piano Forte/ der Freifrau Elise von Munk/ hochachtungsvoll gewidmet/ von/ I. M. Marx/ herausgegeben von Fried. G. Schulz in Stutgart. [n.d.]; [25 x 33.5 cm. 6 pp.music. Bound in green paper with butterfly label inscribed: "The First Psalm/ arranged for the piano/ by I.M.Marx/ Stuttgart 1825."]

VP1.9—The/ Apollo/ containing/ Sacred, Moral, Sentimental, and other songs, duetts, trios etc./ in/ seventy-five numbers/ with/ an Accompaniment/ for the/ piano forte/ New York:

Published by T. Birch/ at his Piano Forte and Music Saloon/ Copyright 1825. [34 x 25 cm. 42 sheets. Printed on spine: "Cecilia."]

Contents:

Bailey, Johanna.- O Swiftly Glides the Bonny Boat—New York, T. Birch. [n.d.]; Bishop, H.- Home Sweet Home—Philadelphia, Willig. [n.d.]; Anon.- Auld Lang Syne—Liverpool, Hime & Son. [n.d.]; Wiesenthal, T.- The Harper's Song—Philadelphia. Willig. [n.d.]; Reeve, G. W.- Oh, 'Tis Love—New York, Dubois & Stodart. [n.d.]; Anon.- C'est L'amour—London, Lavenu & Co. [n.d.]; Mannering, Guy.- Scots Wha Hae ni Wallace Bled—Liverpool, Hime & Son [n.d.]; Stevenson, J. A.- Has Sorrow Thy Young Days Shaded—Philadelphia, Willig. [n.d.]; Bishop, Henry.- Though Tis All but a Dream—Philadelphia, Willig. [n.d.]; Bishop, H.- The Pilgrim of Love—Philadelphia, Willig. [n.d.]; Bishop, H.- Home Sweet Home—London, Goulding, L'lmaine & Co. [n.d.]; May, J.D.- The Lord's Prayer—Philadelphia, Willig. Copyright 1817.; King. M.- The Minute Gun at Sea—Philadelphia, Willig. [n.d.]; Clarke, William.- Where Shall the Lover Rest?—Edinburgh, J. Hamilton. [n.d.]; Bishop, H.- Bright Be Thy Dreams—Philadelphia, Willig. [n.d.]; Mozart-Forget Me Not—Philadelphia, Willig. [n.d.]; Mozart.- Ehelicher Guter Morgan und Ehelicher Gute Nacht—Amsterdam, J.H. Henning. [n.d.]; Schoor, H.D.- La vie est un éclair—Amsterdam, Henning. [n.d.]; Braham, Mr.- William Tell—Philadelphia, Willig. [n.d.]; Moschelles, J.- The Switzer's Song of Home—New York, J. Hewitt. [n.d.];

VP1.10—A Collection of sheet music bound in boards and leather. On cover in gold letters: "Miss Herron/ No. 2." 34 x 25 cm. 160 pp.

Contents:

Craven, J.T.- The Light barke—New York, Hewitt. [n.d.]; Stevenson, J.A. [arr.].- Fallen is thy throne—New York, Dubois. [n.d.]; King, M.P.- Father thy word is Past—Philadelphia., Willig. [n.d.]; Mozart [arr. T.W.H.BB.- Go forget Me—New York, Dubois & Stodart. c; 1828; Anon.- Follow, Follow Me—Philadelphia., Willig. c; 1826; T.W.H.B.B.- Lassie wi' the lint white lock—Phila., Willig. [n.d.]; Bayly, Thomas H.- We Met—Phila., Klemm. [n.d.]; Anon.- The Castilian Maid—New York, E. Riley. [n.d.]; Wade, I.A.- Love was once a little Boy—Baltimore, John Cole. [n.d.]; Bishop, H. Home sweet Home—Philadelphia., Willig. [n.d.]; Lee, Alexander- Harrah for the Bonnets of Blue—Philadelphia, Klemm. [n.d.]; Stevenson, J.- Oft in the Stilly Night—Phla., Klemm. [n.d.]; Stevenson, J.- The harp that once thro' Tara's Halls—Phila., Willig. [n.d.]; Millard, Mrs. P.- Alice Gray—New York, Dubois & Stodart. [n.d.]; Anon.- Who'll be king but Charlie—Phila., G.E. Blake. [n.d.]; Greene, J.G. [arr.]- O swiftly glides the Bonnie Boat—New York, Riley. ct. 1827; Bishop, H.- Oh! I'll never Mention Him—

Phila., Klemm. [n.d.]; Hime, B.- I see them on their Winding Way—Phila., Klemm. [n.d.]; Hansen, E.R.- Cadets March—Phila., Klemm. [n.d.]; Johnson, F.- Capt. J. Mountfort's March—Phila., Willig. [n.d.]; Anon.- Russian March and the Emperor Alexander's Waltz—Phila., Klemm. [n.d.]; Anon.- The Boston Cadets' March—Phila., Klemm. [n.d.]; Coppock, W.R.—Favorite waltzes—[arranged] by the author & Firth & Hall. [n.d.]; Anon.- Bonaparte's Coronation—Phila., Willig. [n.d.]; A member of the St. Cecilia Soc. of Phila.- Air with vars.—Phila., Willig. ct. 1825 pf. solo; Coppock, W.R.- Oh, no, we never mention Her—New York, Bourne, ct. 1829 pf. solo; Haydn.- Military movement for the pf. or organ—New York, Firth & Hall. [n.d.]; An Eminent Professor. Le tout Ensemble—New York, Firth & Hall. [n.d.] pf solo; Coppock. The village Wake—New York, Firth & Hall, [n.d.]; Rossini/Herz. Henri (arr.). Chorus from William Tell pf solo—Phila., Klemm. [n.d.]; W. C. P. [Peters, Wm. C.]. Pittsburgh March—New York, Hewitt. [n.d.] pf. solo; Clifton, A. La Fayette's Welcome—Baltimore, Willig. c. 1824; pf. solo; Pirsson, Alex. T. Grand March—New York, Riley. [n.d.] pf. solo; Krietzer, Me. Favorite Overture to Lodoiska—New York, Dubois. [n.d.] arr. pf solo.

VP1.11—We Met by Chance/Lauf der Welt/Song/ The English words by/W. Bartholomew/the music by/F. Kucken/Phila., A. Fiot. [n.d.] [35 x 27.5 cm. 3 sheets.]

VP1.12—Hours there were/a favorite song/written/ and arranged for the/piano forte/by Joseph Wade Esqr./Philadelphia, Kretschmar & Nunns. [n.d.] [37 x 26.5 cm. 2 sheets.]

VP1.13—Oh! No and Oh! Yes/a Ballad/sung by/ Miss Lewis/composed by/A. Lee/New York, Published by Monson Bancroft. [n.d.] [36 x 27 cm. 2 sheets.]

VP1.14—The Neva Boatman's Song/for three voices/composed and arranged by/Charles E. Horn/New York/published by Hewitt. [n.d.] [34.5 x 27.5 cm. 4 sheets.]

VP1.15—From Greenland's Icy Mountains/A Missionary Hymn/by the late Bishop Heber of Calcutta /composed and dedicated to/Miss Mary W. Howard /of Savannah, Georgia/by/Lowell Mason/Boston, Published by James L. Hewitt. [n.d.] [27 x 35.3 cm. 2 sheets.]

VP1.16—Come ye Disconsolate/a sacred song/arranged and dedicated to/Mr. George Dutton/by/ D. Dutton/New York, published by Dubois & Stodart. [n.d.] [27 x 36 cm. 3 pp.]

VP1.17—The Young & Blooming Bride/sung by/ Mr. Brenan/composed by/J. Addison/Phila., Published and sold at G. Willig's musical magazine. [n.d.] [25 x 35.5 cm. 3 sheets.]

VP1.18—Paul and Mary/taken from a fragment/ in/Paul and Virginia/words by A.A.H./Music by

S.M.H./Philadelphia, Published & sold by C. Willig. [n.d.] [incomplete] [25 x 35 cm. 2 sheets.]

VP1.19—Twilight Dews/a/favorite song/with an accompaniment for the/Piano Forte/Philadelphia, Kretschmar & Nunns. [n.d.] [26.5 x 37.5 cm. 2 sheets.]

VP1.20—By the margin of fair Zurich's Waters/ the much admired song/a la Suisse/as sung by/ Miss Watson/ at/ Niblo's Garden concerts/ composed by/ Alexr. Lee/ arranged with symphonies & accompaniments by/ J. Watson/ New York, Firth & Hall. c. 1835. [36.5 x 27 cm. 2 sheets.]

VP1.21—Die Trennung [title page missing]. A work in three sections for voice and keyboard accompaniment (Die Trennung: Das spinnende Mädchen: Lottens Leiden). [25 pp. bound in cardboard.]

VP1.22—Now Rest Thee Here My Gondolier/poetry by/H. S. Gibson/composed & arranged for the/Piano Forte/by/R. Culver/Philadelphia, Barclay & Culver. [n.d.] [37 x 27 cm. 2 sheets.]

VP1.23—When Other Friends are Round Thee/ Song/composed and arranged/for the/Piano Forte /by A. Schmitz/Philadelphia/Published by Klemm & Brother. c. 1846. [35.5 x 27.8 cm. 3 sheets.]

VP1.24—Queen of My Soul/Rizzio's Last Song/ as sung by/Mr. F. Webster/the words by/Miss Costello/the music composed by/Miss Wollaston/ Boston, published by G. P. Reed. c. 1843. [35.5 x 27 cm. 2 sheets.]

VP1.25—The Old Sexton/words by/Park Benjamin, Esq./music composed and respectfully dedicated to/William Babcock, Esq./by/Henry Russell/Boston/published by Oliver Ditson & Co. c. 1841. [35 x 27 cm. 4 sheets.]

VP1.26—The/Vocal Beauties/of/Lucia di Lammermoor/with English & Italian text/translated by /J. E. A. Smith, Esq./adapted & arranged by/ Edward L. White/Boston/Oliver Ditson. c. 1848. [35 x 27 cm. 4 sheets.]

VP1.27—The May Queen/or/Youth, Spring & Flowers/words by/Mrs. A. H. C. Phelps/the music composed/& respectfully dedicated to/Dr. J. G. Wood/ by/ Henry Rohbock/ Baltimore/ published by F. D. Benteen. [n.d.] [36 x 27.5 cm. 3 sheets.]

VP1.28—Simon the Cellarer/words by/W. H. Bellamy, Esq./music by/J. L. Hatton [no. pub., no. date]. [27 x 35.5 cm. 3 sheets.]

VP1.29—Serenade Through the Leaves, composed by/Franz Schubert/Philadelphia/published by G. Andre & Co. [n.d.] [35.5 x 27 cm. 2 sheets.]

VP30.1—Beautiful Dreamer/One of the latest songs/of/Stephen C. Foster/composed a short time before his death/published by Wm. A. Pond & Co. New York/c. 1864. [34 x 26 cm. 3 sheets.]

VP1.31—Popular songs/from over the/ ocean/The Naughty young man—A. G. Vance/ Marshall, Mich./J. S. White & Co. [n.d.] [35 x 27 cm. 4 sheets.]

VP1.32—The German Fatherland/Wo ist des Deutschen/Vaterland?/German National Song/ for Singing and Piano Solo/Philadelphia/ Louis Meyer. c. 1870. [35.5 x 27 cm. 3 sheets.]

VP1.33—Nordland/Ballad/words translated from the/Swedish/by/Frederick Peterson/Music arranged by/Mme Hilma Berg/New York/William Pond & Co. c. 1879. [35.5 x 27 cm. 3 sheets.]

VP1.34—Moore's/ Irish/ Melodies/ with the celebrated and unsurpassed/symphonies and Accompaniments/of/Sir John Stevenson, Mus., Doc.,/and/Sir Henry Bishop/Commemorative/ Edition (1879)/ The London Printing and Publishing Co. [34.5 x 25 cm. 400 printed pages of music.]

VP1.35—Nonpareil Collection/ of/ Vocal Music/Three Fishers went Sailing/Music by Mr. John Hullah/Published by/National Music Co./Chicago—New York. [n.d.] [35.5 x 26.5 cm. 2 sheets.]

VP1.36—Campaign Song/1880/While we are Marching/for/Garfield/words and music by Thomas D. Story/. cr. 1880. [36 x 27 cm. 3 sheets.]

VP1.37—Ave Maria/à Mme Miolan-Carvalho/ Mélodie Religieuse/adaptée au/ler Prelude de J. S. Bach/par/Ch. Gounod/New York, G. Schirmer (B. Schott's Sohne in Mainz) [n.d.]. [34.5 x 28 cm. 6 sheets.]

VP1.38—Songs by/American Composers/Gottschalk, Louis Moreau—Slumber on, Baby Dear—/ Boston/Oliver Ditson Company. c. 1891. [35 x 27 cm. 5 sheets.]

VP1.39—Roll, Jordan Roll/This is one of the oldest Ethiopian Melodies/and is now sung by the contrabands at Port/Royal, South Carolina/ arranged and adapted/by/C. Everest/Philadelphia, Lee & Walker. cr. 1892. [35.5 x 27 cm. 3 sheets.]

VP1.40—Save, Or I perish!/Bass Song/words by/ Fanny Crosby/ music by/ George S. Banger/ copyright 1894 by A. M. Banger, Hounslow, N.Y. [35.5 x 27 cm. 3 sheets.]

VP1.41—Crossing the Bar/words by/Tennyson/ music by/A.M.B./copyright 1894 by A. M. Banger, Hounslow, N.Y. [35.5 x 27 cm. 3 sheets.]

VP1.42—Don't Be Cross/Sei Nicht Bös/Song from the Opera "Der Obersteiger"/Carl Zeller/ Copyright 1896. Bosworth & Co. Leipzig. [34 x 26.5 cm. 2 sheets.]

VP1.43—The Boston Weekly Journal of/Sheet Music/February 10, 1897/"De Swanee Ribber"/ Old Folks at Home/written and composed by/ Stephen C. Foster/Boston/F. Trifet, Publisher. [35.5 x 27 cm. 2 sheets.]

VP1.44—One Sweetly/ Solemn Thought/ Sacred Song/for Mezzo-Soprano or Baritone/composed by/R. S. Ambrose/Pittsburgh, Pa./Published at Basler's Music House/ published 1897 by H. R. Basler. [35.5 cm x 27 cm. 3 sheets.]

VP1.45—Happy Days/ in Georgia/ March/ two step/ and Cakewalk/ by/ Chas. Kuebler/ composer of/KahKwa Club two step etc./Published by/Brehm Bros./Erie, Pa./. c. 1900 by Brehm Bros. [35.5 x 27 cm. 3 sheets.]

VP1.46—Dreams/ words and music by/ Dave Fitzgibbon/ Supplement/ to/ the/ New York/ Herald/April 5th/1903/. c. 1909 Witmark & Sons New York, London & Chicago. [35.5 x 25 cm. 2 sheets.]

VP1.47—When Our Boys/ Come Marching/ Home/ words and music by/ Gilbert Eberhart/ Philadelphia, Pa./ published M. D. Swisher. c. 1899. [35 x 27 cm. 3 sheets.]

VP1.48—Whose is the Picture?/ Query/ Nellie M. Shevlin/copyrighted 1903 by Nellie M. Shevlin. [no publisher]. [30 x 22 cm. 2 sheets.]

VP1.49—Blue Eyes/words by/Edward Hoopes/ music by/R. T. Townsend/published by Wm. C. Ott & Co., Beaver Falls, Pa. Copyright 1897. [35.5 x 27 cm. 3 sheets.]

VP1.50—The/ Angelus/ written and/ composed by/ "Roma"/ Supplement to the/ New York/ Herald,/ October 5/ 1902/ published by/ permission of/M. Witmark,/& Sons. [35 x 26 cm. 2 sheets.]

VP1.51—The/ Roses'/ Greeting/ Supplement to/The New York Herald,/November 30th 1902/ Music by Julius J. Lyons. [35 x 26 cm. 2 sheets.]

VP1.52—My/ Love/ Am'abel/ Words by/ Miss Rae Kopelman/Music by/Carmelo Trusiano/. Published by permission of C. Trusiano, Hartford, Conn./Music Section New York American and Journal, Sunday, Sept. 24, 1905. [35 x 26 cm. 2 sheets.]

VP1.53—The/ March of Time/ Souvenir of Old Economy/ (Words and Music/ by J. S. Duss) Souvenir edition of 1000 copies, June, 1921. Dedicated by permission to His Excellency William C. Sproul, Governor of Pennsylvania. [31 x 23.8 cm. 5 pp.]

VP1.54—The Trolley/ Song March/ and/ Two Step/J. S. Duss. Dedicated to W. L. Mellon. Pres't of the Monongahela Street Railway Co. Pittsburgh, Pa./Published by W. C. Ott & Co./ 225 4th Ave. Copyright, 1901. [35.3 x 27 cm. 5 pp.]

VP1.55—Life's/ Voyage/ Waltz/ Song/ and/ Refrain./By J. S. Duss/published by/Wm. C. Ott and Co./Beaver Falls, Pa. Copyright, 1895. [35.3 x 27 cm. 5 pp.]

VP1.56—The Tourist's Song of Florida/ Florida/All-Hail/By J. S. Duss/Published by/Volkwein Bros. Inc. Pittsburgh, Pa. Copyright, 1935. [31 x 23.5 cm. 5 pp.]

VP1.57—The/ Cross/ and/ Crown/ March/ Song/Two Step/By/J. S. Duss/Pittsburgh, Pa./ Published by/Wm. C. Ott & Co./Copyright 1898. [35 x 27 cm. 5 pp.]

VP1.58—Trio From The March G.A.R. in Dixie/ J. S. Duss/Copyright, 1895, Wm. Co. Ott & Co./ Beaver Falls, Pa. [35 x 27 cm. 1 sheet.]

VP1.59—March/ G.A.R./ in/ Dixie/ or/ North / And South/ Two Step/ by J. S. Duss/ of the/ Harmonie Society-Economy, Pa./ Published by Wm. C. Ott. & Co. Beaver Falls, Pa. Copyright 1895. [35.5 x 27 cm. 5 pp.]

VP1.60—Shot and Shell March/Two Step/Dedicated to Rear Admiral George Dewey/The Hero of Manila/by/J. S. Duss/Published by W. C. Ott & Co./Pittsburgh Copyright 1898. [35 x 27.3 cm. 5 pp.]

VP1.61—America/ Up/ to Date/ Song/ Two Step/by/J. S. Duss/Published by/Wm. C. Ott & Co., Beaver Falls, Pa. Copyright 1897. [35.5 x 27 cm. 5 pp.]

VOCAL: PRINTED PART-BOOKS

VP2.1—3 und 4 Stimmige Lieder. Verlag von Joh. André in Offenbach a.M. [n.d.]; 1. Franz Abt, Op. 369, Nos. 1-5; 2. E. F. Richter, Op. 14, Nos. 1-6; 3. H. Kurth, Op. 2, Nos. 1-3 [Alt., sop., bass part-books. 17 x 27 cm. Ea. 16 pp.]

VOCAL: PRINTED SCORES

VP3.1—Collection of anonymous sacred choruses. Four copies. Three inscribed: 1. Jacob Henrici 2. Gertrud Rapp 3. J. C. Mueller. No publisher, [n.d.] [31.7 x 33.3 cm. 17 sheets, 34 pp. music.]

VP3.2—Collection of sacred choruses (continuation of VP3.1). Pagination from 37 to 68. 2 copies. One inscribed: "Henrici."

VP3.3—Choruses/solos/duets/and recitatives/ from the works of/Handel, Haydn, Mozart, Beethoven/arr. in/Full Vocal Score/and Interspersed with noted and explanatory remarks by Samuel Dyer. J. D. Auner, Philadelphia. Copyright 1830. [36 x 19.6 cm. 240 pp. music.]

VP3.4—German songs for SATB and piano accompaniment. Contents: Drei Gesänge von Gellert . . . Joseph Haydn; XII Gesänge . . . von J. Amon; Sprichwörter . . . von A. André and Haydn's Schwanengesang. J. André, Offenbach a.M' [n.d.] [32.6 x 23.9 cm. 32 sheets. 44 pp. music.]

VP3.5—Sammlung/Religioser Deutscher Gesänge/nebst einem kurzen fasslichen/unterricht zum Singen/eingerichtet für/oeffentlichen Gottesdienst und/Singeschulen. I. G. Schmauk, Philadelphia. 1824. [34.9 x 25.4 cm. 108 pp. music.]

VP3.6—Cantata/nach Moses Mendelssohns Uebersetzung des 31ten Psalm's/für/4 Singstimmen mit Begleitung des Orchesters und der Orgel/in musik gesetz/. . . von J. G. Schade/Offenbach a/M bey Johann André. [n.d.] [32.8 x 25.1 cm. 76 pp. music.]

VP3.7—Hymne/ Danket dem Herrn/ für/ Sopran, Alt., Tenor und Bass/ in Musik gesetz . . . von/ G. H. Rink/ B. Schott Sohne [n.d.] [35.1 x 25.7 cm. 14 pp. music.]

VP3.8—Charfreytags Cantata/für Sopran, Alt., Tenor und Bass/mit Obligater Orgel oder Clavierbegleitung/Seinem Freunde/dem/Grossherzogl. Hessischen Hof-Kapellmeister/Herrn Appold zu Darmstadt/gewidmet von/G. H. Rinck/B. Schott Sohne. [n.d.] [32.3 x 26.5 cm. 23 pp. music.]

VP3.9—Die Worte des Glaubens/von/Schiller/ als Cantata bearbeitet/und/dem Caecilienverein in Frankfurt a/M gewidmet von Aloys Schmitt/ 30tes Werk. J. André, Offenbach a/M. [n.d.] [34.4 x 25.3 cm. 22 pp. music.]

VP3.10—[Mozart's Requiem. Title page lost. Pub. Plate No. 3206 32.6 x 23.6 cm. 59 pp. music.]

VP3.11—Vierzehn/Vierstimmige Figural-Gesänge/für Kirchen und Schulgebrauch/von/ Stifts/Musik-director Concertmeister/L. Abeille/ 1 Heft/Stuttgart [n.d.] [27.7 x 21.3 cm. 15 pp. music.]

VP3.12—Te Deum Laudamus/Francisco I/Dei Gratia Austriae Imperatori/Submisse dedicat/ Andreas Romberg/N. Simrock. [59 pp. Bound with] La Primavera: Der Frühling/Vierstimmige Cantata/mit Italienischem und Deutschem Text/ in Musik gesetz/mit Begleitung des Pianoforte/ von/L. Cherubini/Leipzig/chez H. A. Probst. [n.d.] [25.7 x 32.6 cm. 86 pp. music.]

VP3.13—Die Jahreszeiten/ von/ Joseph Haydn/Clavierauszug/Breitkopf & Härtel/Leipzig, 1801. [34.4 x 27.2 cm. 174 pp. music.]

VP3.14—The/ Messiah/ composed by/ G. F. Handel/arranged for the/Organ or Piano Forte/ by Dr. John Clarke/of Cambridge/Philadelphia/ G. E. Blake. [n.d.] [25.4 x 34.4 cm. 213 pp.]

VP3.15—Die Zehn Gebote/Das Unser Vater/ und Das Appostolische Glaubens-Bekenntnis/ componiert von/Jacob Henrici/in/Economy, Pa./Copyright 1891. [25.3 x 33.8 cm. 9 pp.]

VP3.16—Anonymous Choruses inscribed in ink: "Verschiedenartige 3 und 4 stim. Gesänge/Religiosen Innhalts." [No pub., n.d. 17.5 x 25.5 cm. 16 sheets.]

VP3.17—Am Kreuz erblasst der Marterlast. [No pub., n.d. Anonymous chorus (SATB). Bass part has watermark: "B. Schott Soehne in Mainz." 26.5 x 17 cm. 12 pp.]

VP3.18—Esther,/The Beautiful Queen/A Cantata or short oratorio/designed for/Musical Conventions, Festivals, and Musical Societies./ Composed by William Bradbury/New York/ Mason Brothers. Copyright 1856. [16.8 x 25 cm. 88 pp.]

VP3.19—Frost Queen/and/Santa Claus/A Christmas Cantata/Words by/Fannie J. Crosby/ Music by W. Howard Doane/New York and Chicago/Copyright 1890. [20.5 x 19.4 cm. 80 pp.]

VP3.20—Shattuch's/Male Quartette/Folio/A collection of Standard and Popular Music/arranged for male voices by/Chas. F. Shattuck/ New York. Copyright 1891. [27.5 x 19.4 cm. 80 pp.]

VP3.21—The Harvest time is passing/for Contralto or Baritone/(and mixed chorus)/c. 1875 by W. L. Thompson & Co.,/East Liverpool, Ohio. [35 x 27 cm. 3 sheets.]

VP3.22—Swinging in the/Summer Air/Song and chorus/Music by Jno. B. Grant/New York/ Published by Wm. A. Pond & Co./Copyright, 1877. [35 x 27 cm. 3 sheets.]

VP3.23—Come where the Lilies Bloom/A Beautiful/Quartett/Written &/Composed by/Will L. Thompson Music Co./c. 1878. [35 x 27 cm. 6 sheets.]

VP3.24—Come, Holy Spirit;/Sacred Quartette/ by/ Will Thompson/ East Liverpool, Ohio/ copyright 1881. [35 x 27 cm. 4 sheets.]

VP3.25—Vox Angelorum/ A Collection of/ Sacred Music with Latin and English Words/ for / Quartette Chorus/ arranged by/ H. Bialla/ New York, Wm. A. Pond & Co./ Copyright 1879. [35.5 x 27.5 cm. 5 sheets.]

VP3.26—Beautiful/ Sacred Songs/ for the Choir and Home Circle/by/Will L. Thompson/ Like as a Father Pitieth His Children. Quartette/ Will L. Thompson & Co./East Liverpool, Ohio. Copyright 1879. [35 x 27 cm. 3 sheets.]

VP3.27—Millard's Selections/ Vol. II/ New York/Published by S. T. Gordon & Son/Copyright, 1878. A Collection of/Anthems, Motets, Sentences and Offertory Pieces/ for/Quartette and Chorus Choirs/By Harrison Millard. [30 x 23.5 cm. 152 pp.]

VP3.28—Florodora/A Musical Comedy/Lyrics by/ Ernest Boyd Jones and Paul Rubens/Music by/ Leslie Stuart/Copyright 1899 by Francis, Day & Hunter/[title page missing]. [22.5 x 28.5 pp.]

VP3.29—The/Songs/of England. Vol./I/Edited by J. L. Hatton/New York. W. A. Pond & Co.

[n.d.]. A Collection of 200 English Melodies, including the most popular Traditional Ditties, and the Principal Songs and Ballads of the Last Three Centuries. Edited, with new symphonies and accompaniments, by J. L. Hatton. In Two Volumes; each containing 100 songs. London: Boosey & Co., New York: William A. Pond and Co. [n.d.] [18 x 26 cm. 240 pp.]

VP3.30—Sacred Songs,/Ancient and Modern/A Complete Collection of/Sacred Vocal Music,/By/ Celebrated Composers,/Suitable for Home Use/ Edited by/John Hiles/London: Boosey and Co./ New York: William A. Pond and Co. [n.d.]. [17.5 x 26 cm. 252 pp.]

VP3.31—The/Psalm of Psalms/Anthem/with/ Bass Solo, Recitative/ and/ chorus for Mixed Voices/ by/ J. S. Duss/ Volkweins/ Pittsburg, Pa. Copyright 1934. [17.5 x 26 cm. 9 pp.]

VP3.32—Mass/ in Honor of/ St. Veronica/ by/ J. S. Duss/ Volkwein Bros./ Pittsburgh, Pa. Copyright 1929. [26.7 x 27.5 cm. 56 pp.]

VP3.33—O Sacred Book/Duet/For Tenor (or Bar.) and Bass/with Chorus/Words by/John Mc-Kee/Music by/J. S. Duss/Volkwein Bros./Pittsburgh. Copyright 1929. [17.5 x 26.5 cm. 4 pp.]

VP3.34—O Salutaris/ Latin text and English Text/ Solo/ for/ Alto or Baritone with Chorus/ or Duet for Soprano and Alto with Chorus or/ Solo and Duet (as above) with Chorus/ by/ J. S. Duss/ Volkwein Bros./ Pittsburgh, Pa. Copyright 1929 by John S. Duss, New Smyrna, Fla. [17.5 x 26.5 cm. 7 pp.]

VP3.35—Lucia Di Lammermoor/Opera in Three Acts/by/G. Donizetti/Copyright 1898 by G. Schirmer, New York. [19.5 x 28 cm. 240 pp.]

VP3.36—Handel's Sacred Oratorio,/The Messiah,/Vocal Score/Edited by V. Novello./Boston [n.d.] [25.5 x 17.5 cm. 182 pp. (covers missing).]

VP3.37—Sänger-Freund/herausgegeben von F. Meckel/für Christliche Vereins und Kirchen-Chöre: Cleveland, Ohio. [A monthly publication of choral music by various composers. Pagination is continuous from January through December. 19.5 x 26 cm. Unbound. Copies here: Jan., Feb., Oct., 1888; August, Sept., Oct., Nov., Dec., 1889.]

VP3.38—Tempel-Musik und Poesie/Die Lösung des Volkes Gottes/Von Christophorus Hoffmann in Jerusalem/Choral und Figural Gesang für gemischte Stimmen mit Orgel-Begleitung . . . von /Wilhelm F. Schmilk/Tempelleher, Organist und Pastor./Im Selbstverlag des herausgebers/Schenectady, New York/1888.[25.5 x 19.5 cm. 14 pp.]

VP3.39—The Lord is My Shepherd/Schubert, F. Copyright 1872 John Church Co., Cincinnati, Ohio. [16.8 x 25.3 cm. 6 pp.]

VP3.40—O Saving Victim/ Soprano Solo, with quartette/ and Chorus, ad lib./ composed by S. B. Whiteley./ New York/ Wm. A. Pond & Co. Copyright 1880. [17 x 27 cm. 9 pp.]

VP3.41—Thou Lovely Maid/ (English version by Louis C. Elson) F. Lynes, Op. 6 No. 2/ Copyright 1887 by Arthur Schmidt & Co. [Collection of songs with keyboard acc. 19.5 x 28.5 cm. Covers and 32 pages missing. Pagination here begins with p. 33 and final page is 51.]

VP3.42—Wilson's Sacred Quartetts/ composed and arranged with separate accom. for/ Organ or Pianoforte/ and adapted to the/ Psalms and Hymns/ Including the Additional Hymns, together with other portions of the service of the/ Protestant Episcopal Church/ by Henry Wilson/ organist of Christ Church, Hartford, Conn./ New York/ Gordon & Son. Copyright 1867. [23.5 x 28 cm. 18 pp. sample of bound, 2 vol. set].

VP3.43—A Spring Song/ Mixed Quartet/ Pinsuti, C. Oliver Ditson Co./ Boston [n.d.]. [27 x 17.5 cm. 3 sheets.]

VP3.44—Selections/ from. Ulysses/ Opera Comique/ in 3 Acts/ the music by/ W. H. Neidlinger/ The Book by/ R. E. Phillips/ New York, G. Schirmer. Copyright 1898. [28 x 19.5 cm. 19 pp.]

VP3.45—Farewell to May/ Madrigal for two trebles, alto, tenor and Bass. Florio, C. Wm. Pond & Co. New York, C. 1871. [17 x 27 cm. 4 sheets.]

VP3.46—Songs of the Flowers/ Twelve/ Two-part Songs/ for/ Women's Voices/ by/ Ciro Pinsuti/ New York/ G. Schirmer [n.d.]. [17.8 x 26.5 cm. 49 pp.]

VP3.47—The/ Daughter of Jairus/ A Sacred Cantata/ Music/ by/ John Stainer/ New York/ G. Schirmer. [n.d.] [26.5 x 17.5 cm. 56 pp.]

VP3.48—Benedictus in D./ Wilson, Henry, Wm. A. Pond & Co. Copyright 1877. [Part of larger work; pagination begins with p. 19. 27 x 17 cm. 4 sheets.]

VP3.49—How Sweet the Answer Echo Makes/ Four part song/ music by Frank A. Howson. Ponds Collection/ of Madrigals and Glees/ New York/ Copyright 1876. [17.5 x 27 cm. 4 sheets.]

VP3.50—Song of the Vikings/ Part song with Pf or orchestral acc./ by Eaton Faning. London: Novello and Co. [n.d.] [17 x 26 cm. 7 sheets.]

VP3.51—Moonlight and Music/ Serenade [SATB] Composed by Ciro Pinsuti. London: Novello and Co. [n.d.]. [17 x 26 cm. 4 sheets.]

VP3.52—The Watchword/ a four part song/ composed by Ciro Pinsuti. London: Novello & Co. [n.d.]. [17 x 26 cm. 4 sheets.]

VP3.53—The Last Rose of Summer [SATTBB]. Parks, J. A. [arr.]. The J. A. Parks Company/

York, Nebraska, U.S.A. [n.d.] [27 x 17.8 cm. 3 sheets.]

VP3.54—The Old Oaken Bucket [male quartet]. M.C.J. [arr.]. Boston, Oliver Ditson Company. Copyright 1888. [27 x 17.5 cm. 2 sheets.]

VP3.55—Two Pilgrim Choruses from "Tannhäuser." Wagner, R. G. Schirmer/ New York [n.d.]. [26 x 17.5 cm. 4 sheets.]

VOCAL: PRINTED SCORES AND PARTS

VP4.1—Motette / Befiehl dem Herrn deine Wege/ für/ Sopran, Alt, Tenor und Bass / mit / Clavier oder Orgelbegleitung/ Componirt und dem Herrn Doctor/ August Hopmann/ grosherzoglich hessischem geheimenstaatsrath / mehr höher Orden Commandeur erster Classe/ Hochachtungsvoll gewidmet / von / Ch. H. Rink/ Schott Sohnen, Antwerpen, Mainz und Paris. [n.d.] 34.1 x 26.2 cm. 21 pp. music.]

VP4.2—Der Friede/ Ein Quartett/ für 2 Sopran, Tenor und Bass/ mit obligater Clarinett oder flöte/ und Piano-forte Begleitung/ componirt von Xaver Schnyder von Wartensee/ in Frankfurt am Mayn/ Bonn und Cöln bei N. Simrock. [n.d.] [34.3 x 26.4 cm. 11 pp.music.]

VP4.3—Luft und Licht/ Richard Kieserling Jr., Op. 12/ Copyright 1905 by Luckhardt & Belder, New York. [19.5 x 26.5 cm. Pf. score, 11 pp. 27 x 17 cm. Vocal parts, 16 pp.]

VP4.4—Grüsse an die Heimat [TTBB] Kromer, Carl. G. Schirmer, New York. [n.d.] [26.5 x 17.5 cm. 4 sheets per set.]

VP4.5—Sonntag ist's [TTBB] Breu, Simon. Published 1899 by Carl Fischer, N.Y. [27.5 x 17.5 cm. 4 sheets per set.]

VP4.6—Drei Röselein [TTBB] Silcher, F. F.A. Rockar, New York. Copyright 1893. [18 x 27.5 cm. 13 sheets per set.]

VP4.7—Weisst du Muatterl / was i träumt hab'/ Text und Musik von/ Alois Kutschera, Op. 4/ Rozsavolgyi & Co./ Budapest und Leipzig. [n.d.] [26.5 x 17 cm. 6 sheets per set.]

VP4.8—Op. 6, No. 1. Beim Liebchen zu Haus. No. 2. Mein Heimatthal [TTBB] Pheil, H. C.F. W. Siegel, Leipzig. [n.d.] [17.5 x 27 cm. 7 sheets per set.]

VP4.9—Sonntag, Op. 16. [TTBB] Birseck, L. New York, Luckhardt & Belder. Copyright 1894. [17 x 27 cm. 6 sheets.]

VP4.10—Mein Himmel auf der Erde/ Heinrich Pfeil, Op. 16./ [TTBB] New York. Carl Fischer, 1903. [27 x 18 cm. 6 sheets.]

VP4.11—Weihnachtslied/ Werner Nolopp, Op. 35/ TTBB/ Liepzig/ Gebrüder Reinecke/ 1870 [27 x 17 cm. 6 sheets.]

VP4.12—Heimkehr / Johannes Gelbke, Op. 16, No. 1/ TTBB New York, Carl Fischer, 1899. [27.5 x 17.8 cm. 6 sheets.]

VP4.13—Frühling, du Gold'ne Zeit./ Engelskirchen, P. New York, Carl Fischer. Copyright 1905 [Männerchor. 27 x 17.5 cm. 6 sheets.]

KEYBOARD: PRINTED

KP1.1-A—Collection d'Ouvertures/ pour à quatre mains/ revues par/ Hugo Ulrich/ Leipzig & Berlin/ C.F. Peters/ Bureau de Musique. [n.d.] [27.5 x 19.5 cm. 280 pp. bound in red boards. Name of Dr. B. Feicht on cover in gold letters. Contains overtures by Beethoven, Herold, Mozart, Bellini, Rossini, Boeildieu, and others.

B—Collection / D'Ouvertures / pour piano Seul/ Leipzig & Berlin/ C.F. Peters Bureau de Musique. [30 x 23 cm. 61 pp.] Bound with: "Collection d'Ouvertures / pour Piano à deux Mains/ . . ." [69 pp.] First section contains overtures by Beethoven. Second contains overtures by Bellini and Rossini, Auber, Spontini, and others.

KP1.2—Two Hundred and Fifty/ Easy Voluntaries and Interludes for the/ organ, Melodeon, Seraphine, etc./ By John Zundel/ Boston/ Published by Oliver Ditson & Co. 1851 [27.6 x 20.1 cm. 88 pp.]

KP1.3—Goodman's Rudiments/ for the/ piano forte/ with a collection of easy Lessons/for/ Young beginners/ and the most fashionable/ Waltzes, Marches, Airs, Dances/ published for the author by/ J.A. & W. Geib./ Manufacturers & Importers of Piano Fortes and Organs etc./ at their Pianoforte Warehouse & Wholesale and Retail Music/ store No. 23, Maiden Lane, New York. [n.d.] [33 x 25.2 cm. 27 pp.]

KP1.4—A Collection of duets for four hands. 24.7 x 33.1 cm. 91 pp. Contains pieces by Latour, Rossini, Mehul, Kirkman, Challoner, and Weber. Most published by Geo. Willig, Phila., and G. Blake, Phila. [n.d.] Table of contents in Dr. Mueller's hand on flyleaf. Watermark: "FELLOWS & SONS, 1821."

KP1.5—Sammlung/ Beliebter/ Tänze/ für das/ Piano-Forte/ Heidelberg/ bei Wil. Thiese. Husaren Galopp-J. Strauss. [n.d.]. [26.5 x 17 cm. 2 sheets, 3 pp of music.]

KP1.6—Gutenberg's Marsch / für das / Piano-Forte / von / Heilmann / Mainz, bei B. Schott's Sohnen. [n.d.] [27.5 x 17.4 cm. 2 sheets, 2 pp. of music.]

KP1.7—Walse / composée pour le / Piano Forte / sur des motifs de l'opera / Le Philtre / Der Liebestranck / dediée a Mademoiselle / Henriette Schott / par Jos. Kuffner / Mayence, Paris & Anvers / chez les fils de B. Schott. [n.d.]. [27 x 17.5 cm. 2 sheets, 2 pp. music.]

KP1.8—Walzer / für das / Piano-Forte / von / S.A. Zimmermann / Kraehwindliade No. 1 / Mannheim / bei K.F. Keckel. [n.d.]. [26 x 17 cm. 2 sheets, 2 pp. music.]

KP1.9—Walzer / für das / Piano-Forte / von / S.A. Zimmermann / Kraehwinkliade No. 2 / Mannheim / bei K.F. Heckel. [n.d.]. [26.5 x 17 cm. 2 sheets, 2 pp. music.

KP1.10—Walzer / für das / Piano-Forte / von / S.A. Zimmermann / Kraehwinkliade No. V / Mannheim / bei K.F. Heckel. [n.d.]. [26.5 x 16 cm. 2 sheets, 2 pp. music.]

KP1.11—2me Valse Favorite / de / Francfort / pour le / Piano Forte / Francfort a / m chez Fr. Ph. Dunst. [n.d.]. [25.8 x 16.5 cm. 2 sheets, 2 pp. music.]

KP1.12—Favorit Walzer / für das / Piano Forte / ueber den chorgesang / Der Herbst am Rhein / von / Jos. Panny / Mainz, Paris & Antwerpen / bey B. Schott's Sohnen. [n.d.]. [27 x 17.5 cm. 2 sheets, 2 pp. music.]

KP1.13—Laendler. Mannheim bei K.F. Keckel. No. 373. [n.d.]. [27 x 17 cm. 2 sheets, 2 pp. music.]

KP1.14—Laendler. Mannheim, K.F. Keckel, 240. [n.d.]. [26.7 x 16.5 cm. 2 sheets, 2 pp. music.]

KP1.15—Weiner / Pracht Walzer / für das / Piano-Forte / Heidelberg / bei Wilh. Thiese. [n.d.] [27 x 17.3 cm. 2 sheets. 2 pp. music.]

KP1.16—A. Petites Pièces, Airs et Rondeaux / pour Piano Forte et Violon ad libitum / formant quatre Suites / d'une difficulté graduelle / à l'usage des Jeunes Elèvea / extraits des Ouvrages / D'Ignace Pleyel. / Revus et corrigés par l'auteur / Bonn, Cologne chez N. Simrock / 1824. Livre 111-1V. [26.1 x 17 cm. 72 pp. music. Inscribed on cover: "Leichte stück, Arien und / Rondeux für Piano Forte / von I. Pleyel pro Gertrude Rapp / Pars III-IV."]

B. Petites Pieces. [Violin part to KP1. 16A. Inscribed on cover: "Violino für /

I. Pleyel's leichte / clavier stücke / pro Gertrude Rapp / Pars III-IV."]

KP1.17—Collection of piano pieces. Table of contents in Dr. Mueller's hand. 33.4 x 23.9 cm. 83 sheets.

Contains:

Kohler, H.- Sonate pour le pf. ou Harpe, oeuv. 83.—Hambourg, Boehm. [n.d.]; Mozart, W.A.- Ouverture d l'Opera Cosi Fan Tutti—Hambourg, Rudolphus. [n.d.]; Latour.- Duettino a quatre mains—Offenbach a/M, André s/m. [n.d.]; Vanhall, J.B.- Trois Sonatines—Offenbach a/M, André s/m. [n.d.]; Moscheles, J.- Trois Rondeaux—Offenbach a/M, André s/m. [n.d.]; Neithardt, A.- Des Menschen Singmeister— Hamburg, Cranz. [n.d.]; Mozart, W.A.- Die Zauberflöte—Hamburg, Cranz. [n.d.]; Mozart, W.A.- Don Juan—Hamburg, Cranz. [n.d.]; Von Weber, C.M.- Romanze Hamburg— Cranz. [n.d.]; Winter, P.- Romanze— Hamburg, Cranz. [n.d.]; Keller, Carl- Gesang für Guitarre od. pf.—Hanover, Bachmann. [n.d.]; Ebers, C.F.- Sechs Schottische Taenze—Offenbach a/M, André s/m. [n.d.]; Bornhardt, I.H.C.- Eccossoisen Hamburg, Boehme. [n.d.]; Schmitt, A.- Douze Walses—Offenbach a/M, André s/m. [n.d.]; C.S. [?]- Favorite Tänze—Offenbach a/M, André s/m. [n.d.]

KP1.18—School / for the / Parlor Organ, Melodeon / and / Harmonium by / J.A. Getze / Organist of Grace Church / Boston, O. Ditson & Company. 1896. [29.7 x 24.1 cm. 144 pp.]

KP1.19—Airs / Favorites / variés pour P. Forte / par / Kirmayr / à Worms / chez J.M. Götz. [n.d.] [23 x 31 cm. 5 pp. music.]

KP1.20 A.—Sammlung / Auserlesener Klavierstücke / mit angemerktem Fingersätze / von Haydn, Mozart, Clementi, Pleyel, Vogler, Knecht, etc. / für Geübtere / Neue, verbesserte Ausgabe / Einstes Heft / Freyburg und Konstanze / 1814. [25 x 21 cm. 24 pp.]

B.—Sammlung / Auserlesener Klavierstücke... Sechstes Heft. Freyburg, 1816.

C.—Sammlung / Auserlesener Klavierstücke... Fünftes Heft. Freyburg, 1816.

KP1.21—Collection of sheet music for piano. 25 x 34.5 cm. 138 pp. On spine in gold letters: "Overtures / Variations." Several sheets signed "W. C. Peters" in pencil.

Contains:

Mozart / Burrowes.- Select Airs from Celebrated Operas—Philadelphia, Klemm. [n.d.]; Mozart, W.A.- Ouverture to marriage of Figaro—Philadelphia, Willig. [n.d.];

Arne.- Overture to Artaxerxes—New York, Riley. [n.d.]; Clifton, W.- Overture to the Enterprise—Philadelphia, Willig. [n.d.]; Fodor.- Overture to Blaise and Babet— Philadelphia, Blake. [n.d.]; Bishop, H.R.- Overture to Guy Mannering—Philadelphia, Willig. [n.d.]; Ware, W.- Overture to Enchanted Harp—Philadelphia, Willig. [n.d.]; Martini.- Overture to Henry 4th—Philadelphia, Willig. [n.d.]; Hayden.- Overture for Piano Forte—Philadelphia, Willig. [n.d.]; Latour.- Overture on "Hope Told a Flattering Tale."—Philadelphia, Bacon. [n.d.]; Anon.- The Marquis de La Fayette's Gr. March—Philadelphia, Klemm. [n.d.]; A Lady of Philadelphia.—La Fayette's Gr. March—Philadelphia, Klemm. [n.d.]; Weber.- Hunter's Chorus [arr. Darley]—Philadelphia, Willig. Jan. 1826. Valentine, Thomas.- And We're a 'noddin'.—Philadelphia, Blake. [n.d.]; Anon.- The Live Long Night —Philadelphia, Willig. [n.d.]; Valentine, Thomas.- Home Sweet Home—Philadelphia, Willig. [n.d.]; Latour.- Since Then I'm Doom'd—Philadelphia, Willig. [n.d.]; Jay, J.- The Vienna Waltz—Philadelphia, Willig, [n.d.]; Lauter, Ferdinand.- Days of Absence—Philadelphia, Willig. Copyright May 1826. Latour.- The Blue Bells of Scotland—Philadelphia, Willig, [n.d.]; McFadyen, J. Jun.- Coming Thro' the Rye— Philadelphia. Willig. [n.d.]; Gelinek.- Hope Told a Flattering Tale— Philadelphia, Willig. [n.d.]; Meineke, C.- Le Petit Tambour—Baltimore, Cole. Copyright 1828.

KP1.22—Collection of music for piano forte, 33 x 25.5 cm. 270 pp.

Contains:

Kozeluch.- Duett for two Performers— Philadelphia, Willig. [n.d.]; Von Weber, Carl Maria.- Der Freyschütz, arr. Diabelli— Philadelphia, Klemm [n.d.]; Meineke, C.- La Fayette's Gr. March and Quickstep— Baltimore, Cole. 1824. Bonnhorst, C. von Esq.- Pres. Jackson's Gr. March—Philadelphia, Blake. 1829. Anon.- Overture to la Caravane—Philadelphia, Willig. [n.d.]; Rossini.- Overture to La Gazza Ladra— Philadelphia, Willig. [n.d.]; Hunten, F.- German Air—New York, Stodart & Dubois. [n.d.]; Moran, P.K.- Honi Soit Qui Mal y Pense—New York, Dubois & Stodart. 1830. Rawlings, T.A.- Oh! No, We Never Mention Her!—Boston, Hewitt. [n.d.]; Knapton, Philip.- Russian Pas Redoublé London, Goulding, D'Almaine & Co. [n.d.]; Rossini, G.- The Most Admired Subjects from His Operas—New York, Hewitt. [n.d.]; Moore, Kiallmark.- She Never Blamed Him—New York, Hewitt. [n.d.]; Cramer, J. B.- Les Bagatelles—New York, Dubois & Stodart. [n.d.]; Pixis, J. P.- Les Charmes de Vienne—Paris, Pleyel. [n.d.]; Davy, John.- New Claret—London,

Preston. [n.d.]; Latour, T.- La Biondina in Gondoletta—Paris, Pettibon; Pixis, J. P.- Favorites from Tancredi—Paris, Pleyel. [n.d.]; Dussek/ J.B. Cramer.- Dussek's Favorite Sonata—New York, Dubois & Stodart. [n.d.]; Rhein, L.- Rondoletto—Paris, Arnaud. [n.d.]; Segura, T.- New Year's Gift— Philadelphia, Willig. 1829. Haydn.- A Waltz by Dr. Haydn.—New York, Hewitt. [n.d.]; Schroeder, R.- A. Popular Swiss Air—Philadelphia, Willig. [n.d.]; Rossini.- Gr. Waltz from La Gazza Ladra— New York, Hewitt. [n.d.]; Rossini/ Metz.- Cavatina from Italian in Algeria—New York, Hewitt. [n.d.]; Rossini.- Two Airs from Barber of Seville—New York and Baltimore, Hewitt. [n.d.]; Opinsky, Count.- Two Polonaises— Philadelphia, Klemm; Fisher, C. F.- Light Brigade March—Baltimore, Willig. [n.d.]; W.C.P. W.C. Peters- Pittsburgh March— New York, Hewitt. [n.d.]; Voigt, Augustus.- Gipsy Dance—New York, Hewitt. [n.d.]

KP1.23—Collection of Organ and Choral Works 34.5 x 25.2 cm. 286 pp.

Contains:

Stanley, John.- Thirty Voluntaries for the Organ or Harpsichord—London, Harrison. [n.d.]; Handel, G.F.- Six Concertos for Harpsichord or Organ (2nd set)— London, Harrison. [n.d.]; Handel, G.F.- Six Concertos for Harpsichord or Organ— London, Harrison. [n.d.]; Handel, G.F.- Six Concertos for Harpsichord or Organ (3rd set)—London, Harrison. [n.d.]; Handel, G.F.- Acis and Galatea London, Harrison. [n.d.]; Handel, G.F.- Dryden's Ode on St. Cecilia's Day—London, Harrison. [n.d.]; Handel, G.F.- The Anthem Performed in Westminster Abbey at the Funeral of Queen Carolina—London, Harrison. [n.d.]

KP1.24—Collection of Music for the Piano. 25 x 34 cm. 139 pp.

Contains:

Purcell.- Purcell's Ground—Philadelphia, Blake. [n.d.]; Christiani, S.- Commodore Decatur's Funeral March—Philadelphia, [No pub., n.d.]; Anon.- Emperor Russia's/ Emperor of Austria's & Maria Louisa's Favorite Waltzes—Philadelphia, Blake. [n.d.]; Anon.- A Favorite Waltz—Philadelphia, Blake. [n.d.]; Kelly, Mr.- March and Quickstep in the Forty Thieves—Philadelphia, Blake. [n.d.]; Goeneke, J.F.- Grand Masters March of N.C.—Philadelphia, Willig. [n.d.]; Anon.- Maria Louise's Two Favorite Waltzes—Philadelphia, Willig. [n.d.]; Taylor, R.- America and Brittannia Peace—Philadelphia, Willig. [n.d.]; Pittes, Gen. M.- Pres. Monroe's March—[No pub., n.d.]; Goeneke, J.F.- The Raleigh Blue's

March—[No pub., n.d.]; Gyrowitz, A.- The Orange Regiment March—Philadelphia, Willig. [n.d.]; Bray, John.- Gen. Harrison's Gr. March—Philadelphia, Blake. [n.d.]; Goeneke, J.F.- General Calvin Jones' March—Philadelphia, Willig. [n.d.]; Thompson, D.- Song to Memory of Mozart—Philadelphia, Willig. [n.d.]; Anon.- One Fingered Sliding Waltz—Philadelphia, Blake. [n.d.]; Anon.- Gen. Graham's Grand March—Philadelphia, Willig. [n.d.]; Goeneke, J.F.- Gov. Miller's Gr. March—Philadelphia, Willig. [n.d.]; Goeneke, J.F.- Quick March—[No pub., n.d.]; Panormo, Francis.- The Bird Waltz—Philadelphia, Blake. [n.d.]; Kiallmark, G.- Danish Waltz—New York, J.A. and W. Geib. [n.d.]; Kiallmark.- Fleuve du Tage—Philadelphia, Willig. [n.d.]; Ricksecker, P.- The Battle of New Orleans—Philadelphia, Willig. 1816 Weber, C.M./Leidesdorf- Excerpts from Der Freyschütz—[No pub., n.d.]; Moran.- Moran's Favorite Variations to the Swabian Air—Philadelphia, Willig. [n.d.]; Rossini, J.- Gr. March from Tancredi—Philadelphia, Willig. [n.d.]; Huerta, A. T.- The Hymn of Riego-Philadelphia, Willig, 1824. A Young Lady of Charleston, S.C.- March composed for and dedicated to the U.S. Marine Corps—Philadelphia, Willig. [n.d.]; Johnson, Francis.- Colonel C.G. Child's Parade March—Philadelphia, Willig. 1820 Latour.- Di Tanti Palpiti with Var.—Philadelphia, Willig. [n.d.]; Parry, John.- Venetian Rondo—Philadelphia, Blake. [n.d.]; Moreau, J. A.- Russian National Dance—Philadelphia, Willig. [n.d.]; Anon.- March dedicated to the Phila. Volunteer—Philadelphia, Willig. [n.d.]

KP1.25—Matilde de Sabran, A Waltz. Hutet, C. S. arr. Philadelphia, Tiet, Meignen & Co. [n.d.] [36.5 x 26.5 cm. 4 pp.]

KP1.26—Trois/ Airs de Ballets/ du/ Dieu et La Bayadère/ de D.F.E. Auber/ Herz, Henri arr. Mayence et Anvers, B. Schott [n.d.] [35.8 x 27.5 cm. 10 pp.]

KP1.27—Twenty Lessons/ for the/ Piano forte/ composed and arranged/ by/ C. Meineke. Philadelphia, Willig, c. 1826, [35 x 25.5 cm. 14 pp.]

KP1.28—Orpheus/ Collection/ de/ nouvelles Ouvertures favorites/ arrangées d'une manière brillante/ pour/ piano-forté/ de l'opéra/ La Muette de Portici par Auber./ A Offenbach s/M, chez J. André. [n.d.]. [33 x 26.5 cm. 11 pp.]

KP1.29—Trois/ Rondeux Brillants/ pour/ piano-forté/ sur des motifs du Vaudville:/ Die Wiener in Berlin/ par/ J. Moscheles/ A Offenbach s/M, chez J. André [n.d.]. [33.5 x 26.5 cm. 9 pp.]

KP1.30—Choix/ D'Airs Favoris/ des Opéras les plus nouveaux/ arrangés d'une mannièr facile/ pour le/ piano-forté/ par/ Charles Vollweiler/ A Offenbach s/M, chez J. André [n.d.]. [26 x 32.5 cm. 8 pp.]

KP1.31—Sounds From Kentucky/ Impromptu/ composé pour le/ Piano/ par/ Henry Rohbock/ published by F. D. Benteen, Baltimore;/ W. T. Mayo, New Orleans, c. 1851. [35 x 28 cm. 5 pp.]

KP1.32—Sechs/ Walzer/ für das Piano-forte/ zu 4 Händen/ von/ M. Henkel/ Offenbach a/M, bei Joh. André. [12 pp. Bound in laminated paper. Butterfly label on cover: "6 Walzer/ für das Piano Forte/ zu 4 Händen von Henkel/ Harmonie, June 1823."] [24 x 33 cm. 14 pp.]

KP1.33—Collection of four-hand piano music by Hunten, Meyerbeer, Auber, Rossini, Bellini, and others. 25 x 21 cm. Only a few pieces complete. [n.d.]. Binding is broken and covers missing as is title page and many pages from the volume. This is a part of "Magazine of Music Euterpe Neues Museum für piano-forte spielen, zu vier Händen, Erster Jahrgang."

KP1.34—Orgelbuch/ von/ Moritz Brosig/ Op. 32./ Leipzig, Verlag von F. E. C. Leuckart. [n.d.]. [22.5 x 26.5 cm. 79 pp.]

KP1.35—Daniel/ Fantaisie/ d'après E. Depas/ pour Saxophone/ et Piano Concertants/ par/ H. Klosé/ Alphonse Leduc, Paris, [n.d.]. [27.5 x 35 cm. 10 pp.]

KP1.36—Cagliostro/ Walzer/ Johann Strauss/ Thos. Hunter, Lith. Phila. [n.d.]. [27 x 34.5 cm. 12 pp.]

KP1.37—Lockvöglein [The Bird Call]/ Th. Oesten. Op. 413/ G. Andre & Co. Phila. [n.d.]. [27 x 35 cm. 9 pp.]

KP1.38—Krug/ Easy Arrangements for Piano/ Martha-Flotow. [no pub., n.d.]. [27.5 x 35 cm. 5 pp.]

KP1.39—Amusement pour le pianoforte/ No. 2/ Preciosa Valse/ J. C. Viereck. Geo. Willig. Philadelphia and E. Johns & Co., New Orleans. [n.d.]. [25.5 x 34.5 cm. 2 pp.]

KP1.40—Grand March/ in/ Billini's Admired Opera/ of/ Il Pirata. Hewitt, New York, [n.d.]. [26 x 35 cm. 2 pp.]

KP1.41—Flow on Thou Shining River/ arr. with vars. for the Piano Forte/ by Chs. Chaulieu/ Hewitt. New York. [n.d.]. [26.5 x 35.5 cm. 9 pp.]

KP1.42—Clic Clac/ Des Omnibus/ Rondoletto / pour le piano/ par/ Adolphe Adam/ Philadelphia/ Fiot, Meigner & Co. [n.d.]. [26.8 x 37 cm. 9 pp.]

KP1.43—A Grand Royal Divertimento/ for the/ piano forte or harp/ with an accompaniment for the Flute/ in honour of his Majesty's most gracious visit to Ireland/ composed and Humbly inscribed to/ The King's most excellent majesty/

George the Fourth/ by/ J. Blewitt. Dublin-published by J. Willis. [n.d.]. [26 x 36 cm. 16 pp.]

KP1.44—Souvenir/ de/ Vienne, Paris, et Londres/ Trois Fantaisies/ pour le/ Piano Forte/ Composé par/ Henri Herz/ Op. 75./ Philadelphia/ Kretschmar & Nunns. [n.d.]. [26.8 x 36 cm. 11 pp.]

KP1.45—Beauties of the Opera/ Being a Collection of/ Favorite Potpourris/ arranged from celebrated Operas of/ Donizetti, Bellini, Meyerbeer, Halevy, Verdi, Auber, etc./ Philadelphia, Lee & Walker. [n.d.]. [27.5 x 35.5 cm. 13 pp.]

KP1.46—Little Wanderer/ G. Lange, Op. 78, No. 2. [No pub., n.d. No title page: 6 pp. from a collection. 26.8 x 35 cm.]

KP1.47—Latest and Correct Editions/ Songs Without Words/ by/ Felix Mendelssohn Bartholdy./ Erie, Pa., Frank Brehm. [n.d.]. [27.5 x 35.5 cm. 3 pp.]

KP1.48—Les/ Elegantes/ A/ Collection of Popular/ Piano Solos/ Bohemian Girl Potpourri- H. Cramer. [No pub., n.d. 27.5 x 35.5 cm. 15 pp.]

KP1.49—Abend-Lied/ componirt von/ Rob. Schumann/ aus Op. 85 nr. 12 apart/ Eigenthum der Verleger: J. Schuberth & Co./ Leipzig und New York. [n.d.]. [26.8 x 34 cm. 4 sheets.]

KP1.50—Over the Waves/ Sobre las Olas/ Mexican Waltz/ by/ Juventino Rosas/ published by National Music Co., Chicago. [n.d.]. [26.5 x 35.5 cm. 9 pp.]

KP1.51—Ouvertures/ Favorites/ par/ Rossini/ arrangées/ pour/ Piano-Forte/ No. 3/ de l'opéra / L'Inganno Felice/ A Offenbach s/M chez Jean André. [n.d.]. [27 x 34 cm. 9 pp.]

KP1.52—Fantaisie/ Sur le Duo/ Il Faut aimer/ du Dieu et la Bayadere/ de D.F.E. Auber/ composée pour le piano/ par/ H. Karr/ Mayence & Anvers/ chez les fils de B. Schott. [n.d.]. [27 x 35.5 cm. 9 pp.]

KP1.53—Leaves and Blossoms/ A collection of the Latest Piano Music. Fatinitza March—Suppe Arrang: von Rich. Genee. [No pub., n.d.]. [27 x 35.5 cm. 5 pp.]

KP1.54—Compositions & Transcriptions of/ Brinley Richards/ for the/ Piano-Forte./ Beautiful Bells (melody by Glover). New York, Wm. A Pond & Co. [n.d.]. [25.3 x 35 cm. 7 pp.]

KP1.55—Le/ Pianist/ au Salon/ Le Jet D'Eau—Jules Egghard, Philadelphia/ Louis Meyer. [n.d.]. [27.3 x 35.4 cm. 7 pp.]

KP1.56—Collection of Chorales. [n.d.]. Covers and title page as well as many pages missing. At bottom of each page is: "P.J.T 2." No other marks of identification. [17.4 x 27.3 cm. 77 pp.]

KP1.57—Frankfurter-Wiesbader. Eisenbahn Action Walzer/ für das/ Piano Forte/ von/ Mina-Lust/ Frankfurt a/m bei Fr. Ph. Dunst. [n.d.]. [17.2 x 27.1 cm. 2 sheets.]

KP1.58—Collection of various pieces, songs and Rondos. 33 x 25.7 cm. 116 pp. of music. [n.d.]. Contains: Kauer. Arie/ Kinder des Frühlings etc./ aus dem Donaunveibchen/ für's Forte-Piano/ von/ Kauer/ Altona bey L. Rudolphus. [n.d.]. Methfessel, A. Zwei Gesänge/ mit Ialianischem und deutchem Texte/ für zwei Stimmen/ mit/ Begleitung des Pianoforte/ in Musik gesetzt von/ A. Methfessel/ Hamburg bei August Cranz. Meyerbeer, G. Le Danz des Vaches d'Appenzel/ paroles de Mr. Scribe/ Appenzell Kuhreigen/ ein und zweistimmig/ mit/ Pianoforte Begleitung./ In musik gesetzt/ von/ G. Meyerbeer./ Mit französischem und deutschem Text./ Hamburg bei A. Cranz [n.d.]. Potpourri/ Pour la Piano Forte/ No. V./ sur des Themes/ de Mozart,/ L. v. Beethoven, Paer,/ etc./ Leipzig, C. F. Peters. [n.d.]. Moscheles, J. La Petite Babillarde/ Rondeau/ Pour le Piano-Forte/ composée par/ J. Moscheles/ Oeuvre 65/ A Offenbach s/M, chez J. André. [n.d.]. Moscheles, J. Trois/ Rondeaux Brillants/ pour/ Piano-Forte/ sur des motifs du Vaudeville/ Die Wiener in Berlin/ par/ J. Moscheles/ Oeuvre 67/ A Offenbach s/M, chez J. André. [n.d.]. Nos. 1, 2, 3. Schmitt, Jacques. Andante/ avec Variations/ tire de la grande Sonate; Oeuvre 50/ pour/ Piano-Forte/ compose par/ Jacques Schmitt/ A Offenbach s/M, chez J. André. [n.d.]. Diabelli, Anton. Sonatine/ für das Pianoforte zu 4 händen/ nach dem duett: Wenn mir dein Auge strahlet/ aus der Oper/ das unterbrochene Opferfest, von Winter./ eingerichtet von/ Anton Diabelli/ Braunschweig. [n.d.]. Sonatine/ für das Pianoforte zu 4 händen/ nach der Cavatine des Figaro/ Ich bin das Factotum, aus der Oper/ der Barbier von Sevilla von Rossini/ Eingerichtet von/ A. Diabelli/ Braunschweig. [n.d.]. Sonatine/ für das/ pianoforte zu 4 händen/ nach der Romance/ Ich war, wenn ich erwachte/ aus der Oper/ Das unterbrochene Opferfest von Winter/ Eingerichtet von/ Anton Diabelli/ Braunschwein. [n.d.].

KP1.59—Hering, C. G. Praktische/ Praeludirschule/ oder/ anweisung/ in der Kunst/ vorspiele und Fantasien selbst zu bilden/ Zweyter Band/ Leipzig, bey Gerhard Fleischer dem Jungern. [n.d.]. [26.5 x 20.5 cm. Volume in two parts: 96 pp. in part I; more than 108 pages in part II, some pages missing from part two.]

KP1.60—Douze/ Variations/ sur un Air de l'opera/ Preciosa/ Pour le Piano-Forte/ composée et dedices/ a Monsieur Charles Maria de Weber/ par/ D. S. Siegel/ Chez Breitkopf & Härtel à Leipsic. [n.d.]. [34 x 26.5 cm. 4 sheets.]

KP1.61—Picture of Youth/ (Jugendleben)/

Twelve Progressive / and / Melodious Pieces / by / H. Lichner / Op. 84 / National Music Co., Chicago. [n.d.]. [26.5 x 35.5 cm. 3 pp.]

KP1.62—Collection of fragments, loose leaves, unidentifiable portions of keyboard works from various periods. Wrapped in manilla folder. 36.5 x 38 cm.

KP1.63—Lieblingstanz aus Preciosa von C. M. v Weber. Single sheet originally part of volume. [No pub., n.d.]. [23 x 32 cm.]

KP1.64—Deux / Rondeaux / pour le Piano / sur les motifs de Rossini / par / François Hünten / Mayence & Anvers / chez les fils de B. Schott. [n.d.]. [26 x 34 cm. 9 sheets.]

KP1.65—The Sacred Harmonist. No. 27 / London: Musical Bouquet Office. Luther's Chant; and the Hallelujah Chorus—Handel. [n.d.]. [26.5 x 35.5 cm. 2 sheets.]

KP1.66—Overture / Il Pirata / as performed at the / Italian Opera House New York / arranged for the / Piano Forte / composed by / Bellini / New York, Hewitt. [n.d.]. [36.8 x 27 cm. 5 sheets.]

KP1.67—The / Battle / of / Paris / for the / Piano Forte / New York / Firth & Hall. [n.d.]. [37.5 x 27 cm. 6 sheets.]

KP1.68—Un Moment de Récréation / Collection de Marches, Danses et autres pièces / pour le / Piano Forte / Marche / sur deux motifs favoris / Les souvenirs du pouple par Berton / par Carulli / arrangée par / J. P. Heuschkel / Mayence, Paris et Anvers. chez les fils de B. Schott. [35 x 26 cm. 2 sheets.]

KP1.69—La Réplique / Divertissment / for the / Piano Forte / With an Accompaniment for the / Flute or Violin / Composed by / T. Latour / Boston / New York / J. L. Hewitt & Co. [n.d.]. [36 x 27 cm. 5 sheets.]

KP1.70—Rousseau's Dream / An Air with / Variations / for / Two Performers / on the / Piano Forte / composed / by / I. Latour / Philadelphia / G. E. Blake. [n.d.]. [26.3 x 37 cm. 9 sheets.]

KP1.71—Grand March & Chorus / from the Opera / Il Poliuto / the martyrs / by Donizetti / arranged for the / Piano Forte / by / Charles Fradel. / New York / published by Wm. Hall & Son. c. 1859. [35 x 27 cm. 4 sheets.]

KP1.72—Alleghany March / composed and respectfully dedicated to / Miss Sarah J. Liddall / by / V.H.G. / New York, published at Millet's Music Saloon / W. D. Smith Pittsburgh. [n.d.]. [37.7 x 26 cm. 2 sheets.]

KP1.73—Les Clockes du Monastere / Nocturne / Lefebura-Wely / New York / published by Wm. Pond & Co. / Copyright 1866. [35.8 x 27 cm. 4 sheets.]

KP1.74—Lamartine / Waltzes for Piano by / Will L. Thompson / East Liverpool, Ohio / published by W. L. Thompson & Co. Copyright 1874. [35.5 x 27 cm. 4 sheets.]

KP1.75—Le Sourire / the smile / Nocturne / par / Francois d' Auria / Philadelphia, Lee & Walker / Copyright 1875. [35.5 x 27.5 cm. 5 sheets.]

KP1.76—Operatic Gems / potpourris / from / Favorite and Popular Operas / For two performers on the / Piano-forte / arranged / J. A. Getze / New York / Wm. Pond & Co. / Copyright 1877. [35.5 x 27 cm. 6 sheets.]

KP1.77—A. F. Hays Collection of Sheet Music. One Volume of sheet music for pianoforte, collected and bound by Alden F. Hays, Sewickley, Pa. 34 x 28 cm. On front cover: "A. F. Hays, / 1878." Bound in boards and leather. Contents: Kunkel, J. Germans / Triumphal March. St. Louis, c. 1871. Wagner / Thomas. Grand / Festival March. Cincinatti, John Church Co. c. 1876. Rubenstein, A. Ruins of Athens March. Philadelphia, F. A. North. [n.d.]. Wallace, W. V. Grande Polka / de / Concert. New York / William Hall & Son, c. 1850. Ascher, J. Fanfare Militaire. Philadelphia, Lee & Walker. [n.d.]. Litolff, H. Spinnlied / pour Piano Forte Op. 81. Philadelphia, G. Andre. [n.d.]. Wollenhaupt, H. A. Impromptu / Polka. New York, W. A. Pond, c. 1862. Wollenhaupt, H. A. Spinning Song / from / Wagner's Opera. Flying Dutchman. New York, Wm. A. Pond. c. 1863. Wollenhaupt, H. A. Souvenir de Niagara. New York, William Hall. [n.d.]. Wollenhaupt, H. A. Une Perle de nuit. New York, Wm. A. Pond, c. 1863. Wollenhaupt, H. A. Murmuring / Zephyrs. New York, Wm. A. Pond, c. 1863. Wollenhaupt, H. A. La Gazelle. Phila., Lee & Walker. [n.d.]. Wollenhaupt, H. A. Galop di Bravura. Phila., F. A. North Co. [n.d.]. Heller, Stephen. The Art of / Phrasing. Boston, Russell & Tolman. [n.d.]. Heller, Stephen. Tarentelle. [no pub., n.d.]. Moelling, Theo. Retour de Printemps. New York, S. T. Gordon, 1862. Mendelssohn, F. Minuet / from the / Reformation Symphony as performed by Carl Sent's Orchestra. Philadelphia, Lee & Walker. [n.d.]. Hoffman, R. La Gazelle. Pittsburgh, H. T. Knake. [n.d.]. Mattei, Tito. Grande Valse. Philadelphia, Lee & Walker. [n.d.]. Bach, J. S. Well-Tempered Clavichord. (P & F, 1 & 2) Boston, O. Ditson. [n.d.]. Wely, Lefebure. Titania. Philadelphia, Lee & Walker. [n.d.]. Smith, Sydney. La Cascade de Rubis. Philadelphia, F. A. North. [n.d.]. Lange, Gust. Perles et Diamants. Boston, O. Ditson. [n.d.]. Spindler, Fritz. Charge of the Hussars. [no pub., n.d.]. Spindler, Fritz. Rhapsodie, Air Louis XII. Phila., W. H. Boner. [n.d.]. Ketterer, Eugene. Galop de Concert. Phila., G. Andre. [n.d.]. Ketterer, Eugene.

Defile Marche. Phila., G. Andre. [n.d.]. Ketterer, Eugene. Boute-en-Train. Phila., F. A. North. [n.d.]. Gounod, Chas. March Funebre d'une Marionette. Phila., F. A. North, c. 1877. Zundel, John. Grand-Festival March / for the Organ. N.Y., W. Pond, c. 1870. Costa, M. March of the Israelites. Boston, O. Ditson. [n.d.]. Read, Edward M. Offertoire in A flat for the Organ. Burlington Vt., E. M. Read, c. 1873. Clark, Scotson. Procession March. Phila., F. A. North. [n.d.]. Gounod, Ch. March Romaine. Phila., W. H. Boner. [n.d.]. Meyerbeer. Marche du Sacre. Phila., F. A. North. [n.d.]. Mendelssohn / Maylath. War March of the Priests. Boston, J. White, c. 1872. Knight, J. S. Love's Request (Reichart). Boston, J. White, c. 1872. Abt / Knight (arr.). Slumber On. Boston, J. White c. 1870. Kücken / Knight (arr.). Good Night, Farewell. Boston, J. White, c. 1872. Gottschalk, L. M. Slumber on Baby dear. New York, Wm. Hall, c. 1863.

KP1.78—Fairy Serenade / and / Idylle / for the / piano forte / by Joseph Sieboth / New York, Wm. A. Pond & Co. / Copyright 1880. [36.5 x 27.3 cm. 7 sheets.]

KP1.79—Celestial Dreams (Reverie) by George Fox, Op. 40 / Copyright 1879, by White, Smith & Co. [title page missing]. [35.5 x 26.5 cm. 4 sheets.]

KP1.80—Souvenirs d'été / Dolce far Niente / Serenade / for / Piano Forte / by / Richard Hoffman / New York / Wm. A. Pond & Co. / Copyright 1880. [35.5 x 27 cm. 4 sheets.]

KP1.81—Blue Bells of Scotland arr. by Jules Egghard. [no pub.]. Copyright 1882 by R. A. Saalfield. [35 x 26 cm. 2 sheets.]

KP1.82—Nearer / My God To Thee / Variations for the Piano / by Fred S. Chandler, Jr. / National Music Co., / Chicago and N.Y. / Copyright, 1884. [36 x 27 cm. 3 sheets.]

KP1.83—Carnival / Schottisch / composed by / Miss Ada Koppitz / Pittsburgh / Published by JNO Riebling / Copyright, 1885. [36 x 26.5 cm. 3 sheets.]

KP1.84—The / Ellington / Two Step / (E. K. Bennett) / published by / D. H. Baldwin & Co. / Cincinnatti. Copyright, 1898. [35.5 x 27.5 cm. 2 sheets.]

KP1.85—Honeysuckle Polka / by J. O. Casey / Philadelphia / Harry Coleman. Copyright, 1891. [34.3 x 27 cm. 5 sheets.]

KP1.86—Facilita / Air with Variations / for the Cornet and Piano / J. Hartmann. Car. Fischer's / Selected compositions / for / Cornet and Piano / New York. Copyright, 1890. [34.5 x 27 cm. 6 sheets.]

KP1.87—The / Star / Dance Folio / two steps, Waltzes, etc. . . arranged by J. Bodewalt Lampe / New York and Detroit / Jerome Remick & Co. Copyright, 1910. [30.2 x 23 cm. 83 pp.]

KP1.88—Du, Du Liegst Mir im Herzen (with variations). Cornet solo with piano accompaniment by Herbert L. Clarke. Copyright, 1912. New York, M. Witmark and Sons. [35 x 27 cm. 7 sheets.]

KP1.89—Rose Song (Rosenlied) by J. A. Wallace. Copyright, 1900, by Lechner & Schoenberger. [no title page]. [31 x 23.8 cm. 2 sheets.]

KP1.90—The Rover / by Carl Bruno / Copyright, 1901, by the Walrus Co. [no place of publication]. [31 x 23.8 cm. 2 sheets.]

KP1.91—The Love of / One Fond / Heart / Supplement to the Old Song Series / Section 4 / Feb'y 22nd / 1903 Philadelphia. Song by Alice Hawthorne [no pub.] [34 x 28.3 cm. 2 sheets.]

KP1.92—The Bride of the Waves / Polka Brillante / Herbert L. Clarke. Copyright 1914 by Lyon & Healy, N.Y. [35 x 26.5 cm. 8 sheets.]

KP1.93—Beyond the Gates of Paradise / Solo for Cornet, Baritone or Trombone with piano accompaniment / by Robt A. King / copyright 1901 by Carl Fischer, New York. [35 x 27 cm. 4 sheets.]

KP1.94—Hiawatha / A summer Idyl by Neil Moret, Op. 6. Detroit, Whitney-Warner Pub. Co. Copyright, 1901. [incomplete]. [35 x 27 cm. 2 sheets.]

KP1.95—Rhapsodies / Hongroises / pour le piano / par / Fr. Liszt / Mayence les fils de B. Schott / Lodres-Bruxelles. [n.d.]. [27.5 x 34 cm. 27 pp.]

KP1.96—Diana / Polonaise / Cornet Solo / by / John S. Duss. (pf. accompaniment) Published by Wm. C. Ott & Co., Beaver Falls, Pa. Copyright, 1895. [35.5 x 27 cm. 7 pp.]

KP1.97—Sounds from Beaver / Valley—Waltz / Composed for Piano by / J. Markus H. Winteringer / Published by The Winteringer Music Co., Limited, Pittsburg, Pa. Copyright 1902. [34.5 x 27 cm. 7 pp.]

KP1.98—Song. "Dear Heart" / Cornet Solo with piano Acc. / Tito Mattei / Arr. / by J. F. Zimmermann / Philadelphia; Pa. / Published by Harry Coleman. [n.d.] [27 x 35.5 cm. 5 pp.]

KP1.99—The / Pittsburgh Dispatch March / Two Step / J. S. Duss / of the / Harmony Society / The John Church Company / Cincinnati / New York / Chicago. c. 1896. [27 x 35 cm. 4 pp.]

KP1.100—Liberty / Chimes / March / Two Step by / J. S. Duss / of the Harmony Society—Economy, Pa. / Arranged / by / W. C. Ott. Beaver Falls, Pa. / Published by W. C. Ott & Co. Copyright 1894. [27 x 35 cm. 5 pp.]

KP1.101—The Limited Express / March-two step / by / J. S. Duss / Published by Wm. C. Ott & Co. Beaver Falls, Pa. 1894 [27 x 35 cm. 5 pp.]

KP1.102—The Brownies/ Dance Characteristic/ by/ J. S. Duss/ Published by Wm. C. Ott & Co. Beaver Falls, Pa./ Copyright 1895. [35 x 27 cm. 5 pp.]

KP1.103—Festival/ March/ written expressively [*sic.*] for and in Honor of the/ Beaver County Centennial Held at Beaver, Pa./ June 19th to 22nd 1900/ by/ J. S. Duss. Copyright J. S. Duss 1903. [no pub.]. [26.5 x 16 cm. 3 sheets.]

HYMNS: PRINTED ENSEMBLE PARTS AND PARTITUR

HP2.1—Kneckt, Justin Heinrich. Volständiges/ Württembergisches Choralbuch/ welches/ in allen Vaterländischen Kirchen und Schulen ausschliessend, alergnädigst verordnet ist./ von/ Justin Heinrich Knecht./ Königlich Württembergischem Musik-Direktor/ Zweiter Theil/ Stuttgart, 1816. [21 x 24 cm. 321 pp; 266 four-part choral settings with figured bass. Instructions for using wind and string instruments as well as keyboard. Complete indices of composers and authors.]

HP2.2—Greenwood, John. Modulus Sanctus/ A Collection of/ Sacred Music/ arranged for one or four voices with an accompaniment for the/ Organ or Piano Forte/ by John Greenwood/ late organist of the Parish Church, Leeds / Published by Sykes & Sons, at their music warehouse, 72, Briggate/ and may be had of Clementi & Co. Cheapside, Birchall & Co. and/ Mayhew & Co. Bond Street, London, 1828. [22 x 27.8 cm. 61 pp.; 37 hymns.]

HP2.3—Hering, M. Carl Gottlieb. Musikalisches/ Volksschulengesangbuch/ von/ M. Carl Gottlieb Hering./ Leipzig, bei Gerhard Fleischer, 1821. [19.8 x 12 cm. 284 pp.]

HP2.4—Choralbuch/ zu dem/ Gesangbuche für protestantisch-evangelische Christen, vierstimmig ausgesetzt/ Im verlage der allgemeinen Pfarr. Wittn. enkasse des Rheinkreises/ Speier/ 1824. [23 x 33 cm. 76 pp.]

HP2.5—Schmauk, J. G. Deutsche Harmonie,/ oder/ Mehrstimmige Gesänge/ für/ Deutsche Singeschulen und Kirchen./ Enhaltend:/ Eine Anzahl der beliebtesten Choral-oder Kirchenmelodien; drei und vierstimmiger Gesänge für Anfänger und geübtere Singer/ nebst einer kurzen Anleitung zum Gesangunterricht./ von/ J. G. Schmauk/ Organist an der deutsch lutherischen St. Michaelis Kirche, in Philadelphia. 1833. [20.3 x 27 cm. 233 pp; 108 hymns and choruses.]

HP2.6—Die/ Union Choral Harmonie/ enhaltend:/ drei und vierstimmig ausgesetze Melodien,/ mit deutschem und englischem Texte;/ sowohl zum Gebrauche beim "öffent-lichen Gottesdienste aller Christlichen Confessionen, als auch für/ Singschulen und Privatgesellschaften./ Von H. C. Eyer./ Zwölfte vermehrte und verbesserte Auflage./ Am Verlag von Schafer & Koradi. Philadelphia, 1829. [16 x 25.5 cm. 192 pp. of music in shape notation.]

HP2.7—Annonymous. 28.5 x 14.8 cm.; 106 pp. German texts with three-part settings in shape notation. Complete index but title page missing.

HP2.8—Sechs/ Bücher/ deutscher Lieder/ mit/ bewährten Sangweisen./ Zunächst für Schulen/ Viertes Buch./ Dreistimmige Lieder für oberklassen enhaltend./ Ausgabe in Ziffern./ Gütersloh,/ Druck und Verlag von G. Bertelsmann. [n.d.]. [Ea. 10.5 x 17.5 cm. Book I: 9 copies in numerals; 6 copies in notes. 32 pp. Book II: 5 copies in numerals; 2 copies in notes. 39 pp. Book III: 4 copies in notes. 39 pp. Book IV: 2 copies in numerals; 3 copies in notes. 32 pp. Book V: 7 copies in notes. 32 pp. Book VI: 4 copies in notes. 32 pp.]

HP2.9—Mason, Lowell. Carmina Sacra: or/ Boston Collection of Church Music. Psalm and hymn tunes in general use; new tunes, chants, sentences, motets and anthems. Boston, New York, and Philadelphia. 1841. [15 x 24.5; 348 pp.]

HP2.10—Hastings, Thomas. The Manhattan Collection/ of/ Psalm and Hymn Tunes and Anthems./ of the/ New York Academy of Sacred Music/ and adapted to the/ use of classes, choirs and congregations,/ with a/ figured bass for the organ./ by Thomas Hastings/ professor of musical elocution. New York. [c. 1840]. [17.3 x 27 cm. 351 pp.]

HP2.11—White, Edward L. The/ Boston Melodeon/ Vol I A collection of secular melodoes,/ consisting of/ Songs, Glees, Rounds, Catches, Fifth edition/ Boston, [copyright 1846]. [17.5 x 25.5 cm. 223 pp.]

HP2.12—Mason, Lowell. The/ New Carmina Sacra;/ or Boston Collection of Church Music./ Comprising the Most popular/ Psalm and Hymn Tunes in General Use./ Together with a Great Variety of/ new tunes, chants, sentences, Motets, and Anthems;/ Principally by distinguished European Composers;/ The whole being/ one of the Most complete Collections of Music/ for Choirs, congregations, singing schools and societies, Extant./ By Lowell Mason./ Boston, 1851. [15.5 x 24.5 cm. 390 pp.]

HP2.13—Dewey, T. M. The Romberg Collection of Sacred Music;/ Consisting of a/ Large variety of Psalm and Hymn tunes,/ with a choice of/ Anthems, Sentences, Chants . . ./ selected and arranged from the most distinguished European Composers;/ Together with/ Many original compositions,/ a/ few choice voluntaries for the Organ,/ and a/ progressive system of elementary instruction/ Philadelphia, Boston, Cincinatti and Baltimore. Copyright 1852. [15.8 x 25 cm. 320 pp.]

HP2.14—Mason, Lowell. The Hallelujah:/ A book for the service of song in the house of the Lord; containing tunes,/ chants and anthems, both for the choir and the congregation;/ to which is prefixed/ The Singing School;/ A manual for classes in vocal music, with exercises, rounds, and part songs for choir practice;/ also/ Musical notation in a Nutshell;/ a brief course for singing schools; intended for skillful teachers and apt pupils./ By Lowell Mason/ New York, and Boston, [copyright 1854]. [16.5 x 25 cm. 368 pp.]

HP2.15—Woodbury, I. B. The/ Anthem Dulcimer:/ constituting A large and choice variety of new tunes, chants, anthems, Motets, etc./ from the best foreign and American composers, with all the old tunes in common use;/ together with a/ new and greatly improved elementary course,/ and a choice collection of original anthems./ The whole comprising the most complete collection of sacred music ever published./ By I. B. Woodbury/ editor of "Musical Pioneer." New York, [c. 1856]. [17 x 25 cm. 352 pp.]

HP2.16—Wolle, Peter. Hymn Tunes,/ used in the Church of the United Brethren,/ arranged for four voices and the organ or piano-forte;/ to which are added/ chants for the Litany of the church,/ and/ A number of approved anthems for various occasions./ By Rev. Peter Wolle./ Philadelphia/ 1857. [16 x 25 cm. 145 pp.]

HP2.17—Gregor, Christian. Choral-Buch/ enthaltend alle/ zu dem/ Gesangbuche der evangelischen Brüdergemeinen/ vom Jahr 1778 gehörigen Melodien./ Vierte neu revidirte Auflage./ Gnadau,/ im verlage der Buchhandlung der evangelischen Brüder-Unität, sowie in allen Brüdergemeinen./ 1859. [21.5 x 25.5 cm. 257 pp; 575 settings in two voices with figured bass.]

HP2.18—Waters, Horace. The Sabbath School Bell;/ A New Collection/ of/ Choice hymns and Tunes, original and standard: carefully and simply/ arranged as solos, duetts, trios, semichoruses and choruses,/ and for organ, melodeon or piano. [No. 1]/ Compiled by Horace Waters./ Published by C. M. Tremaine. New York, [copyright 1859]. [12 x 15 cm. 139 pp.] [Four copies].

HP2.19—Waters, Horace. Sabbath School Bell. (No. 2), 1859. [11.7 x 15 cm. 185 pp.]

HP2.20—Waters, Horace. The Sabbath School Bell. (Nos. 1 & 2), 1860. [12 x 15 cm.]

HP2.21—Wichern, Dr. Unsere Lieder./ Dritte Auflage/ Hamburg 1861/ Agentur des Rauhen Hauses. [10 x 14.5 cm.; 320 pp.]

HP2.22—Schaff, Philipp/ G. F. Landenberger. Choral-Buch für die Orgel/ mit zwischenspielen versehen,/ und für den vierstimmigen Gesang eingerichtet./ Bearbeitet von G. F. Landenberger,/ Organist an der St. Paulskirche./ Phila. 1861. [18.5 x 26 cm. 203 pp.]

HP2.23—Fink, G. W. Musikalischer/ Hausschatz der Deutschen./ Eine Sammlung von 1000/ Liedern und Gesängen mit Singweisen und klavierbegleitung./ Gesammelt und herausgegeben/ von/ G. W. Fink/ Neu umbeanderte und verbesserte stereotyp-Ausgabe/ dritter Abdruck./ Leipzig/ 1862. [first printing 1842]. [27 x 19 cm. 736 pp.]

HP2.24—Beecher, H. W. Plymouth Collection / of/ Hymns and Tunes; for the/ use of Christian Congregations./ New York:/ 1862. [14.5 x 21.5 cm. 507 pp.]

HP2.25—Haas, J. C. Siona,/ Sammlung vierstimmiger Gesänge:/ chöre/ Hymnen, Motetten, Psalmen etc.,/ für/ Kirchliche Sing-Chöre./ Gesammelt von J. C. Hass/ Gesanglehrer und Organist./ Erster Anhang zu J. G. Schmauch's "Deutscher Harmonie."/ Vierte Auflage./ Phila., [n.d.]. [17 x 24 cm. 100 pp.]

HP2.26—Kraussold, Dr. L. Liedersammlung/ für/ Schule und Leben./ von/ Dr. L. Kraussold. / Erster Theil./ Zweite Auflage./ Erlangen/ Verlag von Andreas Deichert./ 1863. [21.5 x 15 cm. 80 pp.]

HP2.27—Endlich, John. Das/ Sonntagschulbuch/ Liturgische Gesänge zum Lutherischen Hauptgottesdienst,/ Bearbeitet von John Endlich./ Philadelphia and Allentown, [n.d.]. [16.5 x 12.5 cm. 350 pp. (binding missing)].

HP2.28—Heim, T. Siona, Sammlung von drei- und vierstimmigen/ Volksgesängen/ für/ Knaben, Mädchen und Frauen./ Liederbuch für Schule, Haus und Verein./ Philadelphia, [n.d.]. [17.5 x 11.5 cm. 392 pp.]

HP2.29—Hass, J. C. Siona/ Sammlung vierstimmiger Gesänge. [copyright 1863]. [17 x 24 cm. 220 pp. (16 copies)].

HP2.30—Heppe, C. J. Gesänge für Sonntag-Schulen./ Mit/ ausgemählten Melodien und Liedern./ freundlich gewidmet allen deutschen evangelischen Sonntag-Schulen./ Gesammelt und bearbeitet/ von/ C. J. Heppe/ herausgegeben/ von der Amerikanischen Tracktat-Gesellschaft./ Philadelphia, 1866. [13 x 16.5 cm. 112 pp.] [7 copies].

HP2.31—Johnson, A. N. The/ Alleghany Collection/ of music, for/ public worship, choirs, singing schools,/ musical conventions, musical associations/ and the social circle./ Containing also/ Johnson's method for teaching the art of reading music. New York, [c. 1868]. [17.5 x 24.8 cm. 384 pp.]

HP2.32—Methfessel, Ernst. Enrst Methfessel's / Liedersammlung/ für gemischten Chor./ Neue vermehrte und verbesserte Auflage./ Philadelphia/ 1868. [13 x 19 cm. 274 pp.]

HP2.33—Kraussold, Dr. L. Liedersammlung/ für/ Schule und Leben/ von/ Dr. L. Kraussold/ Zweiter Theil/ Zweiter Auflage/ Erlangen / Verlag von Andreas Deichert/ 1868. [15 x 22 cm. 92 pp.]

HP2.34—Geistliches Saitenspiel/ oder eine/ Sammlung/ . . . für gemischten Chor./ zum Gebrauch/ für/ kirchlichen und hauslichen Gottesdienst./ Reutlingen/ 1869. [17.2 x 11.5 cm. 384 pp.]

HP2.35—Bickel, P. W. Das Singvögelein/ oder/ Melodien und Lieder/ für/ Sonntags-Schulen/ von/ P. W. Bickel/ Cincinnati, O., 1869. [10 x 14 cm. 96 pp.]

HP2.36—Palme, R. Partitur/ Deutsches Liederbuch/ für/ gemischten chor./ Eine Sammlung der beliebtesten Lieder/ älterer, sowie der hervorragendsten jetzt lebenden Tondichter,/ herausgegeben von/ R. Palme/ königl. Musikdirektor und Organist/ Leipzig 1870. [12 x 18.2 cm. 367 pp.]

HP2.37—Wichern, Dr. Unsere Lieder/ Herausgegeben/ von/ Dr. Wichern/ vierte Auflage/ Hamburg/ Agentur des Rauhen Hauses/ 1870. [10 x 152 cm. 376 pp.]

HP2.38—Kummerle, S. Neue/ Zionsharfe/ Eine Sammlung/ geistlicher Lieder, Gesänge, choere und Motetten/ für gemische stimmen/ Für kirchengesangvereine gesammelt und bearbeitet/ von/ S. Kummerle/ Neue, ganzlich umgearbeitet und vermehrte Auflage/ Neu folge/ Erste Hälfte Philadelphia, Koradi-Schäfer, [n.d.]. 2 vols: [1: 16.5 x 24.1 cm. 112 pp. 2: 16.2 x 23.1 cm. 11 pp.]

HP2.39—Kummerle, S. Zionsharfe/ Eine Sammlung/ geistlicher Lieder, Gesänge, Chöre und Motetten,/ für gemischte stimmen/ für kirchengesangvereine gesammelt und bearbeitet/ von/ S. Kümmerle/ Lehrer an der Höhern Töchterschule zu Schorndorf./ I Theil/ Philadelphia [1871] bei Schafer und Koradi. [16.3 x 24 cm. 86 pp.]

HP2.40—Liebhart, H. Neue Harfe/ Sang und Klang/ für/ Schule und Haus/ Bearbeitet von/ H. Liebhart/ Cincinnati, Chicago und St. Louis/ [1871]. [12.8 x 20 cm. 104 pp.]

HP2.41—Schaaf, Julius. Die Harfe/ Sammlung ausgewählter religioser Gesänge/ mit und ohne Begleitung der Orgel/ für/ gemischte kirchliche Sing-Chöre./ Gesammelt von Julius Schaaf,/ organist. Philadelphia [n.d.]. [2 vols.: 24.7 x 19 cm. 128 pp. 1 vol.: 26 x 19 cm. 96 pp. 2 vols.: 26 x 19.6 cm. 32 pp.]

HP2.42—Landenberger, G. F. Kirchen-Chöre/ eine Sammlung der beliebsten und besten/ Gesangstücke für kirchliche Gesang-Vereine/

Bearbeitet von G. F. Landenberger, Organist an St. Paulus,/ Philadelphia/ 1872. [18.5 x 23.8 cm. 235 pp.]

HP2.43—Vierstimmige/ Choralmelodien/ zu dem/ Gesangbuch/ für die/ evangelische Kirche in Württemberg,/ zum gebrauch/ in Kirchen und Schulen./ Zehnte Stereotyp Auflage./ Stuttgart, 1873. [12.9 x 19.8 cm. 160 pp. 10 copies.]

HP2.44—Lützel, J. Heinrich. Chorgesangbuch/ für/ Kirchen und Schulen/ herausgegeben/ von J. Heinrich Lützel/ Kaiserlautern/ 1874. [18 x 12 cm. 296 pp. [24 copies].]

HP2.45—Bliss, P. Gospel Songs/ a choice collection of/ Hymns and Tunes,/ New and Old,/ for/ Gospel Settings, Prayer Meetings, Sunday Schools, etc./ by/ P. P. Bliss. Cincinnati, 1874. [13 x 19.5 cm. 128 pp. 3 copies].

HP2.46—Bliss, P. P. and Sankey, I. D. Gospel Hymns and Sacred Songs/ by/ P. P. Bliss and Ira D. Sankey,/ as used by them in/ Gospel Meetings/ Cincinnati, O. 1875. [22 x 13.3 cm. 112 pp. 3 copies.]

HP2.47—Schmauk, J. G./ Haas, J. C. Deutsche Harmonie/ oder/ Mehrstimmige Gesänge/ für/ Deutsche Singschulen und Kirchen. Durchgesehen und vermehrt von J. C. Haas, Philadelphia, [c. 1875]. [16.5 x 26.5 cm. 286 pp. [23 copies].]

HP2.48—Johnson, A. N., and Tenney, J. H. The Singing School Banner/ New York [copyright 1875]. [24.5 x 16 cm. 8-page advertisement.]

HP2.49—Bliss, P. P., and Sankey, I. D. Einige/ Evangelische hymen/ und/ Gottesdienstliche Gesänge/ von P. P. Bliss und Ira D. Sankey gebraucht in den/ Evangelischen Versammlungen von herren D. L. Moody und Ira D. Sankey. Deutsche text mit den original-Melodien./ New York, Cincinnati,/ 1876. [21.5 x 14 cm. 12 pp.]

HP2.50—Bliss, P. P. and Sankey, I. D. Gospel Hymns #2. Cincinatti, 1876. [20.3 x 13.3 cm. 112 pp.]

HP2.51—Choralbuch/ für die/ evangelische Kirche in Württemburg/ Dritte, durchgesehene auflage. Stuttgart/ 1876. [27 x 22.3 cm. 244 pp.]

HP2.52—Gundlach, W. Liederbuch für Schul und Volksgesang in Worten und Weisen. New York, 1872. Ein/ sammlung zwei und dreistimmiger Lieder. [18.5 x 12.4 cm. 174 pp.]

HP2.53—Gundlach, W. Liederbuch für Schul- und Volksgesang in Worten und Weisen. Eine/ sammlung zwei und dreistimmiger Lieder. New York, 1876. [19 x 13 cm. 174 pp.]

HP2.54—Haas, J. C. Liederkranz für Christliche Schulen/ 10te Auflage Philadelphia & Leipzig, 1876. [17.5 x 11.7 cm. 46 pp.]

HP2.55—Haas, J. C. Liederkranz für Christliche Schulen / 10te Auflage Philadelphia & Leipzig, 1876. [18.5 x 11.7 cm. 62 pp.]

HP2.56—Heim, Ignaz. Neue Volksgesange für den Männerchor. / Liederbuch für Schulen und Vereine. Zurich, 1878. [17.4 x 11.5 cm. 296 pp.]

HP2.57—Zionsharfe / Gesangbuch / für die / deutschen Wesleyanisthen Methodisten / Cannstatt, 1878. [19 x 12.5 cm. 444 pp. 25 copies].]

HP2.58—Landenberger, G. F. Kirchen-Chöre / Zweiter Theil / Philadelphia, 1879. [19 x 25.5 cm. 220 pp.]

HP2.59—Bickel, P.W. Das Singvögelein / eine / Sammlung von Melodien und Liedern / für / Sonntags-Schulen, / von / P. W. Bickel / Siebente, stark vermehrte und verbesserte auflage / Cleveland, O., 1879. [15.7 x 11.2 cm. 282 pp.]

HP2.60—Hofer, Samuel. Pilgerharfe / oder / Christlicher Glaube in Liedern / für gemischten Chor. / Bearbeitet / von / Samuel Hofer / Siebente Auflage. Basel, 1880. [18 x 11.4 cm. 320 pp.]

HP2.61—Haas, J. C. Templeklänge / Neu Sammlung Vierstimmiger Gesänge / Chöre, Hymnen, Motetten, Psalmen, etc. / für / Kirchliche Sing-Chöre / Gesammelt von J. C. Hass / Gesanglehrer und organist (Nos. 1-27). Phila., 1880. [18.5 x 25 cm. 128 pp. Bound in boards and buckram.]

HP2.62—Haas, J. C. Templeklänge. [see HP2.61]. pp. 129-160. [19.9 x 26.2 cm.]

HP2.63—White, Stone, & Oyen. Better than Pearls / Sacred Songs expressly adapted for Gospel Meetings / J. E. White, Battle Creek, Mich., 1881. [19 x 13 cm. 110 pp.]

HP2.64—Gebhardt, Ernst. Zions / Perlenchöre / Eine Sammlung / Auserwählter, lieblicher Compositionen / für gemischten Chor, / von / Ernst Gebhardt. Bremen / 1883. [18.8 x 12.5 cm. 345 pp.]

HP2.65—Shaker Music / original / Inspirational Hymns and Songs / illustrative of the / Resurrection Life and Testimony / of the / Shakers. New York, 1884. [21.3 x 14.5 cm. 250 pp.]

HP2.66—Hartmann, Wilhelm. Der Mannerchor / sammlung / der / neuesten anerkannt besten deutschen Compositionen / fur den / vierstimmigen Männergesang / herausgegeben für die deutschen Gesang-Vereine in Nord-Amerika / von / Wilhelm Hartmann Vierte Auflage. Phila., 1884. [25.2 x 16 cm. 296 pp.]

HP2.67—Schmelz, Reinhard. Vierzehn Grabgesänge für Männerchöre. Phila., 1885. [19.2 x 13.3 cm. 31 pp.]

HP2.68—Singet Dem Herrn! / Bundesharfe / für / Evangelische Jünglings-und Männervereine

/ herausgegeben / vom / Komittee des Rheinisch-Westfälischen / Junglingsbunds / Zweite unveränderte Auflage. Gutersloh / 1885. [18.2 x 12 cm. 380 pp.]

HP2.69—Wonnberger, C. Unsere Lieder / Geistliche und weltliche / Männerchöre / 2te auflage, Reading, Pa. [Copyright 1885]. [18.5 x 13.5 cm. 350 pp.]

HP2.70—White, J. E. Joyful Greeting / for the / Sabbath School / by / J. E. White Battle Creek, Michigan / 1886. [13.8 x 19.5 cm. 216 pp.]

HP2.71—Haas, J. C. Templekänge / neue Sammlung vierstimminger Gesänge Philadelphia, 1886. [18.5 x 25.2 cm. 256 pp.]

HP2.72—Wonnberger, C. Jauchzet Gott in Allen Landen / Festgesang auf das Heilige Osterfest / für / gemischten Chor. / componiert von C. Wonnberger / Reading, Pa. [c.1887]. [19 x 26 cm. 8 pp.]

HP2.73—Klee, Hans. Gesangbuch / für / die dritte Stufe der Primarschule / des / Kantons Bern / verfasst / von / Hans Klee, Bern / 1887. [20 x 13.5 cm. 200 pp.]

HP2.74—Schneider, C. G. Sonntagsklänge / Sammlung leichter und ansprechender Gesänge für Kirchlicher Sing-Chöre. Phila., 1888. [20 x 26.3 cm. 130 pp.]

HP2.75—Leslie, C. E. Leslie's Male Quartet and Chorus Book. Chicago. [Copyright, 1889]. [12.5 x 22.8 cm. 144 pp.]

HP2.76—Sankey, Ira D.; McGranahan, J.; Stebbins, G. Gospel Hymns #5. Chicago, Cincinnati, New York. [copyright, 1890]. [20.5 x 14 cm. 211 pp.]

HP2.77—Hauschild, Ernst. Männerchöre / zum Gebrauch der evangelischen Missionschule in Basel. Philadelphia, [n.d.]. [17.8 x 24.8 cm. 328 pp. 27 copies.]

HP2.78—Anonymous. 6 sheets, pages numbered 545 to 556; 16 hymns a4. Unbound and uncut. 17.5 x 24.3 cm. [12 copies].

HP2.79—Kleine / Missionsharfe / im / Kirchen und Volkston / für / festliche und auserfestliche Kreise / Philadelphia, [n.d.]. [15.5 x 11.7 cm. 136 pp. 32 copies.]

HP2.80—Nageli, Hans Georg. Männerchöre / Jubiläums—Ausgabe / zur hundert-jährigen Geburtstagsfeier / des Tondichters / herausgegeben von der Musikkommission / der Züricher Schulsynode. Philadelphia, [n.d.]. [17.5 x 12 cm. 94 pp.]

HP2.81—Liederbuch / für / Sonntag-Schule und Haus / Eine Sammlung der besten älteren und neueren Lieder / herausgegeben vom / Verein der Prediger der Deutschen Evang / Protestantischen Kirche von Nord-Amerika / Zweite vermehrte und verbesserte / Auflage. Pittsburgh / 1900. [21.2 x 14.5 cm. 328 pp.]

HP2.82—Sankey, I.S. Gospel Hymns No. 6. New York, Cincinatti, Chicago. [copyright, 1891]. [20.5 x 13.8 cm. 208 pp.]

HP2.83—Leason, Ls.; Lafferty, W. A. Leason & Lafferty's/ Graded Collection/ for/ Choral Union classes,/ singing schools, institutes/ conventions and public schools/ Chicago, New York. [copyright, 1891]. [23.5 x 17.5 cm. 176 pp.]

HP2.84—Anonymous. Die Hoffnungsterne. [n.d.]. 18.5 x 27 cm. 12 sheets printed on recto only. Covers are light blue paper. Pagination given on some sheets but not consecutive. This apparently a sample section of a larger collection.

HP2.85—Kinderharfe/ Liederbuch für Christliche Sonntags-Schulen/ herausgegeben/ vom/ Verein für Christliche Erbauungsschriften./ Neu Auflage/ Phila., [n.d.]. [14.3 x 11 cm. 112 pp.]

HP2.86—Gloor, Gottlieb. Jugend-Chöre/ Sorgfältige Auswahl/ zwei, drei, und vierstimmiger Gesänge/ für/ Schule und Haus/ gesammelt, arrangirt und herausgegeben/ von/ Gottlieb Gloor/ Lehrer/ Philadelphia, [n.d.]. [16.5 x 12.3 cm.]

HP2.87—Rodeheaver, H., Ackley, B. D. Great/ Revival Hymns/ for/ The Church, Sunday School and/ Evangelistic Services. Chicago, [c. 1911]. [20 x 13.5 cm. 256 pp.]

HP2.88—Bowen, C. A. The Cokesbury Worship Hymnal. Pittsburgh, [Copyright, 1938]. [20.5 x 14.5 cm. 348 numbered hymns and readings. 8 copies].]

HP2.89—Wurst, Jakob Raimund. Fünfzig zweistimmige Lieder/ für die/ Mittel-Klassen der Elementarschulen/ Ein hülfsmittel/ zur / method, Behandlung des ersten Unterrichtes im Gesänge/ In/ Tonziffern gesetzt und methodisch geordnet/ von/ Raimund Jakob Wurst/ ehemal Professor und Seminardirektor in St. Gallen, jetzt Lehrer in Ellwangen. Reutlingen, 1839. [11 x 15 cm. 47 pp. songs in number notation.]

HP2.90—The/ Harmonie/ Collection of Compositions/ by various heads of the Harmony Society/ Economy Centennial-Souvenir Edition/ June, 1924. [26.5 x 17.5 cm. 25 pp. 14 copies.]

PRINTED PSALTERS: MELODIES IN NOTATION

PP.1—Freylinghausen, H. Anastas. Geistreiches/ Gesang-Buch Den Kern/ Alter und Neuer/ Lieder/ Wie auch die Noten der/ unbekannten Melodeyen - und dazu gehörige nützliche Registern/ in sich haltend/ In gegenwärtiger bequemer/ Ordnung und Form/ samt einer/ Vorrede zur/ Erweckung heiliger Andacht/ und Erbauung im Glauben und gott-seligen Wesen,/ zum achten mal/ herausgegeben von/ H. Anastas Freyling-/ hausen, Past. Adj./ Halle/ Getruckt und Verlegt im Waysen/ hause 1714. [16.5 x 7.5 cm. 1,158 pp. plus 42 pp. of indexes. 758 hymns. Where tunes are not given there is cross-reference to melody on another page. Music consists of melody with bass figures.]

PP.2—Sultzburgeren, Joh. Ulrich. Vier Stimmiges/ Psalmenbuch/ das ist/ D. Ambr. Lobwassers/ Psalmen Davids,/ transponiert durch/ Joh. Ulrich Sultzburgeren./ Direct. Mus. und Zinckenisten Lobl./ Statt Bärn/ Mit Verbesserung der undeutlichen/ Redens-Arten, sammt gewöhnlichen und einichen/ neuen Fest-Gesängen./ Aus Hoch-Oberkeitlichem Befehl und Approbation./ Worbey eine kurtze Musicalische/ Unterweisung, sammt etlichen schönen Gebätten enthalten/ Cum Gratia & Privil. Magist. Bernensis/ Bärn, in Hoch-Oberkeitl. Druckerey/ Bey Wagner und Muller, 1736. [16.5 x 9 cm. 675 pp. 20 pp. of musical instructions, exercises based upon "ut re mi fa sol la si ut," followed by index of psalm settings in four parts: Discantus, Altus, Bassus, Tenor. Bound in boards and dark leather with brass corner braces and latch.]

PP.3—Wülffing, Petrus. Ronsdorffs/ Silberne Trompeten/ oder/ Kirchen-Buch/ Abgefasst von Petrus Wülffing,/ Predigern der nach Gottes Wort Reformir-/ ten Gemeine in der Stadt Ronsdorff,/ Wie auch Königl. Preussisch Consistorial-Rath./ Mülheim am Rhein/ gedruckt mit Properischen Schriften/ Im Jahr 1761. [17.6 x 10.5 cm. 732 pp.]

PP.4—Geistliches/ Blumen-Gärtlein/ Inniger Seelen:/ oder kürze/ Schluss-Reimen,/ Betrachtungen und Lieder/ Über allerhand Wahrheiten des/ Innwendigen Christenthums;/ Zur Erweckung, Stärckung/ und Erquickung/ in dem/ Verborgenen Leben/ Mit Christo in Gott;/ Vierdte und vermehrte Edition/ Nebst der/ Frommen Lotterie/ in verlag der Heilmannischen Buchh./ 1766. [14.5 x 9 cm. 477 pp. plus index and 23 pp. of "Zugabe."]

PP.5—Geistlichen/ Blumengärtleins/ Drittes Büchlein/ oder/ gestliche/ Lieder und Andachten/ mit noten Versehen/ Achte Auflage./ Frankfurt und Leipzig/ Bei Petrus Dan Schmitz, Buchh. in Solingen/ 1779. [14.2 x 8 cm. 562 pp. plus "Zugabe" and "Tersteegen's Erklärung."]

PP.6—Chur-Pfältzisch/ Allgemeines Reformirtes/ Gesang-Buch,/ bestehend aus denen/ Psalmen Davids,/ nach/ D. Ambrosii Lobwassers/ hin und wieder verbesserter Uebersetzung,/ und 700 Auserlesenen Liedern,/ samt deren Inhalt und verschiedenen Melodien,/ mit/ Chur-Psältzischen Kirchen-Raths/ Approbation/ zum offentlichen Kirchengebrauch und besonderer hausandacht / herausgegeben / auch denen nöthigen Registern / und Chur-Pfältzischen Kirchen-Agendis / versehen. / Mit Chur-Pfältzisch- allergnädigstem Privilegio / Franckfurt am Mayn, / ·in der Andreäischen Buchhandlung, 1783. [16.2 x 8.8 cm. 166 pp. of psalms and melodies.] Bound with: Des / neu-eingerichteten / Chur-Pfältzisch / Reformirten / Gesäng-Buchs / Anderer Theil, / welcher / aller Glaubens-Lehren / und / Lebens-Pflichten / in 700 Auserlesenen geistreichen / sowol / alten als neuen Liedern / in sich hält . . . / Franckfurt am Mayn, / in der Andreäischen Buchh., 1782. [538 pp. plus index.]

PP.7—Des / Geistlichen / Blumengärtleins / Drittes Büchlein, [See PP.5], Neunte Auflage. 1786. [14.5 x 8.5 cm. 562 pp. plus Tersteegen's declaration and "Grabschrift."]

PP.8—Des seligen / Gerhard Tersteegens / hinterlassene / Erklärung / seines / Sinnes / seinem Testamente beigelegt / nebst dessen / Ermahnung zur Liebe, / kurz vor seinem Ende / Den zten April 1769. Erfolget von ihm geschrieben / Solingen / bei Pet. Dan Schmitz, Buchh. 1793. [In three books, the third of which contains melodies for 111 hymns. 14.2 x 8.5 cm. 562 pp. plus indexes.]

PP.9—Ein / Neues, unparthenisches / Gesangbuch / zum / allgemeinen Gebrauch des wahren Gottesdienstes / Auf Begehren / Brüderschaft der Menonisten Gemeinen / aus vielen Liederbucher gesammelt. / Mit einem dreifachen Register versehen / Zweyte verbesserte Ausgabe Lancaster / Gedruckt bey Georg und Peter Albrecht, 1808. [80 pp. of psalms with melodies; 448 pp. of hymns with tunes noted. 18 pp. of indexes with melody register. 18.5 x 11 cm.]

PP.10-1—Gesangbuch / zum / gottesdienstlichen Gebrauche / für / Protestantisch-evangelische Christen. / Zweybrücken, 1823 / Gedruckt und in Commission bey G. Ritter und Comp. [18 x 11.5 cm. 569 pp.]

PP.10-2—Gesangbuch / zum / gottesdienstlichen. . . . [see pp.10-1]. 1829 ed. [16.9 x 10.5 cm. 568 pp.]

PP.11—Anon. Gesangbuch und Gebete. . . . [title page missing through p.5] The register gives dates of composers, the latest of which is 1841. [11.8 x 8 cm. 618 pp. 266 hymns with tunes.]

PP.12—Das neue / Gemeinschaftliche Gesangbuch / zum / gottesdienstlichen Gebrauch / der / Lutherischen und Reformirten Gemeinden / in / Nord Amerika / Mit einem / neuen vermehrten Anhange, / der herrlichsten Kirchenlieder aus den Jahren / 1400 bis 1850 / New York: / Wilhelm Radke, 550 Pearl Str. / 1870. [19 x 12.5 cm. 707 pp. of texts and indexes; 30 pp. of tunes.]

PP.13—Davidsches / Psalter-Spiel / der Kinder Zions / oder / Sammlung / von / Alten und neuen auserlesenen / Geistes-Gesängen / Allen wahren heilsbegierigen Seelen und Säuglingen der Weisheit / insonderheit aber / denen Gemeinden des Herrn / zum / gesegneten Gebrauch mit Fleiss zusammen getragen / nebst den dazu nöthigen und nützlichen / Registern / Nunmehro zum acten Male an's Licht gegeben / und gedruckt / Dritter Abdruck / Amana, im St. Iowa, 1871. [19.2 x 12.5 cm. 1170 pp. of texts and indexes; 111 pp. of music.]

PP.14—Sammlung / geistlicher Lieder / zum Gebrauche / bei dem öffentlichen Gottesdienste / in den / evangelischen Gemeinden / Mit hohen obrigkeitlichen privilegien. / St. Gallen. / gedruckt und zu haben in der Zollikofer'schen Offizin / 1858. [18.5 x 11.5 cm. 288 pp. plus indexes.]

PP.15—Das neue / Gemeinschaftliche Gesangbuch. . . . [see pp.12]. Mit einem / neuen vermehrten Anhänge . . . 1863. [18 x 11.5 cm. 707 pp. with 30 pp. of melodies.]

PRINTED PSALTERS: MELODY NAMES ONLY

pP.1—Hallischen Gesang Buch [title page missing. Vorrede is dated "Halle, Den 1 May, 1711." 17.2 x 7.8 cm. 926 pp. with 715 hymns.]

pP.2—Anmuthiger / Blumen-Krantz / aus dem Garten / der Gemeinde Gottes / in sich fassend / allerhand Göttliche / Gnaden und Liebes Wurkungen / ausgedruckt in / geistlichen lieblichen / Liedern zum Dienst / der / Liebhaber des Lobes Gottes / gesamlet / Ans licht gegeben / Im Jahr 1712. [14 x 8.5 cm. 757 pp. of hymns. 777 hymns and indexes. 2 copies].

pP.3—Schütz, Christoph. Des / geist Harpfen-Spiels / der / Kinder Zions / ander Theil / oder / Dass innige Verlangen und Seuffzen / des / Geistes / welches / in etlichen Gebetern / Liebes und Hertzens / Seufftzern ausegedrucket / und seinem / Rachsten zur Erbauung und ermunterung ans / Licht gegeben / der autor / Christoph Schütz / Im Jahr Christi 1725. [14 x 8 cm. 475 pp.]

pP.4—Anon. Gesangbuch . . . . [title page missing] to which is bound: Geist-Reiches / Gebet-Büchlein / darin zu finden / Morgen und Abend / Wie auch / Buss-Beicht Communion / Krank-Sterb-und andere / schöne Gebete / Frankfurt / Bey Metzlern und Erhardt / Buchhändler in Stuttgardt / 1738. [14.3 x 8.7 cm. 646 pp. of hymns plus index and Register of melodies. 2 copies].

pP.5—Der / Cöthnischen / Lieder / Erster und Anderer Theil, / zum Lobe / des Dreyeinigen / Gottes / und zu gewünschter / reicher / Erbauung vieler Menschen / mit Innhalts-Spruch, und / Anfangs-Registern / herausgegeben / Reuttlingen, / bey Johann Jakob Fleischhauer. [17.5 x 7 cm. 472 pp. and index 3 copies n.d.]

pP.6—Evangelisches / Gesang-Buch, / In einem hinlänglichen / Auszug / der Alten, Neuern und Neuesten / Lieder, / Der / Gemeine in Ebersdorf / zu öffentlichem und besonderm Gebrauch / gewidmet. / Die zweite und vermehrte Auflage. / Ebersdorf / Zu finden im Waysen-Haus / 1745. [17.3 x 9.5 cm. 720 pp. 785 hymns.]

pP.7—Evangelisches / Gesang-Buch . . . . [see pp. 6]. [16.5 x 10.2 cm. 790 pp. [2 copies].

pP.8—Der / Cöthnischen / Lieder, / Erster und Anderer / Theil / zum Lobe . . . [see pp. 5]. Esslingen / zu finden bey Gottlieb Mantlern / 1756. [17 x 1.5 cm.]

pP.9—Geistliches / Blumen-Gärtlein / Inniger Seelen; / oder, kurtze / Schluss-Reimen, / Betrachtungen und Lieder, / Ueber allerhand Wahrheiten des / Inwendigen Christenthums; / zur / Erweckung, Stärckung und Erquickung in dem / Verborgenen Leben / Mit Christo in Gott / . . . . Neuste Auflage / Reutlingen und Fürth. [n.d.]. ["Vorbericht" dated 1756 and author given is Gerh. Tersteegen. 422 pp. hymns; 42 pp. scripture and religious poetry. 16 x 10 cm. 2 copies.]

pP.10—Herzquickendes / Lobopfer Gottes / oder / Geistreiches / Gesang-Buch, / wie solches / in unsern Evangelischen Kirchen / gebrauchlich, / und als ein Kern / aus / D. Martin Luthers / und anderer / Gottesgelehrten Männer Liedern / zusammen getragen / und in alphabetische Ordnung, nebst einem / Register eingetheilet worden. / Tübingen, / Druckts und verlegts Joh. Heinrich Phil Schramm. / Anno. 1758. [18.8 x 11.4 cm. 212 pp.;]

pP.11—Eines / Hungrigen Bettelkindes / einfältige / Trauben-Nachlese / nach dem, reichen Lieder-Herbst / auf verschiedenen Weinbergen / gesammelt / Anno. 1759. [16.2 x 10.7 cm. 78 pp. of hymn texts and tune names. No compiler or printer.]

pP.12—Der / Cöthnischen / Lieder / erster und anderer / Theil . . . . [see pP.5]. 1760. [17.5 x 7.5 cm. 460 pp.]

pP.13—Der / Cöthnischen / Lieder / . . . . [see pP.12]. [Title page missing but similar to above. Last page has imprint of angel figure which is not in pP.12 17.5 x 6.5 cm. 460 pp. hymns.]

pP.14—Die / Cöthnische / Lieder / zwey Theile, / zum Lobe / des Dreyeinigen Gottes / und zu gewünschter reicher / Erbauung vieler Menschen, / mit / Dreyfachen Registern / herausgegeben / Stuttgart, / bey Johann Philipp Erhard / Buchdruckern. / 1769. [16.5 x 7 cm. 471 pp. plus indexes. 3 copies].

pP.15—Geistliches / Blumen-Gärtlein / Inniger

Seelen / . . . . [see pP.9]. Fünfste und vermehrte Edition / nebst der Frommen Lotterie / Germantown, / Gedruckt und zu finden bey Christoph Saur / 1769. ["Vorbericht" has date 21 June, 1744. G.T. St. (Gerhardt Teersteegen?) 14.2 x 8.5 cm. 546 pp.]

pP.16—Würtembergisches / Gesang-Buch, / nthaltend / eine Sammlung / reiner und kräftiger / Lieder, / welche ein Herzoglicher Synodus / zum Gebrauch der Gemeinden aus / dem heutigen Ueberfluss erlesen und / angewiesen. / Mit Herzoglich-Höchster Freyheit / wider das Nachdrucken / Stutgard, / bey Christoph Friedrich Cotta, Hof-und / Canzley-Buchdrucker / 1770. [18.5 x 10.5 cm. 746 pp.]

pP.17—Würtembergisches Gesang-Buch, c.1770. [see pP.16] [7 copies, all with title pages missing]

pP.18—Geistliches / Liederkästlein / zum Lobe Gottes, / aus 366 kleinen Oden über so viel biblische / Sprüche. / Kindern Gottes zum Dienst aufgesezt / von / M. Philipp Friedrich Hillern / Erster Theil / Stutgard / in Verlag Johann Benedict Metzlers, 1771-1775. [9 x 11 cm. 366 pp. of hymns and readings plus indexes] [3 copies.]

pP.19—Würtembergisches / Gesang-Buch . . . . [see pP. 16] 1772 [17.5 x 10.5 cm. 746 pp. 393 hymns.]

pP.20—Würtembergisches / Gesänge-Buch . . . . [see pP.16]. c. 1772. [title page missing] [17. x 10 cm. 744 pp. plus register.]

pP.21—Würtembergisches Gesangbuch [see pP.16]. 1774. [16 x 9.5 cm. 380 pp; 393 hymns. 6 copies].

pP.22—Davidsches / Psalter-Spiel / oder / Sammlung / von / Alten und Neuen auserlesenen- Geistlichen-Gesängen / wahren Heilsbegierigen Seelen / insonderheit aber / Denen Gemeinden des Herrn / zum gesegneten Gebrauch mit Fleiss / zusammen getragen / Nebst dazu nöthig und nützlichen / Registern / Zum fünftenmal ans Licht gegeben / Büdingen / Gedruckt bey Johann F. Stohr / 1775. [17 x 11 cm. 943 pp. plus indexes.]

pP.23—Stimmen / aus / Zion, / oder: / Erbauliche / Lieder, / zur / Verherrlichung Gottes / und Erbauung vieler / Seelen / heraus gegeben. / Neue revidirte Auflage / Erster Theil / Kopenhagen und Stargard, / Verlegts Christian Gottlob Proft. / 1775. [16.5 x 7.8 cm. 756 pp.; 280 hymns, the last of which by D. Spener, has 205 stanzas.]

pP.24—Würtembergisches Gesangbuch. [See pP.16]. [17.5 x 10.5 cm. 554 pp., 393 hymns plus "Kürze Gebet." 1776.]

pP.25—Würtembergisches Gesangbuch. [See pP.16]. [16 x 9.5 cm. n.d. on title page. Has bound to it Johann Christian Storrens' "Beicht und Kommunion Buch", Stuttgart (5th ed., 1771.) 342 pp. here. Back cover and some pages missing.]

pP.26—Würtembergisches Gesangbuch. [See pP.16] 1779. [16 x 9.5 cm. 393 hymns to page 268. Pagination then skips to 305 and continues to 380. 6 copies].

pP.27—Würtembergisches Gesangbuch. [See pP.16]. 1780. 17.8 x 10.2 cm. 754 pp. plus Register; 393 hymns. 2 copies].

pP.28—Würtembergisches Gesangbuch. [See pP.16]. 1784. [17 x 9.5 cm. 369 pp; 393 hymns. 3 copies].

pP.29—Sammlung/ einiger/ geistlichen/ Gedichte und Lieder/ für diejenigen/ welche ihren Heiland/ Jesum Christum/ über alles schätzen/ und das rechtschaffene Wesen lieb haben/ das in ihm ist/ Magdeburg/ in Commission bey dem Buchhändler Creutz/ 1785. [16.5 x 11 cm. 536 pp. plus indexes.]

pP.30—Würtembergisches Gesangbuch. [See pP.16]. 1786. [16.9 x 9.3 cm. 387 pp.; 393 hymns.

pP.31—Einige christliche/ Lieder und Gebete/ für/ die protestantische Gemeine/ in Prag/ Neue Auflage/ Prag/ Verlag der Lochner und Mayrischen Buchhandlung/ 1788. [16.6 x 11 cm. 180 pp.]

pP.32—Anonymous Gesangbuch. Covers and title page missing. Vorrede by D. Heinrich Melchior Mühl(hausen?), New Providenz, 1786. [17 x 10.5 cm. 602 pp.]

pP.33—Anonymous. 520 pp. texts bound with "Einer Himmlischgesinnten/ Seelen/ Erquickstunden/ welche sie sucht und geniesst in einem glaubig-/ und vertraulichen Gespräch mit Gott . . . . Stuttgart, verlegt Bernard M--[?] [n.d.]. [14.5 x 8.5 cm. 178 pp.]

pP.34—Würtembergisches Gesangbuch. [See pP.16]. Title page missing. "Vorbericht" dated Stuttgart, June 14, 1791. 16.4 x 9.5 cm. 552 pp.]

pP.35—Das Kleine Davidische Psalterspiel . . . . (Covers and title page missing but see pP.40.) Bound with: Die Kleine/ Harfe,/ Gestimmet von unterschiedlichen Lieblichen / Liedern oder Lob-Gesangen/ welche gehöret werden/ von dem Enden der Erden, / zu Ehren dem Gerechten/ Diese Kleine Harfe klinget zwar lieblich/ aber doch noch im niedrigen Thon;/ Bis das grosse/ Harfen-Spieler Heer/ den Gesang erhöhen wird/ Gott und dem Lamm sey die Ehre und/ das Lob in Zeit und Ewigkeitl Amen/ Zum ersten mal ans Licht gegeben/ Chesnuthill. Gedruckt bey Samuel Sauer, 1792. [17.5 x 10.5 cm. 572 pp. with 576 hymns in first part. This followed by Regis-

ter and 55 pp. of hymns (Kleine Harfe); 57 hymns and another Register.]

pP.36—Das Kleine Davidische Psalterspiel . . . . (Title page missing but see pP.40.) Bound with: Die Kleine Harf . . . (see pP. 35.) Schaffer & Maund, Baltimore. [n.d. 17 x 10.5 cm. 576 pp. 576 hymns plus additional 57 hymns and registers.]

pP.37—Geistliches/ Liederkästlein/ zum Lobe Gottes,/ [see pP.18]. 1792. [10.7 x 9 cm. 366 pp.]

pP.38—Geistliches/ Blumengärtlein/ inniger Seelen:/ [see pP.9]. Frankfurt und Leipzig, 1794/ in commission bei Dav. Friedr. Hartmann,/ Buchbinder in Schorndorf. [14.5 x 8.9 cm. 558 pp. plus indexes. 10 copies].

pP.39—Geistliches/ Liederkästlein/ zum Lobe Gottes/ [see pP.18]. Stuttgart, 1795. [8.5 x 10.5 cm. 366 pp. of hymns.]

pP.40—Das Kleine/ Davidische/ Psalterspiel/ der/ Kinder Zions,/ von alten und neuen auserlesenen - Geistes Gesängen/ Allen wahren heilsbegierigen/ Säuglingen der Weisheit,/ insonderheit aber denen/ Gemeinden des Herrn/ . . . . Germantaun/ Gedruckt bey Michael Billmeyer, 1797. [17.3 x 10.3 cm. 572 pp. plus registers and Zugabe. 2 copies.]

pP.41—Würtembergisches Gesangbuch (see pP.16). Stuttgart, 1799. [16.5 x 10 cm. 520 pp. of hymns plus Epistles and indexes.]

pP.42—Vollständiges/ Marburger/ Gesangbuch/ zur/ Uebung der Gottseligkeit/ in 615 Christlichen und Trostreichen/ Psalmen und Gesängen/ Hrn. D. Martin Luthers/ und anderer/ Gottseliger Lehrer/ . . . Philadelphia:/ Gedruckt bey Carl Cist, Num. 104 in der Zweyten strasse, nah am Eck der Rehs Strasse, 1799. [17.2 x 10.5 cm. 258 pp.; 615 hymns plus indexes.]

pP.43—Kern/ Geistlicher lieblicher Lieder/ dem/ Herrn mit Hertz und Mund zu singen/ Oder/ Neu-auserlesenes/ Gesang Buch/ in welchem/ Tausend derer besten alten und neuen/ Kirchen-Lieder, deren die meisten nach bekannten Melodien können gesungen werden/ enthalten sind/ Nebst einem kleinen/ Gebet Buch/ und einem/ Anhang/ von/ Sonn-und Fest- Tags . . . . Nürnberg [remainder of title page missing., n.d.]. [16.5 x 10 cm. 419 pp. of hymns; 1,000 hymns plus Zugabe of additional 18 hymns and 17 pp.]

pP.44—Frankfurtisches/ neues Gesangbuch/ zur/ Beförderung/ der/ öffentlichen und hauslichen/ Andacht/ Mit Obrigkeitlicher Freiheit/ Frankfurt am Main, 1800/ Zu finden in der Andreaischen, der Brönnerischen und der Jägerischen Buchhandlung. [17.4 x 19.4 cm. 536 pp. hymns [666 hymns] plus 56 pp. of prayers and indexes. 2 copies.]

pP.45—Sammlung/ von/ geistlichen Liedern/ zum/ gemeinschaftlichen Gesang/ zusammen getragen [No place of publication] 1801. [15.6 x 9.2 cm. 144 pp.; 68 hymns with melody names plus index of first lines.]

pP.46—Würtembergisches Gesangbuch. [See pP.16]] Stuttgart, 1801. [16.5 x 9.5 cm. 520 pp.; 620 hymns.]

pP.47—Sammlung/ von/ Geistlichen Liedern. [see pP.45] [No place of publication] 1801. [14 x 8.5 cm. 348 pp. 3 copies].

pP.48—Knecht, Justin Heinrich. [Title page missing. "Vorrede" dated "Biberach, April, 1802." 19 x 11.5 cm. 788 pp. of hymns; 993 hymns.]

pP.49—Klopstocks/ Werke/ Siebenter Band/ Oden/ Geistliche Lieder/ Epigramme/ Leipzig/ Bey Georg Joachim Göshen, 1804. [21 x 13 cm. 402 pp.]

pP.50—Würtembergisches Gesangbuch. [See pP.16). Stuttgart, 1805. [18 x 10.5 cm. 671 pp. of hymns plus "Sonn-Fest und feyertägliche Evangelien und Episteln."]

pP.51—Gesangbuch/ zum gottesdienstlichen Gebrauch/ in den/ Königlich Preussischen Landen/ Mit Königlich Allergnädigst ertheiltem Privilegio/ Heiligenstadt/ im Verlag der Dülleschen Buchdruckerey/ 1807. [17 x 10 cm. 408 pp.]

pP.52—Anonymous. [No means of id.]. 13.5 x 8.3 cm. 114 pp. here but many missing.

pP.53—Hillern, M. P. F. Geistliches/ Liederkästlein/ zum Lobe Gottes. . . . [see pP.18]. Stuttgart, 1810. [11.5 x 9 366 pp.]

pP.54—Würtembergisches Gesangbuch. [See pP.16]. Stuttgart, 1812. [16.7 x 10.3 cm. 520 pp. hymns; 628 hymns.]

pP.55—Das/ Kleine/ Davidische/ Psalterspiel/ der/ Kinder Zions/ . . . . [see pP.40]. Schaffer und Maund, Baltimore, 1816. [17.5 x 10.5 cm. 600 pp.; 576 hymns plus "Die Kleine Harfe" which has 56 pp. 14 copies.]

pP.56—Neues/ Hamburgisches/ Gesangbuch/ zum/ "öffentlichen Gottesdienste/ und/ zur hauslichen Andacht/ ausgefertiget/ von dem/ Hamburgischen Ministerio/ Mit Eines hochedlen und Hochweisen Raths/ Special-Privilegio/ Achte Auflage/ Hamburg, 1816/ Gedruckt und verlegt von Gottlieb Friedrich Schniebes. [17.6 x 10.5 cm. 392 pp. of hymns: 441 hymns plus 112 pp. of "Sammlung von Gebeten und Andachtübungen."]

pP.57—Erbauhliche/ Lieder-Sammlung/ zum/ Gottesdienstlichen Gebrauch/ in den Vereinigten/ Evangelisch-Lutherischen Gemeinen/ in/ Pennsylvanien/ und den benachbarten Staaten, / Gesammlet, eingerichtet und zum Druck befordet/ durch das hiesige/ Deutsche Evangelisch-Lutherische/ Ministerium/ Die Siebente vermehrte und mit einem melodien Register versehene Auflage./ Philadelphia;/ Gedruckt bey G. und D. Billmeyer 1818. [14.7 x 9 cm. 463 pp.; 746 hymns plus 26 pp. of "kürze andachten. . . ."]

pP.58—Würtembergisches/ Gesangbuch/ zum gebrauch/ für/ Kirchen und Schulen./ von dem/ Königlichen Synodus/ nach dem Bedurfness der gegenwartigen Zeit/ eingerichtet . . . . Stuttgart./ Bei Hof und Kanzleibuchdrucker Cotta's Erben./ 1819. [16.7 x 19 cm. 520 pp.; 628 hymns plus 128 pp. "Evangelien und Episteln."

pP.59—Sammlung/ auserlesener/ geistlicher Lieder/ zum/ gemeinschaftlichen Gesang/ und/ eigenen Gebrauch/ in/ christlichen Familien/ Neunte vermehrte Auflage/ Leipzig/ bei C.H.F. Hartmann/ 1819. [16.2 x 10.3 cm. 216 pp., 90 hymns.]

pP.60—Harmonisches/ Gesangbuch/ Theils/ von/ Andern Authoren/ Theils neu Verfasst./ Zum Gebrauch von Singen und Musik/ für Alte und Junge/ Nach Geschmack und Umständen zu wahlen gewidmet/ Allentown, Lecha Caunty, in Staat Pennsylvanien./ Gedruckt bei Heinrich Ebner/ 1820. [18.7 x 11 cm. 200 pp.; 196 hymns in first section with 58 additional in "Anhang/ zum/ Harmonischen Gesangbuch."]

pP.61—Harmonisches/ Gesangbuch/ . . . . [See pP.60]. 1820. [18.7 x 11 cm. 287 pp. of hymns and indexes; 196 texts in first section; Hymns 197 to 254 in "Anhang"; Hymns 255 to 371 in "Zweyter Anhang"; last page has "Johann Herman/ Buchdrucker, Lancaster, Ohio."]

pP.62—Gesangbuch/ für den öffentlichen Gottesdienst/ der/ evangelisch-protestantischen Gemeinden/ der/ freien Stadt Frankfurt/ Frankfurt am Main, 1824/ Gedruckt und Verlegt bei Johann David Sauerländer. [18.2 x 11.3 cm. 656 pp.; 860 hymns.]

pP.63—Feurige Kohlen/ der aufsteigenden Liebesflammen/ im Lustspiel der Weisheit/ Einer nachdenkenden Gesellschaft gewidmet/ Gedruckt zu Oekonomie/ im Jahr/ 1826. [18.2 x 11 cm. 335 pp.]

pP.64—Harmonisches/ Gesangbuch/ Theils/ von Andern Authoren/ . . . . [see pP.60). Oekonomie,/ Beaver County, im Staat Pennsylvanien/ Gedruckt, im Jahr/ 1827/ [17.5 x 10.5 cm. 420 pp.; 518 hymns.]

pP.65—Psalms/ carefully suited/ to the/ Christian Worship/ in the/ United States of/ America/ Being an improvement of the old Version of the / Psalms of David/ Stereotype ed./ Pittsburgh/ Published by H. Holdship & Son/ 1828. [13.8 x 7.8 cm. 274 pp.]

pP.66—Würtembergisches/ Gesangbuch/ zum Gebrauch/ für/ Kirchen und Schulen/ . . . . [See pP.58], Stuttgart, 1828. [17.3 x 10.7 cm. 520 pp. of hymns; 628 hymns; 128 pp. of "Evan. und Epist."]

pP.67—Würtembergisches/ Gesangbuch. . . . [See pP.58]. Stuttgart, 1829. [16.8 x 10.5 cm. 520 pp. of hymns; 628 hymns; 128 pp. of "Evan. und Epist."]

pP.68—Geistliches/ Blumengärtlein/ inniger Seelen- oder:/ Kurze Schlussreimen/ Betrachtungen und Lieder/ über/ allerhand Wahrheiten des/ inwendigen Christenthums;/ zur/ Erweckung, Stärkung und Erquickung/ in dem/ Verborgenen Leben/ mit Christo in Gott/ . . . Dreizehnte Auflage/ Esslingen/ im verlag bei J. M. Seeger, Buchdrucker,/ 1834. [17.8 x 11 cm. 381 pp.]

pP.69—Union Hymns/ Revised by the committee of Publication of/ The American Sunday School Union/ Philadelphia/ American Sunday School Union/ No. 146 Chestnut Street. Entered in copyright by Paul Beck, Treasurer for S.S. Union in 1835. [11 x 7.5 cm. 337 pp. of hymns and metres and indexes; 520 hymns. 4 copies].

pP.70—Gesangbuch/ für die/ evangelischen Kirchen und Schulen/ des/ Königreichs Württemberg./ Stuttgart/ in dem J. B. Metzler'schen Gesangbuchs-Comtoir./ 1836. [19 x 11.2 cm. 670 pp. of hymns; 629 hymns; indexes, and "Die Leidens-Geschichte Jesu Christi," 185 pp.]

pP.71—Knapp, Albert M. Evangelischer/ Liederschatz/ für/ Kirche und Haus/ Eine Sammlung geistlicher Lieder/ aus/ allen christlichen Jahrhunderten/ gesammelt und nach den Bedürfnissen unserer Zeit bearbeitet/ von/ M. Albert Knapp,/ Diakonus an der Hospitalkirche in Stuttgart./ Stuttgart und Tübingen./ Verlag der J. G. Cotta'schen Buchhandlung/ 1837. [23.5 x 15.5 cm. Two-volume set: 1:682 pp.; 2:912 pp.; 3,572 German hymns with texts and complete indexes, biographical sketches of authors, etc.]

pP.72—Anonymous. [Title page missing]. 17.3 x 10 cm. 554 pp. plus index; 393 hymns but pages containing 1-90 missing.

pP.73—Neues/ Psalter-und Harfenspiel/ der/ Kinder Zion/ oder/ zweiter Theil/ der/ Sammlung/ auserlesener/ geistlicher Liedern/ Basel, bei J. J. Wurz,/ Reutlingen, [n.d.]. [13.2 x 9 cm. 368 pp.; 129 hymns.]

pP.74—Anonymous. [title page missing]. 16.4 cm.; 327 pp. of hymns plus Register; 718 hymns.

pP.75—Starck, Johann Friedrich. Johann Friedrich Starcks/ gewesenen Evangelischen Predigers und Consisistorial-Raths zu Frankfurt/ am Mayn/ Tägliches/ Handbuch/ in guten und bösen Tagen/ Enhaltend:/ Aufmunterungen, Gebete und Lieder,/ zum Gebrauch gesunder, betrübter, kranker/ und sterbender Christen/

Welchem beygefügt ist,/ Ein Tägliches Gebetbüchlein/ für/ Schwangere, Gebärende und Unfruchtbare/ Durchgesehen, verändert und vermehrt, von/ M. Johann Jacob Starck/ . . . Neu (20te) Auflage/ Philadelphia:/ Verlag von Schäfer & Koradi, [n.d.]. [19 x 12 cm. 538 pp., in first section followed by "Gebet-Büchlein" of 106 pp.]

pP.76—Anonymous. [title page missing]. 11.5 x 6.8 cm. 214 pp. of hymns plus index. Most of index missing from this volume. First section of volume has hymns for each day of the week.

pP.77—Fünfzig Betrachtungen/ über das/ Leiden und Sterben/ des/ Herrn Jesu Christi/ Herausgegeben von der/ Amerikanischen Tractat-Gesellschaft/ Neu-York, 150 Nassau-Stresse / [n.d.]. [15.8 x 10.5 cm. 319 pp.]

pP.78—Anonymous. [title page missing]. [n.d.] 14.5 x 9 cm. 348 pp; 85 hymns, the last of which comprises the "Anhang" (27 stanzas). First page has: "Lied/ über die Offenbarung Johannis/ Das, was droben ist."

pP.79—Liturgische/ Gesänge/ der/ evangelischen Brüdergemeinen/ neu/ durchgesehen und vermehrt/ Zweite unveränderte Auflage/ Gnadau/ im Verlag der Buch-handlung der Evangelischen Brüder-Unitat/ bei Hans Franz Burkhard/ 1839. [19 x 11.7 cm. 247 pp.]

pP.80—A Collection/ of Hymns/ for use of the / Methodist Episcopal Church/ Principally from the collection of the/ Rev. John Wesley, a.m. Late fellow of Lincoln College, Oxford/ Revised and corrected/ with a supplement/ New York. Published by G. Lane and P. P. Sanford,/ J. Collard, Printer/ 1842. [13 x 8 cm. 616 pp. 2 copies.]

pP.81—Erbauliche/ Lieder-Sammlung/ zum/ Gottesdienstlichen Gebrauch/ in den Vereinigten/ Evangelisch—Lutherischen Gemeinen/ in/ Pennsylvanien/ und den benachbarten Staaten . . . . Philadelphia, Mentz und Kovoudt, 1845. [13.8 x 7.8 cm. 512 pp.]

pP.82—Das/ Gemeinschaftliche Gesangbuch/ zum/ gottesdienstlichen Gebrauch/ der/ Lutherischen und Reformirten Gemeinden/ in/ Nord America/ Sechste Aufflage/ Philadelphia/ Mentz und Kovoudt/ 1846. [15.5 x 9.8 cm. 374 pp.]

pP.83—Gesangbuch/ zum Gebrauch/ der/ evangelischen Brüdergemeinen/ Philadelphia/ gedruckt bei J. J. Schwacke, 226 Nord 3te Strasse/ zu haben in sämmtlichen Brüdergemeinen in dem Verein. Staaten/ 1848. [15.5 x 10.5 cm. 289 pp.]

pP.84—Gesangbuch/ für/ die evangelische Kirche/ in Würtemberg/ Stuttgart, 1850. [16.2 x 10.4 cm. 441 pp. of hymns and indexes.]

pP.85—Sammlung/ auserlesener/ Geistlicher

Lieder/ zum/ gemeinschäftlichen Gesang/ und/ eigenen Gebrauch/ in Christlichen Familien/ Reutlingen/ Fleichhauer & Spohn/ 1850. [16.8 x 10.5 cm. 244 pp. of hymns, scripture, and indexes.]

pP.86—Sammlung/ auserlesener/ Geistlicher Lieder/ zum/ gemeinschaftlichen Gesang/ und / eigenen Gebrauch/ in/ Christlichen Familien/ Neu Ausgabe/ Zoar, O./ 1855. [17.5 x 12 cm. 141 pp. of hymns and indexes.]

pP.87—Die/ Wahre Separation,/ oder die/ Wiedergeburt/ Dargestellet in/ Geistreichen und erbaulichen/ Versammlungs-Reden/ und/ Betrachtungen./ Besonders auf das gegenwärtige Zeitalter anwendbar/ Gehalten in der Gemeinde in Zoar,/ im Jahr 1830/ Erster Theil/ Gedruckt in Zoar, O. 1856. [18.5 x 20 cm. 409 pp; 52 "Lessons" with hymns given for each but only a few have the texts printed. "Zugabe" consists of three hymns, the second of which has 39 stanzas.]

pP.88—Sammlung/ auserlesener/ Geistlicher Lieder/ . . . [see pP.86]. 1867. [18.5 x 13 cm. 169 pp.]

pP.89—Dreizehn Tempellieder/ für/ die Gemeinde in Schenectady, und/ andere Jerusalemsfreunde./ . . . Herausgegeben/ von/ W. F. Schwilk, Hirte, und Lehrer/ Gedruckt in der Offizin der "Reichs Posaune"/ Schenectady, N.Y./ 1867. [19.3 x 12.5 cm. 30 pp.]

pP.90—The New/ Evangelical Hymn Book/ adapted to/ Public, Social, and Family,/ Devotion/ and designed for the Members/ of the/ Evangelical Association/ and/ All Lovers of Jesus/ First Edition/ Cleveland, Ohio/ Published by Charles Hammer for the Evangelical Association/ 1867. [13.5 x 8.5 cm. 860 pp.; 1,262 hymns.]

pP.91—Church Book/ for the use of/ Evangelical Lutheran/ Congregations/ Philadelphia:/ Lutheran Book Store/ 1868. [16 x 11 cm. 465 pp. 588 hymns.]

pP.92—Kleines Lutherisches/ Schul-Gesangbüchlein/ Lieder und Lieder-Verse/ aus dem/ Gesangbuche der Evangel. Luth. Kirche/ in der Ver. Staaten/ . . . . Herausgegeben/ von. J. Hardter/ New York/ Verlag von E. Steiger/ 1873. [13.5 x 8.5. cm. 48 pp. 49 copies].

pP.93—Gospel Hymns/ and/ Sacred Songs/ [words only]/ by/ P. P. Bliss and Ira D. Sankey/ as used by them in/ Gospel Meetings/ Biglow & Main, and John Church & Co., New York and Cincinatti. [Copyright, 1875]. [12 x 8 cm. 95 pages. 2 copies].

pP.94—Gesangbuch/ für die/ Evangelische Kirche/ in Würtemberg. . . . [Title page missing. See pP. 95. 19.8 x 12.4 cm. 658 pp; 651 hymns.]

pP.95—Gesangbuch/ für die/ Evangelische Kirche/ in/ Wurtemberg/ Stuttgart/ 1877. [16.5 x 10.3 cm. 651 hymns; 419 pp. of hymns plus "Verzeichniss der Bibelstellen," to p. 434. 3 copies].

pP.96—Kirchenbuch/ für/ Evangelisch-Lutherische Gemeinden/ Herausgegeben von der Allgemeinen Versammlung/ der Evangelisch-Lutherischen Kirche/ in Nord Amerika/ Zu beziehen durch, Wartburg Publishing House Paulus List, Manager/ Waverly, Iowa. Binder & Kelly, Phila., 1877. [18 x 12 cm. 824 pp.]

pP.97—Deutsches/ Taschen-Liederbuch/ enthaltend/ 510/ Volks-Vaterlands-Turner, Schützen-Studentent-Trink-und Gesellschaftslieder,/ Operngesänge, geistliche und Concertlieder/ . . . Herausgegeben/ von/ Hermann Mendel/ Sechzigste Auflage/ Berlin, G. Mode's Verlag. [n.d.]. [11.5 x 8 cm. 464 pp. of texts.]

pP.98—Sonntagschul-/ Gesangbuch/ der/ Reformirten Kirche/ in den Verreinigten Staaten/ Herausgegeben von den deutschen Synoden obiger Kirche/ Cleveland, O./ 1886. [13 x 8.5 cm. 313 pp. plus indexes.]

pP.99—Harmonisches/ Gesangbuch. . . . [see pP. 64], 1889. [Reprint of 1827 hymnbook of the Harmonie Society. 18.3 x 11.5 cm.]

pP.100—Achtzig Kirchenlieder/ in Unordnung und Text/ nach den/ Geistlichen Liedern für Kirche, Schule und Haus/ Herausgegeben von/ F. Anders und W. Stolzenburg/ Nebst/ achtzehn Psalmen, Luthers kleinem Katechismus/ und/ den feststehenden Teilen des liturgischen Gottesdienstes. Breslau 1905/ Druck und Verlag von Carl Dulfer. [19 x 12 cm. 96 pp.]

THEORY AND PEDAGOGICAL BOOKS: PRINTED

TP.1—Clifton, Arthur. New/ Vocal Instructor/ containing/ Exercises/ For Improving and Modulating the Voice, Correcting and familiarizing the Ear,/ To Harmony and Intonation;/ And facilitating the inflective powers of Execution:/ also/ Lessons/ For the Acquirement of/ Graces, Ornaments, and Cadenzas . . . etc./ Philadelphia / Published and sold at G. Willig's Musical Magazine/ Copyright December, 1820. [25.5 x 35.5 cm. 15 pp.]

TP.2—Preceptor/ for the/ Spanish Guitar. [No author, date, or publisher. 27.5 x 37 cm. 14 pp.]

TP.3—Albrechtsbergers, Johann G. Johann Georg Albrechtsbergers/ K. K. Hoforganistens in Wien/ Anweisung/ zur/ Composition,/ mit/ ausführlichen Exempeln/ zum Selbstunterrichte,/ erläutert/ nebst/ einem Anhange/ von der Beschaffenheit und Anwendung aller jetz üblichen/ musikalischen Instrumente/ Leipzig / bey Breitkopf und Härtel. [n.d.]. [25.2 x 14.5 cm. 404 pp.]

TP.4—Koch, Heinrich Christoph. Musikalisches / Lexikon/ welches/ die theoretische und praktische Tonkunst, encyclopädish bearbeitet, alle alten und neuen Kunstwörter erklärt, und die alten und neuen Instrumente beschrieben, enthält/ von/ Heinrich Christoph Koch/ Fürstl: Schwarzburg-Rudolfstadt; Kammer-Musikus./ Johann André, Offenbach a/m. [Vorrede" dated 1802]. [22.4 x 13.7 cm. 903 pp.]

TP.5—Marx, Adolf Bernhard. 1. Die Lehre/ von der/ Musikalischen Komposition./ praktisch theoretisch/ von/ Adolf Bernhard Marx/ Sechste verbesserte Ausgabe/ Leipzig/ Breitkopf und Härtel/ 1863. [Four-volume set. Ea. 22.7 x 14 cm. 1. 620 pp.; 2. 616 pp.; 3. 634 pp.; 4. 630 pp. 2. Marx/Saroni. Theory and Practice/ of/ Musical Composition/ by/ Adolph Bernhard Marx/ Translated from the Third German Edition/ and edited by/ Herrman S. Saroni/ New York, F. J. Huntington and Mason & Law/ 1852. [21.5 x 15 cm. 406 pp.]

TP.6—Hummel, Johann, N. Hummel's Klavierschule [first volume missing and subsequent volumes do not contain title page]. Eigenthum u. Verlag von T. Haslinger in Wien. [n.d.]. [Four volumes here. Ea. 36 x 26.5 cm.] 1. II-Theil, 1 Kapitel [paginated 115-172]; 2. II-Theil, 2, 3, 4, Kapitel [paginated 173-296]; 3. II-Theil 5-10 Kapitel [paginated 297-381]; 4. III-Theil [paginated 385-444].

TP.7—Czerny, C. 100 Exercises/ for the/ Piano Forte/ Intended to make Instruction/ Easy for the Young/ by/ C. Czerny/ Published J. L. Peters & Bros./ St. Louis, A. C. Peters & Bro., Cincinnati, [n.d.]. [27 x 35.5 cm. 45 pp.]

TP.8—Mozart, Leopold. Leopold Mozart's/ Violinschule/ oder/ Anweisung/ die Violin zu spielen/ Neue umgearbeitete Ausgabe/ Leipzig, C. F. Peters, 1804. [24.8 x 32 cm. 69 pp.]

TP.9—Bach, Carl Philipp Emanuel. Versuch/ über die wahre Art/ Das Clavier zu Spielen/ mit Exempeln/ und achtzehn Probe-Stücken in sechs Sonaten/ erläutert/ Leipzig [Erster Theil] / 1787. [22 x 18 cm. 280 pp. Bound with "Zweiter Theil" which is dated 1797.]

TP.10—Baillot, Rode et Kreutzer. Methode/ de/ Violon/ par Messrs./ Baillot, Rode et Kreutzer/ rédigée/ par/ Baillot/ Français avec la traduction allemande/ A Offenbach sur le Mein / chez Jean André [n.d.]. Plate No. 2524. [31 x 24 cm. 110 pp.]

TP.11—Knecht, Justin Heinrich. Elementarwerk der Harmonie/ als/ Einleitung/ in die/ Begleitungs-und Tonsetzkunst,/ wie auch/ in die Tonwissenschaft/ Zweite, ganz umgearbeitete und vermehrte Ausgabe/ München, 1814. [25 x 21 cm. 264 pp.]

TP.12—New Instructions/ for the/ German Flute/ containing/ The Easiest and most Modern Method for Learners to Play/ to which is added/ a favorite collection of Minuets, Marches, Song tunes, Duets etc. . . as played by the two eminent Masters/ Florio and Tacet/ G. Willig, Phila. [n.d.]. [15.8 x 26 cm. 35 pp.]

TP.13—Schubart, Christ. Fried. Dan. Ideen/ zu einer Ästetik/ der/ Tonkunst./ Herausgegeben/ von Ludwig Schubart/ Wien/ 1806. [21 x 12.8 cm. 382 pp.]

TP.14—Kummer, C. Flöten-schule/ von/ C. Kummer/ Op. 106. [title page in Ger., Fr., and Engl.]. The Amateur's Instruction Book for the Flute/ containing/ Preparatory lessons and exercises, the scales/ chords, tables of scales with fingering, table of shakes,/ and instructive remarks/ also a selection of short lessons arranged as/ duets for two flutes. G. Andre, Phila. [n.d.]. [33 x 26.5 cm. 67 pp. plus fingering chart.]

TP.15—J. W. Pepper's Self Instructor. [n.d.]. [26.2 x 17 cm. Binding broken, covers missing as are many pages. This an instruction manual for a brass instrument (treble clef), 12 sheets here.]

TP.16—Pick, Dr. Bernhard. Dr. Martin Luther's / Ein Fest Burg ist unser Gott/ in 21 Sprachen/ Zu Seinem 400 jahrigen Geburtstage/ Chicago, Ill./ Severinghaus & Co./ 1883. [20.7 x 14.5 cm. 46 pp.]

TP.17—Standard/ Exercises/ By/ Eminent Authors/ Cincinnati/ John Church & Co. [n.d.] [35.5 x 27 cm.] 1. Kohler's Studies, Op. 50, Bk. I [paginated 1-9]; 2. Kohler's Studies, Op. 50, Bk. II [paginated 10-17]; 3. Czerny's Etudes de Velocity. Op. 299, Bk. 3. [paginated 32-45]; 4. Duvernoy's 15 Etudes. Op. 120 Bk. 3 [paginated 20-33].

TP.18—Alexander's/ Complete Preceptor/ for the/ Flute/ First American/ from the/ Third London Edition/ New York/ Firth & Hall, [n.d.]. [34 x 24.5 cm. 48 pp. Butterfly label on cover: "Alexander's/ Flöten-Preceptor/ Oeconomie/ November, 1830." In ink on first title page: "Dem Music band gehörig/ Economy, November 22d, 1830." Pasted to 2d title page in Müllers hand are 10 features of the preceptor. The paper is signed: "Economie Museum Dec. 16, 1830, J. Chr. Müller."]

TP.19—LX/ Notentafeln/ zu/ Knecht's-Elementarwerk/ der Harmonie/ Ite [bound with IIte] Abtheilung/ München/ Falter und Sohn. [n.d.]. [Watermark: "Canzlei Stuttgart." Also has figures "B" and "2" and shield with crown on top. Butterfly label on front cover: "Economy Musical Society/ Economy." 26 x 34 cm. 98 pp.]

TP.20—Cramer, J. B. Practische/ Pianoforte-schule/ von/ J. B. Cramer/ Neue Ausgabe/ Breitkopf & Härtel in Leipzig. [n.d.]. [26 x 34 cm. 48 pp.]

TP.21—Burgmüller. Burgmüller's Instructions/ for the/ Piano Forte/ With French & English Text/ Phila./ A Fiot [n.d.]. [27 x 24 cm. 59 pp.]

TP.22—Plaidy, Louis. Technical Studies/ for the/ Piano Forte/ by/ Louis Plaidy/ Professor of the Piano Forte at the Conservatorium of Leipzig/ Translated from the latest corrected and improved/ German Edition/ Cleveland/ S. Brainard & Sons/ Copyright 1870. [31.3 x 23.5 cm. 58 pp.]

TP.23—Getze, J. A. Getze's/ New and Improved School/ for the/ Parlor Organ/ New York, S. T. Gordon & Son/ c. 1876. [23.3 x 28 cm. Unbound Advertisement of 8 sheets.]

TP.24—Brainard's/ Dollar Method/ for the/ Piano-Forte/ containing/ complete and thorough instructions and/ a choice selection of vocal and/ instrumental music/ S. Brainard's Sons/ Cleveland and Chicago/ c. 1880. Cover advertises volume as "Hamilton's/ New Method/ for the/ Piano-forte/ S. Hamilton/ Pittsburgh, Pa." [23.5 x 30.4 cm. 96 pp.]

TP.25—Carcassi, M. Method/ for the Guitar/ carefully revised and enlarged by/ Walter Jacobs. Copyright 1884, White, Smith & Co. Revised 1896. [25 x 32 cm. 152 pp. here. Front cover missing. Originally bound in boards and buckram. In pencil: "This must have belonged to Walrath Weingartner. The only guitarist in the Harmony Society. He made the guitar on which he performed. J. S. Duss." Weingartner died 1873—23 years before this book was printed!]

TP.26—Ludden, W. School for the Voice/ being an/ Analytical, theoretical and practical treatise/ upon the/ proper use and development of the vocal organs: together with a progressive/ course of Etudes and Exercises/ written expressly for the education of the voice in/ the art of singing/ by/ W. Ludden/ Boston/ Oliver Ditson & Co. Copyright 1871. [25.8 x 32 cm. 176 pp.]

TP.27—Langey, Otto. Tutor for the/ Cornet/ selected/ arranged and/ composed by Otto Langey/ Phila., Pa. published by Harry Coleman/ copyright 1890. [23.5 x 29.2 cm. 126 pp.].

TP.28—Bibl, Rudolf. Theoretisch praktische/ Harmonium-Schule/ Mit besonderer Rücksicht auf den Selbstunterricht/ von/ Rudolf Bibl/ Berlin/ Schlesinger'sche Buch U. Musikhandlung ["Vorwort" dated 1881]. [24 x 30.5 cm. 52 pages here. Unbound. Binding broken and some pages missing.]

TP.29—Ryan's True Banjo/ Instructor/ Published by John Church & Co., Cincinnati, O. Copyright, 1874. [17.6 x 25.3 cm. 63 pp.]

TP.30—Mason, Lowel. Dr. Lowell Mason's Music Charts./ First Series. [106.5 x 73.5 cm. 15 sheets.] Published by Mason Brothers, N.Y. & Boston. Copyright 1868.

TP.31—Mason, Lowell. Dr. Mason's Music Charts/ Series II. [see TP.30].

TP.32—The New York Musical Pioneer/ and/ Choristers's Budget/ Vol. V., October 1859 to September 1860. Published by F. J. Huntington, No. 7 Beekman St. [25 x 17.5 cm. Each vol. is paginated separately. Contains music, advertisements, news, etc. contemporary to printing of each vol.]

TP.33—The New York Musical Pioneer. Vol. XI (No. 2) November 1865, to Vol CII (No. 12) December 1867. [see TP.32].

TP.34—The Century Magazine. Vol. XXXI, No. 6, April, 1886. Contains article: "Creole Slave Dances: The Dance in the Place Congo" by George W. Cable. Arrangements of Creole music. Also article: "Creole Slave Songs," by G. W. Cable. [17.5 x 25 cm. 964 pp.]

TP.35—New & Complete/ Preceptor/ for the/ Spanish Guitar/ with/ Progressive Exercises/ Selected from the works/ of/ The Best Authors/ Philadelphia/ John G. Klemm/ Copyright 1827. [26 x 35.5 cm. 15 pp.]

TP.36—Winner, Sep. Winner's/ Easy System,/ for the/ Guitar/ by Sep. Winner/ Philadelphia/ Lee & Walker/ copyright 1866. [17.5 x 25 cm. 80 pp.]

TP.37—Baker, Theodore. A Supplement to the/ Biographical Dictionary/ of/ Musicians/ by/ Theodore Baker, Ph.D./ New York: G. Schirmer/ 1905. [22.3 x 15.5 cm. Pagination 649-95.]

TP.38—Chevalier Giuseppe/ Ferrata, Mus, Doc./ Director of Music of the/ Beaver College and/ Musical Institute. [Booklet published by Beaver College Feb. 1903, announcing appointment of Ferrata to the faculty. Contains letters of commendation, programs from Italian and American concerts and recitals; published works, etc. 18.5 x 11.5 cm. 31 pp.]

TP.39—Kuhlo-Bethel, Johannes P. Posaunen-Fragen/ beantwortet von/ P. Johannes Kuhlo-Bethel/ Dritte verbesserte und vermehrte Auflage/ 1909/ Zu beziehen durch die Buchhandlung der Anstalt Bethel bei Bielefeld. [19 x 12.8 cm. 144 pp.]

TP.40—Taylor, H. Hits and/ Hitters/ or/ secrets of the music publishing/ Business/ by/ John Philip Sousa, Paul Dresser Harry von Tilzer, Chas. K. Harris, etc./ published by Herbert H. Taylor/ New York/ copyright 1900 [13 x 19 cm. 53 pp.]

TP.41—President's Annual Address/ to the members of the/ Musical Mutual Protective

Union/ of New York/ N.Y., [Alexander Bremer], January 9th, 1902. [21.2 x 28.5 cm. 4 sheets.]

TP.42—Konzert-Handbuch/ Lager von/ Breitkoph & Härtel/ in Leipzig/ VI. Militar (harmonie) Musik/ deutschen und ausländischen Verlages/ Leipzig, 1899. [16.7 x 12 cm. 50 pp. Covers missing.]

TP.43—Bartlett, M. L., and Kinsey, J. F. The Echo Musical Supplement/ The Song Circle/ The Echo Music Co./ Lafayette, Ind. [n.D.]. [18 x 26 cm. 4 sheets. Unbound.]

TP.44—Conn, C. G. C. G. Conn's/ Truth/ Elkhart, Ind., July, 1901. [Magazine of advertisements, photographs of bands, etc., articles on instruments, music and musicians. 34 x 25 cm. 32 pp.]

TP.45—Der/ Musikfreund/ Illustrierte Zeitschrift/ für/ Folkstümliche Hausmusik/ Herausgeber: H. Jenne's Velag, Copenick-Berlin/ Nummer 1, 1. Jahrgang/ 1904. [Contains music and articles about music and musicians. 27.5 x 35 cm. 6 sheets.]

TP.46—The Etude/ For the teacher-Student/ and Lover of Music/ Theodore Presser, Phila. February 1903. [26.5 x 35 cm. Pagination from 41-80.]

TP.47—The Etude/ May 1903 [see TP.46]. Pagination from 165 to 208.

TP.48—Every Month/ Song and Story/ Fashions, Household/ etc/ $2 worth of Music for Ten Cents/ New York, August, 1902. Vol XIV No. 5. [25 x 32.3 cm. 33 pp.]

TP.49—Every Month [see TP.48]. September, 1902. 32 pp.

TP.50—The Dominant/ A Journal for Musicians and Music Lovers/ Arthur A. Clappe/ Editor and Proprietor/ Vol. VII. No. 4, June 1899. [35 x 26.5 cm. 28 sheets.]

TP.51—The Dominant [see TP.50]. Vol. VII, No. 7, Sept. 1899. 30 sheets.

TP.52—Bulletin of New Music/ published and imported/ by/ G. Schirmer/ New York, October, Nov., Dec. 1902.

TP.53—Programs, news articles, photographs, and communication of John Duss. Carton 1: 13 x 27 x 42 cm.

TP.54—Carton 2 [see TP.53].

TP.55—Carton 3 [see TP.53].

TP.56—Catalogue/ of/ Music/ for/ Standard/ Piano/ Players [rolls]/ Manufactured by/ The Chase & Baker Co./ Buffalo, N.Y. U.S.A./ 1904/ Hallet & Davis Piano Co./ Boston, Mass. [13 x 19.5 cm. 286 pp.]

TP.57—Deutch-Amerikanische Chor-Zeitung/ Musikalische Monatschrift für Kirche, Schule und Haus/ Mai (1892) Number 8. [25.5 x 17.5 cm. Pagination from 226 to 255.]

INSTRUMENTAL: MANUSCRIPT ENSEMBLE PARTS

IM2.1—Benda, Georg. Amynts Klagen Über die Flucht der Lalage. Instrumental and vocal parts to cantata for soprano and orchestra. 20.9 x 32.9 cm. 15 sheets. [n.d.].

IM2.2—Hiller, J. S. Horatu Carmen ad Aelium Lamium. Instrumental and vocal parts to cantata for soprano, alto, chorus and orchestra. [n.d.]. 22.4 x 24.5 cm. 19 sheets.

IM2.3—Anon. Short pieces for three flutes. [n.d.]. 20.8 x 34 cm. 15 pp. of music.

IM2.4—Lanner, Schumann, Eggers, and Anon. Songs and waltzes arranged for 2 clarinets, 2 horns, tenorhorn, and bass. [n.d.]. 21.2 x 34.2 cm. 18 sheets.

IM2.5—Lochner, Hamm, Newmann, Beethoven, and Anon. Dances, marches, etc., all incomplete. [n.d.] 34 x 21.5 cm. 22 sheets.

IM2.6—L. Beme, Romney, Brown, Holden, and Anon. Treble instrument parts to marches and waltzes. All incomplete. [n.d.]. 25 x 30 cm. 8 sheets.

IM2.7—A series of four part-books containing the secular series, including pieces and arrangements by W. C. Peters and C. v. Bonnhorst. All 11.5 x 20.5 cm., Bound in leather and boards.

1 Corno Primo. Butterfly label on cover reads: "Corno Primo/ pro/ Jonathan Lentz in/ Economy." Inside front cover is written: "Jonathan Lenz, Corno Primo." Holdship watermark (circle). 229 pp. music.

2 Flute. Inside cover has drawing of flute and fingering chart. 103 pp. music.

3 Violoncello/ Basso/ Bugle. On front cover: "Violin cello/ Basso." This section of volume contains 67 pp. of music. Reversed book becomes Bugle part-book with 144 pp. music.

4 Flute. Drawing of flute on inside front cover. Many pp. torn from volume. 113 pp. of music remain. Also contains songs with texts for Harmonist festivals.

IM2.8—A series of 14 part-books representing the secular and sacred music repertories of the Economy orchestra c. 1822-1830.

1 Bassoon. On flyleaf: "Basoon bekommen den 26 April 1828." Page 372 dated Sept. 3, 1827. 20.5 x 11.5 cm. 393 pp.

2 Viola. 31 x 20 cm. 285 pp. with indexes.

3 Canto and Violin Primo. On cover in gold letters: "J. C. Muller." Parts to 320 pieces in numbered series as well as violin 1 parts to quartets and ensemble works, some in numeral notation. 28 x 42.5 cm. 187 pp., pp. 132-151 cut from book.

4 Bass Viol. Inside cover: "Jonathan Lenz fur das Bassgeigen." 137 pp. of music from

front to middle. Inverted book contains 25 pp. of hymns. 38 x 22.8 cm.

5 Faggotte/Bass Book. Parts to hymns and secular series. 30.5 x 18.8 cm. 266 pp.

6 Flauto Secondo. On spine in gold letters: "Flauto/ Secondo/ Elias/ Speitel." 208 pp. of music from front to middle; inverted 2 pp. of music. Harmonie binding. 32 x 19.8 cm.

7 Clarinet. 31 x 19.5 cm. 164 pp. of music front to back; inverted 45 pp.

8 Bugle 2. 28.5 x 21 cm. 97 pp. of music front to middle. Inverted, 47 pp. Many pp. missing.

9 First Bugle. 21.5 x 29 cm. 103 pp. but many missing.

10 Flauto Primo. Butterfly label on cover: "Flauto Primo/ Marches, Waltzes, etc./ pro Matth. Scholle/ 1827." Flyleaf has "John Wolfnagel, Jr., Economy, Nov. 17, 1872." 11.5 x 21.5 cm. 561 pp. music.

11 Violin, Butterfly label on cover: "Marches pro J. C. Müller [crossed out]. B Schnabel/ Harmonie, Ia. Julie 3/1822." 8.7 x 20 cm. 158 pp.; 136 with music.

12 Violino Primo. 42 x 28 cm. 230 pp.

13 Peiffe 2. Marches and waltzes, 20 x 16.5 cm.; 16 pp.

14 Corno. 11 x 20 cm. 46 pp.; 26 with music.

IM2.9—A series of six part-books (1, Trumpet; 2, Bombarton; 3, Althorn; 4. Trombone; 5, Trombone; 6, Clarinet) containing excerpts from operas by Bellini, Strauss, Hamm, Schweda, Kolb, Adam, and others. Each 24.5 x 33.7 cm. 56 pp. music. No pagination, unbound but pages sewn together.

IM2.10—Treble Instrument Part-Book containing hymns and sacred songs. 20.4 x 32.1 cm. Pagination complete through p. 93 but pp. 2 and 3 missing.

IM2.11—Flauto Secondo. On frontcover: "Harmony den 30 Oct. 1814/ Mr. Millr Bot[anist?]." One piece by Mozart, remainder anon. 31.5 x 25 cm. 12 pp. music.

IM2.12—Flauto Primo. Title page reads: "Einige leichte Duetts/ für Flöten/ von/ Hoffmeister/ Flauto Primo/ Poss./ E. Heidelberg." Watermark "C Graf." 21 x 32 cm. 9 pp. music.

IM2.13—Second Violin. Parts to secular series with many pieces by W. C. Peters. Holdship watermark. 19.1 x 30.8 cm. 54 pp. music.

IM2.14—Bass/Horn. Overtures and sinfonia from secular series, pp. 1 to 20 for Bass; reversed 22 pp. for Horn. Holdship watermark. 18.4 x 30.2 cm.

IM2.15—Violino Primo/ Tenor/ Guitar. Butterfly label on cover reads: "Tenor cum/ violino Primo pro/ [name scratched out]." One page dated August 3, 4, 1834. Front part of book contains tenor voice and 1st violin parts to large

choral works by Haydn, Mozart, and others. Reversed it is an instruction manual for guitar. 27.2 x 21.9 cm. 70 pp. music.

IM2.16—A series of four part-books containing marches and dances, some from the secular series. Compositions by Mozart, Handel, Stamitz, and anon. Instruments not indicated but all in treble clef. 1. 21.4 x 18.2 cm.; 101 pp. music. Bound in grey cardboard; 2. 19.5 x 15.5 cm. 68 pp.; 3. 17 x 20.5 cm. 50 pp.; 4. 20 x 16.5 cm. 36 pp.

IM2.17—Treble instrument part-book containing sacred series in first part and secular series in second. 19 x 15.3 cm. 130 pp. music.

IM2.18—Treble instrument part-book containing entries from IM2.16 and IM2.8. 18.8 x 15.9 cm. 151 pp. music.

IM2.19—Bass and Treble instrument part-book. Pieces from the secular series with bass parts on verso and treble on recto. One page inscribed: "By Saml Beards, esq. 1850." 19.5 x 11.1 cm. 139 pp. music.

IM2.20—Treble instrument part-book containing secular series. Entries on recto only. Inside front cover: "Nicander Wolfangel." 17.4 x 10.2 cm. 104 pp. music.

IM2.21—Treble part-book with name "Jacob Shriver" inside front cover. Contains marches and waltzes from early period. 11 x 19.5 cm. 120 pp.

IM2.22—Violino Primo/Flauto Primo. Butterfly label on cover reads: "Leichte Trio/ für violine od. F[löte]/Violino 1/pro J. [Müller]." First part of volume for flute and dated 1803. Second begins with title page: "Trios faciles/ pour/ deux violons & Violoncelle/ par J. Vanhall/ Violino Primo/ Oeconomie, Augt. 21, 1828." 23.3 x 13.5 cm. 37 pp. music.

IM2.23—Guitar part-book. On front cover: "Friedrich Baumann/ 1876." Contains polkas, waltzes, and songs in a numbered series. Inside front cover: "Charlie Baumann, Economy, Pennsylvania." 23.8 x 16.7 cm. 63 sheets.

IM2.24—Treble part-book containing 5 pp. of hymn tunes from c. 1820. Letters "AA" on front cover. 21.8 x 18.5 cm.

IM2.25—Fagotto/ Basso part-book of anon. rondos and songs. On cover: "Fagotto, Basso/ pro/ Walrath Weingartner/ Harmonie, October/ 1819." 32.5 x 20.2 cm. 9 sheets sewn into wallpaper cover.

IM2.26—Flauto Primo part-book containing Sonatine by Wanhall and other anon. pieces. On cover: "Flauto Primo/ pro/ Jac. Shriver." Four sheets sewn into folded copy of Indiana Centinel and Public Advertiser of Sat., Jan. 20, 1821. 24.5 x 30 cm.

IM2.27—Second Violin/ Keyboard parts to

secular series and hymns. 21.8 x 28 cm. 92 pp. music.

IM2.28—Viola/keyboard part-book containing marches, hymns and choruses. 27.1 x 21.9 cm. 64 pp., 22 with music.

IM2.29—Viola part-book. Most entries are W. C. Peters' arrangements. Holdship watermark. 20.9 x 32 cm. 46 pp. music.

IM2.30—Violin/ Violoncello part-book. [Contains pieces from IM2.8 series.] 20.3 x 32.6 cm. 8 pp. of music.

IM2.31—Bass Posaune part-book containing short pieces, hymns and sacred songs. On front cover: "Bass/ Posaune/ Economie the 24 Merz, 1835 Economy/ Pa. Jacob Henrici." 16 pp. music. 19.4 x 10.2 cm.

IM2.32—1 1st Violin. Challoner, N. B. Duets for two violins. Title page reads: "Twelve/ Duets/ for two/ Violins/ composed, arranged/ and partly/ selected from the works of the best/ Authors/ by/ N. D. Challoner/ Op. 7/ Philadelphia/ Published by F. G. Klemm, Music & Musical Instrument Seller/ 3 South Third Street/ Jacob Henrici/ Aug. 27, 1833." 19.5 x 32.2 cm. 14 pp. music. 2 Violin 2.

IM2.33—Corno Primo part-book containing ländlers, allegros, andantes, all anon. 20.5 x 17 cm. 8 pp. music.

IM2.34—Secondo [violin]. One piece by Vanhall, others anon. Title page is cover and bears inscription: "Poss. J.H.H.." 20.1 x 16.6 cm. 12 pp. music.

IM2.35—Treble part-book containing waltzes, quadrilles, and marches from the secular series. 16.4 x 19.8 cm. 7 pp. of music.

IM2.36—First Horn part-book in which each part is written twice: once in notes and once in numeral notation. 16 x 19 cm. 40 pp. of music.

IM2.37—A series of four part-books (1. Flauto Tertio; 2. First Clarinet; 3. Second Clarinet; 4. Bassoon) containing anonymous marches, waltzes, dances, and sinfonias. All 21.8 x 33.6 cm. 43 pp. of music.

IM2.38—Pleyel, I. Title page inscribed: "basso/ zu Ignatius Pleyel's/ Kleine Clavier-Stücke,/ ausgesetzt zu einer kleinen Privat Music/ von JC Müller/ Harmonie, Ia., Im October, 1823." 16 x 20 cm. 35 pp. of music from front to center. Reversed, 22 pp. of treble parts to dances and marches.

IM2.39—Guitar/ Viola part-book containing marches, airs, etc., for guitar. Inscribed on cover: "Marches/ Waltzes, Airs, Songs, etc./ for the/ Guitare/ Burghard Schnabel." Reversed book contains secular entries for viola. 136 pp. of music. 20.1 x 16.5 cm.

IM2.40—Horn/ 2te Stimm. Entries are large

sacred works, dated 1823 to 1839. Inside cover inscribed: "John Bammesberger." 19.9 x 16.6 cm. 181 pp. music.

IM2.41—Treble/ Bass part-book containing sacred choruses, hymn and chorale melodies. On binding in gold letters: "Music/ Book/ G. Rapp." Treble parts front to middle; bass parts entered from other end with book inverted. 22.8 x 33.8 cm. 89 pp. music.

IM2.42—Second Violin Part-book containing pieces from secular and sacred series, some dated 1828-1830. 19.3 x 31.1 cm. 130 pp. music.

IM2.43—Anon. Cantata, "Preis dem Erretter." Parts here for Flauto secondo; Clarinetto Primo and Secondo; Corno secondo; trombone Basso; Timpani; Violino Primo; Viola. 32.8 x 24 cm. 7 sheets.

IM2.44—Treble part-book containing chorale melodies. 16.4 x 19.8 cm. 9 pp. music.

IM2.45—Book of clarinet duets, inscribed: "Copied for, and/ Presented to/ Mr. A. Shriver, by J.Seetin, Pittsburgh/ Economy." 17.3 x 24.7 cm. 24 pp. music.

IM2.46—Assortment of unidentifiable fragments, loose leaves. Unsorted and wrapped between two cardboard sheets. 41.5 x 54 cm.

IM2.47—Beethoven, L. Symphony No. 5. Parts for wind and percussion [two sets of parts]. One inscribed:"F. Schmida, F/M 1843." Stamped on all sheets: "Reinhard Schmelz." Set 1: 35.5 x 21.5 cm. Set 2: 25 x 33.8 cm.

IM2.48—Collection of pieces for Zither. Pieces by Froshmann, Kuken, Kuhner, and excerpts from various operas. Inscription inside front cover:"Friedrich Bauman, Stuttgart, 1868." 24.3 x 16.8 cm. 78 pp.

IM2.49—Treble parts to pieces in secular series. Numeral notation. 20.1 x 32 cm. 1 sheet.

IM2.50—Duss, J.S.Orchestra parts to "The Cross and Crown March." 34 x 27 cm. 11 sheets.

IM2.51—Strauss/ Rohr. Loreley—Rhein Klänge—Waltzer von Strauss arr. by J. Rohr. Economy Cornet Band Stamp. 26.5 x 34 cm. 18 sheets.

IM2.52—Anon. Overture zu Berlin: Wie es weint und Lacht. Economy Cornet Band. 30.2 x 22.5 cm. 18 sheets.

IM2.53—Duss, J.S./ Neubauer. Life's Voyage/ J.S. Duss,/ arr. Henry Neubauer/ Copyright by Wm. C. Ott and Co./ Beaver Falls. Orchestra parts. 17 x 26.5 cm. 39 sheets.

IM2.54—Duss, J.S. The Brownies [and] The Fair Debutante. Orchestra Parts. 23 x 31 cm. 41 sheets.

IM2.55—Townsend, R.T. Blue Eyes [see VP1.49]. Orchestra parts. 24 x 31 cm. 4 sheets.

IM2.56—Rohr, J. Clarinetto Walzer. Stamped "Economy Cornet Band." 26.5 x 34 cm. 4 sheets.

IM2.57—Anon. The Echo Polonaise/ and The Oriole Schottish. Stamped "Economy Cornet Band." 22.5 x 30 cm. 21 sheets.

IM2.58—Hamm/ Rohr. Die Beiden Schwätzer/ and Militare Ouverture. Arranged for Economy Cornet Band. 18 sheets. 22.5 x 30 cm.

IM2.59—Verdi/ Rohr. Ouverture de Nabuchodnosor. Arranged for Economy Cornet Band. 22.5 x 30 cm. 19 sheets.

IM2.60—Neibig, A. Liederkranz Potpourri. Economy Cornet Band. 32 x 24 cm. 13 sheets.

IM2.61—Rohr, J. [arr.]. Swiss Air für Clarinet. Economy Cornet Band. 26.5 x 34 cm. 14 sheets.

IM2.62—Bach/ Rohr. Inaugeral Polonaise/ and Bellini/ Rohr. Potpourri aus Norma. Economy Cornet Band. 30 x 22.5 cm. 13 sheets.

IM2.63—Hartzing/ Rohr. Potpouri aus Czar und Zimmerman. Economy Cornet Band. 30 x 24.8 cm. 13 sheets.

IM2.64—Donizetti [arr.?]. Potpourri from "Il Poliuto." 1st Clar. part here only. 27.5 x 18 cm. 2 sheets.

IM2.65—Wallace [arr.]. Selections from "Maritano." Economy Cornet Band [incomplete]. 30 x 22.5 cm. 5 sheets.

IM2.66—Suppe/ Rohr. Overture "Dicter und Bauer." Economy Cornet Band. 25 x 30 cm. 12 sheets.

IM2.67—Rice, W.A. Transcontinental March. Parts for band. 26.8 x 34 cm. 6 sheets.

IM2.68—Labitsky/ Rohr. Heimweh Walzer/ and Medley Ouverture Economy Cornet Band. 26.8 x 24 cm. 23 sheets.

IM2.69—Donizeto/ Rohr. Potpouri aus der Oper Lucrezia Borgia. Economy Cornet Band. 26 x 34 cm. 20 sheets.

IM2.70—Beethoven, L. Schlacht. Parts for large concert band. Some inscribed: "Ph., N.Y., 1902." 34 x 27 cm. 17 sheets.

IM2.71—Rohr, J. [arr.]. Economy Potpouri. Economy Cornet Band. 22.5 x 30 cm. 17 sheets.

IM2.72—Graffula Quickstep/ and Moskay Parade Marsch. Economy Cornet Band. 17 x 26 cm. 11 sheets.

IM2.73—Bellini/ Rohr. Ouverture aus Norma von Bellini/ arranged by J. Rohr. Economy Cornet Band. 30 x 22.5 cm. 12 sheets.

IM2.74—Brunet, L. The Cavalier Marsch/ and Graffulla. Quick March "The Tempest." Economy Cornet Band. 30 x 22.5 cm. 26 sheets.

IM2.75—Suppe [arr.?]. Ouverture Leichte Cavalerie. Economy Cornet Band. 34 x 27 cm. 9 sheets.

IM2.76—Bela, Keler. Ungarishe Lustspiel Ouverture/ and Anon. Spring Greeding [sic]. Economy Cornet Band. 34 x 27 cm. 35 sheets.

IM2.77—Pleyel [arr.?]. Pleyel's Hymn/ variations for cornet. Band parts. 22.5 x 30 cm. 14 sheets.

IM2.78—Anon. Finale aus der Operette "Dornroschen." Economy Cornet Band. 26.5 x 34 cm. 18 sheets.

IM2.79—A collection of dances by Aug. Herzog, Labitsky, Wallenstein, and anon. Parts incomplete. 21.5 x 33.5 cm. 11 sheets.

IM2.80—A series of 11 part-books for the Economy Silver Cornet Band (c.1876-1879). Several entries dated. 29.3 x 22.8 cm. All bound in blue buckram and leather. All parts inscribed: "Economy/ Silver Cornet Band." Instrumentation here includes: 2 E-flat cornets; 2 B-flat cornets; B-flat tuba; 2 B-flat tenors; 1 E-flat solo Alto; 1 E-flat Alto; 1 Bariton; 1 E-flat Tuba. The series contains 32 selections, most of which have the titles cut from top of pages indicating binding was done after copy was made. Most pieces are anon.: 1-4 [missing]; 5 Summer March; 6 Lucia de Lammermoor [arr. Rohr]; 7 Atila Quick Stepp; 8 March for Lucrezia Borgia; 9 Polonais; 10 Mountain High; 11 Through the World; 12 Overture to Nebuchodnosor (Verdi-Rohr); 13 Aria from Ermani; 14 Militaire 15 Potpouri (Stradella); 16 Concert March; 17 Waltz; 18 Ov. Calif de Bagdad(arr. Rohr); 19 Come where the lilies bloom; 20 Potpouri aus Martha; 21 Potpouri Araber; 22 Kapitania; 23 Parade March; 24 Tancredi; 25 Abendstänchen; 26 Amboss Polka; 27 Potpouri; 28 Irish Potpouri; 29 Banditenstriche (Suppe/ Beyer); 30 Rage in America (Ringleben); 31 La Bel Flower Walzer; 32 German Medley.

IM2.81—Strauss [arr.?]. Concortia Tanse Waltz. Economy Cornet Band. 30.5 x 27.5 cm. 14 sheets.

IM2.82—Anon. Recollections of War and Peace. Economy Cornet Band. 25.5 x 34 cm. 11 sheets.

IM2.83—Meuller, Gus[arr.]. Fanfare for concert band. Inscribed: "Gus Meuller/ arrg. of Music/ Allegheny, Pa." 24 x 31 cm. 21 sheets.

IM2.84—A series of 19 part-books representing two instrumental groups: the Economy Brass Band; and the Silver Cornet Band. One book has label on each cover with"Silver Cornet Band" on one and "Brass Band" on the other. Contents of both identical but given in different orders: 1 Harmonie du Bruderstadt; 2 Bei der Weisheit; 3 Sei Getreu; 4 Der Todt ist Todt; 5 Erhöhe soll ich dich; 6 So schön wie mein geliebter; 7 Ruhet wohl ihr Todenbeiner; 8 Jesus Meiner Zuversicht; 10 Stiller Kirchhof; 11 Freut euch ihr Kinder; 12 In meinem Hause; 13 Lobe den Herrn; 14 Auf, auf ihr Christen; 15 Jauchzet ihr Christ; 16

Erwach zum neuen Leben; 17 Der schöne Maien-mond began. Most books 11.5 x 15.5 cm.

IM2.85—A series of 4 part-books stamped: "Economy Silver Cornet Band, Economy, Pa." Contents: Die Kappelle von Kreuger; Mahnung [anon.]; Rondo von Rex; Die Post v. Schafer; Auf den Alpen anon.]. Ea. 22.5 x 30 cm. Ea. 9 sheets.

IM2.86—An E-flat Alto part-book containing pieces not found in other series. Dances, marches, by Mozart, Kuchner, Strauss, and anon. Inscribed: "William Seefeldt / 1st E-flat Alto / Manufacturer & Dealer in Musical Instruments / 731 Race St., Phila." 16.8 x 12.8 cm. 18 sheets.

IM2.87—An E-flat Alto part-book containing 8 anon. marches and dances. 17.5 x 13.3 cm. 15 sheets.

IM2.88—Bruno, Carl / Merz. The Pittsburgh Gazette March / Carl Bruno / arr. by Otto Merz. Drum Part only. 34 x 26.5 cm. 1 sheet.

IM2.89—Duss, J.S. / Metzner, W.A. Dreams-Concert Mazurka / by / J.S. Duss. Piano and 3rd B-flat Clar. and drum parts only. 27 x 34 cm. 5 sheets.

IM2.90—Gavotte [anon.]. Two Fagott and Corno II parts. 27 x 34 cm. 3 sheets.

IM2.91—Womit soll ich. . . [anon.]. Setting for five-part brass choir. 8 x 17 cm. 5 sheets.

IM2.92—Nevin / Atherton. Narcissus, arr. by F. P. Atherton. 3rd B-flat Clar. and Tenors 1 & 2 only. 28 x 22 cm. 2 sheets.

IM2.93—Blanquette / Rohr. The Chimes of Normandie. Bass part only. 27 x 34 cm. 2 sheets.

IM2.94—Anon. Frish, Fromm und Froh-Overture. E-flat cornet and treble part marked "leader" here. 27 x 35 cm. 3 sheets.

IM2.95—Anon. Lerchenfelder Walzer. E-flat bass and piccolo parts here. 27 x 35 cm. 3 sheets.

IM2.96—Hartner. Banquet of Sparks Polka and / Wagner, Tannhauser Marsch [arr.?]. 1 E-flat cornet part here. 30.5 x 22.5 cm. 3 sheets.

IM2.97—Neumann / Rohr. Polka Mazurka / and Balfe, Cavatine from the Opera Falstaff. Parts for solo and alto; 1st tromb.; 1st B-flat cornet; Bass drum. 17 x 27 cm. 5 sheets.

IM2.98—Gungle. Dream Waltz and / Salon Polka Mazurka. E-flat tuba, B-flat cornet, and 1st trombone parts here. 17.5 x 26.5 cm. 5 sheets.

IM2.99—Anon. Cavatine from "Ermani." Parts for band. 17 x 26.5 cm. 9 sheets.

IM2.100—Miscellaneous loose leaves and sheets from the Economy Cornet Band and Duss' Band. Unidentifiable fragments of various sizes.

INSTRUMENTAL MANUSCRIPT SCORES

IM3.1—Collection of Music of various types. [No means of id., n.d.], All pieces anonymous. 38.4 x 30.6 cm. 242 pp., 22 of which are blank; 2 contain staves only and the rest have music. Pagination on verso and is continuous through p. 251; however, pp. 128-147 have been cut from book. Bound in boards with grained design and leather spine and corners. Watermark on each sheet. At left side in block letters is word HOLD-SHIP: on right side of sheet is an anchor. Volume contains first, a number of marches and short pieces in full orchestral score; second, short religious hymns and songs; third, works for two pianos; fourth, hymns and chorales written partly in 4-part note notation and partly in number notation. This last section is entered with the book inverted.

IM3.2—Collection of short pieces. Composers: Mozart, Fuchs, Lully, and many anon. 19 x 30.1 cm. 128 pp., 4 of which are blank, the rest contain some music. No pagination. On p. 3 is inscription "Angefangen den 29 Jan. 1829." Hold-ship watermark. Volume contains pieces which were intended to have been scored for small orchestra but only a few are complete, the remainder exist only with pf. score copied and blank staves for the other instruments.

IM3.3—Collection of short pieces. Pleyel, Born-horst [Bonnhorst], Rossini, Mozart. 33.3 x 40.5 cm. 21 sheets or 42 pp., three of which contain staves only. Pagination on verso and complete through p. 38. Cover has butterfly label bearing inscription: "Partitur-buch No. V." Under this in different hand is date 1885. Beneath label in original hand is written "Oden Partitur-Buch pro C.F. Müller. Economie, Nov. 1827." Volume contains scores for various instrumental combinations from quartets to small chamber orchestra with chorus. Many have copying dates, the last of which is Dec. 29, 1829.

IM3.4—Collection of symphonies, overtures, and dances by Gyrowetz, Handel, Weber, Meineke, Meuller, Fuchs, Anon. Several works are dated. 40.9 x 27.5 cm. 202 pp. 23 of which are blank. Pagination on verso and complete through 168. Bound in boards with brown and tan grained design. Butterfly label on cover reads: "Partitur-Buch / der Music Bands / der Oekonomie / Ange-fangen im December / 1828." Book appears to have been Meuller's.

IM3.5—Collection of overtures, dances, and other short pieces. Martini, Wanhall, Fuchs, Mozart. 40.7 x 33.4 cm. 46 pp., 9 with staves only, 2 blank. Bound in boards with grained design but back cover missing. First page has written on it: "To Dr. Müller, Economy," and last page of first section has a letter to Muller from W. C. Peters. Holdship watermark on some pages.

IM3.6—A Favorite German Waltz. Peters, W.C. [arr.]. 24.9 x 33.9 cm. 12 pages, 2 of which contain staves only. At top of first page is written: "Arranged by W.C. Peters, Louisville, March 20th, 1833. A favorite German Waltz in E minor (W.C. Peter's favorite) For the Economy Musical Society." Watermark that of a bird with a twig in its mouth.

IM3.7—Collection of dances, marches, and sketches. Lanner, Kuffner, Feucht, Ascher, Kleber, anon. 22.8 x 35.4 cm. 34 pp., 1 is blank. On cover is written: "Josephine Stevenson, Cleveland." Volume contains pieces scored for band as well as individual instrumental parts and piano parts. One work by Dr. B. Feucht fixing the date of the volume c. 1865.

IM3.8—Partitur of Waltzes and Marches for Orchestra. 40.2 x 33.4 cm. 88 pp. One page contains staves only. Pagination is complete through p. 91 with pp. 2-5 missing. Bound in boards, grained design in blue and cream colors, with leather binding and corners. Last page has; "Script str [Sept.] 7 & 8, 1819." in Mueller's hand. Label on cover is butterfly design.

IM3.9—Overture to Tancredi, Rossini [arr. W.C. Peters]. 24.8 x 35 cm. 35 pp. of music. Title page reads: "Overture Tancredi / composed by Rossini / arranged / for a full / orchestra / by / W.C. Peters / for the / Economie Band / July 11th, 1830."

IM3.10—Two Waltzes. Anon. 18.9 x 31.8 cm. 4 pp. of music. Waltzes are numbered 29 and 212 and scored for 2 vls., 2 bugles, 2 hns., vlc., and bass.

IM3.11—Band scores, piano scores, and individual instrument parts. 19.8 x 31.1 cm. 32 pp. of music, 6 sheets blank. Front cover has name B. Feucht in lower left corner.

IM3.12—Dances and short pieces for Band. Anon. No watermarks or means of id. 22.8 x 34.6 cm. 44 pp. of music. Only a few entries complete; most have score laid out but only melody and bass line given.

IM3.13—Abraham auf Moriah. Oratorio for orchestra, 4 pt. chorus, and 4 solo voices. Breitkopf Catalog lists composer as J.H. Rolle (Partitur 2668). Manuscript here does not give composer. 24.7 x 37.3 cm. 104 sheets, 203 pp. of music, 5 pp. blank. Pagination complete through 203. 14 to 18 hand-drawn staves per page. Unbound. Has fleur-de-lis watermark.

IM3.14—Pastorale Larghetto. Turk, D.G. 20.7 x 34.7 cm. 52 pp. of music. Title on music is "Pastorale Larghetto die hirten bey der krippe von D.G. Turk." Watermarks are upright eagle with spread tailfeathers and name "Halle."

IM3.15—Collection of Polkas, Waltzes and marches. 19 x 24 cm. Scored for cornet band [7 parts]. 19 leaves bound in wallpaper covered boards with cloth spine.

IM3.16—Collection of marches, polkas, and hymns. 17.3 x 27.3 cm. 29 sheets bound in boards with leather spine. Inside front cover: "Mr. Henry Feicht's Book / Bolivar / Ohio."

IM3.17—Vom lieben deutschen Vaterland, von Reutlinger. Instrumentirt von C. Stix. Last page has "C. Stix, Frankfurt a/M Februar 1897." 31 x 34.5 cm. 24 pp.

INSTRUMENTAL: MANUSCRIPT SCORES WITH PARTS

IM4.1—Anon. Cantata for orchestra, chorus, and soloists. No title page, composer, or other identification except for watermark which is a crested eagle with spread wing and tail feathers and HALLE. [see IM3.14]. Text to opening chorus is: "Saiten Rauchet! Pauken Schallet!" 24.7 x 21.1 cm. 36 sheets, 71 pp. of music. Unbound.

IM4.2—Stiegmeyer und Rolle. Lazarus, oder Die Feyer der Auferstehung. Cantata for full orchestra, soloists, and chorus. No watermarks on paper. 22. x 35.4 cm. 127 sheets; 250 pp. of music. Unbound.

IM4.3—Duss, J.S. Jordan's Riffles / Rag-time Two Step / by / J.S. Duss. [band] All parts bear stamp: "Gus. Mueller / Arr. of Music / Allegheny, Pa." Copies dated Sept. 8, '99. 34 x 27 cm. 26 sheets.

IM4.4—Kolbitz, Geo. Two Concert Pieces / by Geo Kolbitz / 1907 / 1. Warum 2. Bagatelle. [Band arr.] 27 x 34 cm. 29 sheets.

IM4.5—Duss, J.S. "Durch Kampf Zum Sieg" / Through Trial to Triumph / Funeral March / by J.S. Duss / composed about mid-February, A.D. 1898 / as a memorial to the members / past and present—of the Harmony Society. Score: 27 x 34 cm. 3 sheets, 3 copies. Parts: 13 x 17 cm. 37 sheets.

IM4.6—Rohr, J. Variations on "Home, Sweet Home." Score and parts for Band. 26.5 x 34.5 cm. 29 sheets.

IM4.7—Kiesler. Schalk. Grosses Potpourri. Score and parts for band. 26.5 x 34 cm. 14 sheets.

MANUSCRIPT: VOCAL SOLOS WITH KEYBOARD ACCOMPANIMENT

VM1.1—Collections of songs by Moore, Ch. M. Weber, Gebauer and anon. 30.8 x 39 cm. 14 leaves or 28 pp. 26 pp. of music.

VM1.2—Choruses by Haydn, Cherubini and others. 29 x 35.5 cm. 174 pp. First entry dated August 1830.

VM1.3—Anon. short pieces with Guitar accomp. 19 x 15.5 cm. 86 pp. Inverted book becomes Fr., Eng. and Ger. grammar.

VM1.4—Anon. Chorus. [n.d.]. 19.9 x 33 cm. 22 leaves, 44 pp. bound in boards. Contains only one piece, incomplete occupying the first 6 pp. No watermarks. Text: "Erhöre Gnädig Herr die deinen zu dir beten."

VM1.5—Die Farben/ 7 Lieder von C. Müller/ in Music gesetzt von F. F. Hurka zu Altona/ Poss. Gertrud Rapp. 19.5 x 32.5 cm. 10 sheets; 20 pp.

VM1.6—Collection of short songs. Heart, fraktur on flyleaf: "Sammlung/ einiger/ Musicalien/ 1801/ Possesor/ Catherina Spor." 17.9 x 22.3 cm. 13 leaves sewn into blue paper cover.

VM1.7—Collection of short songs, by Bishop, Denman, Parry, Moore, and anon. Volume in Mueller's hand. Some pieces dated 1831. 19 x 30 cm. 46 pp.

VM1.8—Collection of short pieces by White, Mozart, and anon. 19.7 x 32.5 cm. 34 pp. in numeral and traditional notation. On cover in ink: "Economy, April 1867."

VM1.9—Collection of solos, duets, choruses by Clark, Braham, Whitton, and others. Dated Economy Feb. 11, 1828. 20.8 x 33.5 cm. 124 pp.

VM1.10—Collection of Choruses, Anthems, and Psalm settings in 4 parts. Title page in middle of volume: "Twelve/ New Psalm Tunes/ In Three, Four, Five and Six Parts;/ with Symphonies and a/ Thorough Bass/ for the/ Organ, Piano Forte/ with two favorite Christmas Hymns/ composed by Mr. W. Gifford of/ South Perton/ Sommersetshire." 20.8 x 33.5 cm. 41 sheets; 82 pp.

VM1.11—Collection of short solos, duets, and choruses by Haydn, Hurka, Schulz, Sterkel, and anon. 20.8 x 33.5 cm. 84 pp.

VM1.12—Collection of songs arranged from the oratorios of Haydn. Arrangements by B. Carr as well as Psalm settings a 4 with accompaniment by Croft, Green, Allison and others. 24.2 x 29.3 cm. 32 sheets with 2 blank pp. and 62 pp. of music. At end of p. 23 is "Script 19 December, 1824."

VM1.13—Collection of solo songs with Keyboard accompaniment. Pieces by Schubert, Christman, Sulzer, and others. 30 x 22.5 cm. 32 sheets with 12 pp. blank and 50 pp. of music. Bound in boards with Harmonie grain. Paper has anchor watermark. Last entry dated May 10, 1830.

VM1.14—Anon. The Orphan's Song. 26.4 x 33.8 cm. 1 sheet; 2 pages of music. Solo song with keyboard accomp.

VM1.15—Duss, J. S. More to Do/ Bass Solo [with keyboard accompaniment]. Text by Douglas Wallock. 32 x 24.5 cm. 3 pp.

VM1.16—Anon. St. Joseph's Feast. 5 stanzas and "chorus." 34.5 x 26.8 cm. 1 p.

VM1.17—Duss, J. S. America The Beautiful. autograph copy contains letter from K. L. Bates. 24 x 32 cm. 1 sheet.

VOCAL: MANUSCRIPT SCORES

VM3.1—Collection of Motets and choruses for voices and instruments by Christman, Horren [Canstatt, 1817] and anon. 30.6 x 24 cm. 16 sheets; 32 pp. of music.

VM3.2—Hässler, Johann Wilhelm. Erfurth/ eine Kantate von Carl von Dalberg/ und/ Erfurth Dankvole Empfindungen für seinen Dalberg/ ein musicalisches gedicht von J. F. Herel/ beide componiert/ von/ Johann Wilhelm Hässler. Cantata for orchestra, solo voices, and 4-part chorus. 31.5 x 22.6 cm. 87 sheets; 171 pp. of music.

VM3.3—Partitur-buch/ No III/ Singstücke [1st butterfly label on cover] "Partitur-buch enthaltend/ Singstücke, Menuets, etc./ für 2 violinen, 2 flöten, und/ 1 violoncello/ Oeconomie, Augs, 1827." Title page reads: "Arien-Partitur-buch/ für das/ Orchester [Musik bande-scratched out] der Oeconomie Angeordunt durch W. C. Peters, Augs, 19, 1827." In center of page in large letters: "Wilhelm C. Peters." 32.3 x 39.1 cm. 29 sheets with 3 pp. blank; 54 pp. of music.

VM3.4—Partitur-buch/ No. VI/ Oden und Gesänge/ Oekonomie Decemb. 1828. Contains scores for Harmonist festival pieces as well as cantatas by Cherubini, Schade and others. 38 x 30.8 cm. 66 sheets; 158 pp. of music. Holdship and anchor watermarks.

VM3.5—Choruses from works of Beethoven, Haydn, and others, in notes and numerals. 20.9 x 33.9 cm. 81 sheets; 138 pp. of music.

VM3.6—Collection of pieces from large choral works of Handel, Knecht, Haydn, Cherubini, and others. Title page reads: "Violino Primo cum Soprano 1/ Verschiedener Cantate/ pro J. Chr. Müller/ Oeconomie, Martius, 1829." 26.9 x 41.3 cm. 53 sheets; 98 pp. of music.

VM3.7—Collection of pieces from large choral works of Beethoven, Cherubini, and others. 26.8 x 41.9 cm. 109 sheets; 201 pp. of music.

VM3.8—Original-Partitur/ "Schön Bist du Harmonie."/ Eigene Melodie. A collection of loose sheets, including score and sketches for the cantata above, psalm settings and Henrici's setting of the Apostles' Creed. 25 x 34.9 cm. 43 sheets plus fragments.

VM3.9—Collection of sacred choral works. All anon. except the first which is "Preis Ihm," by

Horren [see VM3.1], however, composer's name not given here. None of the other pieces, most of which are in two and three parts, relates to those in VM3.1. 33.4 x 20.5 cm. 23 sheets; 43 pp. of music. Watermark "COX."

VM3.10—Collection of Harmonist Festival pieces by Peters, Muller and others. 47.7 x 30 cm. 291 pp. but only 25 contain music.

VM3.11—Henrici, Jacob. Die Zehn Gebote. 34.5 x 27 cm. 4 pp.

VM3.12—Fragments, loose leaves, torn sheets, and unidentifiable pieces. Tied between two cardboard sheets: 41.5 x 54.2 cm.

VM3.13—Duss, J. S. The Psalm of Psalms. Excerpts from various Psalms set for Bass solo and chorus with organ accompaniment. 32 x 24 cm. 10 pp.

VM3.14—Duss, J. S. Vocal Supplement to "The Fighting Tenth" March, set for SATB and keyboard accompaniment. 34 x 26.5 cm. 4 pp.

VM3.15—Duss, J. S. Manuscript drafts of HP2.90. Various sizes. 9 sheets.

VM3.16—Duss, J. S. O Sacred Book. Setting of poem by John McKee, for TB soli, and SATB chorus with keyboard accompaniment. 24 x 32 cm. 3 pp. Bound in manilla folder.

VM3.17—Duss, J. S. The Lord is My Shepherd / Duet for Tenor & Bass (Soprano & Alto) with keyboard accompaniment. 30.5 x 24 cm. 5 pp.

VOCAL: MANUSCRIPT SCORES AND PARTS

VM4.1—Duss, J. S. [orchestrated by Otto Merz]. Mass/ in Honor of/ St. Veronica/ by/ J. S. Duss/ Great House/ Economy, Pa., June 1916. Orchestral parts and choral score. 84 parts. 30.5 x 24 cm. Choral score, 56 pp. 37 x 17.5 cm. Solo vocal parts (4) 24.5 x 31 cm.

VM4.2—Duss, J. S. One Ship Sails East / Baritone Solo / acc. 1st & 2nd Violin, Cornet & Cello. 24 x 32 cm. 8 sheets.

VM4.3—Duss, J. S. (Arr. F. H. Warner) Gethsemane / Baritone Solo and Quartette or chorus (opt. 2 violins). One sheet has in pencil: "Warner was an organist in a New York City Church." 24 x 32 cm. 17 sheets.

VM4.4—Duss, J. S. The Violet. Piece for vocal solo and string trio [2 vls., 'cello]. 27 x 34 cm. 5 sheets.

KEYBOARD: MANUSCRIPT

KM1.1—Anon. Short piece [30 measures] for piano. 16.7 x 20 cm. Unbound. Single sheet.

KM1.2—Collection of keyboard pieces by Schubart, Vogler, Mozart, and anon. 17.8 x 22.8 cm. 42 sheets; 75 pp. of music. Covers missing.

KM1.3—Das Schnee Tröpflein. Anon. piece for keyboard [Menuetto and Trio]. 27.5 x 22 cm. 1 sheet; 2 pp. of music.

KM1.4—Sonate a/ quatre mains/ pour le/ Forte Piano/ composed/ par/ W. A. Mozart. Cover contains dates 1819 and 1817. 33 x 26.2 cm. 6 sheets; 10 pp. of music.

KM1.5—Collection of pieces in various forms by Vanhal, Knecht, Dussek, Mozart, Haydn, Pleyel, Vogler, and others, scored for various instrumental ensembles but most arranged for keyboard. 42.1 x 27.6 cm. 68 sheets; 128 pp. of music.

KM1.6—Nerv und Sinn. Fuchs. 24.7 x 30 cm. 1 sheet; 2 pp. of music. This numbered '56' and originally part of volume.

KM1.7—Collection of short keyboard pieces by Pleyel, Endres, Beethoven, Liedle, and anon. 34 x 20.9 cm. 18 sheets.

KM1.8—Ouverture du Calife de Bagdad. Boeildieu, F. 31.9 x 20.8 cm. 6 sheets. Unbound. Paper maker's name [Owen & Hurlibut/ So Lee/ Mass.] pressed into paper.

KM1.9—Collection of pieces by Vanhall, Gelinek and anon. 33.9 x 21.3 cm. 21 sheets; 39 pp. of music.

KM1.10—Collection of hymns, menuets, and short dances and marches. Cover has butterfly label which reads: "Klavier Stücke/ Burghard Schnabel/ Harmonie, Ia./ Angef. im Febr. 1818." Title page: "This Book/ belongs to/ Burghard Schnabel/ at Harmonie, Indiana/ Begun in February 1818./ Lobe den Herrn meine Seele." Most entries are dated. Composers' names not given but several pieces by J. C. Müller are here. 20.4 x 16.6 cm. 33 sheets.

KM1.11—Collection of pieces from the secular series, preceded by exercises and instructions in keyboard technique. Some pieces arranged for four hands. Most are from the IM2.8 series. 30.1 x 24.3 cm. 76 sheets; 143 pp. of music. Butterfly label on cover reads: "Eine Sammlung verschiedener / Clavier Stücke / Stufenweise/ eingerichtet für Gertrude Rapp. Harmonie, Ia. Juli 1823."

KM1.12—Anon. Theme and variations for keyboard, sewn to flute parts to marches by Kuffner, Meyerbeer, and others. 19 x 31.5 cm. 8 sheets; 17 pp. of music. Unbound.

KM1.13—A. J. McDonald. Three Musical Snuffbox Waltzes. 33.4 x 25 cm. Single sheet.

KM1.14—Collection of keyboard interludes, some apparently for organ, as well as complete pieces from the secular series and some songs with texts. First page serves as cover and has: "Notenbuch für Henrici." 33.3 x 24.5 cm. 9 sheets; 16 pp. of music.

KM1.15—Keyboard partitur to sacred music series, Harmonie festival pieces, cantatas and sacred songs. Cover has butterfly label which reads: "Choral-buch/ für/ Gertrude Rapp/ Harmonie, Ia., A.D. 1822." Melody, bass and figures. 24 x 19.2 cm. 60 sheets; 112 pp. of music. Entry #54 dated Jan. 7, 1828.

KM1.16—Collection of keyboard scores, some for four hands, of the sacred and secular series. Many entries are incomplete sketches; some for orchestra. 31.2 x 39 cm. 147 sheets; 35 pp. of music.

KM1.17—Collection of four-hand piano arrangements of pieces by Mozart, Latour, Rossini, Mehul, and others. Most are arias, overtures, etc. from well-known operas. 30.4 x 46.9 cm. 40 sheets; 63 pp. of music. Some entries dated between June, 1838 and Jan. 1839.

KM1.18—Collection of short pieces for four hands, all anon. and without titles. Entries are listed under tempo markings. 19.4 x 20.6 cm. 16 sheets; 26 pp. of music. Bound in purple laminated paper. Several watermarks appear on the different pages, including a crescent, F.C.O., and an intricate scroll design.

KM1.19—Collection of anonymous waltzes, marches, and short pieces. Cover has in ink: "Henrici in Kaisers/ lautern im lten Janner 1822/ Sammlung von Walz/ für/ Jacob Henrici." 16.1 x 26.1 cm. 21 sheets; 42 pp. of music.

KM1.20—Volume containing music instructions, parts to songs for a treble instrument [violin] as well as keyboard scores to secular and sacred songs and hymns. Stamped in gold letters on spine: "Music/ Book/ Burghard/ Schnabel." 23.5 x 20.5 cm. 127 sheets.

KM1.21—Anon. "Du den meine Seele liebt," "Heilig Sei dein Nam," "6te March," arr. for keyboard. 27.2 x 21.8 cm. 1 sheet on both sides.

KM1.22—Collection of pieces by Beyer, Lanner, Fuchs, and anon. 23 x 35.3 cm. 24 sheets; 17 pp. of music.

KM1.23—Collection of pieces, most by Valentin Endres, but others by Rossini, Held, Beethoven, Mozart, and anon. 27.3 x 22.6 cm. 21 sheets; 42 pp. of music.

KM1.24—Collection of pieces by Knecht, Theodor Smith, J. C. Mueller, and anon. Butterfly label on cover reads: "Auserlesen Stücke/ für Pianoforte/ pro Gertrude Rapp/ Harmonie, A.D. 1823." 31.6 x 19.3 cm. 18 sheets; 25 pp. of music.

KM1.25—Astral Bells/ Intermezzo/ by/ V. Ragone/ From Duss Theme. Includes photos (decorated with rhinestones) of the composer and Duss as well as letter of dedication. 34 x 26.5 cm. 6 sheets.

KM1.26—Collection of keyboard arrangements of songs from secular series. Title page reads: "Overture/ Du Calife de Bagdad/ Musique/ de Boieldieu/ Arrangée pour le piano/ avec Accompanement de Violon obligé/ par l'Auteur." Preceding occupies first 16 pp. but remainder of contents are secular pieces for piano only. 20 x 32 cm. 56 sheets; 106 pp. of music.

KM1.27—Collection containing keyboard scores to pieces in the secular series. Reversed and inverted volume is violin part-book for the secular series. Butterfly label on cover reads: "Violino Primo/ für Privat Music/ pro [name scratched out]." 27.2 x 21.9 cm. 42 sheets; 53 pp. of music.

KM1.28—The Pittsburgh Dispatch March/ composed Nov. 1896 by J. S. Duss/ in honor of said Pittsburgh Daily/ arranged for piano by Gus Meuller. 27 x 34 cm. 3 pp.

KM1.29—Dussology/ March/ F. Fanerielli/ Bandmaster 71st Regt./ N.Y., N.Y./ Dedicated to my friend and collegne/ J. S. Duss, conductor of Duss'/ Famous Band. 27.5 x 34.5 cm. 4 pp.

HYMNS: MANUSCRIPT ENSEMBLE PARTS AND PARTITUR

HM2.1—Bass Part-book. Contains hymns (bass parts) and music for Harmoniefests. There are instrumental bass parts [Vlc.] here as well as vocal parts. [n.d., c. 1827]. 18.7 x 30.8 cm. 146 sheets with 155 blank pp., 4 pp. table of contents and 151 pp. music. Pagination complete through p. 147. 12 to 14 hand-drawn staves per page. Bound in boards and leather with red label on cover reading: "Basso, Daniel Schreiber, Economy, 1828." Paper has the Holdship and anchor watermark.

HM2.2—Bass and Tenor part-book. [n.d. c. 1827]. Contains bass and tenor parts to hymns and music for Easter. 18.5 x 15.8 cm. 134 sheets with 2 pp. of table of contents, 99 pp. blank, 8 pp. with staves only. 159 pp. of music. Pagination only in the last half of volume which runs 1-118. 5 and 6 hand-drawn staves per page with staves running the length of the page.

HM2.3-1—Bass part-book. 20.1 x 11.5 cm. 63 sheets with 20 blank pp. 2 pp. staves only and 104 pp. of music. No pagination but items are numbered consecutively through 52. Butterfly lable on cover reads: "Vokal Musik/ Basso/ für/ Sibilla Hurlebaus, Harmonie, Ia., 1824." Title page has flower wreath design in center of which is: "Bass/ Lobe den Herren/ mein Seele."

HM2.3-2—Bass part-book. 11.2 x 20.5 cm. 211 pp. of music and 3 pp of index. Items numbered to #77, but some entries not numbered. Butterfly label on front cover reads: "Vokal Musik/ Basso/ für/ Sibilla Hurlebaus/ Economy, 1825."

HM2.3-3—Tenor part-book. 20.8 x 11.8 cm. 115

pp. Label on front cover reads: "Vokal Musik/ Tenore/ für/ Logina Hinger, Harmonie, Jan. 1824." Flower wreath design has in center: "Tenore/ Lobe den Herrn meine Seele."

HM2.3-4—Soprano part-book. 20.8 x 11.8 cm. 110 pp. Butterfly label on cover reads: "Vokal Musik/ Sopran/ für/ Gertrud Rapp/ Harmonie, Ia. 1824."

HM2.4—A series of 20 part-books (TTBB) for Maennerchor dating from the late period [1897]. Most entries are compositions by Naegeli copied from printed sources. 23.3 x 18 cm. 52 sheets per volume. Bound in black leather. Some volumes contain the names of singers and possessors. 1. II Ten. (A. Berger, J. Werner-1897, Jacob Boss); 2. Partitur: four-part settings (conductor's score) for Maennerchor; 3. II Ten. (Jacob Boss-1897, W. J. Armer-1898); 4. II Ten.; 5. I Bass; 6. I Bass; 7. II Bass. (Fritz Gerhard). 23.9 x 14.5 cm. Cardboard binding; 8. II Bass (Hastm[?], 1892); 9. II Bass; 10. II Bass (Fred Riethmueller); 11. I Bass; 12. I Bass; 13. I Ten. (Willhelm Mattes); 14. I Ten. (John Somnor[?]); 15. I Ten.; 16. I Ten. (Gustav Kruger); 17. I Ten. (Gottlob Betz); 18. I Bass; 19. I Ten. (Gustav Kruger); 20. II Bass (P.W. Strawle).

HM2.5—Soprano-Bass parts; 2te Stimm; and numeral partitur for hymns & sacred songs. [no id., n.d.]. 19.2 x 16.6 cm. No pagination, 96 sheets with 146 pp. of music. Has name "Friederick Eckensperger" printed on front cover and paper has circle watermark. Number series gives cross-reference to no less than three other sources. One refers to HP 2.1, the source of most of the contents of this volume.

HM2.6-1—Partitur [three treble voices]. On inside cover is name Jacob Shriver. [n.d.]. This apparently an attempt to do a 3 pt. treble-voice setting of the hymn repertoire. 19.6 x 16.4 cm. 59 sheets; 101 pp. of music and/or texts. One page has Patterson & Co. watermark in block letters while others have circle watermark. Bound in boards with leather spine and corners. Contains the most frequently used hymns, but only a few settings complete. Most pp. contain only the texts.

HM2.6-2—Score for two; three- and four-part hymn settings with treble instrument accompaniment. Contents similar to HM2.6-1, but not in same order. Hand is same as preceding and this volume contains only those which were complete in the other volume. 16 x 13 cm. 135 pp. Bound in boards with leather spine. Boards are covered with a multi-colored blotch design common among the Harmonist books.

HM2.7—Treble part-book, contains melodies and texts to 8 *Feurige Kohlen* Poems. [No i.d.]. 19 x 9.7 cm. 22 sheets with 2 pp. blank, 10 pp. of staves only, and 32 pp. of music. Items are numbered consecutively from 1 through 8. Volume is bound in heavy cardboard, the outside of which has a multi-colored grained design.

HM2.8—Tenor, Soprano, Bass Part-book. [No i.d., but one work is dated 1835.] Items are parts to extensive festival works, most by Harmonist composers but composer's names are not given. Some items are in numeral notation. 18.5 x 15.4 cm. 255 sheets with 175 blank pp. 2 pp. of staves only and 335 pp. of music. Pagination complete through 335. Bound in boards and leather. On spine in gold letters: "Tenor/ Sibilla Hurlebaus."

HM2.9—Soprano part-book. Volume contains parts to choral works by Harmonist composers and others. Latest date in book is 1833. Some items in numeral notation. 17.9 x 15.1 cm. 221 sheets with 88 blank pp. and 353 pp. of music. Pagination complete 7-360, first 6 pp. missing. Bound in boards covered with green paper with leather spine and corners. Written on spine: "Soprano/ Mensueta Schmid."

HM2.10—Secondo [2nd Soprano]. Items are parts to festival songs and hymns. A large portion of the book is in numeral notation. 17.8 x 14.8 cm. 262 sheets with 188 blank pp. 2 pp. staves only and 256 pp. of music and texts. Pagination complete through 337. Bound in boards covered with buckram and leather spine. On spine in gold letters: "Secondo/ Paulina Speidel." Latest date in book is 1842. Pages have Holdship and anchor watermark.

HM2.11—Corno Primo and Treble [Tenor] part-book. One item dated 1820. Most items are music to *Feurige Kohlen* poems. 19.1 x 16.5 cm. 41 sheets with 10 blank pp. 4 pp. of staves and 66 pp. of music. Pagination complete through 64. Bound in boards covered with paper of old check books but given a grained design. Binding is leather and inside front cover is name "Jonathan Lenz." Some pp. have small circle watermark.

HM2.12—Flute part-book with texts to festival works and hymns. Contains both first and second flute parts to Harmonist-composed works. Some items have dates from 1822 to 1825. When reversed book contains flute parts to marches and dances. 20.2 x 16.3 cm. 61 sheets with 2 pp. staves and 120 pp. music. Pagination complete through 83. Butterfly label on cover reads: "Haydn's Frühling/ Tenor [?] ives Flauto / Matthew Scholle." Bound in green wallpaper with fern design. No watermarks.

HM2.13—Soprano part-book with some Keyboard settings. 19.5 x 16.2 cm. 37 sheets with 28 blank and 45 pp. of music. Title page reads: "Sammlung einiger Singmusikalien/ für F. Eckensperger." Most items are numbered, but not consecutively, and numbering coincides with page numbers of same items in the *Harmonisches Gesangbuch* of 1827 [pP. 64].

HM2.14—Tenor and Second Soprano Partbook. Most are Harmonist Festival works dating from 1822 to 1827. 19.3 x 15.6 cm. 42 sheets with 2 blank pp. and 82 pp. of music. Pagination complete through p. 37. Bound in boards with leather spine. Butterfly label on cover reads: "Tenore/ Haydn's Jahrzeiten." First two pp. have table of contents and "pro Romelie/ Adam, Schreiber & Scholle." No watermarks and several different hands.

HM2.15—Partitur of Festival pieces. Contains festival music by Müller and Peters. 23.4 x 19.1 cm. 84 sheets with 2 pp. table of contents, 6 blank, and 159 pp. of music. Pagination through 105. Bound in boards covered with grained paper and leather spine and corners. On spine in gold letters: "Oden." Title page reads: "Oden und Fest-Gesänge/ für/ Gertrud Rapp/ in Musikgesetz/ von J. C. Muller/ Harmonie, Ia., AD 1822." At least two hands represented. Title page has colored flower design.

HM2.16—Tenor part-book. Contains several printed texts with dates 1827-1829, printed at Oekonomie by J. C. Müller. When reversed book has what appears to be tenor parts to sacred works as well as treble instrumental parts to secular pieces. 19.3 x 11.4 cm. 63 sheets with 3 blank pp. 1 p. table of contents and 121 pp. of music. No pagination but items are numbered through 33. Bound in leather-covered boards. Title page reads: "Geistliche Vierstimmige Arien und Lieder/ zum Gebrauch der Harmonie 1823/ III pro tenore." Colored flower design.

HM2.17—A series of ten part-books to large choral works, most copied and arr. from printed sources in the collection, by Beethoven, Schade, Cherubini, Romberg, Haydn, etc., as well as Harmonist festival works.

1. 2te Stimm [2nd Sop. & Alto]. 18.8 x. 15.6 cm. 233 sheets with 182 pp. blank. 4 pp. staves only, and 198 pp. of music. Pagination complete through 383. Bound in boards and leather. Square label on cover reads: "Secondo." Dates up to 1839. Has Holdship and anchor watermarks.

2. Bass part-book. 15.8 x 19.5 cm. Square label on cover reads: "Bass/ Jonathan Lenz." Date at top of table of contents is 1829, Jan. 10, indicating that this series probably begun at that time. Pages 1-53 are used, then most of book is blank. Entries in the back of book begin pagination over again (1-44) and another section left blank.

3. Bass part-book labeled: "Bass/ George Bauer." 15.9 x 20 cm. Pagination goes to 444. Bound in boards and leather.

4. 2te Stimm. 15 x 19.3 cm. 389 pp. of music, 35 blank pp. Inside front cover reads: "Jacob Stahl, 1860/ Philibert Laupple."

5. Tenor part-book. 19.5 x 16 cm. 177 pp. of music with 108 blank, then 217 more with music. General index in front and index of Harmonie songs in back. Label on cover reads: "Tenor/ Felix Wolf."

6. Tenor [3te Stimm]. 16.3 x 20 cm. Volume has entries from both ends: One has 141 pp. of music [beginning with "Der Schall von Lobgesang"] and the other 147.

7. Tenor part-book. Contents mixed: 1te stimm, 3te stimm. 15.8 x 19.5 cm. 152 pp. of music then blank to 239. pp. 240 to 326 music. Remainder of book blank except for 3 pp. of index. Label on cover now gone. The word "Tenor" is barely discernible but the possessor's name just below is no longer discernible. Inside front cover is name "W. M. Diethelm."

8. Soprano part-book. 18.5 x 15 cm. 328 pp. of music in notes and numerals. Printed on spine: "Sopran." This volume contains some of the pieces in HM2.18.

9. Soprano part-book. 15.5 x 19.5 cm. 288 pp. of music in notes and numerals. Printed on spine: "Sopran./ Gertrud Rapp."

10. Bass part-book. 15.5 x 19.5 cm. 210 pp. of music, remainder blank except for 4 pp. of index. On spine: "Basso/ Sibilla Hinger."

HM2.18—A series of four part-books, containing music for various Harmonist festivals as well as anthems and large choral works by Graun, Romberg, Cherubini, and Haydn. All dated 1827.

1. Primo [Soprano] part-book. 19.2 x 15.5 cm. 71 pp. with 6 blank, 2 pp. with staves only, and 134 pp. of music. Pagination complete 2-109. Bound in boards with leather corners and spine. Oval label on front cover reads: 'Vokal Musik/ Primo/ pour/ Gertrude Rapp/ Economy Pa., 1827."

2. Tenor part-book. 19 x 15.5 cm. 148 pp. Oval label on cover reads: "Tenor/ für/ Logine Hinger/ Oeconomie 1827."

3. Bass part-book. 19 x 15.5 cm. 166 pp. Oval label on cover reads: "Bass/ für/ Sibylle Hinger/ Oeconomie/ 1827."

4. Alto part-book. 18.5 x 16 cm. 188 pp. Oval on front cover reads: "Alto. für/ Sibylle Hurlebauss/ Oeconomie/ 1827."

HM2.19—Partitur. 17.2 x 26.8 cm. 9 sheets with 18 pp. of music. No pagination. Bound in boards with cloth spine. Inside cover is name: "Carl Mueller, geb. 8 Nov. 1833". Contains keyboard scores and texts to anthems with a cross reference to sources from which they were copied. Entries are in black and red inks.

HM2.20—A series of five part-books for Maennerchor, dated October, 1877. Composers represented: Beethoven, Mozart, Abt, Heim, and others. Contains some of same pieces as HM2.4 series. All five in same hand.

1. Tennor II. 16.9 x 26.5 cm. 23 pp. of music. No pagination. Inside cover has name "Bernhard Kweifel." Square label on cover: "Tenor/II."

2. Bass II. Same size as 1. 26 pp. Names of Georg Karle, Bernhard Baker and Fritz Gerhard on inside front cover.

3. Tenor. Same size as 1. 62 pp. Names: Peter Schwab, John Miller, Markus Knabel, F. Jacobson, and others.

4. Bass. Same size as 1. 34 pp. Jacob Stadelmann.

5. Tennor. 27.2 x 17.2 cm. 60 pp. Bound in boards covered in buckram. The name Gottlieb Reithmüller on flyleaf.

HM2.21—Partitur [SATB]. 26.8 x. 34.3 cm. Setting of "Schön bist du Harmonie," which John Duss attributed to Jacob Henrici. Four sheets of what appears to be commercially manufactured music manuscript paper; "Piano oder Orgelbegleitung" in introduction would indicate late period when reed organs were used.

HM2.22—Partitur [Soprano, Bass and figures for keyboard and texts]. All entries are chorales. 23.6 x 27.8 cm. 46 sheets with 2 blank pp. Title page, and 3 pp. table of contents. No pagination. Items are numbered but not consecutively and inside front cover is listing of pieces with two sets of numbers. These probably refer to two sources with which these accompaniments were to be used. Fly leaf reads: "Choral für Henrici," and in lighter ink which was added later "et Georg Ape." In pencil under the names "1822."

HM2.23—Partitur [numerals]. Most settings in three voices. 15.4 x 18.9 cm. 46 sheets with 4 pp. blank; 3 pp. lines only and 85 pp. of music. No pagination. Bound in laminated paper with leather spine.

HM2.24—Soprano part-book [1st and 2nd]. Contents are two treble parts to the music of *Feurige Kohlen* texts. 11.5 x 18.7 cm. 119 sheets with 88 blank pp.; 50 staves, and 100 pp. of music. No pagination and binding is the same as that of HG 1820.

HM2.25—Treble part-book. 9.7 x 15.6 cm. 4 sheets with 1 p. of staves only and 7 pp. music. No pagination. Treble part to "Lob Sey Gott."

HM2.26—Partitur. 26.4 x 20.8 cm. 45 sheets with 81 blank pp. and 9 pp. of music. Bound in boards with leather spine. Some pages have dates 1844-45. Book was used as sketchbook to plan field crops.

HM2.27—Partitur. 19.7 x 30.8 cm. 89 sheets with 90 blank pp. 7 with staves only and 81 pp.

of music. No pagination. Bound in boards with leather spine. Has Holdship and anchor watermark. Only a few hymns and chorales in staff notation with most of book (reversed) in numeral notation. An uncommon system of figures is used throughout, the code to which is given on inside front cover.

HM2.28—Partitur. This is a very complete collection of early hymn and sacred music repertoire. 19 x 21.5 cm. 116 pp. Bound in boards covered with green fern-design wallpaper. Butterfly label on front cover reads: "Arien und Gesänge/ der/ Harmonie, pro F. R./ July, 1817." Binding is broken but all pages here.

HM2.29—Partitur. 30 x 22 cm. Bound in boards covered with blue cloth, leather spine and corners. Sticker on spine reads: "Music/ John Duss." This keyboard accompaniment to the hymns was copied and used by Jacob Henrici. Texts and metres are given and cross-reference index is given to at least two printed sources and one manuscript source, indicating that they were used simultaneously. Pagination goes to 334 but volume contains only 93 pp. of music. Last entry dated August 13, 1883.

HM2.30—Partitur. Items numbered consecutively and apparently are complete collection of hymn and sacred song repertoire of Indiana period. Many selections have dates and composers' names. 19.3 x 24.5 cm. 212 pp. bound in boards with leather spine and corners. Butterfly label on front cover reads: "Arien buch/ für/ Gertrud Rapp/ Harmonie, Ia. A.D. 1822." Title page reads: "Ein Sammlung/ verschiedener Arien und Gesänger/ für Gertrud Rapp/ Geschrieben zu Harmonie, Ia. A.D. 1822."

HM2.31—Alto part-book. No names or dates. Contents primarily festival music and Harmonist hymns. 16 x 10 cm. 252 pp. of music and texts.

HM2.32—2te Stimm. Contains music for Harmonie Fest 1831 only. 9.5 x 16.5 cm. 22 pp. 5 blank. Pages are sewn to heavier grey paper which serves as cover.

HM2.33—Partitur. From a volume containing keyboard parts and texts to festival cantatas. There are portions of two works here. The first apparently in Müller's hand and has inscribed at close: "Componiert 22-23 december, 1830." Second in different hand entitled: "Ode auf das 26te Harmonie Fest, in 25te Jahr der Harmonie 1830." Second work is complete. 24 x 18.5; 8 leaves.

HM2.34—Maennerchor parts [unsorted] from late period. Most dated 1885-1895. Most contained in HM2.4. All in loose sheets. [Carton 1]

HM2.35—Maennerchor Parts. [Carton 2] See HM2.34.

HM2.36—Partitur in numeral notation. Contains music fundamentals, followed by songs and hymns in 2, 3, and 4 parts. 15.6 x 19.2 cm. 82 sheets bound in laminated paper boards with grained effect.

HM2.37—Partitur. Collection of songs and hymns in one to four parts 16.5 x 21.2 cm. 24 sheets; 14 pp. of music in numeral notation.

MANUSCRIPT HYMNALS: TEXTS ONLY

pM.1—Manuscript hymnal. 21 x 17 cm. 28 pp. texts; 24 pp. blank. (Watermark of crest with crown on top; eagle with outstretched wing on each side and eight-point star at bottom. Bound in paper-covered boards and leather binding. Design on cover is four black dots on brown paper. No pagination and at least two hands. On front inside cover: "Ein aus Schreib buch vor Johann Dietrichs Knodel. In Heittlingen, ist gebohren 16 Mertz Anno 1781. Das ausschreib buch hab ich kauft im jahr 1801." In another hand to right of above: "Johann Dieterich ist gebohren 16 Mertz 1781, ist gestorben den 19 April, 1818."

pM.2—A series of five manuscript hymnals with similar contents, compiled c. 1811 to ca. 1817.
1. 14 x 8.5 cm. Pagination to 165. Bound in boards covered with blue paper with leather binding. Possessor: Elizabeth Schnebberin 1811.
2. 16.4 x 10.4 cm. Handmade book with 52 sheets, 104 pp. but pagination irregular. Sheets are sewn to soft leather cover and volume served as penmanship exercise book as well as psalter. Contains none of Mueller's songs, dating it pre-1816.
3. 15.5 x 11.2 cm. 34 sheets, 68 pp., folded and tied to blue cardboard cover. No owner given.
4. 125 pp. sewn together and tied to blue cardboard cover. 17 x 10.5 cm. No owner given.
5. 15.5 x 9.5 cm. 156 pp. here. Both covers missing. No owner given.

pM.3—A series of five manuscript psalters with similar contents dating from 1816 to c. 1821.
1. 17 x 9.8 cm. 336 pp., 76 blank with 3 pp. of index. Bound in heavy paper. On flyleaf: "Fast und bett tag January 25th 1820." Below this in pencil: "Exhibited at the New Harmony Centenial 1914 have this marked as property of John Duss. J. S. Duss May 22, 1940." On the following page: "Harmonie. Sept. 20, 1816. John Schreiver his hymn book to rite hymns in it. . ." Some entries dated, the latest of which is 1821.

2. 16 x 10.8 cm. 307 pp. bound in leather and pressed paper. Inside front cover: "Dieses gesangbuch gehört Johannes Viehmayer in den Harmonie 1816."
3. 16.5 x 10.3 cm. 191 pp. Bound in paper from the Discount Deposit of Pittsburgh, Engles & Co., Wood St., with leather spine. Flyleaf has: "Joseph Hornle in Harmonie 1816."
4. 16.5 x 10.5 cm. 244 pp. with 13 blank. Bound in pressed fiber board with leather spine and covered with wallpaper. Has elaborate fraktur on flyleaf and in addition to hymns contains directions for making colors [dyes]. In frakturschrift: "Dieses Gesangbuch gehört Walrath Weingartner in Harmonie den 25 Jule: 1816."
5. 16 x 10 cm.; 176 pp. with first 4 pp. missing. pp. 144 to 173 blank. Index incomplete. Bound in leather. Contains several hands and served as grammar notebook as well as psalter.

pM.4—A series of nineteen manuscript hymnals begun c. 1817 and some containing entries as late as 1839.
1. 15.6 x 10 cm. Covers missing. 201 pp. here. In fraktur: "Harmonisches Gesangbüchlein/ für/ Hillarus Henning/ Harmonie, den 1 Merz: 1817/ is gemacht voor den an dem/ Wabasch."
2. 16.6 x 10 cm. 204 pp. bound in pressed paper with leather binding. "Maria Ehmannin, January 1, 1817."
3. 16 x 10 cm. 159 pp. of texts, 21 pp. blank, 3 pp. index. Bound in pressed paper cover with leather binding. In fraktur: "Dieses/ Lieder Büchlein/ gehört/ Adam/ Schreiber / In/ Harmonie/ Juli den 1 1817."
4. 16 x 10 cm. Three books stitched together: 180 pp. in first, 86 in second and 25 in third. On flyleaf: "Hymn Book/ made in/ Harmony/ Anno Domini 1817/ John Bessan."
5. 17 x 9.8 cm. 78 pp. On cover: "Christina Schmid." Below this in pencil: "Dieses buch gehört der Magdalena Wolf."
7. 17 x 10.5 cm. Bound in boards and leather. 405 pp.; 6 blank and 6 of index. pp. 286-317 missing.
8. 16.5 x 10 cm. Two books stitched together; 153 pp. in first and 144 pp. in second. First has festival texts for 1817 and second for 1839. Second also contains a sermon at top of which is: "Mittwoch, den 7 May, 1837."
9. 16 x 9.5 cm. 197 pp. of texts, 6 blank, 9 pp. index. Bound in blue-green pressed paper with leather binding. Fly leaf has: "Joseph Hornle/ in/ Harmonie/ Novem 1, 1817."
10. 16 x 10 cm. 283 pp. 20 blank and first 36

missing; 4 pp. index. Back cover is missing. No owner.

11. 16 x 10 cm. 204 pp. bound in pressed paper covered with paper from bankbook of Pittsburgh Discount and Deposit Co. No owner.

12. 16 x 9.8 cm. Bound in blue-green paper with leather binding. Two books in one: 168 pp. in first, 88 pp. in second. First book has index. Flyleaf has: "Dorothy/ Mahlen/ Harmonie, den 16 Jun: 1817."

13. 17.3 x 11 cm. 128 pp. bound in wallpaper with green fern design. Paper has watermark: "PB." No owner.

14. 16 x 9.5 cm. 266 pp. bound in wallpaper with leather binding. Front cover is missing. Flyleaf has: "Dieses büchlein/ gehört/ Jacobina Königin/ Harmonie den 19th April / 1817."

15. 16.5 x 10.5 cm. 264 pp. bound in boards and leather. No owner.

16. 16 x 9.8 cm. 125 pp. bound in bankbook paper with leather binding. No owner.

17. 16.2 x 10.3 cm. 104 pp. bound in blue-green paper with blotch design. Binding is leather. No owner.

18. 16 x 10.5 cm. 181 pp. bound in paper with blue-green blotch design. Binding is leather. Last part of name on front cover" —"Heiber."

19. 16.3 x 10 cm. 267 pp. bound in blue-green cardboard with leather binding. pp. 5-6 missing. No owner.

pM.5—A series of five manuscript hymnals begun c. 1817.

1. 15.5 x 9 cm. 268 pp. last 44 blank as are pp. 4-10. Both covers missing. No owner.

2. 15.5 x 10 cm. 259 pp. bound in paper with leather binding. No owner.

3. 16.5 x 10 cm. Pagination begins with 163 and goes to 249. No owner.

4. 15.5 x 9.5 cm. 32 pp. of texts, 40 pp. blank. Bound in paper with speckled design and leather spine. No owner.

5. 15.5 x 9.8 cm. Bound in checkbook paper of Discount & Deposit Office of Pittsburgh. 95 pp. On spine: "Spidle."

pM.6—A series of three manuscript hymnals from c. 1819.

1. 15.8 x 9.5 cm. 254 pp. bound in blue-green paper with leather spine. No owner.

2. 15.4 x 10 cm. 108 pp. bound in green and brown wallpaper with leather spine. No owner.

3. 16 x 9.5 cm. Pagination begins with 147 and goes to 331. Covers missing. No owner.

pM.7—Manuscript hymnal. 16 x 10 cm. 80 pp. bound in bank book paper with leather binding. On spine: "Endrus, 1820." Opposite this: "David Lenz."

pM.8—A series of four manuscript hymnals c. 1820-1822.

1. 16.5 x 10.5 cm. 258 pp. bound in boards and black leather. Title page: "Eine Sammlung/ Musicalischer und/ geistlischer Leider/ Der Harmonie/ Angefangen A.D. 1822." Second title page: "Erster Abtheilung/ Enthaltend/ Musicalischer Lieder/ zur Erbauung und/ vergnugen der Jugend." Third title page: "Zweiter Abtheilung/ enthaltend/ geistliche Lieder/ mit choral und/ gewohnlichen Melodien/ Angefangen A.D. 1822."

2. 14.8 x 9.7 cm. 76 pp. 29 blank with 30 pp. of bass vocal part to "Als Gott der Almächter." Bound in leather. Inside front cover: "David/ Wigand/ geborenden/ 8 April/ 1808/ Den 4 October/ 1822."

3. 16.2 x 20 cm. 129 pp. of texts. Paper covered boards with leather binding. Paper has Patterson watermark.

4. 17.8 x 11 cm. 486 pp. bound in boards with leather binding. Entries follow closely those of the printed *Harmonisches Gesangbuch* of 1820 (pP.60) and some hymns crossed out here are omitted from pP.60 indicating that this could have been the model for the 1820 printing. The presence of texts not found in other MS. sources tends to substantiate this. It also contains a complete topical as well as an alphabetical index.

pM.9—A series of three manuscript hymnals begun c. 1823.

1. 16.3 x 10 cm. 294 pp. bound in black leather. In fraktur: "Rosina Rapp/ gehörig, Harmonie, Ia/ 1823." Patterson Co. watermark.

2. 16.3 x 10 cm. 58 pp. of texts, 24 blank. Bound in pressed paper with leather binding. In fraktur: "1823/ Sabina/ Hartmann."

3. 15.6 x 9.5 cm. 98 pp. bound in paper with blotch desion and leather binding. In fraktur: "Logina/ Hingerin/ geboren den 4 Nov. 1806/ 1823."

pM.10—A series of three manuscript hymnals begun c. 1822-23.

1. 15.8 x 9.8 cm. 127 pp. of texts bound in boards and leather. Contains the names of authors of many of the poems and hymns. Back cover has pencil sketch of man below which is the name "D. Michael de Molinos, Sacerdos." This is followed by a eulogy dated Apr. 15, 1822.

2. 16 x 10 cm. 66 pp. of texts, 74 pp. blank. Bound in leather with blotch design paper pasted on covers. Contains names of poets. No owner.

3. 15.3 x 9.5 cm. 372 pp. texts. 72 blank, 15 pp. index. Covers missing. Title page: "Erste Abtheilung/ Enthaltend/ Musicalische

Lieder,/ zur Erbauung und/ vergnugen der Jugend." Poets' names are given as well as directions for performances: "mit vokal stimme den knaben. . . ,"

pM.11—Two manuscript hymnals begun c. 1825.

1. 16 x 10 cm. 144 pp. of texts, 109 pp. blank, 5 pp. index. Bound in boards and leather with blotch design paper pasted on covers. In fraktur: "Dieses Lieder/ Buch gehört/ Margaretha/ Rosdanin/ Economy den 20ten Feber: 1825."

2. 16.2 x 10 cm. 300 pp. of texts, 54 pp. blank, 4 pp. index. Bound in pressed paper boards with leather binding. On flyleaf: R. L. Baker/ Economy/ 1825."

pM.12—A series of three manuscript hymnals from the early 1820s. None gives owner or specific dates.

1. 15.5 x 9.5 cm. First portion of volume missing. Pagination begins with 77 and goes to 84. Pagination begins with 1 again and second section goes to 98. Bound in green blotch design paper with leather binding.

2. 16 x 10.2 cm. 216 pp. of texts, 82 pp. blank. Bound in paper boards and leather binding. No owner. Contains names of poets.

3. 15.3 x 10 cm. 184 pp. of texts, 64 blank, 18 pp. of texts and index. Contains names of poets. Bound in paper boards and leather binding.

pM.13—16 x 10 cm. 127 pp. of texts, 186 pp. blank, 9 pp. index. Final entry dated Harmonie Fest 1839. Bound in leather with green-blue paper with blotch design pasted on covers. No owner.

pM.14—Two manuscript hymnals made c. 1840-50.

1. 16.4 x 10 cm. 218 pp. Inside front cover: "Agnes Müller/ den 1 August 1849/ Diese buch gehört Agnes/ Muler, ist gebornen den 4te/ Januari 1840."

2. 15.7 x 10 cm. 264 pp. of texts. 20 pp. blank, 6 pp. index. On back cover: "Casper Henning/ geboren in Harmonie/ 2th Ap: 1833."

pM.15—Two manuscript hymnals c.1856.

1. 15.8 x 9.8 cm. 18 pp. of texts, 22 pp. blank. First and last pp. serve as covers. First entry texts of Harmonie Fest 1856. No owner.

2. 15.5 x 9.5 cm. 162 pp. texts. Contains texts for Liebes Mahl 1855 and tenor vocal part to "Er Schwebt auf Fittigen." No owner.

pM.16—A series of handmade hymn-text books dating c. 1850-80. Made of lined notebook paper folded, stitched and bound in brown cardboard covers. 22 x 10 cm. 48 pp.

1. No. 8 on cover and name G. Keynen; 2. Regina Bosch; 3. J.H. 4. [cover missing]; 5. No.

28. Anie Lei [?]; 6. Has "A" on cover. Last entry dated "Feb. 8/77." 7. No owner. Texts dated 1864, some use "Vorsänger." 8. K. Krauss. First entry sung 1834. Also funeral music of 1852. Texts by Albert Knapp [see pP.71]. 9. Covers missing; 10. No. 2 on cover; 11. Elizabeth Wintermanst/ geb. den 1 April/ 1858; 12. No. 10 on cover. Last entry dated March 9/75; 13. No. 9 on cover, 25 pp. here only; 14. No. 7 on cover. Entry dated March 75; 15. Fragments & loose pages from books belonging to this series.

pM.17—Manuscript hymnal. 20 x 15.5 cm. 227 pp. of texts, 16 blank. Bound in boards and leather with gold design on covers and binding. Paper has watermark: "Royal Irish Linen/ Marcus Ward/ & Co." Paper is blue-green color. Title page: "Dieses Buch/ gehört/ Jonathan Lenz/ Geboren den 10 Juni/ 1807/ Jahr/ 1886." The entire book is in elaborate fraktur in red, green, blue inks. Last page has: "Amen. Vollende den 4 Januar/ 1886 Gott sey die Ehre."

pM.18—Manuscript hymnal. 17 x 10.5 cm. 192 pp. pp. 99 to 188 blank. Title page: "Lieder Buch für/ Jonathan Lenz Oct 1/88." Cover is red leather with "Records" stamped in gold on front cover. Page 79 has date Jun 9, '89.

pM.19—Manuscript hymnal. 15.8 x 19.5 cm. 4 sheets; 8 pp. Folded and stitched together in blue paper which serves as cover. Contains two texts: "Trost und Klaglied" and "Wie sie so sanft ruhe" both funeral hymns. No date or owner.

THEORY AND PEDAGOGICAL BOOKS IN MANUSCRIPT

TM.1—A series of seven books, 15.6 x 19.2 cm. containing 128 sheets with 23 pp. blank, 28 pp. staves only and 205 pp. of notation. Pagination runs 1 to 77; at page 70 is inserted an additional section of pp. numbered 1 to 32. After page 77 another pagination begins with 10, proceeding by twos [10, 12, 14, etc.] up to page 70. Books contain "Übungs-Stücke aus Kochs Gesanglehr." Exercises begin with melody only, then proceed to 2, 3, and finally 4-part writing.

1. Sibilla Hurlebaus. Inverted and reversed contains "Comfort Ye" from "Messiah." 2. Gertrud Rapp. 3. Logina Hinger. Page 70: "Economy, Jan. 17th, 1834." 4. Paulina Speitel. 5. Sibilla Hinger. Page 70: "January 27th, 1834." 6. Helena Reichert. 7. Mensueta Schmidt. Page 70: "Economy, January 20th, 1834."

TM.2—Manuscript theory book. 15.3 x 18.6 cm. 8 sheets here, many torn from book which is bound in pressed paper covers with leather binding. Contains exercises in various keys. No songs.

TM.3—"Auszug/ aus/ August Bernhard Müller's, kleinem/ Elementar Buch für/ Klavier-spieler,/ Als wesentlese Grundlage der Kunst, das Klavier, od./ Piano-Forte zu Spielen, verbessert von/ Carl Czerny./ Abgeschrieben von Joh. Chr. Müller/ für seine Freundin, und ehmälige Schulerin/ Gertrude Rapp,/ in Oekonomie in Monat Februar 1832." 30 x 18.5 cm. 122 pp. Paper has Holdship and anchor watermarks. Bound in boards with Economie grain and leather binding. Red butterfly label on front cover.

TM.4—19.4 x 15.5 cm. Exercise book explaining triads, scales, etc. 20 pp. 10 blank. Pagination begins with No. 9. Covers missing.

TM.5—"Auszug aus/ August Eberhard Müllers/ Elementar Buch für Clavier/ Spieler (remainder illegible) . . ." Preceding on butterfly label on cover. 32 x 19.5 cm. 60 pp. bound in boards with Economie grain with leather binding. Title page: "Musicbuch/ für/ Hr. Thalia Bentel/ in/ Freedom,/ Als ein geschenk und Andenken von/ ihrem Freund J. C. Müller/ Bridgewater, December 21, 1843." Paper has Holdship watermark. pp. 41-46 contain songs of Müller. At top of page 41: "Arien und gesänge, componirt von JCM in Harmonie/ am Wabbasch und Oeconomie, unter der despotischen herrschaft, (the greatest monopolist I ever knew)

viz. George Rapp & his adopted son Fredk Reichert.) Yet, the Lord seeth the Heart!"

TM.6—"Kurzgefasste/ Clavier Schule/ für Anfänger/ von F. Kauer,/ in Wienn/ Zu finden bey Artaria Comp." 22 x 35 cm. 8 sheets of heavy blue colored paper, sewn together, unbound. Watermark is oval decorated with intertwining ribbons. [n.d.] 2 copies, the second of which is on white paper No watermarks.

TM.7—Theory exercise book. [n.d.]. 19.5 x 16 cm. 64 pp. 33 blank bound in folded paper sheets. No watermarks. Contains: "Kürze Auszug aus Knecht's Elementarwerk der Musik."

TM.8—[No owner, n.d.]. 19.5 x 16 cm. 29 sheets bound in blue cardboard with leather binding. Exercise book on triads, intervals, scales, etc.

TM.9—Exercise book. 31.5 x 39 cm. 16 sheets. Unbound, containing numeral notation exercises. Size would indicate they were used by instructor in classroom.

TM.10—33 x 19 cm. One sheet; one page showing drawing of a flute with various keys and holes, and a complete fingering chart with staff showing the notes which can be played on the instrument.

BIBLIOGRAPHY

Albrecht, H. F. *Skizzen aus dem Leben der Musik-Gesellschaft Germania.* Philadelphia: King und Baird, 1869.

Andrews, Edward D. *The Gift to be Simple.* New York: J. J. Augustin, 1940.

Arndt, Karl J. R. *George Rapp's Harmony Society 1785-1847.* Philadelphia: University of Pennsylvania Press, 1965.

Arndt, Karl J. R. *George Rapp's Successors and Material Heirs.* Cranbury, New Jersey: Fairleigh Dickinson University Press, 1971.

Arndt, Karl J. R. *A Documentary History of the Indiana Decade of the Harmony Society 1814-1824* Indianapolis: Indiana Historical Society, 1975.

Arndt, Karl J. R. and Wetzel, Richard D. "Harmonist Music and Pittsburgh Musicians in Early Economy." *The Western Pennsylvania Historical Magazine,* 54: 2,3,4, 1971.

Bailey, Albert Edward. *The Gospel in Hymns.* New York: Charles Scribner's Sons, 1950.

Baines, Anthony. *European and American Musical Instruments.* New York: Viking Press, 1966.

Bauman, The Reverend Joseph H. *A History of Beaver County, Pennsylvania.* 2 vols. New York: The Knickerbocker Press, 1904.

Baynham, Edward Gladstone. "The Early Development of Music in Pittsburgh." Ph.D. dissertation, University of Pittsburgh, 1944.

Bernhard, Duke of Saxe-Weimar Eisenach. *Travels Through North America During the Years 1825 and 1826.* 2 vols. Philadelphia: Carey, Lea and Carey, 1829.

Bestor, Arthur Eugene, Jr. *Backwoods Utopias. The Sectarian and Owenite Phases of Communitarian Socialism in America, 1663-1829.* Philadelphia: University of Pennsylvania Press, 1950.

Bole, John A. *The Harmony Society: A Chapter in German American Culture History.* Philadelphia: American Germanica Press, 1904.

Brook, Barry S. *The Breitkopf Thematic Catalog 1762-1787.* New York: Dover Publications, 1966.

Buckingham, J. S. *The Eastern and Western States of America.* 2 vols. London: Fisher, Son and Company, 1842.

Cincinnati Commercial, 22 April, 1866.

Cincinnati Daily Gazette, 21 April, 1866.

Cist, Charles. *Cincinnati in 1851*. Cincinnati: Wm. H. Moore and Co., 1851.

Connor, S. V. *The Peters Colony of Texas*. Austin, 1959.

Duss, John S. *George Rapp and His Associates*. Indianapolis: Hollenbeck Press, 1914.

Duss, John S. *The Harmonists: A Personal History*. Harrisburg: The Telegraph Press, 1943.

Duss, John S. Unpublished Manuscripts found among the Music of J. S. Duss. Economy Archives, Ambridge, Pennsylvania.

Eaton, Quaintance. *The Miracle of the Met*. New York: Meredith Press, 1968.

Economy Archives, Ambridge, Pennsylvania.

Business Accounts:

26 May, 29 December, 1814.

3 February, 1 March, 8 May, 1815.

30 December, 1817.

4 May, 17 July, 12 November, 1818.

26 May, 9 September, 1819.

6 April, 1820.

28 April, 30 May, 1823.

3 November, 1824.

17, 27, 30 July, 1827.

30 January, 17 March, 1828.

11, 12, 13, 14, 15 September, 13 October, 2 November, 1830.

20 February, 22 September, 1846.

9 March, 15, 29 April, 1885.

29 April, 14, 27 May, 20 June, 8 July, 1887.

3 June, 1900.

20 November, 1902.

Letters:

22 May, 1826.

18 September, 1827.

26 November, 1838.

9 October, 1854.

9 May, 1895.

13, 17 December, 1900.

10, 26 January, 8, 11 February, 1901.

Eitner, Robert. *Biographisch-bibliographisches Quellen Lexikon der Musiker und Musikgelehrten der christlichen Zeitreichnung bis zur Mitte des 19. Jahrhunderts. . . .* 10 vols. Leipzig: Breitkopf und Härtel, 1898-1904.

Ernst, James. *Ephrata, A History*. Ed. John Joseph Stoudt. Allentown: Schlechter's Press, 1963.

Fink, Gottfried W. *Musikalischer Hausschatz der Deutschen*. Leipzig: Gustav Mayer, 1862.

Foster, Morrison. *My Brother Stephen*. Indianapolis: Privately Printed for the Foster Hall Collection, 1932.

Gaul, Harvey. *Minstrel of the Alleghenies*. Pittsburgh, 1934.

The Harmony Society in Pennsylvania. Federal Writer's Project. WPA Beaver County, Pennsylvania. Philadelphia: William Penn Association of Philadelphia, 1937.

Hinds, William. *American Communities*. (New York, 1878). New York: Corinth Books, 1961.

Johnson, Earle H. "The Germania Musical Society." *The Musical Quarterly*. New York: G. Schirmer, 39: 1953.

Julian, John. *Dictionary of Hymnology.* (London, 1892). 2 vols. New York: Dover Publications, 1957.

Klees, Frederick. *The Pennsylvania Dutch.* New York: Macmillan Company, 1952.

Knapp, Albert. *Evangelischer Liederschatz für Kirche und Haus.* 2 vols. Stuttgart und Tübingen: J. G. Cott'schen, 1837.

Kolodin, Irving. *The Story of the Metropolitan Opera, 1883-1950.* New York: Knopf, 1953.

Krohn, Ernst C. *Music Publishing in the Middle Western States Before the Civil War.* Detroit Information Coordinators, 1972.

Larner, John W., Jr. "Nails and Sundry Medicines." Master's Thesis, University of Pittsburgh, 1961.

Leiser, Clara. *Jean de Reszke and the Great Days of Opera.* New York: Minton, Balch and Co., 1934.

Louisville City Directory, 1843-1844. Louisville, 1844.

Melish, John. *Travels in the United States of America in the Years 1806-1811.* 2 vols. Philadelphia, 1812.

Morneweck, Evelyn Foster. *Chronicles of Stephen Foster's Family.* 2 vols. Pittsburgh: University of Pittsburgh Press, 1944.

Morning Telegraph. New York. 17 May, 1904.

Musical Courier. New York. 11 December, 1901; 22 January, 1902.

Joshua Nachtrieb v. Romelius L. Baker and Society. Circuit Court of the United States. Beaver County, 3 August, 1852. Pittsburgh: W. S. Haven, 1852.

New York News. 13 June, 1902.

New York Telegraph. 9 November, 1907.

Nordhoff, Charles. *The Communistic Societies of the United States.* New York: Schocken Books, 1966.

Owen, William. *The Diary of William Owen from November 10, 1824, to April 20, 1825.* Edited by Joel W. Hiatt. Indianapolis: Indiana Historical Society Publications, 1906.

Pleasants, Henry. *The Great Singers.* New York: Simon and Schuster, 1966.

Pittsburgh Dispatch. 21 June, 18 August, 1902.

Pittsburgh Gazette. 29 June, 1906.

The Pittsburgh Leader. 28 October, 1902.

Pittsburgh Mercury. 8 June, 1814.

Printer's Ink. New York, 27 August, 1902.

Pratt, Waldo Selden, and Boyd, Charles N. *American Supplement to Grove's Dictionary of Music and Musicians.* New York: Macmillan Company, 1934.

Proceedings of the Lehigh County Historical Society. Allentown, 1947.

Randall, E. O. *History of the Zoar Society.* Columbus, 1904.

Ritter, Frederick Louis. *Music in America.* New York: Charles Scribner's, 1883.

Robertson, William. *The History of the Reign of Emperor Charles the Fifth.* 2 vols. Philadelphia: J. B. Lippincott Company, 1856, 1890.

Town Talk. New York, 27 August, 1902.

The Twentieth Century Bench and Bar Association of Pennsylvania. 2 vols. Chicago: H. C. Cooper, Jr., & Bros. and Co., 1903.

Wetzel, Richard D. "Some Music Notation Systems in Early American Hymn-Tune Books." *Keystone Folklore Quarterly,* XII:4, 1967.

Wetzel, Richard D. "The Music of George Rapp's Harmony Society 1805-1906." University of Pittsburgh, 1970.

Williams, Aaron, D.D. *Harmony Society at Economy, Pennsylvania. Founded by George Rapp*. Pittsburgh: W. S. Haven, 1866.

Wiseman, C. M. L. *Centennial History of Lancaster, Ohio*. Lancaster, 1898.

Zahn, Johannes. *Die Melodien der Deutschen Evangelischen Kirchenlieder aus den Quellen geschöpft und mitgeteilt*. 6 vols. Gütersloh: C. Bertelsmann, 1889.

Index